BOB DYLAN
TOO MUCH OF NOTHING

DEREK BARKER

FIRST PUBLISHED IN HARDBACK BY RED PLANET BOOKS IN 2018

THIS REVISED AND UPDATED PAPERBACK EDITION PUBLISHED BY RED PLANET BOOKS IN 2020

TEXT COPYRIGHT © DEREK BARKER 2018-2020

THIS EDITION COPYRIGHT © RED PLANET BOOKS 2020

ISBN: 978 1 9127 3314 9

PRINTED IN THE UK BY TJ INTERNATIONAL

redplanetbooks

Red Planet Books, PO Box 355, Falmouth TR11 9ER   redplanetbooks.co.uk

Cover image of Bob Dylan in Woodstock © Elliott Landy (elliottlandy.com)

CONTENTS

Introduction

When Bob Dylan picked up a silver cross thrown on stage in San Diego and found Jesus in late 1978, it ended a search that had begun when his career had crashed to a halt in 1966. *Too Much of Nothing* begins with that motorcycle accident and traces Dylan's long journey of discovery that culminated with his finding Jesus in 1978-79.

Reports of his condition after the accident were, to say the least, vague and shocking rumours inevitably began to circulate: Dylan was badly disfigured; he was paralysed; he was insane. There was even talk that he was dead. Although the motorcycle crash brought his career to an abrupt halt, ultimately this time out of the public's gaze would prove transformative and the music he made after 1966 was far removed from what had gone before.

Dylan later recalled, "The turning point was back in Woodstock, a little after the accident." Sitting quietly outside one night he made up his mind that "Something's gotta change."

Too Much of Nothing charts those many and varied changes. While the six months to December 1967 was one of the most fertile and creative periods of Dylan's entire career, the music he produced in the cinder-block basement of the Hawks Big Pink home was not immediately offered for public consumption. Nevertheless, this time out of the spotlight only made Bob Dylan more mysterious and his music more sort-after. This, however, was not Dylan's intention.

The summer of '67 brought with it a radically altered music scene and Dylan found the complex compositions, overblown production values and elaborate album sleeves too much to bear. With the release of *John Wesley Harding* in December 1967 – his first album since the motorcycle accident – Dylan responded to the excesses of the psychedelic revolution with a stripped down album. He even requested that his record label should release the record with "no publicity and no hype."

Dylan knew that to stand still musically would be to stagnate, but his response was not to leap onto the out of control industry rollercoaster but instead, if I can borrow a line from a Basement song, 'to strap himself to a tree with roots.' The time spent making music in Big Pink reintroduced Dylan to his cultural heritage and that music would set the tone not only for the back to basics *John Wesley Harding*, but also for The Band's début record, *Music from Big Pink*.

While many artists were content to hang on to the white-knuckle rollercoaster ride, others like Dylan and The Band were able to see that you could move forward by looking back. Eric Clapton cites the roots rock approach of *Music from Big Pink* as persuading him to quit Cream and pursue other avenues of music with Blind Faith, Delaney & Bonnie, and Derek and the Dominos. According to Clapton: "The Band brought things back into perspective. The priority was the song." Like Dylan, Clapton was now intent on debunking the superstar cult that had formed around him. Others, including George Harrison and even Pink Floyd's Roger Waters, were also greatly influenced by *John Wesley Harding* and *Music from Big Pink*.

While Dylan raised a family in upstate rural Woodstock, his fans and the press were clamouring for music or information; preferably both. *Rolling Stone* wrote that from late 1971 to early '74 the once venerated songwriter was more like a "rumour than a luminary." By the time he hit the road in 1974, Dylan had been away from touring for eight years. Presented on a grand scale, his so-called 'comeback tour' with The Band was light years away from his experiences in 1965 and '66. Gone were the town halls and cinemas with seating for a couple of thousand and in were sports arenas with typical capacities of 15,000-20,000. The cash that rolled in from tickets sales looked great but the experience wasn't all that it might have been.

An old rock'n'roller at heart, Dylan was a devotee of the Rolling Stones' music and when he saw the band perform in July 1972 he was gripped by the concert. The next time he went to see them, however, it was a very different story. The Stones had fully embraced the decadence of the times and Dylan was disappointed with their June '75 concert. After that Madison Square Garden show Dylan met ex-Mott the Hoople front-man Ian Hunter in Greenwich Village. Dylan asked Hunter what he thought of the Stones' concert and Ian replied, "Insipid," to which Dylan said, "Yeah apathy for the devil." That comment moved Dylan to write 'Black Diamond Bay' while Hunter took the phrase and shortly after wrote 'Apathy 83.' Hunter's song succinctly summed up the mood of the times with the lyric: "There ain't no rock'n'roll no more just the sickly sound of greed."

After experiencing the excesses and polish of his 1974 tour and witnessing the Stones at Madison Square Garden, Dylan was determined that he should bring to fruition an idea that had occupied his mind for quite some time. That idea was a multi-act revue involving a loose caravan of musicians that might roll from town to town without too much fuss. The tour would be the complete antidote to corporate '74. The Rolling Thunder Revue tours of 1975-76 were partly successful in achieving this, but when they ran out of steam, it was time for further exploration.

In the Sixties, in a quest for answers to life's difficult questions, many musicians had experimented with drugs and eastern mysticism. In the Seventies, the seekers of enlightenment turned to the New Age movement, meditation, tarot and Jesus. Some attained spiritual or religious contentment but many others were either apathetic or merely content to immerse themselves in the newly established riches of the music industry. Self-indulgence and arrogance flourished to the extent that music journalist Nick Kent described the scene as being a kind of "bankrupt time." It was far from bankrupt money wise, but there is no denying that the often desolate world of Seventies rock had become spiritually bankrupt. Dylan, however, was no longer buying into the rockstar lifestyle and his wife never had. Sara hated being in the spotlight and looked for happiness through New Age practises, psychic energy and the tarot, elements of which Bob would become drawn to in his search for enlightenment. While most other artists were striving for superstardom, he was eagerly attempting to be Mr Ordinary. According to his memoir *Chronicles*, after the trials of his 1966 tour all he wanted was a "house on a tree-lined block with a white picket fence."

Too Much of Nothing covers a 12-year period during which Dylan achieved some monumental highs even though for much of this time he was simply dodging lions and wastin' time. Some writers have christened this time the "lost years." In a 1978 interview, Dylan referred to it as a period of "amnesia." This book puts into context Dylan's disappearance from view in the late Sixties, his numerous and sometimes tentative efforts to return and a final chapter that focuses on Dylan finding Jesus and a comprehensive examination of where his faith lies today. Along the road, with its dead ends and desert hideaways, there are in-depth examinations of the Basement Tapes recordings, *John Wesley Harding, Nashville Skyline, New Morning,* the filming of Sam Peckinpah's epic western *Pat Garrett & Billy the Kid, Planet Waves, Blood on the Tracks, Desire* and *Street-Legal*. There are also extended commentaries on two significant landmarks along the way: The 1969 Isle of Wight music festival and the 1978 Picnic at Blackbushe.

Too Much of Nothing encompasses research conducted by me for *ISIS* magazine over the past 35 years, including interviews with the likes of Dylan confidants, Al Aronowitz and Allen Ginsberg;

Woodstock neighbour, John Brandt; co-author of 'Desire', Jacques Levy; Rolling Thunder band member, Mick Ronson; producer Bob Johnston, manager, Jerry Weintraub; road managers, Arthur Rosato and Jonathan Taplin; Woodstock promoter, Mike Lang and ex-lover Faridi McFree.

This edition of *Too Much of Nothing* was revised and updated in August 2019. Newly discovered information was added to Chapter 5, mostly in the *Pat Garrett and Billy the Kid* section; Chapter 7, 'Rolling with the Thunder,' was also added to as was the final chapter, 'You Changed My Life.' Many other small amendments have been made including to some typos that appeared in first printing of the 2018 hardback edition.

Derek Barker, October 2019

Chapter One

Something's Gotta Change

"The turning point was back in Woodstock. A little after the accident. Sitting around one night under the full moon. I looked out into the bleak woods and I said, 'Something's gotta change'." (Bob Dylan, January 1974)[1]

With *Bringing It All Back Home*, *Highway 61 Revisited* and *Blonde on Blonde*, in the space of 15 months Bob Dylan had released what would be hailed as three of the greatest albums in rock music history. Just six days after *Blonde on Blonde* debuted on the Billboard Album Chart, however, Dylan took a spill from his motorcycle and with that event his whole world began to change and with it so did the world of rock music.

There are many conflicting accounts about what happened to Bob Dylan on the morning of Friday July 29, 1966. Wild rumours circulated, and still do, about the extent of his injuries. Like much of Bob Dylan's life, this incident is cloaked in mystery. We know that Dylan and his wife of eight months, Sara, had driven Bob's Ford station wagon from their Hi Lo Ha home in Byrdcliffe, two-and-a-half miles to his manager's house at 18 Striebel Road, Bearsville.

The reason for the short trip to Albert Grossman's home was to collect some items for their new home that were in storage at the Grossmans, including Bob's motorcycle which at the time was garaged there.

According to biographer Howard Sounes, Dylan was taking "an

old motorcycle"* to a "repair shop."[2] He doesn't give his source for
this information and he may have taken it from another biographer.
Anthony Scaduto and Dylan's friend Robert Shelton had both
previously written that Dylan was taking the bike for repair. Quite
where this information originally came from is not at all clear but at
less than two years from the date of manufacture, Sounes' inference
that the bike was "an old motorcycle" is way off the mark.

Sounes investigations convinced him that the accident happened
north on Striebel Road, which runs directly outside of the Grossman
estate, or a mile or so further on at Glasco Turnpike. Either way, this is
the exact route that Dylan would have taken if he were riding home
from the Grossman house. Had he been heading for a repair shop
as stated by others, he would not have been travelling north into
the depths of the Byrdcliffe countryside, where there were no repair
shops, but south towards route 212 and the town of Woodstock.

In February 2013, I talked with John Brandt, the adopted son
of Bruce Dorfman, who at the time was Bob Dylan's next door
neighbour in Byrdcliffe. John confirmed, as Sounes had speculated,
that the accident did take place on Striebel Road. John called the
accident a "spill," but stressed that Bob did indeed break his neck (in
some way). It seems that for a while Dylan was walking with a cane
while he underwent therapeutic ultrasound treatment for the injury.
John told me that Bob, "simply lost control of his bike on one of the
most treacherous roads in town." He went on to say that Striebel
was "steep and hazardous" and "paved with shale and not asphalt."[3]

Striebel Road is heavily tree-lined, narrow, steep and dangerous;
even today the speed limit on the new asphalt surface is just
30mph. The trees that run along the entire route create dappled
sunlight that can be almost strobe-like and on this Friday morning
the sun was bright, low and dazzling. Dylan himself has given

* *Often said to be a Bonneville 500, the bike was a red-and-silver 1964 Triumph
Tiger 100-SS*

several different accounts as to the cause of the accident. He told Robert Shelton: "I'd been up for three days. I hit an oil slick."[4] He nonetheless gave a different and much longer account to the playwright Sam Shepard, who published it in *Esquire* as part of a one-act play. "It was real early in the morning on top of a hill near Woodstock," he told Shepard. "I can't even remember exactly how it happened. I was blinded by the sun for a second. This big orange sun was comin' up. I was driving right straight into the sun... I just happened to look up... I went blind for a second and I kind of panicked or something. I stomped down on the brake and the rear wheel locked up on me and I went flyin'."[5]

Dylan was notorious for his driving skills; or lack thereof. In her autobiography, Joan Baez recalled, "He was a terrible driver, just terrible... I always feared for us... He drove sloppy, he used to hang on that thing like a sack of flour. I always had the feeling it was driving him, and if we were lucky we'd lean the right way and the motorcycle would turn the corner. If not, it would be the end of both of us."[6]

Only a short time after collecting the bike, Bob arrived back at the Grossman house, being driven by Sara who had been following Bob in the station wagon. Grossman's wife, Sally, who at the time was on the phone to her husband Albert, saw Bob making his way back toward the house, "kind of moaning and groaning."[7] She says that he made it to the front door but then, "sort of lay down on the porch." There were no apparent signs of injuries and there is no police record of an accident having taken place. Perhaps of more significance, no ambulance was called. The nearest general hospital in Kingston was a short 25-minute drive but Sara drove Bob to Middletown; more than 60 miles from Bearsville and over an hour and 15 minutes driving time. More than this, she would have had to drive past the suburbs of Kingston to reach Middletown! We can only deduce from this that Bob was not badly injured. Researchers are again divided as to what happened next, with some saying that Sara took Bob straight to the Middletown home of one Dr Ed Thaler. In actual fact, she took Bob to Middletown Hospital for an x-ray and then to the Thaler's house. Dylan told Sam Shepard: "Spent a week in the hospital, then they moved me to this doctor's house in town."

Dylan had been seeing Dr Thaler since being referred to him by the singer Odetta. The good doctor seemed like the perfect choice to care for Dylan. He was very leftwing, a civil rights activist, played the guitar, was an admirer of Woody Guthrie's politics and music, and like Dylan, he was something of a Guthrie jukebox. Thaler was also quite unconventional, which is probably why several musicians preferred to use his services. He was not board certified, refusing to comply with what he called unnecessary bureaucracy (Board certification is not a legal requirement in the United States).

The Thalers' had an attractive six bedroom Victorian house on Highland Avenue. Bob was given a third-floor room there. Dylan arrived "very upset" the doctor's widow, Selma, said in an interview with the Associated Press. "He didn't want to go to the hospital, so we said, 'You can stay here'... He was sweet and quiet," Selma said. Like Sally Grossman, Selma couldn't remember Dylan showing any visible signs of injury but she believed he had "broken his neck."

Dylan remained at the Thalers' for between four and six weeks. He ate dinner with them and had friends over to the house on Friday nights, including Allen Ginsberg who brought Bob a pile of reading material. Dylan's time at the house was a closely guarded secret. The family had to be especially careful because their neighbour, Al Romm, was the editor of the *Times Herald-Record*. He didn't discover that Dylan had been living next-door until the stay was over. Shortly after returning home from the Thalers,' Dylan told Robbie Robertson that the doctor was a "genius" and a "miracle worker." Thaler had ordered Dylan a neck brace and Bob told Robbie that the brace was great but that he couldn't turn his head to see who was behind him.

Friend and journalist Al Aronowitz later said: "I never really believed the story about Bob breaking a vertebra in his neck. Later on, [Dylan] claimed that was just an expression that his brother used at the time. I always felt a strange twinge of guilt about the spill Bob took because I was the one who had driven him to pick up his new Triumph bike in the first place. I remembered an ominous foreboding as I followed him while he rode the motorcycle home. But I never told him about this feeling. He wouldn't have heeded my warning, anyway."[8]

The extent of Dylan's injuries was never disclosed, but news of his accident quickly got out. The first Bob's parents knew of the accident was when they received an out of the blue phone call from a Minnesota radio station asking for information about the crash. The station had received a news wire informing them there had been a motorcycle accident. Dylan's father called Sara but couldn't get an answer. This was of course because she was with Bob in Middletown. In desperation, he called Dylan's friend, the *New York Times* music journalist Robert Shelton, to ask if he knew anything. Bob's father told Shelton that he had already called Albert Grossman's office but they were unable to help. Shelton knew nothing about the accident but said he would call the Times in the hope that the paper had some information. They didn't.

On the afternoon of Saturday July 30, the day after the motorcycle spill, music radio stations across the United States were breaking the news. Initial reports were extremely sketchy. Nevertheless, news, or at least rumours of the accident, was quick to circulate. Albert Grossman issued an official short statement on Monday, August 1 and the following day what little information he had given to the press was printed, including a two-sentence "story" in *The New York Times* under the headline, "Dylan Hurt in Cycle Mishap." This piece stated that Dylan was under a doctor's care, but very little else. With Dylan holed up, first in Middletown and then back home in Woodstock, the rumours began to grow. In London, a group of hippies printed a memorial poster with a space left blank for the time and place of the funeral service.

Writing about the accident eight months later in the short-lived pop magazine *Cheetah*, Ellen Willis summed up the situation: "Reports of his condition were vague, and he dropped out of sight... Gruesome rumours circulated: Dylan was dead; he was badly disfigured; he was paralyzed; he was insane. The cataclysm his audience was always expecting seemed to have arrived. Phil Ochs had predicted that Dylan might someday be assassinated by a fan. Pete Seeger believed Dylan could become the country's greatest troubadour if he didn't explode. Alan Lomax had once remarked that Dylan might develop into a great poet of the times unless he killed himself first... As months passed, reflex apprehension turned to suspense, then irritation... Not since Rimbaud said 'I is another' has an artist been so obsessed with escaping identity. His masks hidden by other masks, Dylan is the celebrity stalker's ultimate antagonist."[9]

Once back in the bosom of his family, Bob gradually began to take stock of his life. The last 18 months had been frenzied, especially the lengthy 1966 world tour. The music was completely groundbreaking; it set a precedent. Nevertheless, the price Dylan had to pay was way too high. His once angelic face was now sunken, his eyes were dark and his skin a whiter shade of pale. It was quite apparent that liberal quantities of 'medicine' had been consumed during the tour. Filmmaker D.A. Pennebaker told biographer Clinton Heylin: "Bob was taking a lot of amphetamines and who-knows-what-else ... He was very edgy, very uptight, and he stayed up for days on end, without sleep."[10]

Dylan's Guitarist Robbie Robertson said that by Belfast (May 6, 1966) he had begun to worry about Bob's health. "It became obvious," Robertson said, "that Bob was maintaining his performance level with the help of amphetamines..."[11]

Talking about Dylan's May 26 performance at the Royal Albert Hall, music journalist and musician Mick Farren alleged: "[Dylan] was obviously exceedingly stoned and probably taking a lot of pills, that's what we all figured... Little did we know – amphetamine and heroin."[12]

After the second night at the Albert Hall, the final show of the world tour, Robbie Robertson said that Dylan appeared to have "fainted" or was "deliriously exhausted." Robertson and Albert Grossman helped Dylan into a bath to bring him round before putting him to bed.[13]

With the tour now completed, there were compelling rumours that Dylan was treated for exhaustion by an English nurse in Paris.

"You were right on it when you described all those pressures," Dylan told Anthony Scaduto. "But you really only touched the surface. The pressures were unbelievable. They were just something you can't imagine unless you go through them yourself. Man, they hurt so much."

In 1969, Dylan told *Rolling Stone* co-founder Jann Wenner: "I was on the road for almost five years ... It wore me down. I was on drugs, a lot of things. A lot of things just to keep going.."[14]

Over the years, it has been suggested that Dylan's stay with Dr Thaler was to wean him off drugs. There is no evidence to support this however and Thaler has flatly denied the claim: "He did not come here regarding any situation involving detoxification," Thaler told Howard Sounes. Robbie Robertson: "People say, 'Oh, he didn't have an accident, this was just so he could kick heroin or whatever.' No, no, no! He fell off the motorcycle and fractured his neck ... and he had to wear this brace on his neck for quite a while..."[15]

Dylan spoke to Sam Shepard about his time at the Thalers: "I started thinkin' about the short life of trouble. How short life is. I just lay there listenin' to birds chirping. Kids playing in the neighbour's yard or rain falling by the window. I realised how much I'd missed. Then I hear the fire engine roar, and I could feel the steady thrust of death that had been constantly looking over its shoulder at me."[16]

Now installed back at Hi Lo Ha, these thoughts gathered pace. Bob continued to have visitors in the shape of DA Pennebaker, Robbie Robertson, Allen Ginsberg and Al Aronowitz. All of these people believed that Dylan had been injured, but no one thought the injuries were in any way serious. In his memoir, *Chronicles Volume One*, Dylan wrote: "I had been in a motorcycle accident and I'd been hurt, but I recovered. Truth was that I wanted to get out of the rat race. Having children changed my life and segregated me from just about everybody and everything that was going on. Outside of my family, nothing held any real interest for me and I was seeing everything through different glasses."[17]

For most of the remainder of 1966 – about four-and-a-half months – Dylan mainly stayed home with his family. He watched films, often brought up to him from New York City by Al Aronowitz, and he read a lot. Ginsberg had brought books to Thalers' for Dylan, but he delivered a second parcel to Hi Lo Ha; mostly poets: German poet Bertolt Brecht, Lebanese poet Khalil Gibran, the Romantic poet Percy Shelley; ancient lyrical poets like Sir Thomas Wyatt and Thomas Campion; Emily Dickinson, Arthur Rimbaud, William Blake, Walt Whitman, García Lorca and Guillaume Apollinaire. Also included in the parcel was *The Outsider* by Colin Wilson.

In May 1967, Dylan told Michael Iachetta that he'd been, "poring over books by people you never heard of, thinking about where I'm going, and why I'm running and why I'm mixed up too much...."[18] By far the most important book to surface during this period, one not delivered by Ginsberg, was *The Bible*. Several visitors to Dylan's home at that time mentioned seeing a Bible prominently displayed on an impressive looking lectern. A volume of Hank Williams' lyrics was also said to be close at hand.

In a contemporary 1968 interview with Toby Thompson, Dylan's mother, Beatty Zimmerman, mentioned her son's mounting interest in the Bible. "In his house in Woodstock today," she said, "there's a huge Bible open on a stand in the middle of his study. Of all the books that crowd his house, overflow from his house, that Bible gets the most attention. He's continuously getting up and going over to refer to something."[19]

Dylan's thoughts about his life and career were beginning to run deep. For the first time in years he had time to reflect on his situation and he didn't like what he saw. Now, however, he realised that there might be a way out. It had taken a few months to dawn on him, but Bob now recognised that it might be possible to use the motorcycle accident to his advantage. Dylan's 'to-do list' was long and he was now determined to jettison as much of it as possible. For starters, Dylan's recording contract with Columbia Records would soon expire and much consideration was being given to his switching to MGM. He nonetheless owed Columbia 14 tracks (an album's worth of songs). For a time, confusion reigned while Albert Grossman did what Albert Grossman did best– negotiate. Initially, Dylan signed a contract with MGM only for his lawyer to then send a letter rescinding the signature. As it happened, that didn't matter because MGM had already gotten cold feet and hadn't yet countersigned the document. Allen Klein, a member of MGM's board, felt that the offer the company had made to Dylan, a reputed advance of $1 million, would set a dangerous precedent. Then, when Columbia lawyer Clive Davis supplied Klein with Dylan's actual sales figures, Klein quickly ran to the board informing them that signing him would indeed be "a huge mistake."

MGM had based their initial decision to sign Bob mainly on his status and the chart success of his last three albums; all of which had been Top Ten. What they failed to grasp, however, was that Dylan's fan base, then as today, bought his albums upon release, sending them straight up the charts, but their stay there was short-lived and overall sales were nowhere near as big as MGM had imagined. In any event, it would be July 1967 before this whole affair was settled. In the end, Dylan would, of course, remain with Columbia.

Grossman had signed a television deal with ABC. Dylan was supposed to deliver a 90-minute special for the final instalment, Episode 27, of their *Stage 67* series. *Eat the Document*, as the film was later titled, never aired. In April 1967, a spokesperson for the television company said the show had been cancelled because it was delivered late and because there was also a disagreement over the format. The choice of art house camera techniques was said to be "totally unsatisfactory" and "un-television." In 1971, when the film was screened at the Academy of Music, Jonathan Taplin reiterated this when he introduced the film as being "a little too freaky for ABC at that time, and they rejected it." Hubbell Robinson, who at the time was the executive producer for *Stage 67*, flatly denied this statement saying, "We didn't know what we had because when we saw the film in the fall of '66 it wasn't yet edited." Robinson said by that time they had to finalise programming and that's why they couldn't use the film. "Dylan didn't know what the film would be and when it would be finished," Robinson said. "But we were definitely interested in the film."[20] Nevertheless, ABC had already paid Grossman an advance of $100,000 and the company considered taking legal action.

While the record deal was bubbling along below the surface, there were other matters that needed attention. A Broadway show called *The Pied Piper* had been written for Dylan and there was even a vague rumour that he might play the part of James Dean in a New York musical. Then there was the question of his novel,

Tarantula, which had been promised to US publisher Macmillan. Again, a contract had been entered into and a significant advance paid. By the middle of '66, however, Dylan appeared to have lost his enthusiasm for the book. If Bob is to be believed, he had been manoeuvred into writing the book by Albert Grossman. During his July 2001 Rome Press Conference, Dylan said: "My manager at the time had some offers and he was the one that kind of pushed me into it." At any rate, the crash provided Dylan with an excuse and Macmillan's senior editor, Robert Markel, was given some cock and bull story that Bob "couldn't use his eyes for a period of time [which] made it difficult for him to work." Whether Markel believed this tall tale isn't clear, but in any event he wasn't about to start hassling a guy with a supposed broken neck and dodgy eyesight over a book deadline. Bob told one friend that the books was "meaningless" and that he was sure that the publisher wouldn't accept it and that was the reason he was "dropping it." Dylan told *Sing Out!*: "There was no difficulty in writing it at all, it just wasn't a book, it was just a nuisance."[21] In any event, the book would not see the light of day for another five years. He told Scaduto in early '71 that he planned to release the book "because I dig it now. It's a good book. I didn't dig it back then, but I dig it now."

It was glaringly obvious to anyone, though apparently not to Albert B Grossman, that Dylan could not meet all of these commitments. Above everything else, Dylan wanted to avoid going back out on tour. Grossman had lined up a series of concerts spanning from August 1966 until early '67. Robert Shelton has said there were as many as 64 concerts and Dylan's road drummer Mickey Jones is adamant that they were scheduled to play a gig in Moscow and were due to fly out on August 14, 1966.[22]

Although it was soon apparent that Dylan would not be able to play the scheduled August / September dates, it was assumed he would be back in harness soon after that. In fact, *The New York*

Post had reported shortly after the accident that Dylan, "Will be laid up for at least two months, according to his manager, Albert Grossman." This would have meant no shows before October 1966. On October 8, 1966, *Billboard* published an article about the Third Festival of the Roses of Italian Song. This event was held in Rome from October 12-14. While Dylan was not mentioned in the article itself, there was a brief separate report about some of the singers who would be present. This report said: "Bob Dylan and Joan Baez will headline the third annual Festival of the Roses, which begins Oct 12." A few days later, however, CBS issued a denial: "The story that appeared in the trades ... was erroneous." CBS then stated that: "Although Bob Dylan is feeling much better after suffering fractures and concussion in a motorbike accident on July 29th in Woodstock, New York, he has not scheduled any performances before March 1967."

From all accounts, Dylan's management was not happy about the extent of the cancellations. Grossman is reported to have said, "How could he do this to me?," while Charlie Rothschild at ABGM (Albert B Grossman Management) complained to Robert Shelton, "Do you know how much work was involved in setting up 60 concerts?" Regardless, March 1967 came and went and there were no signs of Dylan showing any willingness to go play concerts. In May '67, he uncharacteristically gave Michael Iachetta of *New York Daily News* an interview.

This was Dylan's first interview since the accident. Others had tried; four months previously, the *New York Post*'s Barry Cunningham had arrived at Hi Lo Ha without invitation and Sara threatened to phone the police. Iachetta had gotten nowhere repeatedly calling Grossman for permission to talk to Dylan so like Cunningham he went to Dylan's home without an invitation. After driving up to Woodstock, Iachetta spent almost two days trying to prise directions to the house from the defensive locals. Luckily for

Iachetta, when he did eventually find the house it was Bob who answered the door and he recalled their previous meeting, an interview in October 1963.

Dylan was vague about any future work projects. He told the reporter: "[I'm] Thinkin' about where I'm goin,' and why am I running,' and am I mixed up too much...." This statement was the first clear indication that Dylan was embarking on a journey of discovery. At this stage, however, the notion that this search might persist for the next decade was unthinkable! He said that like always songs were in his head but they were "not goin' to get written down until some things are evened up. Not until some people come forth and make up for some of the things that happened."[23] Although veiled, this was surely an indication that all was not well between Dylan and his manager.

Woodstock Notion
Apart from working on editing what would become unused film footage for *Stage 67*, Dylan mostly continued to escape from work and the world, taking on the role of a family man and country squire. The Dylans had moved from the hubbub of New York City to their rural Byrdcliffe retreat in July 1965. Bob bought the property for the bargain price of $12,000. He later said that he had decided to buy the property after visiting John and Cynthia Lennon at their spectacular Kenwood mansion near London. Four months after the house purchase, on November 22, 1965, Bob and Sara married during a secret ceremony. The wedding was conducted on the lawn under an oak tree outside a judge's office in Mineola, Long Island. The only guests to attend the wedding was Albert Grossman and a maid of honour for Sara, Bob's parents did not receive an invite. At the time, Sara was just six weeks away from giving birth to the couples' first child together, Jesse Byron. For the next three months the marriage would remain a closely guarded secret, even from

friends, until journalist Nora Ephron broke the story in the *New York Post* on February 9, 1966 with the headline: "Hush!!! Bob Dylan is wed."

Sara was a friend of Sally Grossman and she met Bob for the first time when they both attended the Grossman's wedding. "Bob's desire to get married to Sara surprised me," Dylan's close friend Victor Maynudes said. "I asked [Bob] ... why Sara? Why not Joan Baez? ... He responded with 'Because Sara will be home when I want her home, she'll be there when I want her to be there, she'll do it when I want her to do it. Joan won't be there when I want her'."

Bob had first visited Woodstock a few years before with his then-girlfriend Suze Rotolo. They were invited there by Peter Yarrow of the folk music trio Peter, Paul and Mary. Although Peter was born in Manhattan, as a child he fell in love with Woodstock after spending several summers there with his mother and sister. Peter's aunt had a house a short distance from what was then the village centre and Peter took art lessons there. Later, when his mother acquired a property in Woodstock, Yarrow spent much of his free time there and claims to have invited Dylan to stay at his mother's two-room 'shack' in the summer of 1963. Yarrow remembers, "It was a scorcher in New York City in June and July ... I called up Bobby and said, 'Let's get out of the city." According to Yarrow, "Bobby fell in love with the place."[24]

Albert Grossman soon joined Dylan in his love of Woodstock. In fact, Dylan has said that it was he who introduced his manager to the tranquil little town, which at the time had a population of less than 4,000. On the backs of the successes of Dylan and Peter, Paul and Mary, Grossman was rapidly becoming a wealthy man and he therefore decided to invest in a property somewhere in the Woodstock area. So, when a large stone-built house came up for sale in the hamlet of Bearsville, two miles west of Woodstock, Grossman took ownership of the property.

Since first discovering the delights of Woodstock, Dylan had spent time in the Yarrow cabin on Broadview Road and then in a space above the Café Espresso. Dylan had regularly frequented the Espresso, sometimes seated outside or at one of the tables near the door, playing chess and drinking coffee. He quickly became good friends with the owners, Bernard and Mary Lou Paturel, and in the winter of 1963-64 they asked if he would like to work in the space above the cafe. The room was large, about 30 feet by 20 with windows overlooking Tinker Street, Woodstock's main drag. Later still, after Grossman had established himself in Bearsville, Dylan moved into one of the three guest cottages on his manager's 60-acre estate.

The Grossman home was a party house always buzzing with visitors. Albert certainly appreciated the finer things in life and the house, probably better termed as a 'mansion,' was extensively furnished with antiques. Al Aronowitz told me: "When the house was comprehensively refurbished, a vast new kitchen was installed. It had a huge table and that became the main room in Albert's house. It was stocked with rare and expensive gourmet delicacies. That's where all the parties happened. Albert would take great pleasure in slicing off a sliver of the best Italian salami or a portion of fine cheese giving it out for his guests to taste... I've said this before, but I'm sure I'm not the only one to believe that Albert eventually ate himself to death."[25]

By the summer of 1965, Dylan had decided that he would move full-time to Woodstock and after knocking out arguably the best single record ever written he spent June and part of July house-hunting. By the time he found what he was looking for, the six-minute-plus "long piece of vomit," which is how Dylan referred to his draft of 'Like a Rolling Stone,' had reached number 2 on the *Billboard* singles chart, thwarted only by The Beatles' 'Help!.' Described as "revolutionary" by critics, Bob's latest single would spend 12 weeks on the US chart.

Dylan was tipped off about the Byrdcliffe property by Shirley Glaser, wife of Milton Glaser the well-known graphic artists who, a year later, would design the psychedelic poster for *Bob Dylan's Greatest Hits* LP. It seems that Shirley should have been in the real estate business because it was she who had alerted Albert Grossman to his Bearsville property! The rambling 11-room cedar-wood ranch house that Dylan would soon buy was on the mountainside in the East Riding of Byrdcliffe. Built by architect and stage director Ben Webster, the property was on Camelot Road, a narrow gravelly tree-lined lane off Upper Byrdcliffe Road, just past the Byrdcliffe Theater. All of the houses in the area had names and Dylan's property was no exception. The house was named Hi Lo Ha after the first two letters of the first names of the previous owner's children.

Established in 1902, the Byrdcliffe Arts & Crafts colony, one of the nation's oldest, was created as an experiment in utopian living. The original settlement, 30 buildings spread over 300 acres, took its name from an amalgam of the founders' middle names (Ralph Radcliffe Whitehead and his wife, Jane Byrd McCall Whitehead). A wealthy Englishman, Whitehead's dream was to create a self-sufficient arts community where all the arts would come together, including painting, sculpture, pottery, textiles, metalwork, furniture making and music (mostly classical). In the beginning the colony was a great success. It became host to numerous writers, artists, and musicians who came and stayed, sometimes for two or three summers. Some even bought land from Whitehead and built permanent summer residences there. Unfortunately, the place grew to be restrictively expensive and his domineering personality became a confining force. The colony nevertheless endured for almost 30 years under Whitehead's vision until his death in 1929, after which his widow, Jane, and son Peter, struggled to keep the place alive. After his mother's death in 1955, Peter sold most of the land in order to pay taxes. He nonetheless managed to keep the heart of the colony together.

The area had a profound spiritual vibe to it. The Catskill Mountains, which begins at Overlook Mountain, was a sacred place for the Native Algonquin Indians who knew it as Wall of Manitou – Manitou being the "Great Spirit." Tibetan Buddhists built a spiritual centre, the Karma Triyana Dharmachakra monastery, at the top of Mead Mountain Road because it is on one of the major ley lines on the east coast of the United States. Dylan had quickly grown to love the place and as Howard Sounes rightly points out, the Byrdcliffe house was Dylan's first major purchase since becoming famous. His new surroundings had a haunting beauty and there is no doubt that for a time he was extremely content there.

His young neighbour John Brandt told me in 2013: "In Woodstock Bob was a very ordinary guy; a real family man. Our families spent three New Year Eves hanging out." Brandt said that a typical New Year was spent sitting with the Dylans watching TV in their kitchen, "waiting for the Times Square ball to drop marking the New Year." "There was no fanfare," Brandt said. "No big party like you might imagine a famous rock star would have. It was just our small family and the Dylans."[26]

There's No Success Like Failure

While there is no doubt that Dylan had desperately sought success, like many people, both before and after him, he had no real idea just how much baggage came with fame. Although in the early Sixties he had enjoyed living in New York's Greenwich Village and frequenting the folk music cafes that lined the streets there, after acquiring celebrity status it became far more difficult to walk those same streets without being hassled. It seemed that everyone wanted a piece of the newly appointed 'spokesman for a generation.' By contrast, he found that in Woodstock virtually no one recognised him and he was able to go about his daily business without any problems.

One of the hardest things for Bob Dylan to come to terms with in the mid-late Sixties was trying to rescind a mantle that he had never sought-after. Although he had not wanted the role of counterculture leader or spokesman for a generation, these labels had been applied to him because of his unique ability to combine political comment with art. His songs were readily embraced by a youth culture that was beginning to reject political convention, war, racism and conservative resistance to change. His song 'The Times They Are A-Changin'' had become a counterculture anthem. "The world was absurd," Dylan wrote in his wonderful 2004 memoir *Chronicles Volume One*. "I had very little in common with and knew even less about a generation that I was supposed to be the voice of."[27]

Hugh Romney, who would later become Wavy Gravy, the legendary master of ceremonies at the 1969 Woodstock Festival and had shared a room with Dylan in 1962 said: "Bob, in my opinion, was a conduit for the divine... The Bobster, I don't think he was ever [a hippie]. He always turned away from that."[28]

"I was always more tied up with the Beat Movement," Dylan informed Lynne Allen in December 1978. "I don't know what the hippie movement was all about, that was a media thing, I think, 'Rent a Hippie'– I don't know what that was about..."[29]

Talking about the hippies who in the late Sixties invaded his Woodstock privacy, Dylan wrote: "I wanted to set fire to these people." Apart from the strange (for him) attire that he wore during his visit to the 1972 Mariposa Folk Festival, Dylan never dressed in hippie garb. During the mid-Sixties he was uber cool and as he settled into family life in Woodstock he wore his hair short and dressed mostly in casual clothing. If he took Sara out for a meal he might even don a pair of cufflinks. You could even say he was a 'clean-cut kid.' For her part, Sara dressed mainly in suburban casuals rather than the hippie gear that was de rigueur for other musicians' wives, girlfriends and hangers-on. Time, however, seems to have somewhat mellowed Dylan. In June 1999, during a show at the University of Oregon, he introduced the song 'Blind Willie McTell' with, "I wanna say hello to all the ex-hippies tonight. I've never been a hippie myself but ... I'm an honorary hippie!"

Dylan's left-looking stance had been significantly influenced by his old Greenwich Village girlfriend, Susan Rotolo. Suze, as she was known by just about everyone, was a child of radical parents – a so-called red diaper baby – during the McCarthy Era and she worked as a political activist in the New York office of the Congress of Racial Equality (CORE).

In truth, Dylan was far more in tune with Woody Guthrie than the hippie counterculture. His early topical songs like 'Man on the Street' and 'The Death of Emmitt Till' contain elements that are very close to those employed by Guthrie. Dylan's great strengths were as an acute observer and chronicler of topical events and many of his Sixties so-called "finger-pointing" songs were personal observations rather than political statements. According to Suze Rotolo: "When we walked down the street, he saw things that absolutely nobody else saw. He was so aware of his surroundings, in every situation, it was almost like he couldn't write fast enough. He would get thoughts and reactions and stop on a street corner and write things down."[30]

In reality, the protest songs for which Dylan is most well-known and with which he continues to be very much associated were written during a very brief period of only 20 months– January 1962 to the latter months of 1963. Although it was certainly not his intention, during that short space of time Dylan's songs greatly advanced the protest music genre and helped it reach a new mass audience. Dylan's refusal to lead a counterculture charge and his rejection of politics in general were not new; he had maintained this stance from the word go. Most Dylan devotees will be familiar with his December 1963 Tom Paine Award acceptance speech. Dylan felt that the Emergency Civil Liberties Committee (ECLC) and other similar organisations were exploiting his fame and using him as a puppet for their causes. Partly fuelled by drink, he delivered a controversial speech that sent shockwaves through those gathered at the Awards dinner. Soon after the speech, however, Dylan wrote a letter to the Committee's chairman, Corliss Lamont, that began with: "It is a fierce heavy feeling, thinkin' something is expected of you...." The long letter continued:

but you dont know what exactly it is...
it brings forth a weird form of guilt

I should've remembered
'I am BOB DYLAN an I don't have t speak
I don't have t say nothin' if I don't wanna.'"

Dylan had now decided just that; he didn't want to. Still very much anti-authoritarian, he was nevertheless hostile to political organisations. In an interview with Nat Hentoff published in *The New Yorker*, October 24, 1964, Dylan clearly stated his position on the civil rights movement: "Me, I don't want to write for people anymore. You know–be a spokesman. Like I once wrote about Emmett Till in the first person, pretending I was him. From now on, I want to write from inside me ... I'm not part of no movement... I just can't make it with any organisation..."[31]

Dylan told left-wing singer-songwriter Phil Ochs, "The stuff you're writing is bullshit, because politics is bullshit. What's real is inside you. Your feelings."

Woodstock allowed Dylan an opportunity to get away from all this "bullshit." He told Robert Shelton that Woodstock was a place where, "We stop the clouds, turn back time and inside out, make the sun turn on and off. The greatest place on earth."[32] In a November 2014 audio interview, Dylan again reflected on the time he spent there by saying, "Woodstock was a place where you could kind of go and get your thoughts together."[33]

Nevertheless, since taking up residence in beautiful Byrdcliffe, Bob had spent very little time there. Directly after the house move he played at the Newport Folk Festival (July 24 & 25, 1965) and four days later he was in the studio recording *Highway 61 Revisited*. By mid-August, he was getting it together with musicians, including Robbie Robertson and Levon Helm of The Hawks, in Bob Carroll's New York rehearsal hall. On August 28 he played the 15,000-seat Forest Hills Stadium and on September 3 he was in LA for a huge concert at the Hollywood Bowl. It was then up to Canada to spend time listening to and rehearsing with the Hawks before embarking on a US tour which ran from September 24 until December 19. Bob was home for Christmas, but by January 21 he was again in the studio – this time for the best part of two-and-a-half months – before leaving on his 1966 world tour. The chaotic and drug-fuelled "Judas" tour finished at the end of May 1966; nine weeks before Bob got his passport to a shot at sanity in the shape his motorcycle accident. It took a little while, but after Bob realised he could use the crash to his advantage, he played this Get Out of Jail Free card at every opportunity. He now began to paint and sculpt. Bob took up painting in earnest after meeting his artist neighbour Bruce Dorfman as the two men walked their respective daughters to the school bus stop on Upper Byrdcliffe Road.* Dorfman had an art

* *Bob would soon adopt Maria, Sara's five-year-old daughter from a previous marriage.*

studio on Webster Road just across the way from Hi Lo Ha.

In March 1967, almost nine months after the motorcycle accident, Dylan recommenced music making in the 'Red Room' at his Byrdcliffe home. The Red Room was a sort of second living room at Hi Lo Ha, so named because at one time it was painted red. The four musicians involved in these informal sessions, members of Dylan's '66 road band and still on a retainer, were: Robbie Robertson, Rick Danko, Richard Manuel and Garth Hudson.*

Although it's not entirely clear when, by spring, probably early May, when the distractions of family life became a little too much, Dylan and his cohort relocated to the cinder-block basement of a property recently rented by the Hawks' bass player, Rick Danko.** Nestling in the shadow of Overlook Mountain and encircled by dense woodland, Big Pink, as the house would become known, had been rented furnished by Danko for $250 a month. To begin with it was home to Danko, Manuel and Garth Hudson– Levon Helm would join them there sometime later. Set in 100 acres of woods and fields with a pond and a creek nearby, the half-shingled pink painted property provided a tranquil and secluded setting, ideal for music making.

The house is located along Parnassus Lane, a hard-to-find crumbling dead-end track, midway between Woodstock and West Saugerties; a 10-minute drive from Dylan's then Byrdcliffe home. Working with the Hawks in their makeshift basement studio became almost a daily ritual. Robbie Robertson: "We used to get

Unable to cope with the fans' negative response to Dylan "going electric," Hawks' drummer Levon Helm had left Dylan's employment in November '65.

**Rick Danko, Richard Manuel and Garth Hudson live in Big Pink. Drummer Levon Helm took up residence there when he eventually returned to the fold. Although Robbie Robertson visited Big Pink almost daily, even before Dylan began recording there, he never lived in the house. Instead, he set up home with his French girlfriend and future wife, Dominique.*

together every day at one o'clock... There was no particular reason for it. We weren't making a record. We were just fooling around."[34]

According to Danko, Dylan would arrive at the house, let himself in, "make a big pot of coffee [and] roll some joints." He would then sit at the kitchen table and type out lyrics and ideas for songs. Around noon, he would wake the Hawks from their slumbers, "make another pot of coffee [and] roll some more joints," before heading down the open wooden stairs to the basement to try out the songs he had written.[35] Recording would usually commence a little later in the afternoon with the sessions lasting for around three hours. In stark contrast to his recent rock star image, Bob would always leave before six o'clock to be home in time for dinner with the family.

With Garth Hudson at the controls acting as engineer, Dylan and the Hawks committed over 150 songs, including at least 30 originals, to tape via a portable Ampex reel-to-reel recorder. The cover of the official *The Basement Tapes* album incorrectly shows a Revox A77 recorder and this Revox machine is erroneously on display in the Cleveland Rock & Roll Hall of Fame. The Ampex machine used for the recordings bit the dust in 1978 when Garth Hudson suffered a catastrophic house fire. The basic recording equipment – a two-track reel-to-reel, a couple of Altec Lansing mixers and a handful of microphones – was all that was needed to capture what went on in the basement 'live room.' These sessions represent the most uncomplicated and informal recordings that Bob Dylan would ever make. Although he would try many times after that, and come close in the late Seventies, he would never again be able to capture the spirit and feeling of those sessions.

This is where our story really begins. Through the basement recordings we can witness the beginnings of a new Bob Dylan. Although these sessions began as informal and without any real purpose, unbeknown to Dylan, this would be the start of his search for something much deeper than the superficial world of fame and fortune. The changes in his life were becoming quite profound: He now had a home in the country away from the turmoil of New York City. He had a wife and the start of family that by December '69 would total five children. The pressures and stresses of the road, too many drugs and not enough sleep, were starting to fade. Gone were the flashy shirts, chamois jacket and skinny stretch jeans. Now with short hair, wire-rimmed glasses and a beard, Dylan's appearance was radically changed and these changes were reflected in his music. In the basement of Big Pink he was making music for pleasure. How different this must have felt from mayhem, catcalling and booing that he and the Hawks had continually endured during their recent world tour. In 1969, Dylan would tell *Rolling Stone* editor Jann Wenner: "You know, that's really the way to do a recording– in a peaceful, relaxed setting, in somebody's basement, with the windows open and a dog lying on the floor."[36]

Recalling those same recording sessions, Garth Hudson told Martin Scorsese in the movie *The Last Waltz*, "Chopping wood and hitting your thumb with a hammer, fixing the tape recorder or the screen door, wandering off into the woods with Hamlet [Rick Danko's dog, given to him by Dylan] ... it was relaxed and low-key, which was something we hadn't enjoyed since we were children."

Robbie Robertson felt the same about his time living in Woodstock. Looking back in 1984, Robertson said that the Hawks were, "influenced by the ambience." "I felt a little easier about things," Robertson continued. "The feeling of the music wasn't as neurotic as it had been when I was living in the city."[37]

The time Dylan spent making music in Woodstock marked the next phase in his evolution, one that would influence the way he viewed both himself and his music for many years to come. The recordings made in Woodstock show Dylan and the Hawks at their understated best. Dylan found that he was able to play music solely for enjoyment. His new environment had moved his songs away from surreal amphetamine-fuelled poetry to a contented country flavoured sound. His voice was warmer than before. He had partly returned to folk music, emphasising the primacy of how music can express emotions. Record producer Clive Davis recalls how Dylan explained that, at the time, his work had become "all about the music."

Although the sessions were begun merely to pass the time at some point it was decided it might be a good idea to get some of this music down on tape. After a very short time and while still in the Red Room, Bob had begun to write songs and this was possibly the primary motive for getting the tapes rolling. These early recordings contain a surprising assortment of songs from the pop charts of prior decades, including Bob's rendition of Frank Sinatra's 'One for the Road' (forty years later he would revisit ol' Blue Eyes with no fewer than five discs of Sinatra related covers). The basements recordings also drew heavily upon the songs of friends and contemporaries: Johnny Cash ('Folsom Prison Blues,' 'Belshazzar' and 'Big River'), Elvis Presley ('I Forgot to Remember to Forget'), Eric Von Schmidt ('Joshua Gone Barbados'), John Lee Hooker ('I'm in the Mood') Pete Seeger ('Bells of Rhymney'), Ian and Sylvia ('Song For Canada,' 'Four Strong Winds' and 'The French Girl'), Charles Badger Clark ('Spanish is the Loving Tongue') and Dominic Behan's ('Auld Triangle') to name but a few. There were also experimental jams and as time went on, more of Dylan's own newly minted originals. As these recording sessions continued, the material amassed not only accounted for the most productive period in Bob Dylan's career but one of the most vivid chapters in American music.

Summer of Love

Recorded popular music came of age in 1967. There were of course pointers along the way, signposts, most of which had Bob Dylan's

name on firmly emblazoned on them: *Bringing It All Back Home*
and *Highway 61 Revisited* (both 1965) and the first ever double rock
album, *Blonde on Blonde* (June 1966). Bold explorations in music were
now well underway; boundaries were pushed, studio wizardry,
some might call it overindulgence or even crass pretension. The
self-proclaimed "adult" music scene was divorcing itself from
teen pop and the three-minute moon and June popular song was
giving way to album tracks. Music was becoming more involved,
lengthy and improvisational. Dylan's withdrawal to Woodstock had
come at the same time that the music scene was undergoing this
seismic change so when close to 100,000 hippies converged in San
Francisco's Haight-Ashbury neighbourhood for the Summer of Love,
Bob Dylan was well and truly ensconced in pastoral Woodstock
with his wife and children. The Sixties were more a mindset than a
period in time, but in 1967 and for some time to come, Bob Dylan's
mindset and his rural existence were polar opposites of the new
youth movement that followed his music. Allen Ginsberg, along
with the LSD evangelist Timothy Leary, had attended the "Human
Be-In" in San Francisco's Golden Gate Park (January 14, 1967), and
although Ginsberg talked enthusiastically about the event with
Dylan, Bob seemed not to be impressed by what was happening in
San Francisco, or elsewhere for that matter.

   The next big event to take place on the West Coast was the
Monterey International Pop Music Festival. Staged June 16-18,
1967, this granddaddy of rock festivals was held at the Monterey
County Fairgrounds, a couple of hours drive from of San Francisco.
Although Monterey is often referred to as the first US rock festival,
that accolade belongs to the Fantasy Fair and Magic Mountain
Music Festival, a two-day event that took place at the summit of
Mount Tamalpais in Marin County and was staged a week before
Monterey. Monterey was nonetheless the largest event of its kind.
Thirty-three acts performed over the three days and the festival

is remembered for the first major American appearances by The Jimi Hendrix Experience, The Who, and Ravi Shankar. The event launched the careers of several bands including Canned Heat and Big Brother & the Holding Company. It also helped propel psychedelic rock into the American mainstream. Albert Grossman attended the festival and soon went onto manage Big Brother & the Holding Company.

The American psychedelic period was underway. In 1967 Jefferson Airplane issued *Surrealistic Pillow* and *After Bathing at Baxter's*, Country Joe and the Fish released their debut, *Electric Music for the Mind and Body*, Love put out *Forever Changes* and the Jimi Hendrix Experience followed *Are You Experienced* with *Axis: Bold as Love*. In 2014, Dylan said: "The events of the day, they were just happening and they seemed to be a million miles away. We weren't really participating in any of that stuff ... so we did our thing. We wrote 'Million Dollar Bash' to go along with the Summer of Love."[38]

Several less well-known be-ins were also held on the East Coast in New York's Central Park to protest against various issues such as racism and the US' involvement in the Vietnam War. The Easter 1967 Central Park be-in drew an estimated 10,000 participants and less than a month later, on April 15, another anti-war rally was staged as a part of the "Spring Mobilization to End the War in Vietnam." By now numbers were rapidly growing and some estimate that up to 400,000 attended this event. My guess is that Dylan would have been thankful he was out of town.

Bruce Dorfman remembers Dylan sitting in his art studio and "dwelling on his notoriety and the inner tension that came from it. He'd sit there and say, 'I can't understand it – all I am is an entertainer.'" Regardless, the new liberal counterculture was convinced that he was very much more than that. Noel Stookey, better known as the Paul of Peter, Paul and Mary, visited Dylan in Woodstock in the fall of 1967. Like the many hippies who believed

Dylan was the one with all the answers, Stookey began quizzing Bob with ridiculous questions asking about the Beatles, love and the meaning of life. Dylan simply replied with a question of his own, "Do you ever read the Bible?."

Bobby's in the Basement

The participants in the basement tapes sessions are: Bob Dylan (acoustic guitar / acoustic 12-string guitar / piano and vocals); Robbie Robertson (electric guitar / bass / drums and backing vocals); Richard Manuel (piano / drums / tambourine and backing vocals); Rick Danko (bass / mandolin and vocals); Garth Hudson (organ / clavinet / accordion / piano) and in later sessions, Levon Helm (drums).

Exactly who plays what on these sessions is a little sketchy and even the official 2014 Columbia release of *The Bootleg Series Vol.11: The Basement Tapes Complete*, perhaps wisely chooses not to attempt attributions. As the liner notes state: "Harmony and instrumentation are unknown because all involved were multi-instrumentalists and vocalists. No written documentation remains." Nevertheless, I believe the above credits to be reasonably accurate. In addition to the above, however, we also appear to have Richard Manuel playing lap and pedal steel guitars on a couple of songs; Rick Danko playing fiddle and euphonium and Bob Dylan playing autoharp on 'Comin' Round the Mountain.' As stated previously, drummer Levon Helm had left the Hawks and Dylan's employment at the beginning of the 1966 tour and only returned to the fold part way through the basement sessions. A large body of these recordings therefore either have no drummer or on other occasions either Manuel or Robertson are on sticks duties.

As already mentioned, at this time Dylan, and for that matter the Hawks, appear to have been mostly indifferent to current events. Sure, Bob was watching television and reading the newspapers and he clearly responded to China exploding its first hydrogen bomb in June '67 by writing 'Tears of Rage,' but if we consider the vast amount of songs he wrote during 1967, very few appear to be topical. 'Too Much of Nothing' may well have been inspired by the Detroit 12th Street riot, which took place in July 1967. The biggest US riot for more than a century, the 12th Street riot resulted in the deaths of 43 people and injury to a further 1,189. There were also over 7,200 arrests and more than 2,000 buildings destroyed. In an attempt to quell the disturbance, Governor George W. Romney ordered the National Guard into Detroit and President Lyndon B Johnson sent in both the 82nd and 101st Airborne Divisions. These events were a fixture in the media at precisely the time that Dylan wrote 'Too Much of Nothing.' In 2014, Dylan said that he wrote the song in response to "rioting in Rochester," New York but considering the Rochester race riot had taken place three years prior to the Basement seasons, Dylan would seem to have confused these two events. In that same audio interview, put out to coincide with the release of *The Bootleg Series Vol.11*, Dylan said, "the first time that anybody ever heard of a human heart being transplanted, that was incredible. That was a real breakthrough, so we came up with a song, and then when we got the lyrics down, we took the song to the basement." Unfortunately, he doesn't say which song he's referring to. What we do know, however, is that Dr Christiaan Barnard carried out the world's first human heart transplant on December 3, 1967, which indicates that the basement sessions continued through into December and possibly approaching Christmas. Over the years, conventional wisdom had suggested that the basement tapes sessions ended in either October (Krogagaard, Bjorner) or November (Heylin, Dundas). It is true to say, however, that in his book, *This Wheel's on Fire*, Helm reported that Danko remembers that the basement sessions ran from "March to December," which although ignored by most, now appears to be correct.

Because the basement songs were not meant for public consumption, we get a much less graded insight into Dylan's psyche at this time. For all their apparent frivolity, there is a clear thread running through many of the songs; that of the 'nothingness' of human existence, 'Too Much of Nothing,' (can make a man feel ill at ease), 'Nothing Was Delivered,' and even 'You Ain't Going Nowhere' spring to mind. Some of the songs also include a strong sense of searching or yearning. But what is Dylan searching for? At this point he appears to be looking for some meaning to his life away from the superficial trappings of stardom.

In 'Too Much of Nothing,' Dylan makes several allusions to the Bible ("It's all been written in the book") and to religious practice ("In the day of confession, We cannot mock a soul.") Many people have noted the Biblical allusions in the title of 'This Wheel's On Fire,' where visions of a descending flaming wheel accompany prophetic visions of 2 Peter 3:7 and Daniel 7:9. Although Dylan seems to have taken lines from a Biblical source the song's narrative appears to be more personal than apocalyptic. He will use this 'wheels of fire' motif again in the 1978 song 'Changing of the Guards.'

The song 'Sign on the Cross' is clearly inspired by the Bible. The sign on the cross in the title of Dylan's song undoubtedly refers to the sign placed above the cross when Jesus was crucified. In the Gospel of John (19:19-20) the inscription is explained, "Pilate also had an inscription written and put on the cross. It read, 'Jesus of Nazareth, the King of the Jews.' Many Jews read this inscription because the place where Jesus was crucified was near the city; and it was written in Hebrew, in Latin, and in Greek."

In this song, which very much reminds me of 'The Old Rugged Cross,' Dylan appears to ask if Pilate's mocking sign is true. Was Jesus of Nazareth the King of the Jews?

...Ev'ry day, ev'ry night, see the sign on the cross just layin' up

on top of the hill. Yes, we thought it might have disappeared long ago,
but I'm here to tell you, friends,
that I'm afraid it's lyin' there still.
Dylan concludes this stanza with:

But I just would like to tell you one time,
if I don't see you again, that the thing is,
that the sign on the cross is the thing you might need the most.

An interesting and perhaps important line in the song seems to
have been changed when transcribed for the various official lyrics
books. The line in question, as it appears in *Lyrics* is, "But I don't know
'bout that any more, because the bird is here and you might want
to enter it, but, of course, the door might be closed." At a stretch,
the bird could be interpreted as the holy ghost, if not, then the line
makes little or no sense; at least not to me. In fact, on the recording,
this particular line is quite indistinct and it sounds like Dylan might
actually sing, "Later you might find a door you might want to enter
it, but, of course, the door might be closed." Either way, this might be
Dylan searching for salvation.

Probably because of the zany eccentric nature of many of The
Basement Tapes songs there are critics who posit that 'Sign on the
Cross' has no connection to Dylan's later Christian conversion and
while in one sense that might be true, as stated by author Stephen
Webb, at this point Dylan is, "struggling for a form in which to
express his ambivalence, perhaps even his confusion, about faith."

In 1967, Dylan was clearly troubled and appeared to be at the
beginning of his long search. Initially, it might seem unlikely that
Dylan would be exploring Christian themes of reckoning and
redemption at this point in his career. Many followers of Dylan's
music seem only to associate Christian themes in his songwriting
from 1979 onward. At this point he's not converted, but as Webb

suggests, "Where does conversion begin, except with a question that starts to worry you?"

Al Aronowitz told me: "Of course, Dylan had always used Bible imagery in his songs but that had nothing to do with his faith. But when I was spending time up in Woodstock with him after the accident it was different. He had a large Bible at home and he was reading it. It seemed to me like he was searching. Not for lyrics this time though, but for something else! Salvation? I don't know, he didn't say anything to me but there was something going on. Bob really changed after the accident..."[39]

One of the biggest basement conundrums is 'Quinn the Eskimo (The Mighty Quinn).' Is this as Dylan has said a "simple nursery rhyme" or is it one of the most complex songs from these sessions? Dylan is widely believed to have derived his Quinn character from actor Anthony Quinn's role as an Eskimo in the 1960 movie *The Savage Innocents*. The song is about the arrival of Quinn, a mighty Eskimo who transforms despair into joy and confusion into respite. That certainly sums up the way Dylan was feeling in 1967 ("guarding fumes and making haste, It ain't my cup of meat.") But who is this saviour? He certainly isn't an Inuit, but neither is he Christ the Saviour.

Quinn has been interpreted by some as being a drug dealer. The line, "Just tell me where it hurts yuh, honey, And I'll tell you who to call," could evoke a Dr Feelgood type solution to a situation. Also, "All the pigeons gonna run to him" could imply that only fools are drawn to Quinn. "Ev'rybody's gonna wanna doze" might be a reference to staying away from drugs. Instead of staying awake for nights speeding along on amphetamines, it's now time to doze. Dylan of course mentions "no doze" (a well-known caffeine stimulant) in the song 'Subterranean Homesick Blues.'

In his book *Performing Artist*, Paul Williams notes that a recurrent theme in The Basement Tapes songs is "anticipation." The word "gonna" is highly prevalent at these sessions and is most often used to suggest that something "big" is going to happen down the road: "Ev'rybody's gonna jump for joy," "Ev'rybody's gonna wanna doze," "It's gonna be the meanest flood," "W're all gonna meet, At that million dollar bash." The list is long but the inference is clear, something is on the horizon for Dylan and he is filled with anticipation.

Chock-full of emotional power, the gospel-influenced 'I Shall Be Released' is another song brimming with anticipation and of a soul yearning for freedom. This, the most well-known of all the basement songs, also stands as a serious statement of Dylan's state of mind. At its most basic level, in this song, Dylan analogises life to prison. At a show in Danbury, Connecticut (May 11, 1991), Dylan introduced 'I Shall Be Released' by saying, "This is one of my prison songs." Prisons of the mind are a feature of Dylan's writing throughout the basement songs and even further down the line. The song may have its origins in the radical Irish playwright Brendan Behan's prison song, '(Banks of the) Royal Canal,' also known as 'The Auld Triangle,' which Dylan also recorded in the Big Pink basement. As part of his play, The Quare Fellow, Behan's song highlights the monotony of a prisoner's life while awaiting execution. The prison in 'I Shall Be Released' may be understood as a metaphor either for society or for a tormented psyche from which Dylan is seeking release. This shining light of deliverance will come from the "west unto the east." This is, of course, the opposite direction from that travelled by the sun. The late Bert Cartwright, an ordained minister and Dylan enthusiast, found several possible Biblical and poetic sources for Dylan's wording and they all suggest that the phrase "west unto the east" may not be meant as a description of a direction of movement. Instead, the phrase may simply describe a light that fills the entire sky, from one horizon to the other. Such a light would fill the heavens, the Bible says, when Christ returns. "For as the lightning comes from the east and shines as far as the west, so will be the coming of the Son of man. (Matthew 24:27)

There is a clear reference to mass culture in the third verse when Dylan refers to, "this lonely crowd." *The Lonely Crowd* was the title of David Riesman's best-selling sociology study from 1950 that analysed the adaptive successes and failures of different personality types in an increasingly bureaucratised age. At the time, the book was hugely important to an increasingly self-scrutinising American middle class. As already stated, it is perhaps surprising that Dylan would assert his faith in song at this point in his career. Bert Cartwright comes to the same conclusion as Stephen Webb: "This, of course, is not Dylan's confession of faith, but it does indicate fresh exploration of new biblical mythic images for him."

At this stage, Dylan has rejected accepting Christ in favour of his pursuit of music, which had often been a kind of substitute for religion anyway. Thirty years later Dylan would say: "All my beliefs come out of those old songs, literally, anything from 'Let Me Rest on a Peaceful Mountain' to 'Keep on the Sunny Side'... I believe in a God of time and space, but if people ask me about that, my impulse is to point them back toward those songs... That's my religion... I don't adhere to rabbis, preachers, evangelists. I've learned more from the songs than I've learned from any of this kind of entity."

Nevertheless, the journey of exploration is beginning. It might be long and arduous but Dylan senses, or at least very much hopes, that relief will eventually be forthcoming. At present, however, he can only describe the source of that faith as a vision of his "reflection" that shines above, transcending the real or (probably) symbolic walls that confine him.

In January 1985, wearing a very Eighties black and white jacket and droplet earring almost as long as the ones wore by one of his girl backing singers, Dylan performed a radically re-written 'I Shall

Be Released' during a live telecast celebrating Martin Luther King Day:

It don't take much to be a criminal,
One more move and they'll turn you into one.
At first the pain is just subliminal,
You protect yourself, and you're forever on the run.

He will find you where you're stayin,'
Even in the arms of somebody else's wife,
You're laughing now, you should be praying,
This being the midnight hour of your life.

During the final weeks of his informal basement sessions, Dylan took a break and flew to Nashville to record his eighth studio album. The three sessions needed to complete *John Wesley Harding* (October 17, November 6 and November 29), required just 12 hours in total. Oddly, he would record the album using session musicians rather than the Hawks and he would not include any of the songs that he been writing and playing over the previous six months! Instead, Dylan appears to have written all the songs for his new album just before recording them. According to the liner notes of the *Biograph* box-set (1985), 'I Shall Be Released' was intended for *John Wesley Harding* but not finished in time. This, however, seems highly unlikely.

Quite why Dylan felt the time was now right to record a new studio album is unclear, but in part, the spur could have come from the death of his first idol, Woody Guthrie, who died on October 3, 1967, just two weeks before Bob began recording *John Wesley Harding*. Before examining the songs on that album, let us first investigate what became of the material recorded during the extensive The Basement Tapes sessions.

Dylan referred to the commercial pressures behind the basement recordings in a 1969 interview for *Rolling Stone*: "They weren't demos for myself," Dylan told Jann Wenner. "They were demos of the songs. I was being pushed again ... into coming up with some songs. So, you know ... you know how those things go."[40]

Dylan doesn't reveal to Wenner precisely who was doing the pushing, but it could only be his manager, Albert Grossman. The simple fact is, Dylan's record label would not earn anything from other artists covering his work. The only people to benefit from this exercise would be Dylan and his music publishing company. After Dylan's three-year Witmark contract had expired in 1965, Dylan had formed his own publishing company. Dwarf Music was, however, part-owned by Grossman and he stood to benefit significantly from other artists recording Dylan's new songs. Dylan has claimed that he was not aware of this and that he signed that agreement without ever reading it. Although this might sound crazy on Dylan's part, this contract was signed while he was in the middle of his chaotic and drug-fuelled 1966 world tour. In addition, if Dylan is to be believed, Grossman prevented him from actually reading the contract!

Attorney David Braun has said that before Dylan signed the agreement, he tried to go through the details with him. Grossman, however, "came...racing into the room...and terminated the discussion." Allegedly, Grosman said there was "no need to explain [the documents] fully to Bob [because] he knew what they were about." Later, this would become a complaint that Dylan used against Grossman in their protracted legal battle. Braun said that he persevered in his attempts to talk to Dylan but that Grossman was "determined that the conversation not continue."[41]

In any event, in October 1967, a 14-song demo tape was copyrighted and the compositions were registered to Dwarf Music. Even today, it is not entirely clear why Dylan made this demo tape. He has been asked on several occasions and his answers have always been hazy. In 1978 he said: "They were written vaguely for other people ... They must have been written at the time for the publishing company." In 1984, he told Kurt Loder, "they were just songs we had done for the publishing company, as I remember."[42]

Several commentators have put forward the suggestion that these 14 songs were chosen because that was the number of songs Dylan owed Columbia Records on his contract with them. While this is indeed true, the 14-song tape wasn't put together until October 1967, some three months after Dylan had re-signed with Columbia. With this new contract now in place, in effect, Dylan no longer owed the label anything. Moreover, this 14-song tape was never sent over to Columbia so it couldn't have been meant for them. It seems the number of songs on the tape was pure coincidence. In any event, the 14 Dwarf songs were sent out to other publishing companies for distribution to recording artists who might be interested in recording these songs.

The tracks were: 'Million Dollar Bash' / 'Yea! Heavy and a Bottle of Bread' / 'Please Mrs Henry' / 'Crash on the Levee' / 'Lo and Behold' / 'Tiny Montgomery' / 'This Wheel's on Fire' / 'You Ain't Going Nowhere' / 'I Shall Be Released' / 'Too Much of Nothing' / 'Tears of Rage' / 'Quinn the Eskimo' / 'Open the Door, Homer' / 'Nothing Was Delivered.'*

Peter, Paul and Mary, who of course were managed by Grossman, were the first act to have success with a basement composition when their cover of 'Too Much of Nothing,' released November 1967, reached number 35 on the Billboard Pop Chart. Ian & Sylvia, also managed by Grossman, released 'Tears of Rage' on their 1968 LP Full Circle. The Canadian duo also recorded 'This Wheel's on Fire' and 'Quinn the Eskimo.'

* It is alleged that compiler Robbie Robertson left 'I Shall Be Released' and 'The Mighty Quinn' off the official 1975 double LP The Basement Tapes because both he and Dylan thought the public already knew the songs too well from the many cover versions.

Albert Grossman wanted to attain the maximum exposure possible for Dylan's basement recordings and to that end, sometime in late 1967, he hand-delivered a 14-song, 7-inch demo tape to the Dean Street offices of Dylan's UK music publisher, B Feldman & Co. Over the following months, Feldman's employee, Brenda Ralfini, played this tape to several interested parties, i.e. British recording artists who had a desire to record unreleased Dylan material. Anyone who expressed such an interest would be given an acetate of the relevant song/songs taken from the 7-inch tape reel. These Emidisc acetates were cut in London at Feldman's request and given to the likes of Manfred Mann, The Brian Auger Trinity, and Fairport Convention. It is believed that somewhere between three and 10 of these acetates were made and distributed.

In January 1968, Manfred Mann reached number 1 on the UK Pop Chart with their recording of 'The Mighty Quinn' and in April, 'This Wheel's on Fire,' recorded by Julie Driscoll, Brian Auger and the Trinity, made it to number 5 on the Chart. That same month, the Byrds issued their version of 'You Ain't Goin' Nowhere' as a single. The song was also included as the opening track on their 1968 country-rock album *Sweetheart of the Rodeo*. And a version of 'Nothing was Delivered' closed the album.

In July 1968, now re-branded as The Band, Dylan's backing group and basement partners The Hawks released 'Tears of Rage,' 'This Wheel's on Fire' and 'I Shall Be Released' on their stunning debut album, *Music from Big Pink*. Fairport Convention, who would go on to be serial coverers of Dylan tunes issued 'Million Dollar Bash' on their 1969 album *Unhalfbricking*.

Some of These Bootleggers, They Make Pretty Good Stuff

(A Detour)

Having listened to the 14-song demo tape, in June 1968, Jann

Wenner wrote a front-page *Rolling Stone* story headlined: "Dylan's Basement Tape Should Be Released." "There is enough material – most all of it very good – to make an entirely new Bob Dylan album," Wenner said: "[A] record with a distinct style of its own ... If this were ever to be released it would be a classic."

Reporting such as this whetted the appetites of many a Bob fan and when in April 1969 Dylan released his country-soaked album *Nashville Skyline*, the marketplace was ripe for new Dylan product and two young men, Ken Douglas and Dub Michael Taylor, soon obliged by making such a product available. Ken and Dub both worked at Saturn Records, a "one-stop" wholesale record distributor supplying independent stores in and around Los Angeles. Like many other Dylan followers, the two youths were far from enthusiastic about *Nashville Skyline*. Ken later said of the album, "I don't know if *Nashville Skyline* was a big record for Columbia, but it was a turkey for Saturn." Reel-to-reel copies of the demo tape could now be bought for $5 at the LA store Records and Supertape and tracks like 'This Wheels on Fire' and 'Quinn the Eskimo' were being played on the popular Pasadena underground radio station KPPC-FM5.

In the summer of '69 Dub had come by the December 1961 Minnesota Hotel Tape, a private recording which had been given out to friends by Dylan way back in 1962, before the release of his first album. With this tape already in hand and with some of the basement songs now doing the rounds, the lads amassed enough material to make a double LP set. Finding a cooperative pressing plant was the easy part. In the Los Angeles area there were several record plants that were not first in line to press LPs for the major labels, usually only getting work when the larger plants were running at overcapacity. One such plant, Korelich Engineering & Manufacturing Co, willingly accepted the Dylan job and in July 1969 the rock music bootleg industry was born with the release *Great White Wonder*, a two-LP set in a plain white sleeve.

There was, however, a major flaw in the plan. As employees of Saturn Records, Ken and Dub were both well known by the local LA record stores so it was not possible them to sell these dodgy looking records themselves. Enter a new member of the team, Jim. A friend of Dub's, Jim reckoned there were better things in life than being shot at by the Viet Cong and he had decided to desert from the US Army. After that, it didn't take much to persuade him that bootlegs were a better proposition than boot camp. He needed money and wasn't known in the record business so Jim became the "face" of the operation, visiting and selling to record stores.

The appearance of the 14-song basement demos is usually stated as being the impetus for the *Great White Wonder*. Much later, however, when those involved were criticised by some for putting out a "cut-and-paste" double album, instead of a single LP containing just the basement songs, Ken Douglas said that at the time they had only managed to get their hands on seven of the 14 available basement tracks. Two months and several pressings later, *Great White Wonder* had generated an enormous amount of interest and Ken and Jim foolishly agreed to a meeting with reporter Jerry Hopkins in Platypus Record Store in Hollywood. The September edition of *Rolling Stone* magazine featured the interview and an article: "More then 2,300 copies of a 'bootleg' Bob Dylan album are now being sold in Los Angeles in what may be the entertainment industry's first truly hip situation comedy ... [The] effect of the album's release on the local record scene has been phenomenal. Five radio stations [in Santa Barbara, Long Beach, Pasadena and two in Los Angeles] immediately began playing the LP thereby creating a demand that often far exceeded a shop's limited supply. The supply line was ragged at best, largely because the two men behind the scheme ... are the 'exclusive distributors.' Not only that say the men ... 'We have to borrow cars to take the records around.' Distribution has been further hampered by the fact that they will not give their names, addresses or a telephone where they might be reached.

As a result, shops are charging whatever they think the traffic will bear. The two producers say they are wholesaling the package at $4.50 each ($4.25 apiece after the first 50), and shops are asking from $6.50 up. One store, The Psychedelic Supermarket in Hollywood ... is even asking and getting, $12.50 for the two-record set ... In the meantime [the people involved are] struggling with their little company's first release and protecting their anonymity.

'What're your names?' I asked.

'Call me Patrick,' said the one with the longest hair.

'Call me Vladimir,' said the one with the bushiest sideburns.

'How do you spell Vladimir?'

'I don't know, man. Make it Merlin.'"[43]

The act of bootlegging Dylan's unreleased songs would soon change the face of rock music forever. The release of *Great White Wonder* spawned an underground industry that would prosper for the next half-century and gain Bob Dylan the dubious distinction of being the most bootlegged popular music artist of all time. On February 15, 1972, the United States implemented the McClellan Bill on anti-bootlegging making it a federal offence to make and sell bootleg records. By then, however, the genie was well and truly out of the bottle.

Chapter Two

Drifter's Escape

The Story of John Wesley Harding

Eighteen months after the completion of *Blonde on Blonde* Dylan began work on his next album, *John Wesley Harding*. He had found recording with the Hawks in Big Pink to be a pleasurable experience and with a new record deal finally in place he was now ready to move forward. The drifter had not escaped, far from it, but he had taken his first tentative steps on a new highway. At the time, Dylan had no idea if this path would lead him to Lincoln Country Road or Armageddon. In the end, there may not be very much difference between those two destinations, but at least his journey had begun.

In his only 1967 interview, Dylan told Michael Iachetta: "I'm trying to be like the medium at a séance. There's mystery, magic, truth and *The Bible* in great folk music. I can't hope to touch that, but I'm going to try."[1]

In 1978, Dylan talked to Matt Damsker about how *John Wesley Harding* was the start of his musical exploration and how in 1978 he might have finally reached his goal with *Street-Legal*: "I've never broke tradition – I've never gone and done something that had no tradition behind it. When I finally broke with it at *John Wesley Harding*, I started out again, and I knew it wasn't where I was gonna stay very long, but I had to explore that territory, and never until I got to *Blood on the Tracks* did I finally get hold of what I needed to get hold of and once I got hold of that, *Blood on the Tracks* wasn't it either, and neither was *Desire*. But *Street-Legal* comes the closest to where my music is going, you know, for the rest of the time..."[2]

It is not known for certain when the songs for *John Wesley Harding* were written. It is interesting though that none of them are to be found on the now fully heard Basement Tapes recordings. According to Robbie Robertson: "As I recall it was just on a kind of whim that Bob went down to Nashville. And there, with just a couple of guys, he put those songs down on tape."[3] Producer Bob Johnston had visited Dylan in Woodstock in September and Bob had indicated a willingness to record a new album. Although Dylan didn't try out any of these new songs during the basement sessions, according to Bob Johnston, when Dylan arrived in Nashville he already had the songs: "He was staying in the Ramada Inn down there," Johnson said. "[A]nd he played me his songs and he suggested we just use bass and guitar and drums on the record. I said fine, but also suggested we add a steel guitar."[4]

Johnston's memory might be a little faulty here. If Dylan did play songs for his producer before he started recording then it surly wasn't the entire album. It has been said that Bob decided to journey to Nashville by train – a two-day ride – and that 'Drifter's Escape,' for one, was written on that train journey. I would guess that other songs were also written either on the way to the three sessions or in-between them.

Conventional wisdom has always had Dylan finishing up the Big Pink basement sessions before going down to Nashville to begin work on what would become *John Wesley Harding*. This notion, however, seems to have been blown out of the water by the aforementioned talk of a human heart transplant. If Dylan's statement is factual, and I see no reason in this instance to doubt him, then he began recording *John Wesley Harding* almost two months before the end of the basement sessions; taking three short breaks to go down to Nashville to record Harding. It is probable, however, that these later Basement Tapes sessions did not take place in Big Pink, but in the new home of Rick Danko and Levon

Helm on Wittenberg Road in Bearsville.

The buzz word for *John Wesley Harding* has to be simplicity. In 1968 Dylan told *Rolling Stone* magazine: "What I'm trying to do now is not use too many words. There's no line that you can stick your finger through; there's no hole in any of the stanzas. There's no blank filler. Each line has something."[5]

According to Allen Ginsberg, Dylan had talked to him about this new approach to writing. Ginsberg: "He was writing shorter lines, with every line meaning something. He wasn't just making up a line to go with a rhyme anymore; each line had to advance the story, bring the song forward ... There was no wasted language, no wasted breath. All the imagery was to be functional rather than ornamental."[6]

There is no doubting that *John Wesley Harding* is autobiographical. In an interview with Anthony Scaduto Dylan said: "Before I wrote *John Wesley Harding* I discovered something about all those earlier songs I had written. I discovered that when I used words like 'he' and 'it' and 'they' and talking about other people, I was really talking about nobody except me. I went into *John Wesley Harding* with that knowledge in my head ... I was writing about myself in all those songs."[7]

Scaduto: "In Harding [Dylan] is describing the fires that almost consumed him. He is saying: this is what I was like; this is what I have gone through.' And, in writing about himself Dylan drew on *The Bible* for the form and content on which to build the poems, further emphasising his search for redemption and salvation."[8]

At a time of enormous pressure, the author of *John Wesley Harding* communicates a surprising sense of musical, mental, and spiritual calm; a clear antidote for the total confusion of the past 12 months. The album sets out the songwriter's reflection on the "old" Bob Dylan and his quest to find, or maybe create, a "new" Bob Dylan who, among other things, would be as independent as possible from the pressures of his management and of the recording industry in general. After the infamous "Judas" tour, he must have also given a great deal of thought to his current relationship with his fan base. Most of the songs either depict the narrator, Dylan, in search of salvation, or offering advice as to how others might find their salvation. Throughout the album there is a battle raging between the old and new Dylan; the two parts of his Gemini self fighting to emerge as a unified entity.

Music critic Jon Landau felt there was a new seriousness in Dylan's lyrics and that the war in Vietnam influenced him. He thought that Dylan was adopting the stance of a religious or conscientious objector. While Landau admits that none of the songs on *John Wesley Harding* are directly about the war or are protests against it, he does believe that "Dylan has felt the war" and that he "manifests a profound awareness of the war and how it [was] affecting all of us." Writing in *Chronicles*, however, Dylan confessed that at the time he couldn't relate to protest or events on the news. Instead, he was merely concerned about being a good family man.

Another significant aspect in which *John Wesley Harding* has been viewed is religion. Two writers in particular, Robin Witting and the late Bert Cartwright, traced countless Biblical allusions, finding references in almost every line. Dylan himself once supported this approach, calling *John Wesley Harding* the "first biblical rock album."[9] Possibly picking up on this comment, early Dylan biographer Anthony Scaduto proclaimed with great confidence that *John Wesley Harding* was in fact "Dylan's version of the Bible," containing "songs written as parables describing the fall and rebirth of one man Bob Dylan."[10]

In 1968, when Dylan sat down to talk with the editors of *Sing Out!* magazine, they likened the songs on *John Wesley Harding* to Kafka's parables. "Yes," Dylan responded, "but the only parables I know are the biblical parables." The response to this was, "When did you read

The Bible parables?" "I have always read *The Bible*," answered Dylan, "though not necessarily always the parables." They then joked that Dylan did not seem to be the kind of person who would pick up a *Gideon Bible* in a hotel room. "Well," he said despairingly, "you never know."[11]

One of the great difficulties in using *The Bible* to interpret *John Wesley Harding* is determining what Dylan intended with all these allusions. Most critics have sidestepped the issue by writing with generalities. In this way, Cartwright concluded simply that, with the album, the singer describes, "his experience of himself and America in the context of the living God."[12]

Understanding the personal components of the songs Dylan wrote for *John Wesley Harding* requires a basic understanding of the issues with which Bob was then dealing. The songs can be seen to tell a story that generally corresponds to Dylan's spiritual odyssey in the months following his motorcycle accident. Dylan's friend and biographer Robert Shelton was perhaps the first to note that there was logic in the album's presentation of themes, suggesting that the songs on the first side of the album conveyed a sense of guilt, while those on the second side suggested atonement.[13] If the songs were indeed written shortly before they were recorded and in the order recorded, it could be highly significant that Dylan's first idol, Woody Guthrie, had died on October 3, 1967, just two weeks before Bob began the *John Wesley Harding* recording sessions.

As well as the desire to withdraw from the madness of the road and to extract himself from a plethora of other business commitments, Dylan was now beginning to learn how much his manager Albert Grossman was earning off him. For instance, Grossman had long been receiving what was said to be a hidden percentage of Bob's royalty earnings and he was allegedly billing Dylan's company for significant personal expenses. Dylan's conflicts with Grossman were growing on other issues as well. Dylan's friend and sometimes road manager Victor Maymudes had already warned Bob that Grossman was making way too much money from Bob's music publishing but Dylan trusted Grossman and so Maymudes' fate was excommunication. It would, therefore, be the summer of 1968 before Dylan discovered the full extent to which Grossman 'owned' him.

To celebrate the birth of his son Samuel (July 30, 1968), Dylan decided that he would like to change the name of his music publishing company. Business administrator Naomi Saltzman informed Bob she couldn't do that without first getting express permission from Albert because Grossman owned 50 per cent of Dwarf Music. As previously stated, Dylan had signed this contract without reading it while on his 1966 tour. The terms of that 10-year contract would eventually be altered on July 17, 1970. Dylan later told Robert Shelton: "I finally had to sue him. Because Albert wanted it quiet, he settled out of court ... He had me signed up for 10 years ... for part of my records, for part of my everything. He only had me for 20per cent. There were others who had to give him 50 per cent."[14]

In actual fact, even after the new July 1970 agreement Grossman still retained a 50 per cent share in Dylan's publishing. Dylan, however, would now be in direct control of the publishing and he would be responsible for the administration of the accounts. In other words, he would be responsible for paying Grossman his share rather than the reverse. It still wasn't a great deal for Dylan but he later said, "I was willing to enter into the July 1970 agreement because I thought that I would finally be rid of Grossman."[15]

The son of Russian Jewish immigrants, Albert Grossman was a financial wizard who would end up completely redefining the role of personal music management. Attorney David Braun said that Albert, "Was the most successful manager ever ... as smart as anyone I ever met regarding business ... the man who invented personal full-time management."[16]

Over the course of his career, Grossman's client list included: Bob Dylan, Janis Joplin, Peter, Paul and Mary, Odetta, Gordon Lightfoot, Ian and Sylvia, Richie Havens, Todd Rundgren, Electric Flag and The Band. When Al Aronowitz asked Grossman how he and Dylan met, Grossman answered, "We were both waiting for the same bus"– just beautiful! In his memoir, *Chronicles: Volume One*, Dylan describes his first encounter with Grossman at the Gaslight café, "He looked like Sydney Greenstreet from the film *The Maltese Falcon*," Dylan said. "[He] had an enormous presence, always dressed in a conventional suit and tie, and he sat at his corner table. Usually when he talked, his voice was loud like the booming of war drums. He didn't talk so much as growl."[17]

By the late Sixties, however, Albert's interest in the business that had made him his fortune was beginning to wane and as the Sixties gave way to a new decade, Grossman's fortunes changed. In the space of six months he was hit by three significant events. In March 1970, Peter Yarrow was convicted of and served three months in prison for taking "improper liberties" with a 14-year-old girl. Because of this, Peter, Paul and Mary broke up and would not work together for the next eight years. Protracted contractual disagreements with Bob Dylan came to a head and Dylan took back control of his affairs in the July 1970 Agreement and on October 4, 1970 Janis Joplin died from a heroin overdose. Those closest to Grossman are of the opinion that Janis' tragic death was the final straw for his losing interest in the music business.

Jonathan Taplin: "In the end it all just got to be more than Albert could handle. [He] lost his heart for the music and started getting into restaurants and real estate."[18]

Al Aronowitz: "After a time, Albert's life revolved around haute cuisine and he paid more attention to building gourmet restaurants than he did to building hit acts."[19] Even Grossman's wife Sally admitted Albert lost interest in management. "Absolutely," Sally told Rory O'Conner. "He couldn't wait to get out by then. He was burnt out."[20]

The questions for consideration here are how much did Dylan know about Grossman's dealings at the time he was writing the songs for *John Wesley Harding* and how much of Dylan's resentment for Grossman found its way into the groves of that album? Although Dylan didn't fully discover how deeply in hock he was to Grossman until some nine months later, there was already a considerable conflict between a manager who wanted to earn from his artist and an artist who wasn't sure he wanted to work.

So, who is the protagonist of *John Wesley Harding* dealing with on these songs, Albert Grossman or Christ? Interestingly, the previously referred to medieval lectern on which Dylan had kept his Bible had been a present to Dylan from Grossman. However, after the falling out, and seemingly unwilling to have any direct contact with his manager, Dylan returned this costly gift to Grossman via friend and Woodstock cafe owner Bernard Paturel. In 1978, Dylan told *Rolling Stone* magazine: "*John Wesley Harding* was a fearful album – just dealing with fear (laughing), but dealing with the devil in a fearful way, almost..."[21]

Although the songs on *John Wesley Harding* are very different from the basement recordings (less light-hearted, much less raucous and very much more focused), they can be said to retain the spirit of the Big Pink sessions and the sense of searching remains very strong. The Bible imagery that was starting to emerge during the basement sessions is, however, now amplified many-fold. A further legacy of the basement sessions was that Dylan continued to write out the words to the songs before finding the tunes.

Short of reverting to 'one man and his guitar,' the move toward musical simplicity on *John Wesley Harding* is taken just about as far as it can go. Over the years, a common observation has been made that this simplicity ran counter to then-popular trends of both complex musical content and production values. In 2012, Bob Johnston recalled: "By '67 music had changed a lot, every artist on the planet was spending all their time in the studio trying to make the biggest-sounding record possible. Not Bob Dylan. When he came down [to Nashville] to record *John Wesley Harding* he tells me he wants the record to be a stripped-down affair."[22]

While there is no doubt that Dylan was in part responding to the excesses of the "psychedelic revolution" and the likes of The Beatles' *Sgt. Pepper's Lonely Hearts Club Band* album, his stripped bare approach to *John Wesley Harding* was mostly Dylan following his own judgment as opposed to reacting against others with a grand statement.

"I didn't know how to record the way other people were recording, and I didn't want to," Dylan told Matt Damsker in 1978. "The Beatles had just released *Sgt. Pepper's*, which I didn't like at all ... Talk about indulgence. I thought that was a very indulgent album, though the songs on it were real good. I just didn't think all that production was necessary..."[23]

"I asked Columbia to release [*John Wesley Harding*] with no publicity and no hype," Dylan said in interview, "because this was the season of hype."[24]

Turning this debate on its head for a moment, guitarist Carlos Santana believes that *Sgt. Pepper's* might have been influenced by Dylan. Santana: "I would dare to say that I blame *Sgt. Pepper's* on Bob Dylan, because they were still singing like a boy band ... until they were exposed to him ... But then they saw this guy in an Afro, singing songs like 'Desolation Row' and 'Like a Rolling Stone,' and I think they went, 'Dang, this is different. This guy is profound, and he's singing for our generation.' ...The Beatles launched into a consciousness and a way of writing lyrics that was different, beginning with *Rubber Soul*, and some of those songs they even sound like Dylan singing ... on those songs you hear Dylan's voice."[25]

Drifter's Escape

The first song that Dylan recorded for the *John Wesley Harding* album was 'Drifter's Escape,' a seemingly simple tale of an accused man (Dylan?) facing a jury. Bob wrote the song while travelling to the first recording session! As mentioned by several commentators, including Robert Shelton, the lyrics provide a Kafka-esque narrative in which an outsider is oppressed by society, but not conquered. The first line of this first song, "Help me in my weakness," sees Dylan turn toward God for help.

The protagonist, who is put on trial without knowing what the charges are against him – just as Dylan did not understand the criticism he received when he 'went electric' – has suffered emotionally. "My trip," he says, "hasn't been a pleasant one." Even after the trial, as in Kafka, the Drifter doesn't know what he has done wrong. Nevertheless, the jury "cried for more," which was "ten times worse" than the trial itself. Then, through the divine intervention of a bolt of lightning, which "Struck the courthouse out of shape," the Drifter makes good his escape. From this, we can assume that true justice comes only from above and not from any earthly judge.

It would not be too big a leap of faith to imagine that the Drifter escaped to a tranquil Woodstock hideaway where he took stock of his life while reading the Bible and Hank Williams' lyrics, including those of Williams' alter ego, Luke the Drifter.

I Dreamed I Saw St. Augustine

The next song to be recorded was 'I Dreamed I Saw St. Augustine.' Many critics have attempted to address the possible significance of Dylan's invocation of the historical figure, St. Augustine of

Hippo, a bishop and philosopher from Roman North Africa who formulated the doctrine of original sin and died in 430 AD. Some feel there is no significance while others note that St. Augustine's autobiographical work, Confessions – an influential model for Christian writers throughout the Middle Ages – recounts his having led a sinful and immoral life and how much he regretted his debauchery and was seeking redemption in a way that might have appealed to Dylan who was now seemingly putting his rock'n'roll lifestyle behind him.

Why Dylan chose to use Augustine's name in his song title is open to debate but Augustine had expressed his clear views about Jews and their persecution by Rome. Although Augustine wrote: "The true image of the Hebrew is Judas Iscariot, who sells the Lord for silver. The Jew can never understand the Scriptures and forever will bear the guilt for the death of Jesus," he provided a theological rationale for preserving Jews and gave a reason as to why they had survived centuries of persecution by Rome. Augustine believed Jewish people would be converted to Christianity at "the end of time" and argued that God had allowed them to survive, albeit "debased," "destitute" and "in dispersion," as a warning to Christians and because of this he argued they should be permitted to dwell in Christian lands.

It should be noted that there were two St. Augustine's; the other being the lesser known 1st Archbishop of Canterbury. In any event, neither Augustine was martyred so clearly the lyrics cannot be taken literally and it would appear that St. Augustine is used here, at least in part, to symbolise another person. The real clues would seem therefore to be in the song's title, first line and melody, all of which plainly evoke the 1936 song 'Joe Hill,' about the labour organiser and poet who, in 1915, was executed by firing squad in Utah on a phoney murder charge in the face of massive protests. The first line of 'Joe Hill,' "I dreamed I saw Joe Hill last night, alive as you or me," is, except for the proper name, identical to Dylan's opening line in 'I Dreamed I Saw St. Augustine.' This provides a clue to Dylan's intent. If Woody Guthrie's recent death had indeed been part of the impetus for the *John Wesley Harding* album then Guthrie's connection to Hill is just one step removed.

Dylan talks at length about Joe Hill, both the man and the song, in *Chronicles*. Bob had read about labour activist Hill in the early Sixties in pamphlets in the back room of Izzy Young's Greenwich Village Folklore Center. Dylan said that as far as protest songs went, he didn't rate 'Joe Hill' highly. "Protest songs are difficult to write without making them come off as preachy and one-dimensional," Dylan said. "[B]ut if there was ever someone who could inspire a song, it was him. Joe had the light in his eyes." Dylan went on to say, "I fantasised that if I had written the song, I would have immortalised him in a different way..."[26]

In Dylan's song, Augustine is cast as the 'old' Bob Dylan, loosely in the role of a Joe Hill / Guthrie-esque saint, and also the 'new' Bob Dylan who has the dream. The fact that Dylan's St. Augustine carries a blanket underneath his arm indicates that like Joe Hill and Woody Guthrie he is a traveller, a wandering prophet, another of Dylan's drifters. But while the blanket suggests poverty, "a coat of solid gold" indicates material wealth. Nevertheless, as we will see later with Dylan's lonesome hobo, a man who had 14-karat gold teeth, material wealth is no guarantee of spiritual happiness.

Dylan wants to make it clear to those that he addresses, his fans, that they should not follow him, "go on your way accordingly." At the same time, Dylan wants to encourage his listeners and let them know that, at some level, he still shares their concerns. The song's final verse tells us that the 'old' Dylan no longer exists. The 'new' Dylan, the author of the song, admits that he "was among the ones / That put him out to death." This makes the new Dylan, upon waking, "alone and terrified." He is isolated in upstate New York and about to change the direction of his life and career. In this song, Dylan strives to find his own new direction and to lead listeners down a path to moral truth.

The Ballad of Frankie Lee
and Judas Priest

The third and final recording at the October session was the lengthy (5:35 minutes) 'The Ballad of Frankie Lee and Judas Priest.' The song, like 'St. Augustine,' features the death of its leading character that again stands for the 'old' Dylan. The song can also be understood as a parable about the relationship and the growing distance between Dylan (Frankie Lee) and Albert Grossman (Judas Priest). The two men begin as the "best of friends" but things soon change when money rears its ugly head. Judas was of course an infamous traitor, which was how Dylan now saw Grossman and the line, "Well, Frankie Lee.../ He soon lost all control / Over ev'rything which he had made," brings to mind Dylan's lack of control over his publishing. Judas Priest's offer of money, "a roll of tens," evokes Judas Iscariot and thirty pieces of silver. When Dylan decided on the name Judas he surely must also have thought about the shout that had accrued at his recent concert in Manchester, England.

In the end, Frankie died in the arms of Judas Priest in order that a 'new' Dylan could be born. As he had on previous occasions, Dylan was describing the evolution of his different 'selves' and the replacement of one by another symbolically. Quite uncharacteristically, Dylan ends this ballad with a clear explanation:

Well the moral of the story
The moral of this song
Is simply that one should never be
Where one does not belong
So when you see your neighbor carryin' somethin'
Help him with his load

And don't go mistaking Paradise
For that home across the road

Dylan returned to Nashville on November 6 and recorded five songs that generally ask the questions "Where am I now?" and "What should I do next?" Some of the songs suggest that Dylan is still uncertain about his new direction while others set out a fresh set of rules that he must now abide by.

All Along the Watchtower

The first song to be attempted at the second *John Wesley Harding* session, 'All Along the Watchtower,' is without doubt the best-known song from the album, though most people probably got their introduction to it through the superb electric guitar driven Jimi Hendrix version. In the liner notes to the *Biograph* album (1985), Dylan said of the Hendrix version: "I liked Jimi Hendrix's record ... and ever since he died I've been doing it that way. Funny though, his way of doing it and my way ... weren't that dissimilar, I mean the meaning of the song doesn't change like when some artists do other artists' songs."

Although initially recorded acoustically, across the years Dylan has always performed the song on electric guitar. With its dark mood and mysterious quality, the song contains the album's most overt biblical allusions. The setting is drawn from chapter 21 of Isaiah in the Old Testament, which tells the story of the fall of Babylon. According to Robin Witting, who has written several booklets about *John Wesley Harding*, "'All Along the Watchtower' is practically a paraphrase of the Book of Isaiah in 12 lines."

The song begins with a dialogue between two characters, the Joker and Thief who, Stephen Scobie has argued at length, can be taken as symbolic aspects of Dylan's character (as well as myths emanating, in Scobie's view, from the universal "trickster"). The scholar Aidan Day, like Scobie, sees the Joker and the Thief as different aspects of a single person, engaged in "self-dialogue," possibly about issues of creativity and business or perhaps about recent events in a rapidly changing America. The Joker may have been chosen for its symbolism used in tarot. As we will see later in our story, Sara Dylan was a believer in tarot and could read the cards, something that Bob would increasingly come to depend on. The Fool, Jester or Joker is a potent card in the tarot deck, usually representing a new beginning and, consequently, an end to something in a persons' old life.

The Joker is numbered 0 in the tarot deck and does not have a specific place in the sequence of the cards. The Joker can come either at the beginning of the Major Arcana or at the end. The Major Arcana is often considered as the Joker's journey through life. On the card, the Joker is shown at the beginning of his journey and the sun rising behind him represents that beginning. He is facing northwest, the direction of the unknown. He is looking upwards, toward the sky, or Spirit. He is about to step off a cliff into the material world but is he prepared?

In the song, Dylan has a definite sense of alienation from a confused world and he plainly seems frustrated. The time has come for change. It's time to escape a bad situation: "'There must be some way out of here,' said the joker to the thief." The Thief endeavours to calm the Joker, pointing out that many among them "feel that life is but a joke" and then adding hopefully: "But you and I, we've been through that and this is not our fate."

The Tower, or Watchtower, is also a tarot card. It is commonly interpreted as meaning danger, destruction, sudden change, higher learning and liberation. The destruction, however, is on a physical scale, as opposed to a spiritual level. The Tower itself represents ambitions built on false premises. We will return to The Tower in 'Changing of the Guards' much nearer the end of our story.

In 1 Thessalonians 5:2, Jesus said: "For you yourselves know full well that the day of the Lord will come just like a thief in the night." In Dylan's 1979 song 'When He Returns,' Dylan sings "For like a thief in the night, He'll replace wrong with right." Jesus was of course crucified between two thieves. One thief mocked Jesus while the other asked him for salvation.

As previously mentioned, the worsening situation between Dylan and his then manager seems to come to the fore in several of the album's songs and here Grossman could be portrayed as one of the "Businessmen" who drink Dylan's wine. Grossman and others in the music business could easily be seen as gorging themselves with the fruits of Dylan's labours. Having just recorded the Basement demos, the "ploughmen" may perhaps be seen as an allusion to other recording artists covering Dylan's songs.

As already mentioned, a great deal has been made, and justifiably so, of the close parallel of the song's imagery to that of the Old Testament's Book of Isaiah (21:8-9), including Dylan's use of the watchtower and two horsemen. It is then quite tempting to cast Dylan, like Isaiah, as an American prophet who is foretelling the destruction of American society for its wicked and corrupt ways. It is equally likely, however, that Dylan is merely talking to himself about the need for change in his life. The allusion to prophecy serves to underline the inevitability of a radical change and perhaps associates this change, as did the prophet Isaiah, with the sinful or corrupt behaviour of others.

Even though 'Watchtower' is just 12 lines in length – the shortest song on an album of mostly short songs – it has unbelievable power and drama through which Dylan communicates a foreboding that "the hour is getting late" (the imminent return of Jesus?). Seen by many as a 'circular' song, 'Watchtower' seems much longer than its 2.02 minutes. Christopher Ricks has commented that, "at the conclusion of the last verse it is as if the song bizarrely begins at last, and as if the myth began again."[27] The song is a fine example of Dylan's manipulation of time. Despite its length, or lack thereof, the song manages to summarise all of the album's themes.

John Wesley Harding

The fifth song to be recorded, 'John Wesley Harding,' will eventually open the album of the same name. The song provides the listener with a partial statement of where Dylan stood at that time. It asserts to be about the Western outlaw John Wesley Hardin whose name Dylan has intentionally misspelt. As a consequence, Andy Gill suggests that Dylan is not singing about a specific historical character, but rather about the "outlaw myth" in general.[28] In an interview with Jann Wenner, Dylan all but confirmed this when he said he chose the name simply because it "fit the tempo."

When Hubert Saal of *Newsweek* enquired if Dylan had added a 'g' to the outlaw's name to make up for all the g's he dropped in his songs, Dylan dignified the question with the response, "No, that's just the way the name always sounded to me."[29] Dylan also recognised that the song sounded incomplete and that it didn't fit well within what he called the "suite" that comprised the rest of the album, which is why it became the lead-off track.

Unlike the real Hardin, a vicious Texas outlaw who claimed to have killed 42 men, including a sheriff and a sleeping man, Dylan's outlaw "was a friend to the poor" and was "never known to hurt an honest man." In complete contrast, Hardin, who was the son of a Methodist preacher and named after John Wesley, the founder of the Methodist denomination of the Christian church, murdered his first victim aged just 15. The fact that Dylan's Harding was a friend to the poor parallels Woody Guthrie's somewhat romantic version of the outlaw Pretty Boy Floyd. Floyd committed bank robberies but then saved poor framers from pen-wielding bankers and mortgage foreclosures by supposedly destroying mortgage documents during his robberies.

There is little doubt that Dylan's Harding is an amalgam of outlaws and there is also a definite hint of John Hardy in there. Dylan writes that Harding "trav'led with a gun in every hand," while 'John Hardy' "carried two guns every day." There might also be some significance in the story that while he was awaiting execution in jail, Hardy found religion and confessed his sins to the Minister. Having made peace with the Lord, the morning before his death, he requested that he be baptised in a river near the town.

It's also true that Dylan thought of himself as an outlaw. Al Aronowitz: "Once, as we were on our way out for the night, Bob looked at himself in the full-length mirror of his suite in the Gramercy Park Hotel, broke into a grin and asked, 'Well? Do I look like Billy the Kid?' ... The Kid is an outlaw whose nature is to be secretive, private, mysterious and deceptive. Bob wasn't famous for spilling his guts or wearing his heart on his sleeve. He kept his emotions to himself because he didn't want to show weakness..."[30]

Al Aronowitz told me: "[Dylan] would put these things into his songs but you had to work them out and you were never sure if you had got it right. I never asked him to explain. He wouldn't have told me anything anyway and prying would have got you excommunicated from the outlaw gang– the Wild Bunch."[31]

Again, some of the lyrics to 'John Wesley Harding' can be read as applying to Dylan's current situation, "With his lady by his side / He took a stand. ... And there was no man around / Who could track or chain him down / He was never known / To make a foolish move."

These lines could describe Dylan's self-imposed exile with his wife in Woodstock where the fans and all those wanting something from him (his novel, a film, further touring), were unable to "track or chain him down."

As I Went Out One Morning

The next song to be recorded, 'As I Went out One Morning,' reflects upon Dylan's career before the motorcycle accident and as such is out of narrative sequence with other recordings from this session, which dealt primarily with then-current events. It is unsurprising therefore, that when the album was finally sequenced, 'As I Went out One Morning' was promoted to track two, next to its bedfellow, 'I Dreamed I Saw St. Augustine.'

The song's beginning is a clear allusion to Dylan's previous association with the Folk Protest Movement. As author Clinton Heylin noted, the song's opening line, "As I went out one morning," is the folk equivalent of the classic blues opening, "Woke up this morning." Dylan's song appears to borrow from the traditional 'Lolly-Too-Dum' ("As I went out one morning to take the pleasant air"), a song performed by the likes of Burl Ives, Pete Seeger and Tommy Makem.

The next line, "To breathe the air around Tom Paine's," is a reference to the Tom Paine award given by the Emergency Civil Liberties Union (ECLU), an award that was given to Bob Dylan in December 1963. The song appears to refer to a Dylan muse from his 'Folk Protest' days. The lady in question is described as the "fairest damsel / That ever did walk in chains." The damsel could be Dylan's Greenwich Village girlfriend Suze Rotolo who had worked as a political activist in the office of the Congress of Racial Equality (CORE) and was the driving force behind many of Dylan's early "finger-pointing" songs. Equally, the lady could be Joan Baez, whose commitment to civil rights and social justice was stoic. A clue could be that Clark Foreman, the then head of the ECLU, was a close friend of Baez and her family. In the end, it matters not who the old muse was because Dylan has now put aside his dedication to a transcendent muse. Moreover, the fair damsel in the song would appear to be chained by society and its expectations.

In the song's final verse, the real Tom Paine makes an appearance. He causes the muse to loosen her grip on Dylan. A symbol of true freedom, in the closing lines of the song Tom Paine apologises, "'I'm sorry, sir,' he said to me, / I'm sorry for what she's done." Dylan was embarking on a new path and would no longer serve his former mistress.

I Pity the Poor Immigrant

This song could be a cautionary tale to those who might be considering making changes in their life, most especially if those changes are purely for the acquisition of material wealth. Here, Dylan could be weighing up what changes he should now be making while also looking back in anger at Grossman's recent conduct? Those who have attempted to interpret this song have taken many very different roads in the hope of making sense of the piece. Is Dylan the narrator, or is it God talking? Wilfred Mellers, author of *A Darker Shade of Pale*, suggests the song "points a crooked finger at the American Dream," while Robert Shelton suggests that we are all immigrants or exiles from the Gates of Eden. One very clear thing is that while writing the song Dylan must have had the Bible open at the Book of Leviticus, especially Leviticus 26, verses 17, 19, 20 and 26.

As an illustration, take the following three quotes from Leviticus 26:19-20: "I will make your heaven as iron." (Dylan: "Whose heaven is like ironsides.") "Your strength shall be spent in vain." (Dylan: "Whose strength is spent in vain.") "You shall eat and not be satisfied." (Dylan: "Who eats but is not satisfied.") Bert Cartwright believes that in 'I Pity the Poor Immigrant' Dylan makes no fewer than eight illusions to the Book of Leviticus. Regardless of where the inspiration for the lyrics came from, it has to be said that gourmet Grossman, the son of an immigrant, is a very good fit for many of them.

That man whom with his fingers cheats
And who lies with every breath

Who eats but is not satisfied
Who hears but does not see
Who falls in love with wealth itself
And turns his back on me

Who builds his town with blood
Whose visions in the final end
Must shatter like the glass

The song's melody is borrowed from the 19th-century Scottish folk tune 'Come All Ye Tramps and Hawkers.' Reputed to have been composed by Besom Jimmy, the song was popular with the likes of The Dubliners during the second folk revival. Robert Shelton noted that Dylan might have got the tune from one of his early Sixties Greenwich Village contemporaries, Bonnie Dobson, who frequently performed the ballad 'Peter Amberley' which uses the same melody. Dobson released the song on her second album, At Folk City (1962). Interestingly, 'Peter Amberly' is the tale an immigrant's journey that ends with Amberly "Awaiting the Saviour's calling on that great Judgment Day."

I Am a Lonesome Hobo

'I Am a Lonesome Hobo' is yet another song about personal change; another slice of 'old Bob,' 'new Bob.' On the face of it, the song evokes the typical riches to rags tradition. The 'hobo' had seen it all, at one time he was "rather prosperous" and "There was nothing [he] did lack." He had 14-karat gold teeth and wore silk shirts. His prosperity had, however, turned him into a selfish man unable to trust others. Unsure of what is now going on around him, Dylan, like the hobo, had become an outcast.

To begin to comprehend the songs 'I Am a Lonesome Hobo' and 'Drifter's Escape,' we must first understand what the terms hobo and a drifter, which are much the same, actually mean. Hobo is an American expression and outside of the United States the word is often confused with tramp and bum. Nevertheless, unlike a 'tramp,' who works only when forced to, and a 'bum,' who does not work at all, a 'hobo is a migrant worker who is often impoverished and homeless. There have been many notable hobos including Joe Hill and Utah Phillips who were both well-known labour organisers and songwriters. Dylan had recorded the wonderful Utah Phillips song 'Rock Salt and Nails' during his Basement Tapes sessions. Another man who hoboed for much of his early life was Harry McClintock. Known to his hobo friends as 'Haywire Mac,' McClintock claimed to have written the song 'Big Rock Candy Mountain' in 1895. Said to be based on tales from his youth hoboing through the United States, his 1928 recording of the song was undoubtedly the first. The song is about a hobo's idea of paradise where all the cops have wooden legs, the Bulldogs all have rubber teeth, hens lay soft-boiled eggs, there are cigarette trees, streams of alcohol and a lake of whiskey. Although Woody Guthrie probably wouldn't be termed as a hobo, he certainly spent time hoboing and looking for work.

Interestingly, and perhaps surprising to some, hobo's lived by a strict ethical code that was voted on and implemented at the 1889 National Hobo Convention in St. Louis, Missouri. Many of the rules were about behaviour: "Always respect local law and officials," "Be a gentleman at all times," "Always try to find work," "Don't allow yourself to become a stupid drunk," "Help your fellow hobos whenever and wherever needed." The first 'rule' on the list was, however, "Decide your own life, don't let another person run or rule you." While I'm not suggesting that Bob Dylan had read the Hobo Convention's rules for life, his lyric, "Live by no man's code," does fit like a glove.

The crux of the matter is, Dylan's hobo probably isn't on the road out of necessity. Instead, like Dylan, the hobo has abandoned his old life and is searching for something new and better and while he may not gain material benefit from this change, he will hopefully gain spiritually.

The Wicked Messenger

The final recording session for *John Wesley Harding* featured four songs; the first was 'The Wicked Messenger' and the fourth was 'Dear Landlord.' In-between these two important songs, Dylan recorded 'Down Along the Cove' and 'I'll Be Your Baby Tonight.' These two simple numbers are nothing more than the joyous outpourings of a modest man. With these songs, rather than continuing a search for the meaning of life, at best the narrator now seeks only wholeness, which he very much hopes to find with his wife and family. As is often the case with Dylan's albums, the final track on an LP can set the tone of his next record. In the case of *John Wesley Harding*, however, we have not one but two tracks that preview the country soaked *Nashville Skyline*. As Paul Williams pointed out in the first book in his *Performing Artist* trilogy, before those two closing numbers – 'Down Along the Cove' and 'I'll Be Your Baby Tonight' – "Some Dylan fans had never heard a steel guitar before."

Sent "from Eli," Dylan's 'The Wicked Messenger' comes in the form of a simple parable. Not surprisingly, as with so much of the album, the fable's main protagonist once again represents the 'old' Bob. Previously, the messenger only ever seemed to bring bad, even apocalyptic news: 'Blowin' in the Wind,' 'Masters of War,' 'Hard Rain,' 'Talkin' World War III Blues,' to name but a few. 'The Wicked Messenger' can be seen as the end of one phase of Dylan's writing and the commencement of the next. He is now done with songs that were seen by many as making political statements; the new Bob has now "opened up his heart." "If you cannot bring good news, then don't bring any," Dylan sings at the song's close. Paul Williams believed this final line might be sarcastic and bitter but I don't see it that way.

Several Biblical references are especially important. First, Proverbs 13:17 states that a wicked messenger falls into mischief (and a good messenger brings healing). Proverbs 6:20-35 is an admonition against adultery: "Can a man walk on hot coals without his feet being scorched? / So is he who sleeps with another man's wife; no one who touches her will go unpunished." (Dylan: "The soles of my feet, I swear they're burning").

In Hebrew, Eli means high and in the Books of Samuel, which form part of the narrative history of Israel, Eli was a High Priest of Shiloh whose sons behaved wickedly resulting in the Lord punishing Eli and his family with all male descendants dying before reaching old age.

Dear Landlord

As with several songs on *John Wesley Harding*, 'Dear Landlord,' a song that has a definite hymnal feel, could be directed toward both Albert Grossman and a higher power (if indeed there was a higher power than Grossman!). While I've always felt that Grossman was a good fit, others have challenged that notion believing the Landlord to be anything from Dylan's record label, to his audience as well as a metaphor for God. Some years later, Sally Grossman would say that neither she nor Albert ever thought that the song was written about her husband.

Dylan told Cameron Crowe: "Dear Landlord was really just the first line. I woke up one morning with the words on my mind. Then I just figured, what else can I put to it."[32] If we are to take that statement at face value, then Dylan presumably did not have a preconceived idea as to who the landlord was. It is, however, revealing that in a 1971 telephone conversation between Dylan and self-appointed Dylanologist AJ Weberman that Dylan came close to admitting the song was, at least in part, about Albert Grossman: "['Dear Landlord'] wasn't all the way for Al Grossman," Dylan told Weberman. "In fact, he wasn't even in my mind. Only later, when people pointed out to me that the song might've been written for Al Grossman, I thought, well, maybe it could've been."[33]

I think the first part of that answer, "wasn't all the way for Al Grossman," before Dylan quickly checks himself, is quite telling.

Written in the form of a letter, the song's splendid opening salvo, "Please don't put a price on my soul," is the universal plea of the artist to the man in the suit and tie who is controlling him. Also, in the real sense of the word, Albert Grossman had been Dylan's landlord as Bob had, for a time, lived at Grossman's property. It is also true, however, that the lyrics could fit Dylan pleading with his audience not to put a price on his soul.

Dylan says his "burden is heavy" and that his "dreams are beyond control." Nevertheless, he promises that "When that steamboat whistle blows" and he's back out on the road he's "gonna give you all [he's] got to give' and he hopes "you receive it well."

Writing in the May 1968 issue of *Crawdaddy* magazine, Jon Landau caught the essence of the song: "While the landlord has been thought to represent all manner of authority – everyone from his manager to the government – that type of speculation is unimportant. What is important is Dylan's attitude toward the subject. He is not out for blood, yet at the same time, he is not willing to give in. He is empathetic but realistic. 'If you don't underestimate me / I won't underestimate you.' I will recognise you but you are going to have to deal with me." Landau continued, "This is a truly incredible transformation in attitude when seen in contrast with 'Ballad of a Thin Man.'"[34]

Landau has that right, the *John Wesley Harding* album is an analysis of Bob Dylan's conversion, not to Christianity but to moderation.

Minstrel Boy

Before we move on from the music from this period we should look
at the often ignored song, 'Minstrel Boy.' This song is overlooked
mainly because its place in history is a little unclear and over the
years there has been considerable discussion as to the date of the
song. The first time Dylan fans knew about 'Minstrel Boy' was
when Bob played it as a surprise encore at the 1969 Isle of Wight
festival. Dylan, however, has placed the song as being written
during The Basement Tapes period. Indeed, when he came to
compile his first official book of lyrics, *Writings and Drawings* (1972),
he placed the song in The Basement Tapes section. The fact that
the song was not copyrighted at that time is not at all surprising,
'I'm Not There' and 'Sign on the Cross' from the same period were
also overlooked for copyrighting. During the early stages of the
Basement sessions registering these compositions couldn't have
been further from Dylan's mind. Nonetheless, as is so often the
case in the 'Bob world' nothing is ever straightforward because
in subsequent editions of *Lyrics* the song was reassigned to 1969.
Then, with the 2013 release of *The Bootleg Series Vol. 10: Another Self
Portrait*, this ongoing game of ping pong continued with the song
being credited as "Unreleased, The Basement Tapes -circa 1967." In
any event, the song's two verses and three choruses very much lend
themselves to an autobiographical interpretation that fits perfectly
with Dylan's 1967 mindset.

In 'Minstrel Boy' Dylan asks to be let down easy and begs to
know who's going to save his soul? In the first verse he says, "Oh,
Lucky's been drivin' a long, long time." Much later Dylan will adopt
the name Lucky when he joins The Traveling Wilburys. For now,
however, his long, long drive is over and "he's stuck on top of the hill
/ With twelve forward gears, it's been a long hard climb." At the time
of the Basement recordings Bob was indeed "stuck on top of the hill,"
that hill being Byrdcliffe Mountain above Woodstock where he was

now living with his wife. The verse ends with the line, "And with all of them ladies, though, he's lonely still." This would seem to be a reference to his past womanising. As with the previously mentioned 'The Wicked Messenger' and Proverbs 13:17 ("He who sleeps with another man's wife ... will [not] go unpunished"). Also, now Dylan has ceased work he asks himself the pertinent question, "Who's gonna throw that minstrel boy a coin?"

The Key is Frank!

"Faith is the key!" said the first king. "No, froth is the key!" said the second. "You're both wrong," said the third, "the key is Frank!."

Written by Dylan, the liner notes to *John Wesley Harding* are presented as a comic fable featuring a list of characters with fanciful names. Reading much like the experimental prose poetry that Dylan had recently employed in his surrealist novel *Tarantula*, the tale has what appears to be three record execs, cast as kings, come to visit and do homage to "Frank" (Bob Dylan). Also in attendance is "Terry Shute" (Albert Grossman), who is sketched as an insatiable philanderer who Frank's wife, Vera, catches "prying open a hairdresser."

The first king addresses Frank, stating: "Mr. Dylan has come out with a new record. This record of course features none but his own songs and we understand that you're the key." Frank replies that he is indeed the key. He then proceeds to confound and mystify his guests by, among other things, ripping off his shirt and punching his fist through a plate-glass window. During this outburst, a light bulb falls from his pocket. This scene brings to mind the ubiquitous oversized light bulb that Dylan had carried to a London press conference in 1965. In the film *Dont Look Back*, a reporter asked, "What is your real message?" to which Dylan replied, "My real message? Keep a good head and always carry a light bulb."

By contrast, in the *John Wesley Harding* fable, Dylan took the bulb and "stamped it out," crushing it with his foot. With this action Dylan seems to be indicating that while he was once seen to be a bearer of ideas or visions, he is now prepared to crush that notion, surrendering his prophetic voice.

In what seems to be a parody of Grossman's notorious obstinacy and negotiating techniques, Terry Shute then gives a speech, elevating the limitless prospects of Dylan's ultimate destiny, if he is only allowed to do as he pleases. Frank, who no longer wants Terry Shute to speak or act for him, turns "with a blast" and tells Shute, "Get out of here, you ragged man! Come ye no more!."

Despite Dylan's efforts to (in Tim Riley's words) "deflate his demigod status," the foolish kings are nonetheless convinced that they have been given special access to something miraculous. At the end of the fable, Frank's wife Vera asks, "Why didn't you just tell them you were a moderate man and leave it at that...?"

Two Bauls, a Carpenter, The Beatles and The Hand of God

(A Detour)

The story of the Bengali Bauls' visit to the United States and the recording of their *Big Pink* album began when Dylan's friend Allen Ginsberg met Nabani Das Baul in 1962 while the poet was living and travelling in India. After returning to America, Ginsberg talked with Sally and Albert Grossman about the possibility of Grossman recording Indian music and recommended that he met Nabani Das Baul. In early 1967, the Grossmans visited West Bengal and the Bauls were invited to meet and perform for them in Grossman's suite at the Oberoin Grand Hotel, Calcutta. Grossman quickly made arrangements for the musicians to visit the United States but regrettably Nabani Das Baul's failing health prevented him from travelling and so he sent his two sons, Lakshman and Purna Das Baul, in his place.

A hauntingly gifted singer, Purna Das had spent his childhood accompanying his father on his travels across Bengal learning traditional songs until he could perform close to 5,000 of them from memory. Although only two of the musicians, Lakshman and Purna Das, appear on the front cover of Dylan's *John Wesley Harding* album, in total five Bauls came to the United States and as unlikely as it might seem, Albert Grossman became their manager.

The Bauls remained in the United States for about a year and during much of that time they lived in a guest apartment over a converted barn on the Grossman estate. Early mornings were spent oiling their bodies while the afternoons were mostly reserved for sleeping. They prepared their own food, called Sally Grossman "sister" and Albert "brother-of-the-heart." According to Al Aronowitz, Sally took them out in the car to see the sights but they were not at ease when walking in the Woodstock countryside, finding it hard to believe that the woods were not home to tigers.

Intrigued by their mysticism, the Bauls had many visitors while in Woodstock including Bob Dylan, who at the time was still recording with The Band in Big Pink. Purna Das remembers Dylan telling him that their singing goals were the same since they both sang about the people and life and times of their respective lands. Dylan told Purna Das that he was a "Baul of America." The two men became good friends and Dylan said he would "put them in his memory" by including them on the cover of his new album.

The front cover photograph to *John Wesley Harding* has Dylan flanked by brothers Lakshman and Purna Das Baul (to Dylan's left). Behind Dylan is Charlie Joy, a local stonemason and carpenter who just happened to be there at the time! The photograph, which was taken on a piece of rough grassland on the Grossman property, was clicked by Columbia Records' staffer John Berg. He used a Polaroid instant camera because Dylan wanted to see the results as quickly as possible. Some colour Polaroids were also taken but after all the photos were spread across a large table in Grossman's kitchen Dylan insisted they use one of the rough and ready black and whites for the cover.

When The Beatles released *Sgt. Pepper's Lonely Hearts Club Band*, the cover featured, amongst many other figures, a cloth doll wearing a sweater emblazoned with the message 'Welcome The Rolling Stones.' *With Their Satanic Majesties Request*, an album jacket partly inspired by *Sgt. Pepper's*, the Stones reciprocated by hiding images of the Fab Four amongst the flowers on the cover. Suddenly, music fans were seeing Beatle faces everywhere, including it seems in the knotty tree bark on the cover to *John Wesley Harding*, but only if you hold the album Jacket upside down. *Rolling Stone* was the first to report this revelation, which came as a surprise to photographer Berg. When the late John Bauldie, editor of *The Telegraph* magazine, asked Berg about this in 1995 the photographer said: "Later on, I got a call from *Rolling Stone* magazine in San Francisco. Someone had discovered little pictures of The Beatles and the hand of Jesus in the tree trunk. Well, I had a proof of the cover on my wall, so I went and turned it upside down and sure enough ... Hahaha! I mean, if you wanted to see it, you could see it. I was as amazed as anybody."

If you want to search for the faces yourself, they are more apparent on the original British cover of the album. It has also been rumoured that the faces were more obvious on the original artwork and conspiracy theorists believe that the image was "brushed over" before press time (hence, the unusually dark features on the most prominent tree trunk).

A deeply deluded AJ Weberman can see much more than just the Beatles in the cover. During his appearance on the Bob Fass show, *Radio Unnameable*, on WBAI-FM in early 1968, Weberman told Fass that the album cover included a picture of Dylan with a suspicious looking cigarette in his mouth, a photo of Donovan wearing his trademark cap, a hand (said by some to be the Hand of God), and "a cop"– assumedly the cop is there to bust Dylan on a drugs charge? In any event, Weberman continued, "Now, if you follow [the picture] so it moves to the left, you dig? ... Can you see something obscuring it here? ... He's hunched over a guitar... It's a really fine job of superimposition. Comparable to a Salvador Dali print, at least." Weberman was so engrossed in his own fantasy world that he failed to mention the Beatles!

With the long wait had come great anticipation. The late author/journalist/singer and counterculture leader Mick Farren remembered fervently waiting during the last week of December 1967 for Dylan to deliver his new album: "The weight of anticipation that was loaded upon the release of *John Wesley Harding* was probably more than any artist should be expected shoulder," Farren told *Record Collector News*. "The clamour for Dylan product had never been higher and even though Dylan had asked Columbia not to go overboard with their promotion the papers grabbed the story with both hands: The *New York Times* gave the album four columns and Time magazine heralded the release with a feature article on Dylan. During the first week of release the album was reported to have sold 250,000 units and within weeks it became one of the most played albums on countless FM radio stations across America. The record reached number 2 on the *Billboard* chart and went all the way to the number 1 slot in the UK. The album has remained a fan favourite ever since because it's underlying quality is one of timelessness."[35]

Chapter Three

Marking Time

I Won't be Giving Any Concerts for a While

The New Year began with the Dylans and their neighbours, the Dorfmans, watching television and toasting each other as the Times Square ball descended to mark the arrival of 1968. Dylan was approached in early January with a view to him playing the part of Woody Guthrie in a film biography. He read the script and loved it but said that he would never want to play the role of Woody. A week later, however, he called to offer his services as director but perhaps unsurprisingly the offer was politely declined. In any event, at the time Dylan was probably thinking more about the upcoming Woody Guthrie Memorial Concert. He had agreed to appear at the Carnegie Hall, New York show and it would be his first live appearance in 20 months.

The February 24 edition of *Rolling Stone* magazine carried the headline, "Bob Dylan Turns Up For Woody Guthrie Memorial." The report continued, "Bob Dylan finally emerged from 18 months (sic.) of self-imposed seclusion at the Woody Guthrie Memorial Concert in Carnegie Hall on January 20. His appearance had been announced and the two performances were sold out weeks in advance. Scalpers were reportedly getting $25.00 per ticket, and at the concert itself people were standing on the sidewalk and in the lobby begging [for tickets]."[1]

Also performing at the concert were: Pete Seeger, Judy Collins, Woody's son Arlo Guthrie, Tom Paxton, Jack Elliot, Odetta and Richie Havens. It was reported that before and after each song,

Robert Ryan, the program's narrator, and Will Geer, did readings from Guthrie's work, accompanied by slides and still photographs of his art. Dylan wore a gun-metal grey silk mohair suit, blue shirt with green jewelled cufflinks and black suede boots. He was sporting his new short hair cut, beard and moustache. According to *Rolling Stone*, he could be seen, "Sprawled in his chair with his eyes closed, seeming to be somewhere else entirely until it was his turn to play." At the end of the concert, the Guthrie family came out on stage and Mrs Guthrie, in an orange dress hugged and kissed each artist – Dylan appeared to blush.

Although there was never any question that Dylan wouldn't appear at the Guthrie tribute – in fact he told event co-ordinator Harold Leventhal that if a tribute was organised he would be the first to say yes – he did fear that his presence might overshadow the concerts' intended purpose, and to a great extent that is precisely what happened. Indeed, *The New Yorker* devoted close to a page of its lead, 'Talk of the Town' section, to the concert with the lion's share of the writing going to Dylan. The Associated Press also heralded Dylan's comeback over the tribute itself.

Dylan, who had rehearsed the previous day and was backed by The Band, performed 'Grand Coulee Dam,' 'Dear Mrs Roosevelt' and 'I Ain't Got No Home.' There was an afternoon and an evening show and Dylan performed the same three songs at both events. He also participated in the ensemble versions of 'This Land is Your Land' at the afternoon show and 'This Train (Is Bound for Glory)' at the evening concert. Between shows he relaxed at the Sheraton Plaza Hotel and after the event he attended a party at Robert Ryan's Dakota Manhattan apartment where John Lennon lived and died. Dylan arrived on the stroke of midnight and just as had happened at the concert, his presence changed the atmosphere of the room.

The Guthrie Memorial Concert was the first time in public that tensions between Dylan and Grossman became obvious. Drummer

Levon Helm, who had now returned to the fold, immediately noticed a stark difference in the two men's attitude toward each other in the time he had been away. Dylan informed Robert Shelton: "I won't be giving any concerts for a while. I'm not compelled to do it now. I went around the world a couple of times. But I didn't have anything else to do then." By this, Dylan was referring to him now having a home life. Bob was now spending an increasing amount of time with neighbour Bruce Dorfman at his Webster Road art studio. At the time, Dorfman was painting life-sized pictures of what he called his "fantasy women" so when Sara bought Bob a box of oil paints for his 27th birthday he took them round to Dorfman and asked for guidance. Dorfman enquired what sort of thing he wanted to paint and Bob produced an art book containing a reproduction of Vermeer's Girl with Flute. Dylan told Dorfman that he didn't want to copy the picture but that he did want to produce something along those lines. The artist explained the rudimentaries of how to apply oils and Bob became totally absorbed. He returned the following day with a book of Claude Monet's paintings and this continued until he brought along a book of Marc Chagall's work. This was the turning point for Dylan. A Russian-French artist of Belarusian Jewish origin, Chagall was an early modernist who painted mostly dream-like subjects with imagery and allegory uniquely his. Dylan especially liked I and the Village, Clock with Blue Wing and Self-Portrait. According to Dorfman, Bob began making a large canvas inspired by Chagall but all of the images were from 'All Along the Watchtower.'

After years in Greenwich Village living hand to mouth and sleeping on peoples' couches, Bob had now begun to amass considerable material wealth. He had bought a limousine, a long black Cadillac Fleetwood with a glass driver's partition separating him from the driver and he had given Bernard Paturel, former owner of the Woodstock Cafe Espresso, a job as his chauffeur. Bob also owned a Ford Mustang and he had bought a Grumman Olson "Step

Van" truck. He bought the van under the pretext that it was useful for hauling equipment but in reality Bob just liked it and would often drive it around Woodstock for pleasure.

Bob was at home on June 5, 1968 when he received a telephone call from his home town of Hibbing, Minnesota. He then asked Bernard Paturel to drive him to New York where he caught a flight to Hibbing-Chisholm Airport. He didn't tell anybody, even Paturel on their two-hour drive, why he had left so suddenly, only later would Paturel discover that Bob's father, Abe Zimmerman, had died from a heart attack at age 56.

As one might expect, Bob was devastated by his father's death and probably felt regret that relations had not been better between the two of them. He later told Harold Leventhal that he had never really known his father. Leventhal encouraged Bob to explore his Jewish heritage as a way of dealing with his grief and as a possible way of gaining closure. Bob spent five nights in Hibbing comforting his mother, Beatty, who then returned with her son to Woodstock. Less than three weeks after Bob and Beatty arrived back at HI Lo Ha Sara gave birth to their second son, Samuel Isaac Abraham. Sam's second middle name was taken from his recently deceased grandfather. Prior to the birth, Bob found the time and energy to grant a lengthy interview to *Sing Out!* magazine. The magazine's editor, Happy Traum, along with John Cohen, visited Dylan at his home and they conducted three interviews during June and July.

After talking about *Eat the Document* with them, Dylan said that he expected to be playing music "endlessly." He told his interviewers that he knew he would be playing live again and that it was just a matter of the right time. The interview, which appeared in Volume 18 / Number 4 of *Sing Out!*, ran for 13 pages. Talking about his current songwriting, Dylan said: "I don't care if I record my own songs, but I can't sometimes find enough songs to put on an album, so I've got to do my own songs, I didn't want to record this last album. I was going to do a whole album of other peoples' songs, but I couldn't find enough."

Discussing how he composed his songs, Dylan told *Sing Out!*: "It's like this painter who lives around here – he paints the area in a radius of 20 miles, he paints bright strong pictures. He might take a barn from 20 miles away, and hook it up with a brook right next door, then with a car 10 miles away, and with the sky on a certain day. A person passing by will be painted alongside someone 10 miles away. And in the end he'll have this composite picture of something which you can't say exists in his mind. It's not that he started off wilfully painting this picture from his experience... That's more or less what I do."[2]

Dylan was uncharacteristically cooperative during the interviews and even offered to paint a picture for the cover of *Sing Out!* in which the interview would appear. The painter of "composite pictures" that Bob was referring to was obviously Bruce Dorfman and Dylan asked Dorfman for help with the *Sing Out!* painting: A man in a hat seated on a green chair playing a guitar, with another figure peering through a window. The picture was also used by *Sing Out!* as a poster to promote the Dylan issue of the magazine.*

In the summer of 1968, Al Aronowitz was asked to write a piece about Dylan for *Saturday Evening Post*. Aronowitz, in turn, approached a young photographer by the name of Elliott Landy to take the photos that would accompany the article. Landy rented a

* *The reason for Dylan's 'uncharacteristic cooperation' with* Sing Out! *magazine was that John Cohen and Happy Traum were both musicians and old friends of Dylan's. Bob knew both Cohen and Traum from his time in Greenwich Village; Cohen was a founding member (1958), of the New York-based old-time string band New Lost City Ramblers and Traum, who had studied blues guitar with Brownie McGhee, was a stalwart of the Sixties Greenwich Village music scene who had moved up to live in Woodstock about the same time that Dylan had. When in Woodstock, the two men continued their friendship begun in the Village and often visited each other's homes. Nevertheless, three lengthy interviews and a cover painting was a massive coup for the magazine.*

Volkswagen Beatle and drove up to Woodstock from New York City.
This would be the first of several important photo sessions that
Landy would do with Dylan. The photo of Bob that appeared on the
cover of the November 2, 1968 issue of *Saturday Evening Post* was
virtually the first opportunity fans had to glimpse the new look Bob
Dylan. Because Landy's surname is an anagram of Dylan, many fans
didn't believe Elliott Landy was real and that the name was simply
an alias for Dylan. This conspiracy theory first raised its head with
the release of The Band's debut LP *Music from Big Pink*, for which
Bob had painted the front cover picture and Landy had taken the
photographs. Bob had seen The Band photos and was pleased that
Elliott was taking the pictures for Aronowitz's *Saturday Evening Post*
asignment. Bob directed the photo shoot, perching on an old tire
with guitar in hand, walking about doing the chores, emptying the
trash and telling Landy, "That's what I do up here. Take a picture."

In part, the "That's what I do up here" comment was pretty close
to the truth. Dylan was now painting almost daily with artist friend
Bruce Dorfman, spending lots of time with his ever-expanding family,
throwing the few small dinner parties and attending one or two gigs.
It seemed that Dylan's resentment for his manager was growing with
every passing day. Al Aronowitz said that everytime Grossman's
name was mentioned Bob would make a cutting comment.
Grossman knew that he had lost Dylan and as a consequence he
began focusing his attention on The Band. On a trip to New York
he could be seen carrying the cover to The Band's upcoming debut
album, *Music from Big Pink*. He showed it to Happy Traum's brother,
Artie, and to Aronowitz; in fact, to anyone who would look and
listen. He began telling people that he'd got the best band ever. Later,
when the money started rolling in he liked them even more and
Robbie Robertson became his new best mate. Michael Friedman,
hired around this time to assist Grossman, said that it was hard to
imagine Dylan achieving everything he did without Grossman, they

were "alter egos" Friedman says. Nonetheless, Friedman also saw Grossman as an opportunist. "He hadn't cared a thing about the Hawks," Friedman said. "[But] when The Band became successful, all of a sudden he started looking at the balance sheet and decided Robbie Robertson was the way to go."[3]

Unfortunately for Grossman, before he and The Band could exploit the positive reviews for *Music from Big Pink* there was another road accident, this time involving Rick Danko. Danko ran his soon to be wife's car off the road around a sharp Woodstock bend and in doing so broke several bones and sustained a severe neck injury. The 'broken neck' put him in traction and left him with lifelong pain. It also put pay to The Band's planned first tour! They were unable to play live until the spring of 1969. This, on top of Dylan's neck injury, must have had Grossman thinking his Groundhog Day was Friday the 13th.

On October 23, Bob and Sara went to New York to see Johnny Cash perform at Carnegie Hall. After the concert, Dylan, Sara, and a few friends went for dinner with Cash. George and Pattie Harrison visited the Dylans at Hi Lo Ha spending a few days with them over Thanksgiving (November 28). George's visit was two-fold, he loved *Music from Big Pink*, which was now four months old, and wanted to talk with The Band about the album and also to spend time with Bob. Robertson told Harrison, "You should stay at Albert's. He's got a big house." This arrangement proved a little awkward for George: "I hung out with [The Band] and Bob and it was strange because at the time Bob and Grossman were going through this fight, this crisis about managing him. I would spend the day with Bob and the night with Grossman and hear both sides of the battle."[4]

The whole episode proved torturous, most especially for Pattie: "When we went to see him in Woodstock, God, it was absolute agony. He just wouldn't talk. He would not talk. He certainly had no social graces whatsoever. I don't know whether it was because he was shy of George or what the story was, but it was agonisingly difficult."[5] The Harrisons were invited to a Thanksgiving dinner party at Hi Lo La and this evening proved to be the most strained meeting of all. The evening's guests included Mason Hoffenberg – co-writer of the satiric novel *Candy* – the Traums, the Dorfmans and the Taplins. It was, says Jonathan Taplin with admirable understatement: "kind of stiff and formal," until after dinner Hoffenberg suggested that 'we get all the boys over on this side, and all the girls over on this side.

The first couple to get their clothes off and screw wins.' "It was funny enough, it broke the ice," says Taplin.[6] By this juncture Bruce Dorfman had apparently left the party because he was annoyed by the general fawning towards Bob. Dylan later told Dorfman quietly that "it wasn't such a hot visit after all."[7]

In January, the Dylan family took a vacation in the West Indies and on his return Bob talked with producer Bob Johnston about recording his next studio album. The two men met at the Nashville Ramada Inn where Dylan was staying and Bob played Johnston the songs he had ready. The two men also talked about what musicians Dylan might use on the album. Having hinted at his intentions with the last two songs on *John Wesley Harding*, Dylan now plunged head-first into deep country.

Nashville Skyline was recorded over four sessions between February 13 and 18, 1969. As was the case with *John Wesley Harding*, the album was recorded in Columbia Studio A in Nashville. Also, as with *John Wesley Harding*, the Nashville musicians Charlie McCoy (bass), Kenneth Buttrey (drums) and Peter Drake (steel guitar) were used. This time, however, a further half-a-dozen musicians were also drafted in. By the time Dylan arrived in the studio on the first day he only had four finished songs to his name. 'To Be Alone With You,' 'I Threw It All Away,' 'One More Night' and 'Lay, Lady, Lay' were all recorded at that first session, although further takes would be required on the following day before Bob was satisfied with 'Lay, Lady, Lay' and even then overdubs were necessary. 'Peggy Day,' 'Tell Me That It Isn't True' and 'Country Pie' were wrapped up on the 14th. After a two-day break, very lengthy sessions on February 17 and 18, yielding 'Nashville Skyline Rag,' 'Tonight I'll Be Staying Here with You' and 'Girl from the North Country,' would finish the job.

At the same time that Dylan was recording *Nashville Skyline*, Johnny Cash was in Columbia's Nashville Studios starting work on his 33rd album, *Hello, I'm Johnny Cash*. Bob Johnston: "I had Dylan at night, and Cash was coming down at midnight. Cash walked in and said, 'What are you doing here?' Dylan said, 'I'm recording,' Johnny said, 'I am, too. Let's go get some dinner... while they were gone, I built a night club out in the studio, with lights and glass and their guitars and all that shit. They came back in, looked out there, saw that, looked at each other... went out there, and started playin'.' They played 32 songs. Dylan said, 'We're done.' They never released it..."[8]

Johnny Cash also took part in the second half of Dylan's session on the 17th and the whole of the session on the 18th. The one song that was released from the sessions was 'Girl from the North Country.' The song was used as the opening track on *Nashville Skyline*.

Even though time seemed to pass by quickly for Bob, the *Nashville Skyline* sessions came a full 15 months after *John Wesley Harding*. Although Dylan's new record deal had been sorted he was in no hurry to follow Harding and Columbia didn't appear to be chasing him for product. Coming at a time when record companies pushed for two or even three LPs a year from their artists, this was an unusual situation. With the vast amount of basement songs recorded and *John Wesley Harding*, 1967 would prove to be the most productive period in Bob Dylan's entire career, yet his fan base were being starved of product.

Dylan has said that he only went to Nashville to lay the

groundwork for an album but that, "pretty soon the whole album started fillin' in together, and we had an album."[9] That, I'm afraid, depends on your interpretation of what constitutes an album. While there is no doubt that *Nashville Skyline* was a commercial success of sorts, in that it made it to number 3 on the Billboard Top 200 and went all the way to the top of the UK album chart, five good songs does not an album make, and certainly not a Dylan album. Let us not forget that at the time Dylan's popularity was riding high, *John Wesley Harding* through *New Morning* – four albums in succession – would all make number 1 in the UK so *Nashville Skyline* topping the UK chart should not be a big surprise. Nonetheless, a total running time of a mere 27 minutes and 14 seconds informs us in no uncertain terms that Bob hadn't got an album's worth of tunes. Remember what Dub Michael Taylor (bootlegger and employee at US wholesale distributor Saturn Records) had to say about the album: "I don't know if *Nashville Skyline* was a big record for Columbia, but it was a turkey for Saturn."

There are many songwriters who would give their right arm to be able to write 'Lay, Lady, Lay,' 'Tonight I'll be Staying Here with You,' 'I Threw It All Away' and even 'To Be Alone with You,' all for inclusion on one album. But Bob Dylan is not any old singer-songwriter he's, well, Bob Dylan, and for him these were days not of plenty but of famine; the amnesia was upon him. This 10-song, 27-minute LP contains the first instrumental that Dylan had ever released, 'Nashville Skyline Rag,' (placed rather awkwardly as the album's second track), a duet with Cash, 'Girl from the North Country,' which was of course originally released in 1963 on the *The Freewheelin, Bob Dylan* LP and 'Lay, Lady, Lay,' which Dylan probably never intended recording himself and certainly wasn't written for *Nashville Skyline*.

Sometime during the summer of 1968, probably around July, Dylan was approached with a view to him providing a song or songs for the film *Midnight Cowboy*. He had the beginnings of one song, 'Lay, Lady, Lay,' so he accepted the commission. Unfortunately, he delivered it too late and director John Schlesinger used Fred Neil's 'Everybody's Talking' in its place. At this point Bob had no intention of recording his next album so rumour has it that he attempted to give the song away, approaching The Everly Brothers for whom it would have been a good fit. Phil Everly, who was said to be unimpressed by the song, declined the offer.

Dylan's release of the song, first on the *Nashville Skyline* album and three months later as a single, would help to widen his appeal with the record buying public. The single reached number 7 on the Billboard chart on August 2 and number 5 in the UK on September 13. These chart positions were very respectable for Dylan. In the United States it was his biggest single success since 'Like a Rolling Stone,' four years before. For whatever reason, and all fans of Dylan's music will recognise that song selection is not his finest attribute, Dylan decided that the first single from the album should be 'I Threw It All Away.' In stark contrast to 'Lay, Lady, Lay,' which would be the second single from the album, 'I Threw It All Away' stalled horribly at number 85 in the US and number 30 in the UK. Although Dylan would go on to perform 'Lay, Lady, Lay' in concert – at the time of writing he has done so 407 times – it took him some time to feel a connection with the song. Having a far better idea of what sells, Columbia boss Clive Davis had pleaded with Dylan to put 'Lay, Lady, Lay' out as his first single from the album but Bob protested vehemently, saying that the song was not representative of what he did. He also later said that he wasn't satisfied with the version he recorded. "I always had a feeling there was more to that song," Dylan told Jonathan Cott.[10]

Released in October 1969, some eight months after it was recorded, 'Tonight I'll Be Staying Here with You' would be the third and final single from the album. Like 'I Threw It All Away,' the single was not a chart success, only making it to number 50 in the US and failing to dent the UK Top 20. The song's sentiments can be taken two ways. In this song Dylan is staying put but for how long. The word "tonight" is significant and interestingly the song mirrors the closing number from the *John Wesley Harding* album where Dylan sings, I'll be your baby "tonight."

Even before the album was released, Jann Wenner previewed it in *Rolling Stone* (March 15, 1969): "Bob Dylan has completed his next album and joined Johnny Cash for a duet or two," Wenner wrote. "They are the songs I've been writing over the past year," Dylan said in a telephone conversation with Wenner. As vague as ever, Dylan continued, "Some are songs that I've sung and never written down and just sort of turn up again. I can't remember where they come from. I was just sitting down trying to write some notes on where the songs came from and I couldn't figure it out myself."

"I can't remember too much about how I wrote the new songs. It depends on where I am, what the weather is like and who is around at the time. The music is a little of everything. You'll know what it is when you hear it. I can't remember that much about it. The new songs are easy to sing and there aren't too many words to remember."[11]

British fans found the songs easy to sing and on the day of Bob's 28th birthday (May 24, 1969), the album went to Number 1. It remained on the UK Top 10 for 18 weeks, three weeks less than *John Wesley Harding*. "The songs reflect more of the inner me than the songs of the past," Dylan told *Newsweek*. "With *John Wesley Harding*," he continued, "I felt like everyone expected me to be a poet so that's what I tried to be." Writing in *The Village Voice*, Robert Christgau thought, "The beauty of the album is that it is totally undemanding," while Paul Nelson writing in *Rolling Stone* said the album was, "a reminder that Dylan has always been capable of tenderness."

"On *Nashville Skyline* you had to read between the lines," Dylan told Jonathan Cott: "I was trying to grasp something that would lead me on to where I thought I should be, and it didn't go nowhere – it just went down, down, down. I couldn't be anybody but myself, and at that point I didn't know it or want to know it. I was convinced I wasn't going to do anything else..."[12]

Chapter Four

Help Bob Dylan Sink
The Isle of Wight

The two largest and most important pop music festivals of the
Sixties were staged just two weeks apart and it comes as no great
surprise that both sets of promoters wanted Bob Dylan as their
headline act.

By July 1969, Dylan was virtually the only one of promoter Mike
Lang's music heroes who hadn't signed a contract with Woodstock
Ventures. Lang had moved to Woodstock in May 1968 from Coconut
Grove, Florida where he had owned a 'head shop.' Shortly before
relocating to Woodstock he had organised the first Miami Pop
Festival, a two-day event featuring amongst others Jimi Hendrix,
Janis Joplin, Santana and Mothers of Invention. The festival had
drawn a crowd of about 80,000 but Lang now had something much
bigger planned. Grossman visited the Woodstock festival site with
Lang and gave his approval of what was planned. Lang was then
able to sign both The Band and Janis Joplin for Woodstock at a cost
of $15,000 each. Richie Havens, another Grossman act, would also
agree to perform. Nonetheless, although he must have been sorely
tempted, Lang did not broach the subject of Grossman's biggest act,
Bob Dylan.

From the onset Lang had deliberately borrowed Dylan's mystique
by naming his festival after the musician's adopted hometown,
even though there was never any intention to stage the Woodstock
Festival in, or for that matter even near to, the town of Woodstock.
There is a popular misconception that the festival was initially

BOB DYLAN TOO MUCH OF NOTHING

planned for Woodstock and then moved out to Bethel. The truth is that the initially proposed site, Mills Industrial Park, which was actually in the town of Wallkill, was some 65 miles from Woodstock. The eventual site for the festival was of course Max Yasgur's dairy farm in White Lake, Bethel, which was almost 60 miles by road from Dylan's home in Woodstock. It would transpire, however, that even that distance was too close for Dylan's liking.

Having already signed The Band to play Woodstock, Lang reasoned that even if he couldn't persuade Dylan to sign for the festival the likelihood was that he would turn up and play with The Band. As you will see, the truth was far from that. It's not at all clear if Mike Lang had any notion that Dylan had been talking to the promoters of the Isle of Wight Festival and even though it may not have precluded him from appearing at Woodstock, by the time Lang talked with his idol about the festival, Dylan had, in all probability, already committed himself to headline at the Isle of Wight.

"I went to see Bob Dylan at his house in Woodstock," Lang told me. "That would have been about three weeks before the festival. I went up there with someone I knew, a friend of Dylan's, a guy named Bob Dacey. It seemed like an okay meeting; very laid-back. We talked about stuff in general and I told him all about the festival; what we were doing and how we would really love to have him play. I really didn't want to try and book him. I simply invited him to come along. I thought that might be the way to go. If he wasn't advertised he wouldn't be under any sort of pressure. I guess we talked for a couple of hours, maybe more. He didn't say very much about the festival and I didn't push him. I left not knowing if he would come or not."[1]

If Lang's date for this meeting (somewhere around July 25) is correct, then by that time Dylan's management had already confirmed to the Isle of Wight promoters, Fiery Creations, that Dylan would play their festival. This confirmation came by way of a transatlantic telephone call to the promoters on Wednesday July 16 in which Albert Grossman's business partner, Bert Block, confirmed that Dylan had accepted their offer to play the Isle of Wight. This verbal acceptance was confirmed in writing the following day with the arrival of a telegram dated "Freshwater, IOW 17 July '69."

Shortly before the Woodstock Festival, Bruce Dorfman asked Bob if he would be taking part. Dylan answered, "I'm not going." "They are all going to be waiting in line for you. They expect you to go!" Dorfman said. Dylan replied along the lines that people's expectations and realities were not always the same thing. He seemed quite adamant; he wasn't gonna work on Yasgur's farm. A little while after Woodstock, Dylan commented to Al Aronowitz' "I met Michael Lang once, but I can't remember anythin' about him."[2]

Interestingly, just three days before Dylan's management confirmed that he would play the Isle of Wight, Dylan, using the alias of Elmer Johnson, made a surprise guest appearance during The Band's encore at the Mississippi River Festival in Edwardsville, Illinois. It was reported that Dylan had soundman Rob Shaw make a tape of the performance to help him decide whether he was ready to go play live again. He told his friend David Amram about the impromptu performance: "Man," Dylan said, "there was something like 30,000 people and they didn't forget me... It was a good feeling." It would seem that this appearance boosted Dylan's confidence and helped him to finally make up his mind to accept the offer of the Isle of Wight gig.

Around half a million people came together to see and hear the 32 acts that played Woodstock and in doing so they demonstrated how a generation could come together and be heard. The aftermath of the festival was, however, quite a different story. While the hippies and even the 'straight' press were talking of Peace & Love, the four festival directors were practically at each other's throats. Even before the dust had settled – or in the case of Woodstock, the mud had dried – it was clear that the ramifications of declaring Woodstock a free festival were going to be immense.

On the Tuesday after the event the president of Sullivan County National Bank rang the organisers informing them that Woodstock Ventures' account was $250,000 in the red and that some of the artists would not be paid. It soon transpired that Mike Lang and his partners were something like $1.3 million in debt (close to $9 million in 2019). Even Max Yasgur got stung over the festival. Initially, he asked promoters for $10,000 for the use of his land but that eventually rose to $75,000 for the land and other facilities. However, some five months after the festival Yasgur was sued by neighbouring farms for damages amounting to $35,000.

Ever the entrepreneur, Albert Grossman quickly began talks with Mike Lang about forming a partnership. He rightly believed that the planned film of the event was going to be huge and that there was a massive amount of value in the corporate name. He told Lang and his partner Artie Kornfeld that he could raise the capital for the film release and suggested that they buy out Woodstock Ventures other two partners John Roberts and Joel Rosenman. Desperately in need of a break and time to think, Mike Lang decided to try to put the 70 lawsuits that were hanging over Woodstock Ventures out of his mind and fly out with Grossman to see Dylan perform at the Isle of Wight (if the mountain wouldn't come to Muhammad...).

There were probably several reasons why Dylan chose the Isle of Wight festival over Woodstock. There is little doubt that he was reluctant, even nervy to play live again after his long layoff. Others have said it, and I concur, that Dylan probably thought he would feel more at ease making his comeback on foreign soil. Also, in the summer of '69, Bob Dylan's feet might have been in the town of Woodstock, but his head was not.

The town had provided the ever-expanding Dylan family with a secluded and relatively safe refuge for several years. In fact, the

time Bob and Sara Dylan spent there would probably turn out
to be the happiest and most stable period of their lives together.
Bob had retreated from the crazy goings on of the mid-Sixties
and the extremes of life on the road but by the end of the decade
the madness of the times had again reached Dylan's door and the
tranquillity of his country idyll was now under sustained attack. Al
Aronowitz takes up the story: "Dylan's very presence had turned
Woodstock into Mecca to which the faithful had to make their
pilgrimages. Soon, that tiny but burgeoning hamlet was turning into
a music capital as well as an art colony ... Sticking the festival in
Dylan's backyard was like shoving it in his face."[3]

In 1984, Dylan told *Rolling Stone* magazine that when he was living
in Woodstock he was, "getting a great degree of notoriety for doing
nothing ... I was representing all these things that I didn't know
anything about ... It was all storm-the-embassy kind of stuff – Abbie
Hoffman in the streets – and they sorta figured me as the kingpin
of all that. I said, 'Wait a minute, I'm just a musician. So my songs
are about this and that. So what?' But people need a leader ... I didn't
want that, though.

But then came the big news about Woodstock, about musicians
goin' up there [to live], and it was like a wave of insanity breakin'
loose around the house day and night. You'd come in the house and
find people there, people comin' through the woods, at all hours
of the day and night, knockin' on your door. It was really dark and
depressing ... It was as if they were suckin' your very blood out ...
We had to get out of there.

This was just about the time of that Woodstock festival, which
was the sum total of all this bullshit. And it seemed to have
something to do with me, this Woodstock Nation, and everything it
represented. So we couldn't breathe ... I got very resentful about the
whole thing, and we got outta there."[4]

Writing in *Chronicles* Dylan said: "Early on, Woodstock had been very hospitable to us. I had actually discovered the place long before moving there ... I had bought [a house there] and it was in this same house that intruders started to break in day and night ... peace was hard to come by ... Roadmaps to our homestead must have been posted in all 50 states for gangs of dropouts and druggies. Moochers showed up from as far away as California on pilgrimages. Goons were breaking into our place all hours of the night ... rogue radicals looking for the Prince of Protest began to arrive [on one occasion Dylan returned home to find a couple in his bedroom]. Peter LaFarge, a folksinger friend of mine, had given me a couple of Colt pistols, and I also had a clip-fed Winchester blasting rifle around ... The chief of police (Woodstock had about three cops) had told me that if anyone was shot accidentally or even shot at as a warning, it would be me that would be going to the lockup ... Everything was wrong, the world was absurd. It was backing me into a corner ... After a while you realise that privacy is something you can sell, but you can never buy it back again."[5]

In addition to the lack of privacy, the town of Woodstock presented other problems for Dylan, one of which was that his soon to be estranged manager lived just down the road from him. In the spring of 1969, Bob moved his family to a remote 12-bedroom residence halfway along Ohayo Mountain Road. Situated on the opposite side of town from his Hi Lo Ha home, the new property was at the end of a long private gated drive. The house had once belonged to Walter Weyl, the intellectual leader of the Progressive Movement in the United States. The property, which sat amongst 39 acres of private land and had views to the Hudson River, was close to where Richard and Garth had moved to after Big Pink. In an attempt to ensure as much privacy as possible, Dylan bought a further parcel of adjacent woodland.

The Dylans' new home was much more modern than the Byrdcliffe house; not only was there less chance of being invaded by hippies, the plumbing and heating in the Byrdcliffe property was antiquated and Sara complained that something or other broke down just about every other day. The new house had a swimming pool, which Bob had extended. He also had a basketball court built.

Al Aronowitz: "It was August 11 and the Woodstock Festival was scheduled to start the following Friday. Earlier that day, I had visited the festival site and now I reported to Bob that, whereas rain had turned Yasgur's farm into a muddy quagmire the day before, the sun now had succeeded in drying the mud so thoroughly that promoters Lang and Roberts had been talking about renting a water truck to spray the road to keep the dust down. 'I wish they'd send the truck my way,' Bob said. 'The motor from my pump broke down and I haven't had any runnin' water for three days. I'm ready to sell this whole place to the land developers.'

Sara's chief complaint about living in Woodstock was that the water always dried up in August. We both knew that he was booked to sail for England in a few days and that he had absolutely no intention of making a surprise appearance at the Woodstock Festival. He just didn't want me to say so in print. When I told him that Lang and Roberts had just spent $16,000 to fly some 100 members of the Hog Farm from Santa Fe, New Mexico, to the festival site to install showers and portable toilets, Bob said he didn't think he'd need to spend that kind of money to do the job over at his place... He walked past the trampoline toward the swimming pool. He couldn't use the swimming pool, either. There was too much algae in it.[6] 'I've had it!' he laughed. 'We need some water and nobody understands!'"

"My opinion of that festival," Dylan said, "is not any different from anyone else's. I think everyone is probably goin' t'have a good time, but I wouldn't blame 'em if they didn't. Why do they have to call it the Woodstock Festival? We like that name – Woodstock. It has a familiar ring to it. That's one of the reasons we moved up here.

There's quite a few towns with that name ... If it's all the same, we may move on to another one."[7]

Aronowitz said that he wasn't sure why Bob didn't play Woodstock. "Maybe it was his contrary nature, Aronowitz said. "Maybe it was his insistence on being difficult and disagreeable. Maybe he wanted to be perverse or he wanted to stay mysterious. Maybe he just wanted to be different. 'Y'gotta be different!' he'd once told me.

Bob always seemed to try to do the unexpected. He liked to swim against the tide ... For America, the site of Dylan's Woodstock would be even more inaccessible than Max Yasgur's alfalfa field after the traffic jam choked the roads. The site of Dylan's big comeback would be across the Solent, that seven-mile-wide appendage of the North Atlantic that reaches between England and the crumbling chalk cliffs of the Isle of Wight."[8]

The British Pop Festival Scene

In 1968, the thought of staging a pop festival, especially somewhere as remote as the Isle of Wight, was a fairly innovative idea. Unlike their counterparts across the pond, Britain was a little slow to adopt the pop festival mentality. There was the long-running annual National Jazz and Blues Festival, which had begun adding pop acts to its bills in 1965 and later became the Reading festival, and starting in 1968 there was a series of free one-day concerts held in London's Hyde Park. The previous year the Duke of Bedford had staged the hideously named Festival of the Flower Children at Woburn Abbey. The bill for that August weekend was almost as appalling as the name suggests.

In a statement to the press the Duke declared, apparently with a straight face, "Only Flower Children will be allowed in. They are nice peaceful young people who like beat music and coloured lights." His Grace told the press in no uncertain terms,

"They are very different people from hippies who take drugs and make trouble. Hippies will definitely be barred." Free flowers and sparklers were dished out by the organisers and there were fireworks displays. The festival was staged again the following year with a far better line-up. Whether or not His Grace allowed any of those nasty hippies in remains a mystery to me.

The first Isle of Wight music festival, staged in August 1968, started life as a fundraiser. In the Sixties there were no indoor municipal swimming pools on the Island, so anyone wanting to swim had to either visit one of the Island's beaches or the outdoor Blue Lagoon pool in Sandown, neither of which was very popular in winter. Therefore, after the Island's Council refused a request for the funding of an indoor pool, local residents decided to take matters into their own hands. A fund-raising committee was formed and several ideas were talked about. Ray Foulk, who would soon become Chairman of Fiery Creations (the promoters that would stage the Isle of Wight festivals) suggested a lottery. Other ideas were put forward and the Isle of Wight Indoor Swimming Pool Association (I-WISPA) promised to allocate funds to stage whatever event the committee decided would be best. Ray's older brother Ronnie Foulk, who would soon become Managing Director of Fiery Creations, wanted to go down the music route and suggested a jazz festival. They approached their younger brother Bill for help and advice and he agreed to provide input but only if the festival was a pop-rock event.

Ray Foulk: "[I-WISPA] ran a mile ... They supported us at first, but when the bad publicity started, which was pretty quick, they disowned it ... but they left their investment in ... They gave us £750, which we paid back afterwards ... they let us keep that in place ... but it became our own event."9

The event made a small profit which was reinvested in the 1969 festival. All three of the Island's festivals were organised and run by more or less the same group of people: Ronnie Foulk, 23; Ray, 22 (named directors), along with their younger brother Bill, 21, who was responsible for technical aspects and festival design. Our Three Musketeers were aided and abetted by Richard Clifton, Company Secretary, and experienced music promoter Rikki Farr, 27, who acted as Show Producer and Compère.

Ray Foulk: "I didn't know much about the current pop scene and my ideas were way out of date. I mean, I was thinking about some of the early people like Billy Fury and Adam Faith. The sort of names that I had grown up with ... but my younger brother Bill was a student at the Royal College of Art and he was pretty well up to speed with what was happening and I think names like Jefferson Aeroplane and The Move and Pretty Things all came from him."10

Tickets for the festival, which was held on Hayles Field, could be purchased in advance for 25 shillings each, £1.25 in these decimal times; attendees numbered around 10,000. The stage consisted of British Road Services (BRS) low-loader trailers pushed together and covered with large sheets of plywood and two large canvas tents were made available to the artists as rudimentary changing rooms. The whole thing was so informal that the audience was able to wander backstage without being challenged. One person was quoted as saying, perhaps a little unjustly, "The Festival wasn't badly organised. It wasn't organised at all."

The line-up for the 1968 Isle of Wight festival, or to give it its official title, "The Great South Coast Bankholiday Pop Festivity," was relatively modest, the big draw being American import Jefferson Airplane. Fresh from their success at the Monterey Festival, they were paid a fee of £1,000. The 1968 festival might have been an amateur affair but there are many old hippies, and maybe even some flower children, who are adamant that this small scale event was the best of the three Isle of Wight festivals. Regardless, it was enough of a success for the promoters to decide to do it all over again in 1969. No offence to Jefferson Airplane, but this time the Foulk brothers would invest most of their time and money in a true 'superstar' name. That name took some time to surface, but when it did, it was Bob Dylan.

Isle of Wight '69

Ray Foulk: "In about January 1969, we put an advert in the Isle of Wight County Press with a small form to reply on, asking who would people like to see at the next festival ... The idea being to try and involve people locally and to get some ideas as to what artists would be in demand. I had not personally thought of Dylan at the time ... The response from the newspaper advert was very small. Surprisingly it didn't produce many big names ... We put this down, at the time, to the fact that it was beyond people's expectations as to just who would appear at a concert on the Isle of Wight ... [after a while Ronnie said] 'What about Bob Dylan? ... He's a big name; he'll pack them in.' I must admit, I didn't know too much about Dylan, he didn't mean too much to me then..."[11]

The burning question was how to get in touch with Dylan's people. The number certainly wasn't in the phonebook and Fiery Creations didn't even know the manager's name. Having heard that there was a recent piece about Dylan's management somewhere in the British underground press, Ronnie Foulk made a trip up to London in the hope of seeking out the information. He did, and the initial approach to secure Dylan's services was made. Ron Foulk contacted Dylan's New York office and received a somewhat negative reply from Albert Grossman. Nevertheless, the answer wasn't a straight 'no' and Grossman even suggested that they should "try back in a couple of months – just in case." Try back they did. This time Ray Foulk, who had become quite enthusiastic towards Dylan as a headliner, made the phone call and he eventually got through to one Bertram Block.

Bert Block receives scant mention from Dylan biographers and in truth, he wasn't handling Dylan's affairs for very long, but, during this period he had taken over the day-to-day running of Dylan's affairs from senior partner Albert Grossman whom, by this juncture, Dylan was virtually refusing to talk to. It was Block therefore who handled all of the negotiations appertaining to Dylan's appearance on the Isle of Wight.

It was now mid-March and try as he might, Ray wasn't making too much progress. Block had, however, made it clear that the management were keen for Bob to play again and suggested that Ray should call back in yet another month. Ray Foulk: "Following this, I got into regular conversation with Block every couple of days. [He] kept saying, 'We'll phone back Friday,' etc. I was getting to know him quite well over the phone. Then Block said that Dylan was getting interested in doing something."[12]

After seeing on television that the new ocean liner Queen Elizabeth 2 was about to make its maiden voyage, Ron Foulk suggested that they might be able to book Dylan and his family onto the ship as part of the holiday they were cooking up to convince Bob to play their festival. So, when Ray next talked with Block he made the suggestion and Bert said he would include this in his updated proposal to Bob. At this stage in the negotiations the subject of money had not been broached. The chances of Dylan coming out of hiding were still quite small so any talk of an appearance fee was somewhat premature. Nevertheless, at this juncture the Foulks had no other names at their disposal and as time marched on worries mounted that the festival might not be a viable proposition.

Ray Foulk: "We had learnt that you were not going to attract people to the Isle of Wight ... unless you got somebody pretty big ... Dylan was the only name we had in the hat of that calibre ... so it became apparent, by about June time, that the event was not going to take place unless we got Dylan. It was as simple as that."[13]

By this time Dylan had been off the road for three years; his last 'proper concert' had been at London's Royal Albert Hall on May 27, 1966. Needless to say, during this period rumours of Dylan coming out of 'retirement' abounded but they had all amounted to nothing. Even if Dylan wasn't yet ready to play live he was beginning to talk and after a year of pursuit *Rolling Stone* founder Jann Wenner got to interview him on June 26, 1969. This meeting was just three weeks before Bert Block confirmed that Dylan would play the Isle of Wight. Regardless, if Dylan had made up his mind at this point he wasn't letting on and Mr Wenner's opening gambit of, "When do you think you're gonna go on the road?," was met with a reply of, "November ... Possibly December."

After what must have seemed like forever, Block rang Ray Foulk on June 28 to say that Bob was "interested" and that he would like as much information as possible about the festival. Fortunately, Ray owned a printing company so the team was able to quickly put together a 12-page brochure detailing everything from the site itself to the sound system and backstage facilities, which this time would be more than a tent. They listed the names of the people involved in staging the event but inflated their ages to appear more mature. Later, Block would ask for film footage of the site and of the house where Dylan would be staying.

Ray Foulk: "We obtained a farmhouse in Bembridge ... It had a swimming pool and a recently converted barn suitable for rehearsing in ... We were offering Dylan a fortnight's stay there, no expense spared; car with driver. Also, we would have him come over on the QE2."[14]

After sending the telegram confirming Dylan had agreed to play the festival Bert Block now spoke of money. He proposed a $50,000 fee for Dylan but there were strings. Albert Grossman wanted two other acts from his roster to be included on the festival bill. The

Band would back Bob Dylan on his performance but Grossman also wanted them to have their own slot on the bill. His price for The Band was $20,000. It was suggested that the third Grossman act should be Richie Havens. Havens' fee would be $7,000. The inclusion of three Grossman acts earned Dylan's manager almost $16,000 in commission. There was also the small matter of the cost of getting all of the personnel to the Isle of Wight which would rack-up a further ten grand. The total would therefore be $87,000 (almost three-quarters of a million pound in 2019). Ray Foulk later said that he thought $50,000 for Dylan quite cheap.

Foulk said he was "absolutely flabbergasted" when Block confirmed they had got Dylan. "I remember having to sit down," he said. Foulk quickly made arrangements to go to New York with Rikki Farr. Block booked them into the famed Drake Hotel which was located quite close to Grossman's office. Ray Foulk: "There wasn't a lot to sort out. Negotiations were quite quick. As far as I was concerned it was all formality ... It was clear that Grossman in particular wanted Dylan to work again... Block made it plain to me that Dylan was contracted to a one-hour performance ... The contract used was an ordinary standard musicians union contract."[15]

The following day, Foulk and Farr met Dylan at the Drake. Ray Foulk: "It was only a very brief meeting, just two or three minutes, in and out. I think Dylan simply wanted to meet and see the sorts of people he was going to be getting involved with. It was just a few pleasantries, nothing more. He struck me as just a very ordinary person."[16]

"Dylan didn't want to be in the sort of spotlight that Woodstock would have provided. He felt that coming to England, to a small Island, a medium size thing, it wouldn't be too big but it would be big enough to do justice to his status. So I believe that was his thinking. Then there was the attraction of coming to see the home of Tennyson and Queen Victoria and all those things that we could lay on for him and it would be a holiday with his family. So, things combined and gelled in a way that suited him."[17]

From the onset, the intention was to record Dylan's Isle of Wight concert and there was specific mention of this in the contract. Dylan's performance could only be recorded by his label, CBS, and any such recording would be at Dylan's own expense. Fiery Creations would make provision for the recording to take place and if a record was released they would receive a one-off royalty payment of $2,000. If, however, a limited number of songs were to be released, not under the banner of the Isle of Wight concert, as turned out to be the case with *Self Portrait*, then no royalties would be due to the promoters. All payments for the Grossman acts were to be made in full seven days in advance and to ensure everything went smoothly the Grossman office hired British lawyer Arnold Goodman to look after their affairs. Lord Goodman was, in every sense, a heavyweight. A leading London lawyer, he was chairman of the Arts Council of Great Britain, Harold Wilson's legal adviser and the pre-eminent establishment fixer.

The first announcement in the music press that Dylan would indeed headline the festival appeared in the British music paper *Melody Maker* who ran the headline: "Dylan here August," on the front cover of their July 26 issue. Also included in the article was a copy of the telegram from Bert Block confirming Dylan's acceptance, which had unwisely been sent to *Melody Maker* by Rikki Farr. The *Melody Maker* announcement couldn't have come at a worse moment for Ray Foulk who at the time was still in New York being entertained by Grossman. It could have scuppered the deal, especially when Grossman rang London and discovered that it was Rikki Farr who had given the details to the paper. Although Rikki was the most experienced of the promoters he was on occasions rash and unthinking and across the three Isle of Wight festivals, he became something of a liability. Farr's primary responsibility at festival time was that of emcee, but even in this role he mostly failed to excel. In his book *The Road Goes on Forever*, Philip Norman commented, "The precise value of Rikki Farr to the team is never immediately clear."

In early August Dylan began talking about his upcoming Isle of Wight concert. The first interview was given to Don Short who spoke with Dylan at his home in Woodstock. The interview was published in the British newspaper the *Daily Mirror* on August 9. Dylan told Short that he was "happy with his new songs," the country drenched *Nashville Skyline*, and that he was "rarin'" to go play the Isle of Wight. He did say, however, that he was "nervous." "Gee – I am," he said. "It's been a long time." Although much of the blame for the later hype surrounding Dylan's festival appearance was down to Fiery Creations press team, it seems that speculation regarding the length of the set may have begun with Dylan. According to Short in his *Mirror* piece – the statement is written as a direct quotation from Dylan – "We're getting together a brand new repertoire and we may be on stage for a full three hours." Remember, the contact he had just signed was for one hour. Then again, past experience would seem to imply that Dylan didn't read contracts!

In mid-August, shortly before he was due to leave for England, Dylan had a chance meeting with well known sound engineer Elliott Mazer at the Carnegie Deli, a New York restaurant on 7th Avenue adjacent to Carnegie Hall. Dylan casually asked Mazer if he would record his performance at the Isle of Wight and Mazer agreed.

Dylan's Troubled Journey to England

Intending to sail to Southampton, England, Bob Dylan, his wife Sara and their two eldest children, Maria and Jesse, boarded the Queen

Elizabeth 2 in New York Harbor on Friday August 15; the first day of the happening on Max Yasgur's farm and 16 days before Dylan's scheduled appearance on the Isle of Wight. The QE2 had made its maiden voyage from Southampton to New York City on May 2, 1969, so at the time of Dylan's journey, the 70,000-tonne liner was less than four months old. The five-day voyage would therefore have been something quite special, even for the likes of Bob Dylan.

Before the vessel set sail, there was a small farewell party during which Dylan's three-year-old son Jesse lost consciousness after hitting his head on a doorknob on the stateroom door. The ship's doctor refused to take responsibility for the boy on the long voyage, so shortly before they were due to set sail the family, Jesse in Bob's arms, disembarked from the ship and went straight to a hospital where the boy was kept under observation.

Al Aronowitz: "My wife and I had driven the Dylans to the ship to see them off and we were in their stateroom when, 30 minutes before the ship sailed ... Jesse went into convulsions. We rushed Jesse to our doctor, who met us in the emergency room of Lenox Hill Hospital, where, taking no chances, the doctor decided to admit Jesse for a day or two."[18]

Ray Foulk: "It was dreadful news. I was, at this stage, in daily contact with Block. He telephoned me with the news that Dylan had left the ship to go to the hospital and was still in New York. Block said that Dylan would obviously have to fly over at a later date. The accident brought home to us the vulnerability of our position ... The event all hinged on this one human being; it shook us a bit."[19]

Fortunately, Jesse was soon well enough for Bob and Sara to feel comfortable about going to England. This they did, minus both children who stayed home in Woodstock with their live-in nanny, Bernice. Bob Dylan, with an obviously pregnant Sara, arrived at London's Heathrow Airport from New York late on Monday August

25. They were accompanied by Robbie Robertson, Al Aronowitz and The Band's new Road Manager, Jonathan Taplin. The first-class airfares for Dylan and his party had cost the promoters £5,000. Bert Block and his wife and child had arrived in England three days before Dylan. According to Chris Hockenhull, Block himself had been involved in a minor car accident soon after arriving in England.

Ray Foulk: "It was very low key. [Dylan] arrived on a regular flight at about 10 pm... We drove down to Portsmouth in two cars ... It was nearly 1 am when we arrived ... We were drinking tea waiting for our hired hovercraft to arrive ... Once we arrived on the Island it was only 20 minutes drive to Forelands. Once there, Bert Block took over."[20]

The Band had arrived on the Island a couple of days before Dylan and their accommodation had proved problematic. Arrangements had been made for them to stay in the relaxing atmosphere of a family home – Newclose House near the village of Blackwater – however, they took one look at the place, said something about it being a "Granny joint," and refused to stay. Ray and chauffer Chris Colley whisked them away to the Halland Hotel but once again they were "underwhelmed." After much debate, it seems that Robbie Robertson and Rick Danko remained at the Halland while Garth Hudson, Richard Manuel and Levon Helm returned to the initially rejected Granny joint! Daisy Hodges: "My mother cooked for them and sorted their every whim... They ate the most enormous quantities of steak and beef... Some of them had their wives with them... They returned the house to us in immaculate condition."[21] Richard Manuel's wife was expecting a baby and after the festival the couple stayed on the Island while the child was born.

Al Aronowitz: "Bob and Sara and I were going to Forelands Farm ... a 16th Century stone cottage within a walled compound ... There was a 24-hour guard and a proper English hostess [Judy Lewis].

She was an almost matronly woman in her early fifties who went around asking for autographs while wearing a badge that read, Help Bob Dylan Sink the Isle of Wight."[22]

Al Aronowitz was an interesting if slightly curious choice of travelling companion. Maybe Bob looked on Aronowitz as a true friend. Al certainly got quite close to Dylan; a feat managed by very few. Or maybe Dylan simply saw Al as his tame journalist – his press attaché. Al's approach was in the tradition of the writers who trailed after the Old West's outlaws or went out with the US Army during the American Indian Wars, capturing major events as they unfolded but then 'embellishing' them a little to delight a willing and eager readership. In fairness to Al, however, he was always much more of an enthusiastic participant than a mere observer. In any event, by 1969 the two men were closer than ever and for whatever reason Dylan decided to invite Al to accompany him to the Isle of Wight.

Ray Foulk: "We were asked to bring Aronowitz over as part of Dylan's entourage. I thought he was somebody that would perhaps help with Dylan's interaction with the press but he didn't seem to do much except hang around. I didn't even see him talk to Dylan that much." According to the *Sun* newspaper, upon arrival Dylan was "slightly disappointed." "I thought the Island would be kinda derelict, with sandy beaches," Dylan said. "But this is just like a normal country."[23]

I Wanted to See the Home of
Alfred Lord Tennyson

Dylan arrived at Forelands in the early hours of Tuesday morning and later that day George Harrison and Beatles' number two road manager 'Mal' Evans arrived at the cottage in a Daimler limousine. Harrison had to return to the mainland the next day but he arrived back at Forelands with his wife on Thursday August 28. The farmhouse had four bedrooms, two bathrooms, a kitchen, a dining room and a moderately large living room. In total, 10 people stayed in the house: Bob and Sara Dylan; Bert Block, his wife Barbara (a former jazz pianist) and their daughter Suzi; George Harrison and his wife Pattie; Mal Evans (invited by Aronowitz); Al Aronowitz and housekeeper Judy Lewis. On Friday August 29 Bob and Sara visited Osborne House, where Queen Victoria had spent many delightful summers. The couple made the 30-minute journey to East Cowes in the chauffeur-driven black Humber Super Snipe provided by the promoters. Chauffeur Chris Colley said Dylan told him, "Not to hang around but come back in a couple of hours." When Colley returned he said the two of them were waiting like a "pair of holidaymakers." Although the press made much of Bob's mention of wanting to see the home of Alfred Lord Tennyson, Dylan didn't make it to Farringford House: "There was no time to get to Farringford," Judy Lewis told the authors of *Isle of Wight Rock*. She intimated that Dylan's habit of rising late, about midday, restricted the time available for sightseeing.

Judy Lewis: "Bob took a liking for blackberry and apple pies and fruitcakes! Sara was constantly going on at him about his diet ... After supper some evenings he would ask if I would like him to sing something. I would demote George Harrison to go fetch things from the kitchen and help me do the washing up so I would not miss anything ... I think Harrison was in awe of Dylan.."[24]

Al Aronowitz: "It wasn't until 1997 that I got to know [Judy Lewis] better. That's when I wrote to surrealist poet David Gascoyne inviting him to the Allen Ginsberg Memorial in Manhattan's Central Park... and got a reply from – of all people – her. The proper English hostess [was now] Judy Gascoyne, wife of the noted Isle of Wight poet... In her letter, Judy wrote me: 'I was put in charge of looking after you all ... Quite a task really ... The menu was mostly vegetarian because of George Harrison. Breakfast started at midday and was that much easier, since George had convinced us that porridge was better for us than bacon and eggs. However, the morning of the big pop festival concert, I decided to buy a juicy steak (to sustain Bob!) It cost 15 shillings (75p in today's money). It put a hole in the 7-pounds-5-pence a week I had been given for food. Anyway, while Bob was eating his steak [you asked] 'Is that good, Bob?' And you looked at it longingly! So he immediately cut the steak in half and shared it with you ... I suggested he go to Quarr Abbey to hear the monks chanting. He and Sara enjoyed that.' Judy described Bob as 'restless and nervous and very polite' ... 'All the time they were here, they didn't take drugs or drink alcohol...' Little did she know!."[25]

In truth, George Harrison had driven a stash of marijuana over to the island in his new blue Ferrari 365 GTC coupe. Al Aronowitz: "This was the care package we were all jonesing for... none of us had enjoyed a toke since we'd gotten to England... George also brought along a dub of the Beatles' Abbey Road album, which he played over one of the amps in the rehearsal shed. The audience included Robbie Robertson and The Band as well as Dylan and myself and, although I can confess that my own mind was blown by the album, I don't remember Bob and the boys lifting George on their shoulders to tell him how much they loved Abbey Road."[26]

They're Planting Stories in the Press

It's the job of the publicity guys to feed the ever hungry media machine with exaggerations and half-truths and the Fiery Creations publicity people were extremely adept in this dubious art. Rumours abounded that Dylan would be on stage for at least three hours, maybe four and that there might be a superstar jam session at the end of his set. *Melody Maker* reported that George Harrison, the Rolling Stones, Blind Faith and Dylan could play together in a grand finale to the weekend event. A spokesman for the Festival told the

Maker: "Blind Faith is flying in from Honolulu after asking if they could appear [with Dylan]. And Jack Bruce has also said he would be ready and willing to join them all on stage. The Rolling Stones, who, – except for Mick Jagger, who is now filming in Australia – are staying on Keith Richard's yacht off the Island, and it is understood they also have expressed a wish to take the stage with Dylan after his performance ... Fiery Creations say that tickets will now be on sale at the Festival gate."

Dylan read the press and complained to Block about the hype. He had been hoping for a relatively low key comeback and as the gig got closer he was becoming more anxious. Ray Foulk: "There was a certain amount of friction between us here ... I wanted to keep Dylan happy ... [but] on the other hand, I was getting word back from our office ... [that] we have to get more publicity out of Dylan. This is how the idea for a press conference came about ... I thought that if we could arrange one main press conference, rather than set up individual interviews, Dylan may well agree to do it."[27]

Al Aronowitz: "The media continually complained about Bob's aloofness, his inaccessibility, his uncooperative behaviour and his camera-shyness. For his part, Bob fed the antagonism, making it clear that he wasn't a trained monkey doing tricks on command to please the press. His attitude was that he wanted the world to judge him on his songs, his music and his performances alone ... The promoters ... kept pleading with Bob to hold a press conference. On the Wednesday before the show, I had to help arrange one. At press conferences, Bob always did his best to sound as if he were mumbling 'noncommittal statements.' At the Halland, the questions certainly were irrelevant ... That night, Bob could be seen on the evening news, looking straight-faced out from the telly... [It was Dylan's first press conference since May 1966]."[28]

Although Bob Dylan's "comeback" performance at the Isle of Wight had placed the Island at the centre of a giant musical coup with worldwide appeal, the local newspaper, the *County Press*, who were very anti hippies invading their peaceful island paradise, had so far steadfastly avoided mentioning the festival build-up or even that there was going to be a festival! Dylan's press conference was packed with eager newspaper reporters and television crews from around the globe but as Alan Stroud of *Yesterday's Papers* pointed out, one newspaper was "conspicuous by its absence." With a major scoop on his doorstep, Mr Ash, editor of the *County Press*, deemed Dylan's appearance not to be newsworthy and failed to send anyone along to the press conference!

Back in the relative safety of Forelands Farm, Chris White of the *Daily Sketch* managed to get a few words from Dylan as he rested in the garden! Al Aronowitz: "There were security guards at Forelands cottage. Two guards were manning the main gates which were over six feet high. These were wrought-iron and had been boarded-up so people couldn't peep through them. [Nevertheless], somehow an English newspaper journalist just ambled up towards Dylan in the cottage garden. Me and Bert both saw him at the same time and we jumped up and began to bundle him away. Dylan being Dylan though, said, 'No, it's okay, he can have an interview'."[29]

Although it was not an interview, more a brief conversation, which was all White was after, the *Daily Sketch* decided not to publish anything. Nevertheless, White later recounted his conversation with Dylan in *Melody Maker*. In reply to a question about "other engagements" Dylan said: "Not at the moment, but we'll consider any offers we get." White said he found Dylan easy and pleasant to talk to. "He was a complete contrast to what the publicity makes him out to be and a contrast to his lack of communication at the press conference. He was a completely different person to what I expected. It was an insight into the person and not the public image ... Basically he is a shy person."

Judy Lewis: "That evening we watched TV to see if part of the press conference was shown. Bob didn't want to watch saying to me that he never liked to see himself on TV. He lost out though and we watched what items were shown. He said he'd rather be watching *Rowan Martin's Laugh In*."[30]

As the day of Dylan's concert drew closer more guests dropped into Forelands including Charlie Watts of the Rolling Stones. Apple Records' employees Chris O'Dell and Bill Oakes had made plans to attend the festival when Oakes received a phone call from George Harrison instructing him to go to a Soho music store and buy a full set of 12 Hohner harmonicas to bring with him to the festival. "You're never going to believe this," Oakes told O'Dell, "Bob Dylan forgot his harmonicas!"[31]

By next morning the plans had changed. Overnight Harrison had called Oakes again telling him that Dylan needed the harmonicas "right away." Oakes told O'Dell: "[George] wants me to put them on a helicopter this morning." Oakes then suggested they should hitch a ride to the festival. They boarded the helicopter at Battersea Heliport and flew out to Isle of Wight. The pilot was instructed to head to Bembridge and then to look for a large stone farmhouse and a white blanket! After circling the Forelands house for a second time, several people appeared holding a large bed sheet. They waved and pointing towards a field next to the house. According to O'Dell: "Leaning out the second-floor window, a little grin on his face, was Bob Dylan."

Ringo and his wife Maureen arrived at the house with John Lennon and Yoko Ono on the afternoon of Dylan's performance, their helicopter landed not in the adjacent field but bang in the middle of the Forelands Farm garden. The Lennons had ordered thousands of peace leaflets to flutter down on the festival crowd but when the pilot nixed that idea they decided to rain down balloons instead. At Apple Records, the staff was given the rush job of inflating several hundred balloons until somebody realised they would never fit into the helicopter! Beatles' aide Tom Bramwell: "I was up in London, hanging out with Eric Clapton and some others. Early in the afternoon, Eric said, 'Let's go to the Isle of Wight to see Bob Dylan.' He organised a coach and we met outside Robert Stigwood's [music entrepreneur] office and trundled down with all of Cream and Jackie Lomax, singing and drinking all the way."[32]

Rikki Farr says that one moment he'll treasure all his life was witnessing the superstar jam session on the afternoon of the concert: "Dylan, The Beatles, Eric Clapton, Jackie Lomax, all just jamming. Ginger Baker would get off the drum stool and Ringo would step in. Eric Clapton would take a solo, and then George Harrison would take the next one. It was amazing."[33]

That same day, and with a videotape rolling, Bob invited the Beatles to a game of tennis on the Forelands Farm courts. Aronowitz said: "Bob and John teamed up against Ringo and George, Pattie Harrison giggled, 'This is the most exclusive game of doubles in the world!'... Ultimately, the game ended and, at around 5:30, Dylan piled into a white van along with Sara, Ringo, Maureen and me for the five-mile drive to the festival site... A year or so later, the Apple Records press agent who had arranged with me for John and Ringo to land in the Forelands Farm garden sent me the bill for the helicopter. He expected that I would give the bill to Bob... The bill amounted to a few hundred dollars, but Bob wasn't talking to me at the time and so I got stuck with paying it out of my own pocket."[34]

Dave Parr: "I drove Bob Dylan and his wife Sara to the festival. They sat in the front with me in the Ford Transit. In the back was Bert Block with John and Yoko Ono. There were no seats in the back, just a piece of 9x4 timber ... We got up the top of St John's Hill in Ryde and stopped at the traffic lights. When we pulled off the Transit juddered and there was a crash in the back, John and Yoko had fallen off the seat. The funny thing was, nobody said a word."[35]

The Festival

Five miles north-west of Bembridge, outside of the cosseted walls
of Forelands Farm, the Isle of Wight festival had got underway on
Friday August 29. The festival was held at Wootton Farm, a 150-
acre site at Woodside Bay, midway between the towns of Ryde and
Newport on the northeast of the Island. By Monday, a full five days
before the festival proper, over 500 fans were already on site and
British Rail was bracing itself for what a spokesman described as "a
second Dunkirk." Boats from across the South coast were preparing
to ferry up to half a million music fans to the Island.

Al Aronowitz: "I went with Band drummer Levon Helm in the 3
am darkness to watch the kids coming off the ferries at the Ryde
terminal ... Although they should have been burnt out from the trip,
they looked bright-eyed and determined, with their rucksacks and
their bedrolls piled on their backs ... Levon and I had hired a taxi
for the ride into Ryde in our own hunt for a food shop... We were
on an expedition to rustle up some candies, snacks... to bring back
to the rest of The Band, trapped at the Halland Hotel without room
servic ... On our way back to the hotel, Levon and I rode along the
road on which this throng walked. The line was endless ... [Levon]
rolled down the window to get a better look at the kids in this line.
Then he broke into an overpowering smile as he said, 'Look at how
beautiful they are!' At the same time, with a few jerky motions, he
grabbed the care package we had bought for the rest of The Band,
reached into it and he started handing out its contents to the kids
through the taxi window."[36]

Edward Trevor reporting for the *News of the World* wrote: "With the
girls heavily outnumbered by boys, I watched as five girls tried to pick
up partners in a country lane. One of them said, 'We've no money
at all... We've hitch-hiked... And we decided that we'll go with the
right kind of boy providing he'll promise to take us to see Bob Dylan's
concert.' Gerda, a 19-year-old Swedish blonde, told me: 'I'm trying to

find a nice boy for the night because I've only got nine-pence left. I don't mind what happens as long as the boy is good to me and takes me to the concert.'"

English music writer Michael Gray had this to say about his experience: "At Woodside Bob Dylan came, no longer as a contemporary, the wicked message, but as Moses came down from the mount ... The walk down to the site on Friday afternoon, in a rare hour of sunshine, was an eerie recreation of that scene in *The Grapes Of Wrath* where the Joad's approach the work camp, still optimistic, and puzzled and then apprehensive because of the line of unhappy-looking people coming away in the opposite direction... At the end of the dirt-track approach, the first view of the arena itself was of twin towers, a closed gate, a high fence with the wiring carrying 2,600 volts and long lines of submissive, uncomfortable people.

Up on stage Rikki Farr spent three days imposing his sanctimonious assumed personality onto 'you people who really count.' On the other side of the barrier, there was the press and the nasty pop aristocracy. Grossman, the only one with style, was there, detached and powerful, dismissing the rumours of a supergroup jam session... 'Of course the Beatles would like to play with Dylan,' he said. 'I would like to go to the moon.'"[37]

The festival had a lot more than just music on offer. The arena contained areas for catering, shopping, a 400-person cinema tent, a 'disco' tent, a big top featuring folk and blues music, a car jousting arena and a so-called 'environmental playground.' Another of the "happenings,' a huge 'Krazy Foam' play area, proved extremely popular and provided some festival goers with an excuse, if indeed one was needed, to strip naked and frolic. Jackie Leishman reporting in *The Guardian* said: "A girl of 19 who gave her name as Vivian and said she came from 'nowhere' took part in the happening which attracted a large audience ... She and a young man, both naked, made love on a bed of foam ... The girl, when asked why she had done it, replied, 'Why not? It's a beautiful thing'."

The live music began on Friday evening with the opening act being folk-rock band Eclection. However, in advance of Eclection talking the stage the unsigned and little known prog-rock band Marsupilami decided that an appearance at the festival would help to further their careers. Accordingly, they simply turned up unannounced, told Rikki Farr they had mislaid their contract, and on they went! Drummer Mike Fourace would later tell author Brian Hinton that a "baffled" promoter apologised for not having them on his schedule and paid them for the performance! The two big attractions on the first night were The Bonzo Dog Doo-Dah Band and The Nice.

The Saturday schedule, which kicked off at 2 pm, consisted of: Gypsy, Blodwyn Pig, Edgar Broughton Band, Aynsley Dunbar Retaliation, Marsha Hunt & White Trash, Pretty Things, Family, and Free. Free only managed to play three numbers before being ushered off to make way for the day's top of the bill act The Who, whose BEA helicopter was approaching the festival site. Pete Townshend later said, "We had wanted to land on the stage, but they wouldn't let us." The unenviable task of following The Who fell to Noel Redding's Fat Mattress. Coming just two weeks after the release of their debut album, this was the band's first UK gig. The penultimate act for Saturday were Woodstock veterans of two weeks before, Joe Cocker and the Grease Band. The Moody Blues closed that day's proceedings.

One unnamed newspaper reporter said of the gathering crowd: "Tomorrow night, nearly 200,000 youngsters are expected to be here. Among them will be weirdies from Germany, France, Italy, Sweden, Denmark and America; and they come, they tell me, to be among beautiful people and to have a groovy experience." The reporter continued, "The IoW has certainly never seen anything like this in its long and sedate history. Queen Victoria, who loved the Island and made it fashionable in a more gracious era, would not have been amused. And for me, I felt rather more at home dodging snipers' bullets in Belfast two weeks ago.

This really is no place for an elderly reporter who danced the Charleston in Oxford bags 40 years ago. My navy double-breasted suit and homburg have caused much amusement as I wandered among the hippies. Many obviously think I look as funny as I think they do – which only goes to prove it takes all sorts: 'Hey there, daddy-o,' they've shouted at me. 'Get turned on, pop,' and, 'Man, you sure look lost!' But it's all been in good fun for everyone ... These young people are indeed providing an object lesson in good manners and discipline to their soccer hooligans and seaside rowdies ... Some of these youngsters, sleeping rough, have been living in conditions of considerable discomfort for 24 hours already. And they have another 24 hours to wait before their idol, the pasty-faced protest singer from America, performs ... A young lady wearing what appears to be a transparent nightgown and a Red Indian headdress has just offered me, with a beautiful smile, one of her feathers."

Sunday August 31 began with a bugle call from the band Gypsy and a "Good Morning Campers." From mid-morning onwards, those who had come to witness the "return of the master" were continually arriving at the arena gates; there was no doubting who the main attraction was. The Foulk brothers were justified in their concerns over the incident aboard the QE2 because without Bob Dylan, there would not have been a festival. At noon, the first act on stage with their unique mix of music and poetry was The Liverpool Scene. The Third Ear Band then played 'world music' before it had been invented. The east meets west theme continued with the ten-piece band, Indo-Jazz Fusions. Next up was Rikki Farr's brother Gary who was backed by Portsmouth band Mighty Baby. Tom Paxton, Pentangle and Julie Felix followed. Felix was well received;

especially so for her performance of two Dylan songs, 'Chimes of Freedom' and 'Masters of War.' By the time the first of the three Grossman acts arrived on stage twilight was creeping in. As always Richie Havens was both powerful and spellbinding.

The audience for Dylan included John Lennon, Yoko Ono, Ringo and Maureen Starr, George and Pattie Harrison, Keith Richard, Bill Wyman, Charlie Watts, Syd Barrett, Eric Clapton, Ginger Baker, Elton John, Steve Winwood, Jim Capaldi, Jack Bruce, Cilla Black, a 17 year old Sting, Jane Fonda, Terence Stamp, Roger Vadim, Francoise Hardy, Peter Wyngarde, Playboy Club owner Victor Lowndes and England Test cricketer Bob Dylan Willis.

The Long Wait

Al Aronowitz: "No one without proper credentials was supposed to be allowed inside the press enclosure... [which] should have been able to accommodate a couple of hundred reporters and photographers. By the time Dylan got to the festival site, more than a thousand persons had managed to sneak in ... and they were packed as tight as asparagus tips in a can. The promoters had placed seats at the front of the enclosure for special guests ... In the press enclosure behind the special guests, the standees were packed too close together to be able to sit down and they were blocking the view of the rest of the audience, who complained with shouts and curses ... [followed by] bottles and beer cans."

The Band were scheduled for 8.30 pm. By 10.00 pm, however, they had not made an appearance.

Al Aronowitz: "In his dressing trailer, Bob, readying himself for the show, sat tuning George Harrison's favourite acoustic guitar... Bob stayed quiet and stone-faced as he tried to be patient... As 8:30 approached, he looked at me with annoyance and said, 'I don't hear The Band on yet. Ain't The Band on yet?' He said it as if it were my fault. He said it as if he wanted me to do something about i ... 'Shit!'

he said suddenly. 'It's past 8.30! Why ain't The Band playin' yet? ...'.Bob exploded. 'Go find out why The Band ain't onstage yet?.'"

The Band's Road Manager, Jonathan Taplin, was engrossed with checking microphone connections on the stage. Aronowitz asked what was wrong to which Taplin curtly replied, "I'm trying to find out!" Caught between a rock and a hard place, Aronowitz then spent what must have felt like an eternity playing wicked messenger between Dylan, who insisted The Band must go on now, and Taplin, who of course insisted he had to find the fault.

Al Aronowitz: "Whatever kind of hot water I was in, Sara played lifeguard... I worshipped Sara as a goddess who not only could calm the storm but who also could turn Bob into a human being... Living in Byrdcliffe, Bob had gotten into the habit of going to sleep early and it didn't surprise me when he started to yawn." Dylan's annoyance was reaching fever pitch. He was adamant that he wanted to, 'Catch the crowd when it was still at the peak of its psychic energy.' 'This is ruinin' ever'thin' that I came here t'do,' he told Aronowitz. 'Ever'thin' I wanted t'accomplish!'"[38]

Robert Shelton, who was also backstage, wrote in his Dylan biography *No Direction Home*: "I have never been able to determine the cause of the delay. Bob later told me he didn't know what it was about either, but felt the festival was run very poorly." Karl Douglas, writing for *Acoustic Music* magazine, bizarrely suggested the delay was due to Bert Block's demand that Dylan and The Band be paid before performing!

The Truth Behind the Delay

Al Aronowitz's story of a fault with the sound system not only flies in the face of conventional wisdom, but also contradicts the plethora of press reports, all of which blame the delay on the emptying of, and readmission to, the press enclosure. Was this then a case of Aronowitz embellishing his story? Asked about this by documentary filmmaker Tom Odell in 2005, Aronowitz insisted the delay was due to a sound problem and reiterated: "He [Jonathan Taplin] never did tell me what was wrong with the sound system so sometimes I wonder if he did that deliberately to screw Bob up!"[39]

Ray Foulk: "I'm surprised that Al Aronowitz says that the lateness of Dylan going on was because the sound system was broken. It was nothing of the sort. There was no one reason why Dylan was late; it was an accumulation of reasons, the main one being the press ... Now, our press people were perhaps a bit naive in the way they handled it but, after Richie Havens had been on and before The Band went on, we cleared the press arena and reissued passes so that took time and caused a delay. Secondly, The Band played for longer than we had expected. They played an hour, or quite a long set, and thirdly there was never a set time that Dylan was going to go on. Dylan was going to close the show ... and we didn't want to close the show at nine o'clock, or whatever ... so we wanted it to be quite late ... The lateness probably only amounted to about an hour ... It might have seemed like an age but it wasn't really that long. These things get exaggerated over time."[40]

Well, either Ray Foulk's memory is faulty or he is intentionally playing down the delay. The hold-up occurred after Richie Havens' set which ended more or less on schedule at 8.00 pm. As Aronowitz rightly stated, the turnaround should have been about 30 minutes with The Band taking the stage at 8.30 pm. In actual fact, The Band didn't arrive on stage until 10.20 pm, so the delay was much closer to two hours than the one hour suggested by Foulk. Also, I'm not at all convinced by Foulk's statement that, "The Band played for longer than we had expected." The Band only performed nine of the eleven songs they had played at Woodstock and their set lasted for well under an hour. Surely no one, including the Foulks, expected a shorter set? Also, in another interview – not connected to the delay – Ray Foulk stated that The Band was "booked" to "do an hour."

In October 2013, in the hope of finally laying to rest the longstanding debate about this delay, I got the opportunity to ask The Band's road manager Jonathan Taplin if there really was a problem with the sound system. Taplin informed me that Aronowitz was correct and that there had indeed been a problem, not with the promoter's sound system, but with The Band's microphones. Taplin told me that: "Two microphones had gone dead" and that "It took quite some time to trace the faulty connections amongst the miles of cables."[41]

It seems therefore that the promoters' decision to clear the press area and to reissue passes before The Band appeared was fortuitous, in that, in the time it took to achieve this, Jonathan Taplin managed to trace and fix the faulty mic connections. It seems that very few people, including promoter Ray Foulk, were aware that any such problem had occurred. Indeed, only one of the promoters, the onstage emcee Rikki Farr, was aware of the sound problem and although it seems to have gone unnoticed, Farr actually apologised to the crowd for the delay by saying: "People, do you want the sound to be perfect? Then cool it, people. You've waited three days. Be cool and wait another five minutes and you'll have the sound a 100 per cent. In fact, you'll have it 200 per cent perfect."

Chauffer Chris Colley was standing close to the Dylans backstage and witnessed just how incredibly tense Bob was before going on to perform: "He was walking up and down... with Sara hanging onto him, strumming his guitar in a manic and tuneless fashion. He seemed really anxious and Sara was comforting him. 'Bob, it's gonna be alright. They want to hear you. Really you're gonna be great.' Sara had her arm around him. It was really shocking, as he was such a big star."[42]

Bob Dylan's Performance

Bob Dylan eventually arrived on stage at 11.08 pm with the words,

"You sure look big out there!" He was dressed in a loose-fitting white suit, which Eric Clapton would later refer to as his "Hank Williams suit," a dark yellow shirt with cufflinks that Sara had bought him, a white tie and white shoes. He was sporting a shortish haircut and a small beard. He played two acoustic guitars during the performance: a Martin D-28 and a gorgeous sunburst Gibson J-200 given to him by George Harrison (the guitar is featured on the cover of *Nashville Skyline*). It had been three years since Dylan had played in Britain. In 1966 a section of his audiences had come to taunt him and to accuse him of being a Judas. This time they came to worship at the feet of the master.

Half a dozen songs from the 1966 tour remained in favour and the song that opened those shows, 'She Belongs to Me,' gets things off to a lively start here. Understandably, Dylan looks nervous, but it doesn't come across in his performance. His vocal delivery is the new rich *Nashville Skyline* voice, the one that everyone here knew from the 'Lay, Lady, Lay' single which had been released the previous month. There's some nice instrumentation from The Band on the opening number and the recording is so clear that you can pick out every instrument. "Great to be here, great to be here!" Dylan says at the song's close. "Thanks very much. Great to be here; sure is."

The heartfelt 'I Threw it all Away' is exceptionally well sung in a lovely deep voice that is even more *Nashville Skyline* than *Nashville Skyline*. As with most of the set, The Band's playing is wonderfully sympathetic to Dylan's vocal. A rocking and confident 'Maggie's Farm' blasts out and Dylan's voice seems to go up an octave. The Band's backing vocals work well throughout much of the set, but the repeated shouts of "no more" in this one are a little cringeworthy. Otherwise, it's a great arrangement.

The fact that there were only three songs performed with The Band before Dylan did his short four-song solo acoustic spot should have foretold that tonight's performance was never going to be anywhere near as long as people had hoped. In any event, 'Wild Mountain Thyme' is just beautiful! Sometimes known as 'Purple Heather' or 'Will Ye Go, Lassie, Go,' the song is based on a traditional Scottish folk number. This surprise inclusion in the set is the only cover song of the night.

The vocal delivery on 'It Ain't Me, Babe' is tantalisingly restrained and without the edginess and bite that so often comes across on this number. This rendition sounds very much like a song of deep regret rather than an attack. There's a strange guitar flourish part way through which sounds as though the song is going to come to a premature close; it doesn't, and Dylan continues to sing his heart out.

The breathtaking rendition of 'To Ramona' is one of the best versions of Dylan's career. This, and the next song, 'Mr Tambourine Man,' are punctuated only by a short blast from Dylan's harp. 'Tambourine Man' is greeted with thunderous applause, which respectfully stops abruptly to allow Dylan to continue singing. This performance falls way short of the wonderful renditions of three years earlier. Gone is the rambling nine-minute version (this one barely makes it to three), and all but gone is the harmonica. The Isle of Wight performance contains just two token blasts on the harp, the second of which doesn't even fit the song. Although Dylan had the harmonicas specially flown in from London by helicopter, this is the only time he picks one up during the entire set!

"Thank you, thank you," Dylan says as The Band again take the stage for the first of what will be two tracks from the *John Wesley Harding* album ('I Dreamed I Saw St. Augustine' and 'I Pity the Poor Immigrant'). 'St. Augustine,' which contains some nice guitar from Robbie Robertson, is wonderfully done. The arrangement is very similar to the album version but of course at the time the record was only two years old.

There seems to be a false start to 'Lay, Lady, Lay.' Bob strums his guitar for a second time and then says, "Yeah." Helm's delicate stickwork brings the song up to speed after which things come together quite quickly. Driven by Robbie Robertson's guitar, 'Highway 61 Revisited' positively rocks and is maybe the highlight of the entire set. This version, which oddly begins with "God said to Abraham give me a son," is simply joyous to behold and, by the song's end, Bob's overall performance has moved up a couple of gears. Partway through the song, Dylan goes over to speak to Rick Danko and then smiles from ear to ear before moving back to the mic with cupped hands doing some sort of megaphone impression! Levon Helm's exquisite Arkansas drawl can be heard as he shouts out the background vocals with great exuberance.

'One Too Many Mornings' slows the frantic pace; the alternate-rhythms of this bouncy little version are not to everyone's taste. In 2019 we are all very used to Bob Dylan's 115th arrangement of many of his songs but less so in '69. Once again Dylan moves over to talk with Danko and again he smiles. This time when he returns to the mic he poses with his guitar, one leg bent for a few seconds, before punching the air with his right hand. Garth Hudson's beautiful accordion accompaniment on 'I Pity the Poor Immigrant' feels just perfect.

'Like a Rolling Stone,' which ups the pace again, is enthusiastically greeted with much applause and Dylan is clearly having fun with the song. Here we have a brave new arrangement that most Dylan fans don't like. The smooth *Nashville Skyline* voice certainly doesn't fit well with the biting lyrics and the vocal delivery lacks punch. Dylan forgets the words in several places and one line is sung twice before a further stumble occurs. Biographer Clinton Heylin referred to this performance as "a runt of a version."

'I'll Be Your Baby Tonight' supplies some down-home Basement vibes – Kick your shoes off and bring the bottle over here, indeed.

"We're gonna do one more for you here," Dylan informs the masses ... "This was a big hit over here we believe by a ... Manfred Mann (clearly not huge Manfred fans, the crowd responds with almost total silence), (long pause) "Great group, great group (a further long pause). We're gonna do it" A slightly funky and lively rendition of 'Quinn the Eskimo,' which was a UK number 1 for Manfred Mann, bounces along quite merrily until Bob calls out, "Well, guitar now." Robertson obliges and the night air is filled with rapid-fire Telecaster notes. The song ends, Bob smiles and waves goodbye and the crowd begins chanting for more; two encores follow.

A new unreleased Dylan composition, 'Minstrel Boy,' is first. Most people could probably guess what the final song would be. In this festival setting, the crowd-pleasing 'Rainy Day Women #12 & 35' with its marching beat and its "Everybody must get stoned" chorus is the perfect song with which to say goodbye. With partially re-written and partly jumbled lyrics, the song ends with: "They'll stone you when you're riding on your bike / they'll stone you when you're singin' in the mic." Dylan, however, is no longer singing. The show is over! People begin to turn to each other asking, "Is that it?" "Where's the big jam?" "Aren't the Beatles coming on?" Chants of, "We want Dylan!" begin to echo around the site, while jeers and booing erupt from certain sections of the crowd. Compère Ricki Farr attempts to pacify these people by informing them, "Bob Dylan came here to do what he had to do and he's done it, and I'm afraid that's the end."

One contributory factor to the brevity of Dylan's set is that the songs themselves are quite short. Gone are the long epic numbers like 'Visions of Johanna' and 'Desolation Row.' In his 1966 sets, 10 of the songs were over five minutes in length; on the Isle of Wight only one number, 'Like a Rolling Stone,' makes it past five minutes. Maybe Dylan was purposely keeping it simple; not too many lyrics to remember on this his comeback!

One thing is for sure, the 2013 release by Columbia Records of the complete Isle of Wight concert, as part of the deluxe *Bootleg Series Vol. 10*, has rewritten musical history. The muddy audience tapes, which had Dylan's vocal buried deep in the mix, and even the four tracks officially released on *Self Portrait* came fully alive after 44 years in exile. For the first time there is separation between the individual instruments and Dylan's vocal is clear and upfront. Also, at long last, the crowd become part of this historically important concert and we get a true sense and feel of what it was like to have been there.

Immediately after the concert Dylan returned to Forelands. Tom Paxton: "I went with him and The Beatles to the farmhouse where he was clearly in a merry mood because he had felt it had gone so well... The Beatles had brought a test pressing of *Abbey Road* and we listened to it and had quite a party."

The following day, Monday September 1, Dylan returned to the mainland on a privately chartered hovercraft. After arriving in Portsmouth, Bob, Sara and George Harrison were collected by an Apple Records' rented helicopter and flown to Tittenhurst Park, a Georgian mansion in Sunningdale, that the Lennons had recently bought from Peter Cadbury. While boarding the hovercraft, Dylan spoke briefly to waiting reporters. Writing for *The Times* newspaper, David Wilsworth said that Dylan had cut short his stay on the Isle of Wight: "We are going to stay here in England and we may go to Ireland, Scotland and Wales too," Dylan said. In actual fact, the Dylans would remain in Britain for one night only! One of the first guests at Lennon and Yoko Ono's 72-acre Tittenhurst estate, this would be the final time that Dylan and Lennon met and from all accounts it was not a great success. John Lennon: "He came to our house with George after the Isle of Wight ... I was just trying to get him to record. We had just put him on piano for 'Cold Turkey' to make a rough tape but his wife was pregnant or something and they left."[43]

On Tuesday September 2, George Harrison drove the Dylans to London's Heathrow. Bob told *The Express* newspaper: "I was shattered by stories that the kids were angry because I was three hours late. I was there at 5:30 as promised. I don't know why we were so long before going on." Fiery Creations' Peter Harrigan told *Disc*: "We expected him to be on stage a good bit longer than an hour. I don't know whether we would want to re-book him after this." Ronnie Foulk told *The Times* newspaper: "I did expect Dylan to sing for a bit longer but he fulfilled his contract." In 2006, Ray Foulk told Tom O'Dell: "I thought the press was frankly ridiculous in the way they tried to make out there was some sort of problem. I think Dylan fuelled the fire a little at the press conference when he mentioned he'd love to jam with the Beatles, but I certainly didn't think he let us down. All that stuff in the press was just tabloid rubbish, quite honestly."

John Lennon thought Dylan's performance was reasonable, though slightly flat, and that the audience was "waiting for Godot or Jesus ... If there had been a jam, we would have got up. It was killed before it happened. It was so late by the time he got on... The crowd was dying on their feet..."[44]

The press' reaction to Dylan's appearance at the Isle of Wight focused almost entirely on the length of the set and the monies he received. One of the more dramatic headlines appeared in the September 1, 1969 edition of the *Daily Mirror*: "A Riot Threat as Dylan Walks Out." *The Mirror* piece continued, "100,000 pop fans threatened to riot late last night when folk singer Bob Dylan suddenly walked out on them. Security guards with dogs raced to the vast concert arena ... There was near pandemonium as outraged fans asked, 'Has he gone?' Dylan, America's 'high priest' of folk and protest song, had already been paid his fee of £35,000 in cash and was supposed to sing for three hours ... Dylan turned up four hours late. The reception he got could only be described as cool. The fans had given a great response to The Who and folk singer Tom Paxton. But when Dylan arrived the fans had waited too long." Leslie Hinton writing for the *Sun* newspaper accused Dylan of sitting back-stage and refusing to play.

According to the September 7 edition of *News of the World*, Dylan's earnings after his profit share came to £10,000 a song!," though how they arrived at that exaggerated figure is something of a mystery. The *News of the World* went on to say, "Nowadays, Dylan gives nothing for nothing. His normal fee for allowing a few lines of his work to be reproduced in a newspaper is 500 dollars. We were offered – and refused – a special rate of £50 for eight lines. Dylan leaves the sordid financial details to Al Grossman, Bert Block and David Braun, who are collectively known in the business as The Management."

The press were not alone in their carping over Dylan's fee. Indeed, the issue went all the way to the Houses of Parliament. It was reported in the *Evening Standard* on October 5 that the Labour MP for Brixton, Marcus Lipton, had been unsuccessful in a motion to ban Bob Dylan from again performing in Britain! Lipton cited the amount of money Dylan was paid for his Isle of Wight concert as not being, "a powerful incentive for workers to accept income restraint." As a man of an entirely different generation – Lipton was born in 1900 – he was renowned for being highly critical, to the point of absurdity, of pop and rock music in general. In response to the Sex Pistols' 'God Save the Queen' he argued that "if pop music is going to be used to destroy our established institutions, then it must be destroyed first."

On September 6, the Isle of Wight *County Press* eventually came out and admitted that a pop festival had taken place on the island! Under the headline: "Pop Festival Invasion," they reported: "The Island was this week slowly recovering from the hammer blow of

pop with its attendant retinue of strangely garbed young people
who gave the impression that it was a Hindu prayer meeting on the
Ganges rather than a music festival in the Garden Isle."[45]

In general, those attending the event were exceptionally well
behaved, a fact that was picked up and repeatedly reported on in
the national press and by British Rail who said: "Everyone was
extremely polite and friendly ... And there was not a single piece
of vandalism ... We would be very happy to carry this crowd again.
They were no trouble and we had fewer complaints than we usually
receive about a normal bank holiday crowd." Not everyone was
entirely happy with their festival experience. On the way back to
the ferry terminal, one young woman, assumedly feeling let down
by the length of Bob's performance, set fire to a Dylan poster and
tossed it into the river where, for a few seconds, Dylan's glowing
face could be seen shimmering on the surface of the water.

The Festival was Over

On his arrival in New York, comments made by Dylan to the
waiting press were reported by Reuter Agency. On September 3,
the *Liverpool Echo* wrote that Dylan had no wish to perform again in
England: "No more,' he declared. 'They make too much of singers
over there."

The 1969 Isle of Wight festival was a bold and costly project for
Fiery Creations, especially based on the comparatively minor event
held the previous summer. "Our profit is not all that big," Ray Foulk
said. "But we have achieved what we set out to do ... We've given
enjoyment to a lot of people."[46] After the success of the 1969 Dylan
event, Fiery Creations promoted just one further Isle of Wight
festival, a lavish five-day affair staged in the August of 1970. For
a myriad of reasons beyond the scope of this book the promoters
were not able to satisfy all of their creditors. As was the case with
Woodstock Ventures, however, the Foulks had hoped to recoup

any losses from the sale of the film and recording rights. Murray Lerner, a name well known to Dylan enthusiasts, had shot almost 200 hours of priceless footage. "Everything was riding on the film," Ray Foulk told Alan Stroud. Sadly, the film didn't happen and Fiery Creations went into compulsory liquidation in February 1971. There would be no more "Fuckin' in the Bushes" on the Isle of Wight for the next 30 plus years!

Chapter Five

Tin Soldiers and Nixon Coming

The Seventies was a turbulent time both for Bob Dylan and for the United States of America as a whole. The new decade was barely four months old when on May 4, 1970 National Guardsmen opened fire on students on the campus at Kent State University, Ohio. The 29 Guardsmen fired 67 rapid rounds killing four students, paralysing a fifth, and wounding eight others. The whole sorry state of affairs took just 13 seconds. Some of the students had been protesting against the Cambodian Campaign – a new twist in the Vietnam War – while others were merely observing the protest or walking nearby.

The US incursion into Cambodian four days earlier had been followed by the most widespread and persistent protests of the entire Vietnam War. Sixty per cent of the country's college students had walked out of classes and The National Guard had been dispatched to 21 campuses across 16 states. These protests had been supported not only by students but by the wider public, including some GIs. After the Kent State killings, anti-war protests escalated with many colleges and universities across the United States cancelling classes and even closing their doors for the remainder of the academic year in fear that violence might erupt on their campuses.

The Kent State shootings were not an isolated incident. Although much less well known, especially outside of the United States, only 11 days after Kent State, police opened fire on protesting students at the State College in Jackson, Mississippi. Tensions on the Jackson campus had been running extremely high, particularly with regards to racism and civil rights issues, and during a violent student protest on Friday May 15, 1970, police opened fire killing two Black youths – one student and one schoolboy – and injuring 12 others. A five-story women's dormitory on campus, Alexander Hall, was riddled with gunfire. FBI investigators estimated that more than 460 rounds struck the dormitory, shattering every window facing the street. At least 160 bullet holes were found in the outer walls of the building. The damage to the façade is still visible today.

During Tom Wolfe's 'Me' Decade, established politics in the US reached an absolute nadir with the infamous and still controversial Watergate scandal. To add to the political woes of the United States, in 1973, the new Vice President Spiro Agnew resigned in disgrace as part of a plea bargain after he was investigated for extortion, tax fraud and bribery and conspiracy dating back to 1967.

For many Americans, the Seventies became a decade of huge transition marked by confusion, frustration, and an overwhelming feeling that their country had utterly lost its way. It seems that following Watergate, many US citizens withdrew from politics altogether. There was, however, a deluded minority who believed the best way to remove the policy-makers was with a gun rather than the vote.

In April 1972, Arthur Bremer carried a firearm to an event intending to shoot President Richard Nixon but was deterred by heavy security. Moving on to an easier target, a month later, Bremer shot Democratic candidate George Wallace four times at close range. Wallace survived the attack but was paralysed from the waist down. In February 1974 Samuel Byck was thwarted in another plan to kill Richard Nixon and in September '75 Lynette Fromme, a follower of the infamous Charles Manson, drew a Colt pistol on President Gerald Ford when he reached out to shake her hand in a crowd. Fromme was restrained by a Secret Service agent but 17 days later there was another attempt on Ford's life when a second woman, Sara Jane Moore, fired a revolver at him. It is little wonder that Bob Dylan had slight or no interest in politics. Nonetheless, was it possible, as Bob Dylan might have us believe, that he, or for that matter any American, could be wholly detached from the political turmoil of the Seventies?

In June 1984, Dylan informed Kurt Loder: "I think politics is an instrument of the Devil. Just that clear. I think politics is what kills; it doesn't bring anything alive. Politics is corrupt; I mean, anybody knows that."[1] In 2009, Dylan told Bill Flanagan: "Politics is entertainment. It's a sport. It's for the well groomed and well-heeled ... Politicians are interchangeable ... Politics creates more problems than it solves."[2]

Unsurprisingly, a number of songs were written in response to the infamous and well publicised Kent State deaths. Along with the Harvey Andrews' song 'Hey Sandy,' which was addressed to Sandra Scheuer, one of the two women killed in the shootings, Steve Miller, The Beach Boys, The Isley Brothers and Quicksilver Messenger Service all wrote rejoinder's to the massacre. The most celebrated and by far the most poignant reaction to Kent State was, however, 'Ohio.' Written by Neil Young and recorded by Crosby, Stills, Nash & Young the song, rush-released in June 1970 by Atlantic Records, was immediately picked up by FM stations. Neil Young's lyrics, especially the line: "Tin soldiers and Nixon coming/ We're finally on our own," was a brilliant description of the emotions felt by large numbers of US youth after this tragic event.

Those still reeling from Dylan's country crooning on *Nashville Skyline* and the double album *Self Portrait* were desperate for their messiah to make another grand musical statement and maybe even return to protest. There had been veiled hints at the Vietnam War in a couple of the Basement recordings but even if you managed to track down a bootleg containing those songs you would need a cypher breaker to decrypt the lyrics. The Kent State killings failed to persuade Dylan back to protest. Instead, his fans in the Movement would have to wait until November 1971, when he would rush release the song 'George Jackson,' just eight days after recording it in New York City.

For many, the single was a surprising return to protest, mourning as it did the killing, in San Quentin Prison, of Maoist-Marxist Black Vanguard co-founder George Jackson. Dylan wrote the song the day after he had finished reading Jackson's best-seller Soledad Brother, a book-length collection of letters from prison which had been published the previous year. Dylan had come to read the book after talking with filmmaker and friend Howard Alk. Alk had recently filmed and directed a documentary that was begun as a portrait of Fred Hampton and the Illinois Black Panther Party. During the making of the film, however, Hampton was alleged to have been brutally murdered by the Chicago Police Department. Released in Chicago in May 1971, the film attracted little attention; it nevertheless had a successful festival run in Europe and opened in New York City in October 1971. Immediately after talking with Alk and seeing the film, Dylan began reading *Soledad Brother* and just weeks after finishing the book he entered Columbia Studio B, New York (November 4, 1971), to record his response.

Written from the heart, or maybe the gut, 'George Jackson' was more a human response than a political statement. In any event, the song was important enough to Dylan for him to release it on both sides of a single in acoustic and big band versions. Never one to take the easy option, Dylan's reaction to George Jackson's shooting was a much less obvious response than a song about Kent State would have been. It was also far more contentious! Political historian Alexander Baron later wrote: "Dylan ... should have put more thought into this one." Baron then went on to say that, "in the final analysis [George Jackson] was little more than a crook, a petty thug, and ultimately a murderer."

It was certainly true that from a young age Jackson had been in almost constant trouble with the law. He had several juvenile convictions including assault, and several for burglary and in 1960, at age 19, he was convicted of stealing 71 dollars from a gas station at gunpoint, for which he was sentenced to serve one year to life in prison.

On August 21, 1971, a week after the completion of his second book, *Blood in My Eye*, which predicted his death in prison, Jackson had a meeting with his attorney Stephen Bingham. After the meeting and while being escorted back to his cell, officer Urbano Rubico noticed something in Jackson's hair, which was later revealed to be an Afro wig, and when ordered to remove it, Jackson pulled a 9mm pistol from beneath the wig and said, "Gentlemen, the dragon has come," a reference to the Ho Chi Minh poem 'Wordplay', which states, "When the prison gates are opened, the real dragon will fly out." Jackson then forced the prison officer to open all of the cells and along with several other inmates he overpowered the guards and took them and two inmates hostage. Five other hostages, three guards and two white prisoners, were killed. Three other guards were shot and stabbed but survived their ordeals.

Jackson, along with fellow inmate Johnny Spain, made a break for the prison wall. Jackson was shot dead by tower guards but Spain surrendered. Jackson was killed just three days before the start of his murder trial for allegedly killing another prison guard, John Mills in 1970. Three days before the escape attempt, Jackson had rewritten his will.

As would later be the case with his 1975 song about the life and death of mobster Joey Gallo, the 'George Jackson' single had many detractors and Dylan was accused of questionable moralising.

Dylan, however, would turn out not to be alone in his support for Jackson, or at least for Jackson's views. Jackson's supporters point to a number of inconsistencies and improbable elements in the official story of the attempted prison break and believe that Jackson was set up and murdered by prison authorities because he had become all too powerful and posed a serious threat to their control. Or as Dylan sang, "because he was just too real." There will never be agreement as to what actually took place on the day George Jackson was killed. Nonetheless, as political moods shift with the passage of time, the idea of a conspiracy against him no longer seems quite as fanciful as it once did.

The biggest puzzlement of all has to be why Dylan chose to release the 'George Jackson' single at all. In the previous June, he had put out a double album of mostly covers, *Self Portrait*, containing the Lorenz Hart and Richard Rodgers standard 'Blue Moon,' Gordon Lightfoot's 'Early Mornin' Rain' and Paul Simon's 'The Boxer.' Dylan's true reasoning for the album's release will never be known and from day one critics and fans have debated his motives. Was the album intended as a serious release or as Dylan would later have us believe, a ploy on his part to throw his obsessive fans and those who had claimed him as their protest leader off the scent? If we are to believe that Dylan did indeed release *Self Portrait* as an attempt to demystify himself and to escape from the clutches of the counterculture, then why now release what would be construed by all as a highly charged protest record? Inevitably, a song like 'George Jackson' was exactly what his old fans in the protest movement were clamouring for. For many, this release would erroneously herald the return of their messiah.

Robert Shelton was perplexed by *Self Portrait*: "I told Dylan that *Self Portrait* confused me," Shelton wrote in 1986. "Why had he recorded 'Blue Moon'? Dylan refused to be drawn on the subject: "It was an expression," was all he said, though he did point out that if the album had come from Elvis Presley or maybe the Everly Brothers ... it wouldn't have been a shock.

In a 1984 interview with *Rolling Stone*, however, Dylan gave very different reasons for the album's release. Here he talked about the "notoriety" he had gained for "doing nothing" and about how he had wanted to do something that his fans couldn't possibly like and would not be able to relate to. He even talked about the album's cover saying: "I knew somebody who had some paints and a square canvas, and I did the cover-up in about five minutes. And I said, 'Well, I'm gonna call this album *Self Portrait*'." We know that Dylan had been a keen artist for some time before this so the part about knowing somebody who had "some paints and a square canvas" is clearly a tall tale. Also, why include four of his own great songs from his Isle of Wight Festival appearance? And why include some quality cover songs like 'I Forgot More Than You'll Ever Know,' 'Days of 49' and the gorgeous 'Copper Kettle' if all he wanted was for the album to fall flat?

It is also interesting and revealing that in January 2014 a long forgotten store of single-sided acetates was discovered in a five-story brownstone at 124 West Houston Street in Greenwich Village. Dylan had rented the ground floor of the building for use as a studio and when he vacated the premises the acetates had been left behind. In total, there were 149 discs appertaining to *Nashville Skyline*, *Self Portrait* and *New Morning*. The acetates were made by producer Bob Johnston after the various sessions, including *Self Portrait*. After Dylan returned home to New York from recording in Nashville, Johnston would periodically send him work-in-progress acetates of the recordings they'd had made together. Dylan would listen to the records and phone changes through to Johnston, who would make new acetates reflecting Dylan's wishes. These discs were also sent to Dylan for him to decide on the final sequencing of the album. This process seems to me to be a great deal work for an album that Dylan didn't care anything about! Whatever his intentions the album received a real hammering. Robert Christgau said: "I don't know anyone, even vociferous supporters of this album, who plays more than one side at a time. I don't listen to it at all."[3]

The fact that Dylan's next album, *New Morning*, was released just four months after *Self Portrait* helped fuel rumours that the record had been rush-released to help quell talk that with *Self Portrait* Dylan had lost his way. Although not a return to form, *New Morning* received a much warmer reception from fans and critics alike. Writing for *Rolling Stone* (November 26, 1970) Ed Ward said: "Put simply, *New Morning* is a superb album. It is everything that every Dylan fan prayed for after *Self Portrait*." The record broke into the Top 10 in the US and gave Dylan his sixth and last UK number 1 album until 2009's *Together Through Life*.

According to Dylan, some of the songs that made it onto *New Morning*, probably 'Father of Night,' 'Time Passes Slowly' and possibly 'New Morning' itself, were written for the Archibald MacLeish play *Scratch*. Based on the short story *The Devil and Daniel Webster*, the play is about a man who sells his soul to the devil in exchange for fame and fortune but then attempts to renege on the deal. In any event, Dylan's collaboration with MacLeish came to nought and none of his songs were used in the film.

Although *New Morning* contained a number of sentimental love songs with Bob still placing some emphasis on country life and domestic bliss, 'Sign on the Window,' 'New Morning,' 'The Man in Me,' 'Day of the Locusts' and 'Went to See the Gypsy' all went to confirm that the album was a renaissance of sorts. 'Went to See the Gypsy' is a song that has sparked debate ever since its release. The song is clearly about Dylan meeting Elvis Presley but the question remains, was this meeting real or imagined?

Clinton Heylin writes that Dylan and his wife took a trip to Las Vegas in the winter of 1970 and while there the couple "caught one of Elvis Presley's shows at the International Hotel." Although no source is given, Heylin goes on to state that the two men later met "backstage." It is quite possible that this belief is derived from a 1971 *Melody Maker* interview with Ron Cornelius, the guitarist on *New Morning*. When *Melody Maker* asked about 'Went to See the Gypsy,' Cornelius replied, "I asked him [Dylan] about that and he told me it was about going to see Elvis in Las Vegas." It seems to me that Dylan is answering a question regarding the song and not whether he had actually met Elvis in person. During the 2001 *Love and Theft* Rome press conference Dylan replied to a question about his meeting Elvis: "No," he said. Then after a pause, added, "That's what I've been told to say."

In a May 2009 Douglas Brinkley article for *Rolling Stone* Dylan talked about Elvis at some length: "I never met Elvis," Dylan says. "I never met Elvis, because I didn't want to meet Elvis. Elvis was in his Sixties movie period, and he was just crankin' 'em out and knockin' 'em off, one after another. And Elvis had kind of fallen out of favour in the Sixties. He didn't really come back until, whatever was it, '68? I know the Beatles went to see him, and he just played with their heads. 'Cause George [Harrison] told me about the scene ... Two or three times we were up in Hollywood, and he had sent some of the Memphis Mafia down to where we were to bring us up to see Elvis. But none of us went. Because it seemed like a sorry thing to do. I don't know if I would have wanted to see Elvis like that. I wanted to see the powerful, mystical Elvis that had crash-landed from a burning star onto American soil. The Elvis that was bursting with life. That's the Elvis that inspired us to all the possibilities of life. And that Elvis was gone, had left the building."[4]*

* A photograph of Dylan meeting Elvis emerged a few years back but that is unequivocally a fake! In reality, the song is about an imaginary, possibly a dream, meeting with Elvis.

Escaping on the Run

Less than a month after his return from the Isle of Wight Dylan decided to leave Woodstock and move the family base to New York's Greenwich Village. On December 9, 1969, Sara gave birth to a son, Jakob Luke. Including Sara's child, Bob's adopted daughter Maria, the Dylans now had five children. Their family was complete and the next chapter of their lives was about to begin.

In a 1970 interview Dylan told Michelle Enghien: "I believe that at certain periods in a person's existence it is necessary, if not vital, to bring about change in your life so as not to go under. I felt that I needed to stop in order to find something new, in order to create – and then again I wanted to live part of my life without being continually disturbed for no valid reason."[5]

"Truth was that I wanted to get out of the rat race," Dylan recalled in *Chronicles*. "Outside my family, nothing held any real interest for me ... I was fantasising about a nine-to-five existence, a house on a tree-lined block with a white picket fence ... That would have been nice. That was my deepest dream."[6]

Dylan's departure from Woodstock also heralded the beginning of the end of his strained relationship with manager Albert Grossman. In April 1970, following the expiration of their management contract, Bob's newly established Gramercy Park office assumed control of the administration of Dylan's music publishing company, Dwarf Music. The office was headed up by administrator Naomi Saltzman who had left Grossman's employment to work for Dylan. Bob also employed music attorney David Braun, and accountants Marshall Gelfand and Marty Feldman, all of whom had previously worked for Grossman. It seemed that given the option, Grossman or Dylan, there was only one choice.

Dylan didn't give up his Ohayo Mountain Road house but by the spring of 1970 the family were spending almost all of their time in New York City. Bob would soon realise however that the move back to the Greenwich Village was a monumental blunder. During the few short years he'd been hiding away in his Woodstock idyll, the Village had changed. One thing Dylan certainly hadn't bargained for was Alan Jules Weberman. The move to MacDougal Street, just a few short blocks from Weberman's place at 6 Bleecker on the Bowery, proved to be a definite case of out of the Le Creuset and into the fire.

A counterculture activist, AJ Weberman was an obsessive Dylan "fan" who had become so disappointed with Bob's lack of interest in radicalism and the counterculture that he formed the "Dylan Liberation Front." Dylan later said that his decision to move back to New York was, "a stupid thing to do." He said that the worst times in his life had always come about when he tried to find something that was in the past. It seems he should have stuck with his own mantra of don't look back.

Weberman fervently believed that Bob Dylan had the power to help change the world and he would do everything within his power to show Dylan the error of his ways. After all, it was his civic duty not to let Bob Dylan "sell out." One of Weberman's aims was to get Dylan to play benefit concerts and he would later unjustifiably claim that Dylan's appearance at the Concert for Bangladesh was at least in part down to him. On August 1, 1971, three months before the release of the 'George Jackson' single, Dylan had, albeit somewhat reluctantly, agreed to perform at George Harrison's Concert for Bangladesh. This would be Dylan's first proper concert appearance since the Isle of Wight festival, almost two years before.

Dylan did not attend rehearsals and no one was quite sure whether he would turn up on the day. "Bob always liked to hedge his bets," production manager Jonathan Taplin said. Dylan eventually put in an appearance at the full technical rehearsal at Madison Square Garden the night before the concerts. Nevertheless, during this rehearsal he told Harrison that he didn't want to perform. Harrison: "He wasn't sure he was coming ... The night before when we got to Madison Square Garden he saw all these cameras and microphones in this huge place and said: 'This isn't my scene. I can't make this ... Got to get back to Long Island, got a lot of business.' Right up to the moment he stepped onstage I wasn't sure if he was going to come on," Harrison said: "So it was kind of nerve-wracking. I had a little list on my guitar and I had a point after 'Here Comes the Sun' – it just said 'Bob,' with a question mark."[7]

Clad all in denim, carrying a Martin acoustic guitar and wearing a harmonica rack, Dylan looked like the folk singer of old. If this was indeed some sort of statement, it would be reinforced by the choice of songs, all of which were pre-accident material. The biggest surprise of all was 'Blowin' in the Wind,' which Dylan begrudgingly performed after an eight-year absence at George Harrison's request. Although the two sets (afternoon & evening) were only 25 minutes each, Dylan inevitably stole the show. If his performance on the Isle of Wight hadn't convinced him to go play concerts again, would this?

A gadfly and obsessive questioner, AJ Weberman tried to contact Dylan as soon as he found out that Bob was back living in the Village. He started by simply knocking on Dylan's door, that door, however, was quickly slammed in his face. Then, one September day in 1970, as he past Dylan's townhouse, he spied a shiny new steel rubbish bin and immediately thought: "Now, there's something that was inside and now it's outside." Weberman made his way over to the container and lifted the lid. He reached inside and pulled out a half-finished letter to Johnny Cash. It was at that point that the dubious art of garbology was born. The basic premise of garbology is that people are what they throw away and to Weberman Dylan's was Million Dollar Trash. Visiting Bob's garbage became a regular pastime for the newly self-appointed garbologist and although there were a few interesting finds, Weberman's main discovery was that it was as he feared, Bob Dylan, the romantic, visionary, revolutionary had become a typical upper-middle-class family man. Instead of discovering letters from other rock stars, first drafts of newly penned songs, or the Rosetta stone that would enable him to unlock the secrets of Dylan's cryptic symbolism Weberman found, beneath the layers of dog shit and nappies, a vet bill for the Dylans' dog, Sasha, an invoice from the Book-of-the-Month Club, and a memo to Bob regarding the upcoming MacDougal Street Garden Association meeting. Weberman nevertheless continued his investigations.

The height all of this absurdity came when Weberman placed an advert in "EVO" (East Village Other) that read: "If anyone has a sample of Bob Dylan's urine, please send it to me c/o EVO, 20 East 12th Street, New York, New York." Weberman wanted Dylan's urine so he could confirm his suspicions that he was a heroin user. At the time, Weberman, who felt betrayed by Dylan, was still reeling from the effects of *Self Portrait*. "In retrospect, it wasn't that bad," Weberman said: "but at the time I said it was used to induce vomiting in free clinics. If somebody poisoned themselves, they'd play them *Self Portrait*!"

About two weeks into the removal of Dylan's garbage, which AJ had been hauling back to his place on Bleecker Street, Dylan discovered that his rubbish was being kidnapped. One day, as he left the house to walk the kids to school, he found an empty wine bottle left on his doorstep which he picked up to throw in the bin. However, when he lifted the lid, the garbage can was empty. All of the rubbish that the maid had thrown away the night before had vanished! Dylan later told Weberman that he thought the phantom refuse collector might have been him but what about if it were someone planning to kidnap one of his children. Dylan took no chances and put the property under 24-hour surveillance. From that time on, Dylan took care over what he threw away and Weberman's pickings became slim. One of the few finds after this was a doctor's prescription for a strong muscle relaxant in Dylan's name. Weberman deduced from this that Bob was still feeling the effects of his motorcycle accident.

In early 1971, still buzzing around like an annoying mosquito, Weberman formed the Dylan Liberation Front (DLF), the purpose of which was to remind Dylan of his failure to support anti-war and civil rights organisations and to try and persuade him to play a benefit concert for political prisoners. The DLF also wanted Dylan to get rid of stocks that they alleged he owned in companies that produced weapons which might be used in Vietnam. The group had badges made with "Free Bob Dylan" emblazoned on them and to press the point home further, they held a huge party, attended by some 1,000 people, in front of Dylan's house, which resulted in the NYPD closing Bleecker Street. The date the DFL chose was May 24, Bob's 30th birthday. Unfortunately for them, the day before the Dylans had left on a trip to Israel so were not there to witness the goings on!

After Bob played the Concert for Bangladesh, Weberman agreed publically that his harassment of Dylan would stop. However, when a reporter from Associated Press, intending to do a feature story on garbology, approached Weberman and asked if she could see "garbology in action," Weberman, always hungry for publicity, took the reporter to a townhouse owned by the millionaire banker, David Rockefeller. Unfortunately, other than a few chicken bones, Rockefeller's garbage offered nothing of interest and so, in the fury of the moment, Weberman took the reporter down to MacDougal Street and began sifting through the now off-limits Dylan household trash. Sara Dylan saw what was happening and an altercation took place. Later that week, while walking down Elizabeth Street, a bicycle stopped just behind Weberman and he felt an arm clasping his throat. He pulled the arm away but was rewarded with a punch to the head.

Weberman: "I turn around and it's Bob Dylan! I'm thinking, 'Can

you believe this? I'm getting the crap beat out of me by Bob Dylan!'
I didn't fight back. Instead I tried to calm him down and block his
punches. In the end I was forced to bear hug him to the ground.
This only riled him up even more and he began banging my head
against the sidewalk. He's little, but he's strong. He works out. I
wouldn't fight back, you know, because I knew I was wrong. He
gets up, rips off my 'Free Bob Dylan' button and never says a word;
just rides off into the sunset. I picked up an empty wine bottle and
ran after him. Seconds later I spotted him waiting for a light ... I ran
up behind him and was ready to let him have it, Brooklyn-style, but
I couldn't do it. Dylan was right. A Bowery bum comes over, asking,
'How much did he get?' Like I got rolled ... I guess you got to hand
it to Dylan, coming over himself, not sending some fucking lawyer.
That was the last time I ever saw him."[8]

Seven years later, Weberman would insist that the *Street-Legal*
song 'Where Are You Tonight? (Journey Through Dark Heat),' which
mentions Elizabeth Street and contains the line: "It felt outa place/
my foot in his face," was about Dylan's altercation with him. In the
meantime, Weberman's activities had come to the attention of John
Lennon who, for a brief time, became associated with Weberman
and the "Rock Liberation Front." This newly formed "organisation,"
an offshoot of Weberman's "Dylan Liberation Front," believed that
by the early Seventies, rock music had ceased to be a force for
radical political change and that many musicians had been co-opted
into the "establishment."

Lennon sympathised with this premise and during the closing
weeks of 1971 he began to formulate a plan to spread the word. The
project would be called the "John & Yoko Mobile Political Plastic
Ono Band Fun Show." With Phil Spector directing, the music would
be supplied by John and Yoko, along with the likes of Eric Clapton,
Klaus Voorman, Nicky Hopkins and Jim Keltner. Local "Peoples'
Bands" would augment the bill in each city. Lennon proposed, for

instance, the MC5 in Detroit and the English anarchist band the
Pink Fairies in London.

Richard Nixon entered his name on the New Hampshire primary
ballot on January 5, 1972, effectively announcing his candidacy for
re-election. Although Nixon's victory was more or less a foregone
conclusion, an extremely optimistic Lennon believed that it might
be possible to change the outcome of the election by persuading
enough young people to vote against him.

Dylan had recorded the 'George Jackson' single amid a series of
improvised sessions with Allen Ginsberg. The sessions, which were
held at Record Plant studios in New York, were being financed by
Lennon, via Apple Records. When Lennon heard Ginsberg's song
'Going to San Diego' (San Diego was to host the 1972 Republican
Convention before it was relocated to Miami) and Dylan's 'George
Jackson' single, he began to ponder on a scenario where he and
Dylan might co-headline a tour. A tour of that stature, Lennon
mused, might well be able to deliver a message powerful enough to
move even the biggest Republican mountain. There was however
a problem. In recent months Lennon had been quite vocal in his
support of Dylan's nemesis, Weberman, and was even pictured on
the cover of the *New York Post* wearing one of AJ's "Free Bob Dylan!"
badges. In an effort to now distance himself from Dylan's adversary,
Lennon wrote a long open letter to the underground press
denouncing Weberman. At the same time, Weberman wrote a short
open letter to the press which he signed "Sincerely, AJ Weberman,
Minister of Defence, Rock Liberation Front.

The language in the letter didn't sound remotely like Weberman,
and he would soon deny having written it. "I didn't write that
apology," Weberman maintained. "John Lennon wrote it and I
signed it, hoping for the best ... I guess one of the reasons I [agreed
to sign it] was 'cause of the 'George Jackson' single – I thought that
Dylan might really be getting back into it – but as it turned out

Dylan kept all the bread from that single and just did it to get me off his back. You see I really want to believe in Dylan – or wanted to … now I'm convinced there's really no hope of getting Dylan back into the movement – he's just too conservative in lifestyle and politics."[9]

At a time when Dylan could seemingly do no right, the 'George Jackson' single turned out to be something of a conundrum in that the ordinary record-buying public simply ignored it, whilst the hardened political activists, whom you would imagine might have welcomed the song with open arms, fiercely attacked Dylan because he didn't donate the royalties from the song to the Soledad Brothers Defense Committee. Lennon's thoughts about the royalties are not in the public domain but in any event he was still eager to work with Dylan. Social activist Jerry Rubin later said: "I thought that when Dylan saw he was free of AJ, he'd be so appreciative that he would agree to tour the country with John and Yoko … The whole thing was going to revive the Sixties. That was my plan."[10]

Lennon invited Dylan down to Record Plant where he was producing David Peel's Apple Records' album *The Pope Smokes Dope* (released April 1972). Peel had written a song, 'The Ballad of Bob Dylan,' which he sang for Dylan. The song asked a series of questions: "Who is coming back again, fighting with his songs?… Who will help us with the answers?… Who will sing against the wrong?" The answer to all of these questions was, of course, Bob Dylan. As one might expect, rather then bring Dylan on board, the song had the opposite effect, especially as Peel had used Dylan's real name, Zimmerman, in the lyrics. Dylan quickly left the studio. He also left New York!

On reflection, it's simply amazing how much faith and hope people invested in Bob Dylan in the Sixties and early Seventies. It might seem ridiculous now, but at the time he was seen by many as some sort of saviour. These people, and there were an awful lot of them, believed, or at least wanted to believe, that Dylan had all the answers. These people were not all cranks or part of the lunatic fringe (Weberman and Peel), many were serious musicians like John Lennon and also David Bowie.

Written by Bowie for his 1971 album *Hunky Dory*, 'Song for Bob Dylan' was a tribute to his hero in the same way that Dylan's 'Song to Woody' had been a homage to Woody Guthrie almost a decade before. It can be no coincidence that the two songs have comparable lines. While Dylan sang: "Hey, hey, Woody Guthrie/ I wrote you a song," Bowie opens with: "Hear this, Robert Zimmerman/ I wrote a song for you." The song continues, "Now hear this Robert Zimmerman/ Though I don't suppose we'll meet/ Ask your good friend Dylan/ If he'd gaze a while/ down the old street/ Tell him we've lost his poems/ So they're writing on the walls/ Give us back our unity/ Give us back our family/ You're every nation's refugee/ Don't leave us with their sanity."

In an interview with Robert Hilburn in 1976, Bowie revealed his intention for writing the song: "There's even a song – 'Song for Bob Dylan' – that laid out what I wanted to do in rock. It was at that period that I said, 'okay [Dylan] if you don't want to do it, I will.' I saw that leadership void ... [That song] represented for me what the album was all about. If there wasn't someone who was going to use rock'n'roll, then I'd do it."[11]

The pressures for Dylan to conform to what people expected of him were immense. In addition to Weberman, tens of thousands of fans and some musicians, even Bob's good friend Allen Ginsberg, were now on Dylan's case!

Weberman talked about, "getting Dylan back into the movement," but what he failed to grasp was that Dylan had never been part of any "movement." Very few people outside of Dylan's family have got closer to Bob than his friend and sometimes road manager, the late Victor Maymudes. Maymudes has spoken about the time David Crosby called to ask if Dylan was interested in participating in a book he was writing about activism and rock'n'roll, focusing on the parallels between them. A politically aware Victor Maymudes thought it was a great idea: "[A]nything promoting social awareness and political activism is a good thing," Maymudes said. Dylan seemingly agreed, but a few months down the line he pulled out of the project and Crosby, incandescent with rage, was on the phone to Maymudes trying to find out why Dylan had changed his mind. "I told him that Bob was never really an activist in the first place," Maymudes said. "He was asking the wrong guy." Crosby screamed that "Dylan was in Selma!" He then slammed the phone down before Maymudes had a chance to explain.

Many years later, in his book *Another Side of Bob Dylan*, Maymudes got that chance. "The thing about Bob being in Selma, Alabama," Victor said, "is that Theodore Bikel bought him a ticket to fly down there, and yes, Bob was there. But from what I know, that was the only real time that he was part of a march like that and engaged with people. Never again did he do that. He made appearances at big demonstrations, but he wasn't really part of it. It really wasn't his thing."

Dylan of course had been distancing himself from the "movement" since as far back as December 1963 when he made his infamous, drunken speech at the ECLC's annual Bill of Rights dinner, the sentiments of which were reinforced six months later when he recorded 'My Back Pages,' which author Mike Marqusee says: "Must be one of the most lyrical expressions of political apostasy ever penned."

When asked about the radical left-wing organisation the Weathermen naming themselves after a line from 'Subterranean Homesick Blues,' Dylan told Jim Jerome: "You'll have to ask them ... It's not for me. I wouldn't have time for that. I'm not an activist. I am not politically inclined."

Pressures were really piling up on Dylan in New York City:

Weberman had become a greater annoyance than the hippies that had been hanging around Bob's Woodstock home, and now, there were increased demands for him to become more involved politically, or even to take part in some sort of anti-Nixon concert tour! To add insult to injury, Dylan was now experiencing problems with his new MacDougal Street neighbours!

In an effort to gain a little more privacy, Dylan had built a decorative stucco-coated wall to section off part of his rear garden. Unfortunately, the tenants' management agreement did not allow the common gardens to be segregated and, while he was out of town, a group of Dylan's neighbours came into the garden with sledgehammers and demolished the wall. "It was very unpleasant," Dylan's next-door neighbour Gloria Naftali told Howard Sounes. While Naftali liked and was sympathetic towards the Dylans, she felt the house was not suitable for someone so renowned: "When you are a superstar among people who are not," Naftali said: "Life becomes very difficult."

Life in The Big Apple was more than difficult; it was becoming intolerable. Dylan had realised that moving back to the Village was a huge mistake and during his May '71 vacation to Israel Bob and Sara visited the Givat Haim kibbutz to explore the possibility of living there for a year. Hauling garbage from Israel back to Bleecker Street might prove too big an undertaking even for someone as dedicated to cause as Weberman!

Dylan and Sara had gone to Israel without their children in the hope of escaping New York, celebrating Bob's 30th birthday, and exploring his Jewish roots, a subject that Bob had become increasingly interested in after his father's death three years before. However, on the day of his birthday and while praying at the Western Wall, he was snapped by a photographer! The press had been searching for Dylan after being tipped off by an advertisement in the *Jerusalem Post* that read: "Happy Birthday Bob Dylan,

Wherever You Are. Call us if you feel like it. CBS Records, Israel." It seemed that even if he put five-and-a-half thousand miles between him and the United States he was still a media target.

On May 22, two days before his birthday, Dylan and Sara had visited the Mount Zion Yeshiva, an educational Kabbalah training centre, where they talked with Rabbi Yoso Rosenzweig. Eve Brandstein, a kibbutz member at Givat Haim, told Clinton Heylin that Dylan wanted his children to go to the kibbutz, "each day ... for the experience," but that he and his wife did not want to work there. Instead, "they would stay in a guest house and pay for the stay and the keep of the children."[12] The kibbutz members weren't prepared to make concessions for anyone, not even Bob Dylan. Their biggest concern however was that if people discovered that Dylan was living there, and they surely would, the kibbutz would become overrun with press and curiosity seekers. The photograph of Bob at the Western Wall confirmed this. It seems that for Dylan, there was simply nowhere to hide and he returned home to New York somewhat dejected. He still owned the Ohayo Mountain Road house, but since leaving his upstate home he rarely visited Woodstock. He had a rented beach house in East Hampton, Long Island, which he used for summer breaks, but a few weeks hiding there was not a long term solution. He had recently rented a house in Malibu, California and had also acquired a ranch house near Scottsdale, Arizona and in the late winter of 1972 he moved the family down there on an extended vacation that included spending time with his mother, Beatrice, who was staying there to get away from the freezing Minnesota winter.

Imitators Steal Me Blind

During his time in Arizona, Dylan managed to achieve anonymity like never before (or after). His lengthy stay there is cloaked in desert dust, which of course was exactly what Bob wanted. He spent much of his time simply immersing himself in the sights and sounds of the Desert; soaking up the history of the Old West, taking the occasional float trip down the lower Salt River and finding some sort of peace with his family.

The only person who has shared anything about Dylan from this period is Bob Finkbine through his 1986 article in the *Scottsdale Progress Saturday Magazine*. In this piece, Finkbine said: "It was in 1972. Bob and his wife, Sara, and their children came to see his mother, Bea, who wintered here, and decided to stay." Finkbine went on to explain that Bob's mother, Beatrice, had known his mother-in-law when they were both "little girls in Minnesota." Finkbine said that Dylan's stay in Arizona was, "a time for [Dylan] to rest, regenerate, draw sustenance from family love and live a nearly normal life."[13]

With room to breath, Dylan now began thinking more about music and what his next move should be. One of the very few songs from this period is 'Forever Young,' which Finkbine says Dylan played for him. "I've been tinkering around with a new song. I wrote it for Jesse" (his son) Dylan informed Finkbine. In fact, according to engineer Rob Fraboni, the song wasn't new at all. At one of the recording sessions for *Planet Waves* Dylan told Fraboni: "[I've been] carrying this song around in my head for five years." Dylan has spoken about his "amnesia" and how around this period he found songwriting difficult, something that was confirmed during his conversation with Bob Finkbine. Finkbine: "[We] were sitting drinking coffee and I asked Dylan: 'Bob, did you ever have a time when you had trouble writing?' Before Dylan could answer, Sara, who was preparing sandwiches, broke in with, 'Try the last two years.'"[14]

Although deep down he always knew he would return to music, Bob was genuinely unsure what direction to take. And there was another thing– the music scene was beginning to change. Not only that, others were now stepping up to try to fill Dylan's vacant shoes. John Prine, who released his debut album in 1971, soon became known as "the next Dylan," whilst Bruce Springsteen, who was signed to Columbia the following year by none other than John Hammond – the man who discovered Bob Dylan – would soon be officially promoted by his record company as "the new Dylan." Then, while in exile in the Arizona desert, Dylan encountered himself on the radio. What he was hearing was Neil Young's breakthrough single 'Heart of Gold' (January 1972), but to Dylan, it was an eerie feeling.

"I used to hate it when it came on the radio," Dylan told Scott Cohen: "I always liked Neil Young, but it bothered me every time I listened to 'Heart of Gold' ... I'd say, 'Shit, that's me. If it sounds like me, it should as well be me.' There I was, stuck on the desert someplace, having to cool out for a while. New York was a heavy place. Woodstock was worse ... I needed to lay back for a while, forget about things, myself included, and I'd get so far away and turn on the radio and there I am, but it's not me. It seemed to me somebody else had taken my thing and had run away with it, you know, and I never got over it."[15]

By the end of May Dylan and the family had moved back to New York City for the summer and on July 15 he went up to Canada for the Mariposa Folk Festival. However, his presence there created problems. The organisers were aware that he intended to be there and the board of directors called a hastily convened meeting. The festival had changed its original structure away from big-name acts and there was a fear that if Dylan asked to play, or even turned up, all hell might break loose. For whatever reason, the 1972 festival attracted some big-name visitors. Joni Mitchell, Neil Young, Gordon Lightfoot, Jackson Browne and now Bob Dylan was coming! The organisers debated long and hard as to whether or not to allow these guests to perform. In the end, Murray McLauchlan opted to forego part of his set so Joni Mitchell could play and Bruce Cockburn did the same for Neil Young. Bob Dylan, however, the festival board thought was a step too far. The event only had a small police and security presence and with six stages they feared if Dylan was announced and everyone dashed from one stage to another it could very well result in total chaos.

With his jeans, droopy moustache and red and white bandana, a very hippie looking Bob Dylan turned up to the festival and for part of the weekend he managed to wander unnoticed through the crowd of 14,000. Slowly, however, word began to spread that Dylan was there and expectations that he would perform grew to almost fever pitch. On Sunday, Star reporter Peter Goddard spotted him and reported "[Dylan] stood briefly in a crowd watching some fiddlers before moving to another area to listen to old blues pianist Roosevelt Sykes and blues guitarist Bukka White."

After Neil Young's unscheduled appearance – he closed his short four-song set with 'Heart of Gold,' which must have pleased Bob no end – he sat down at a picnic table with Dylan and Gordon Lightfoot. "At some point a frenzy started to build," the Star reported in 2007. "Young retreated to the fenced-off performers' compound. [Lightfoot and Dylan did the same but] when it appeared that the crowd might jump the fence," Dylan and Sara, accompanied by Leon Redbone, had to be escorted off the island in a Harbour Police boat. Bob reluctantly returned with Sara to the elegant King Edward Hotel and the festival became just another failed attempt at being "normal!"

On July 26, a few days after returning to New York, Dylan continued with his concert-going agenda when he and Sara attended a Rolling Stones gig at Madison Square Garden. Dylan was hugely impressed with the performance. Rock critic Dave Marsh would later write that the tour was one of the "benchmarks of an era." July 26 was Mick Jagger's 29th birthday and Bob and

Sara attended a party organised for Jagger by Atlantic Records co-founder, Ahmet Ertegun.

A month later, August 26, Dylan went to the Philadelphia Folk Festival to see amongst others David Bromberg and during September he recorded under the alias of Robert Milkwood, contributing piano and harmony vocals for the Steve Goodman album, *Somebody Else's Troubles*. Early October, and still kicking his boot heels, Bob contributed keyboard, guitar and even some vocals for the Doug Sahm and Band album. During the Atlantic Studios Sahm sessions Dylan also attended one of the recording sessions for Bette Midler's debut album, *The Divine Miss M*. Unsure of what to do next, a convoluted set of circumstances would result in him becoming involved in the Sam Peckinpah directed film, *Pat Garrett and Billy the Kid*.

Postcards of Billy the Kid

Dylan was tipped off about the film by Bert Block. Block, who was the mediator for Dylan's appearance at the Isle of Wight festival, was now Kris Kristofferson's manager and Kristofferson had already been given the part of Billy in the film. Dylan's love of westerns, coupled with Kris Kristofferson being a musician and not an actor (he had made one movie before *Pat Garrett*), piqued Bob's interest in the film. When Block then told Dylan that an acquaintance of his, Rudy Wurlitzer, was writing the screenplay, his interest was increased further and so in October Bob decided to talk with Wurlitzer.

Rudy Wurlitzer: "After Sam [Peckinpah] came on board [for the film] I wrote a draft with some stuff I'd been sent by Producer Gordon Carroll ... I was in Cape Breton, Nova Scotia at the time, but when I got back to New York Dylan visited me at my Lower East Side apartment. This was a month or so before we started filming. Bob said he'd heard that I was making a Billy the Kid film with

Sam and that he had always felt that he had a connection to Billy.
I didn't ask him about this but I got the impression that he was
maybe talking about reincarnation. Anyway, the next day I called
up Gordon Carroll who said don't let him get away, we'll get an
amazing great score out of it. He told me to write Dylan a part, and
so I put together a few scenes; totally off the cuff. I gave him the
part of the character Alias, which seemed very fitting. Then I gave
Bob a screening of Sam's work."

That screening was a private New York showing of Peckinpah's
film *The Wild Bunch*. According to Wurlitzer, Bob only expected to
stay for one reel, about 20 minutes but remained in the theatre for
the extent of the film, a full two hours and 23 minutes. Dylan liked
what he saw and Wurlitzer furnished him with his recently written
Billy the Kid screenplay. Dylan read it and quickly wrote a song,
'Billy,' for the film.

Although Wurlitzer had cleared Dylan's participation in the movie
with producer Gordon Carroll, he still had to get the proposal past
the film's notoriously cantankerous director, Sam Peckinpah, who
was already busy in Mexico with preproduction.

In early November, a week or so after *The Wild Bunch* screening,
Dylan flew down to Durango, Mexico with Wurlitzer, Bert Block and
Sara to meet with the legendary Sam Peckinpah, who at the time
had no idea who Bob Dylan was. This first meeting, which over the
years has been recounted slightly differently by those present, was
memorable for all the wrong reasons. Coburn took the party up to
Peckinpah's hacienda for a dinner of roast goat.

Wurlitzer: "We arrived in Durango late one evening and
immediately went out to see Sam, who was living outside of town.
As we approached the house, there was a gunshot from inside,
followed by a terrified maid running out the front door. Hesitating,
we stepped inside as another shot rang out from upstairs. I called
out for Sam, but there was no sound, no answer. Fearing the worst,

we crept upstairs. At the end of the hall we found Sam in his bedroom standing half-naked in front of a broken full-length mirror staring at his shattered image, a pistol in one hand and a bottle of tequila in the other. 'Hi, Sam,' I finally managed to mumble. 'This is Bob Dylan. He wants to be in the film. I've taken the liberty of writing a part for him.'"[16]

There was a long pause, Sam then turned, slowly looked Dylan up and down and said, "I'm a big Roger Miller fan myself." There was a tension in the room as Dylan sat on a stool in front of Peckinpah who gently rocked back and forth in his old rocking chair. According to Coburn, Dylan sang: "two or three" tunes, although Wurlitzer only mentions one, 'Billy,' and tears began to roll down Peckinpah's face. "Goddamn kid!" said Peckinpah, "Who the hell is he? Who is that kid? Sign him up!" It was, however, the following day before Peckinpah offered Dylan a part in the film. From that moment on, Wurlitzer remembers, "Dylan followed Sam around like he was one of the last real outlaws, which, who knows, he probably was..."[17]

Dylan and Sara returned to New York to collect some belongings for what now looked like being an extended stay but were back in Mexico, complete with children and the family dog, Rover, on November 23. The part of Billy the Kid's mysterious knife-throwing sidekick Alias was based on a figure Wurlitzer had read about in the book *The Authentic Life of Billy the Kid*. Published in 1882, the year after the Kid's death, the book was marketed as a first-hand account written by Pat Garrett himself and as such it was considered to be factual. For more than a century the book was the principle historical source on Billy the Kid's involvement in the legendary Lincoln County War with many films, including the Wurlitzer-Peckinpah movie, basing their plots around the text. In truth, the book, a collaboration between Garrett and ghost-writer Marshall Ashmun Upson, is wildly inauthentic and highly fictionalised containing a host of embellishments and inconsistencies with other accounts of the life of Billy the Kid.

Although friend-turned-lawman shoots his old outlaw pal makes for a great tale, it isn't correct. While it is true that Garrett and the Kid knew each other they were not close friends at all. In the book, and doubtless in an attempt to enhance Garrett's triumph over the Kid, Upson states that Billy had gunned down 21 men during his short life. All other sources, however, state that Billy the Kid killed between eight and 10 men. The list of inaccuracies is long.

In the book, Garrett claims that the Kid rode to Fort Bowie in south-eastern Arizona with a pal called "Alias." Nevertheless, there isn't a single shred of historical evidence to back that up and most serious historians believe that Alias is just one of Upson's embellishments. In any event, the part was not as is sometimes claimed created especially for Dylan. The role was in Wurlitzer's original screenplay long before Dylan was cast. Nonetheless, the part of the man with no name was absolutely perfect for Dylan.

During filming, Kristofferson told music journalist Chet Flippo that he thought the Alias character, "was supposed to be like the Fool in *[King] Lear*. He sees it all, he knows the legend, and can see where it's all going, but we never relate as characters." Kristofferson also remarked that Dylan had, "a presence like Charlie Chapin – an observation made by many music critics over the years regarding his stage presence – "You see him on screen and all eyes are on him. There's something about him that's magnetic. He doesn't even have to move."[18]

Commenting in 1974 Dylan said: "I don't know who I played. I tried to play whoever it was in the story, but I guess it's a known fact that there was nobody in that story that was the character that I played."[19] While Bob is right about that, if he knew it in 1974 he was way ahead of the historians! In the notes to *Biograph* (1985) Dylan said: "Rudy Wurlitzer was writing this thing, inventing a part for me, but there wasn't any dimension to it and I was very uncomfortable in the non-role."

Kristofferson said that he'd "never been that comfortable around [Dylan]. He's like a wild card that none of them knew they had," Kristofferson said. "I think he is a genius or somethin'. You can't really understand him completely. He's like a kid in a way ... I never know where his head's at." Kristofferson had never met anyone like Dylan and he found it hard to understand why he was so uncommunicative. "Hell," Kristofferson said, "he doesn't even talk to his old lady sometimes for weeks ... according to her."[20]

"Bob Dylan is strictly off limits," the press agent told Roger Ebert. "No interviews, no pictures. He's appearing in the picture in order to become familiar with the movie-making process." Publicist Larry Kaplan said, "It's a complex situation. At first, you say 'Bob Dylan, the fucking legend.' And it takes a couple of weeks to get past that to the man underneath. He's really shy and withdrawn, and it's genuine. Reporters here have really spooked him. They follow him around and of course he won't talk to them, so they end up interviewing everyone else about him. It gets bad when you have reporters asking Mexican extras about Bob's kids."[21]

Like all the major players in the film, Dylan and family had a house in the suburbs of Durango, the largest city of the Mexican state of the same name and about a four-hour drive from one of the main film locations, El Sauz. The Dylans house was in the district of Yucatan and the children, when not running wild, continued with their studies, attending the American School of Durango.

Infamous for his belligerent nature, Peckinpah had a reputation for behind-the-scenes battles with crew members, producers and most of all film companies; his moods often made worse by alcohol and drug abuse. If he had not realised all of this at that first 'roast goat' meeting, Dylan would soon discover that the making of *Pat Garrett and Billy the Kid* was not going to be the exception to the rule. In 1982, E. Jean Carroll summed up the filming of *Pat Garrett* for *Rocky Mountain Magazine* in a breathless adrenaline-rush piece entitled Last of the Desperadoes: Duelling with Sam Peckinpah:

"Peckinpah wants a 50-day shooting schedule. MGM wants 36 ... Peckinpah wants a Panavision repairman in Durango, Mexico, to fix the cameras. The studio says nothing doing. The first footage is sent to L.A. to be processed. The lab calls Peckinpah. Says the film's out of focus. Panic in Durango. Downtime. The camera is fixed and the paranoia sets in. The actors get sick. The crew gets sick. Peckinpah is puking every day. They fall behind schedule. James Aubrey, president of MGM, wants to save time and forbids Peckinpah to shoot a raft scene. Peckinpah shoots it ... Rudy Wurlitzer starts complaining. Says Peckinpah is rewriting the picture with the help of his old TV scripts. Jerry Fielding, Peckinpah's music composer, can't work with Bob Dylan and quits.

Dylan's unhappy. Kris Kristofferson (the Kid) says Rudy's dialogue is corny. Rita Coolidge (Maria, the Kid's lover) says all that remains of her role thanks to MGM is that of "a groupie." James Coburn (Garrett) says Peckinpah is a creative paranoid who generates tension to give everyone the same experience to feed on during the film. A fight breaks out one Saturday night. Two guys. One is on the phone ordering a couple of gunmen to Durango. Wants the other guy killed for threatening Peckinpah's life ... The hit is cancelled at Peckinpah's insistence. *Pat Garrett and Billy the Kid* is brought in 20 days over schedule and $1.5 million over budget.

MGM ... needs cash. The studio moves the release date up and gives Peckinpah only two and a half months to edit. On the sly MGM duplicates the work print and employs another cutter. Peckinpah's version runs between 122 and 126 minutes. The studio's runs 106. The producer, Gordon Carroll, negotiates day and night. Gets nothing restored. The picture's released. Peckinpah sues for $1.5 million. Orders all the cuts put back or his name taken off.

Nada. Nada. Nada."[22]

It was their own substantially re-edited version of the film that MGM released to the public in 1973 and it would be close to a decade before the film would be presented closer to the way it was meant to be seen. Dylan said of the filming: "That was Peckinpah's kingdom– and he was sort of a madman. He kept saying, 'It's my movie, my movie.'"[23]

"I'd gotten them [the family] out of New York; that was the important thing, there was a lot of pressure back there." Nonetheless, the madness of this filming coupled with being on location with the drunken and combative Sam Peckinpah proved to be anything but a sanctuary. "My wife got fed up almost immediately," Dylan said. "She'd say to me, 'What the hell are we doing here?' It was not an easy question to answer."[24]

Dylan elaborated in the liner notes to *Biograph*: "[T]ime started to slip away and there I was trapped deep in the heart of Mexico with some madman, ordering people around like a little king ... It was crazy, all these generals making you jump into hot ants, setting up turkey shoots and whatever and drinking tequila 'til they passed out. Sam was a wonderful guy though. He was an outlaw. A real hombre. Somebody from the old school. Men like him they don't make anymore."

According to Kris Kristofferson, Dylan and actor-musician Harry Dean Stanton cost Peckinpah's production budget an extra $25,000 just by going for a run! Dylan and Stanton had decided to keep fit by going running but unfortunately one of their five-mile jogs took them through the shot for the film's final scene. Peckinpah had been waiting for the right evening light for some time and on this night, just as Pat Garrett was riding off into the sunset, Dylan and Stanton ran straight through the shot. Stanton apologised to Peckinpah who responded by throwing a knife which flew just inches past the actor's ear and ended up in the door just behind him.

Desperate to get away from Peckinpah's escalating bouts of drunken madness, Sara persuaded Bob to fly over to England for a break and to spend time with George and Patti Harrison. After filming Bob's January 2 scene where Paco is murdered, they left for England to visit the Harrisons at their Friar Park home. George broke off working on his upcoming album, Living in the Material World, and during the second week of January, the Harrisons were seen out shopping with Bob and Sara on Chelsea's King's Road. By the middle of January, however, the family had returned to Durango and a further four long weeks of filming.

At this juncture, a stutter that was originally a trait of Dylan's character had been abandoned. The reason that Dylan's character is called Alias came from this stutter. In the original film draft, Dylan's first line of dialogue reveals his character had a speech impediment. He is asked his name but when he attempts his stuttering response another character interrupts suggesting they simply call him Alias. All revisions of the script made during November and December 1972 preserve the stutter but for reasons that remain unclear by January 2, 1973 it had mysteriously disappeared.

When asked about the vanishing stutter by Michael Watts, who was on the set in Mexico writing about the film for *Melody Maker*, Wurlitzer said: "Yes [there was a stutter] but it will have to be taken out. It becomes too much of a big thing if you only have a small part, and..." Unfortunately, shouting from outside distracted Wurlitzer so we are left hanging as to what the "and" was.

During the shoot, Dylan began work on the soundtrack for the film and in mid-January he decided to go down to CBS' Disco Studios in Mexico City. Resentful of Dylan's pulling power, Sam organised a rival to the weekend away in Mexico City. Wurlitzer noted in his work diary: "Sam knows he's losing to Dylan. He's giving a screening of *The Getaway* – Peckinpah's December 1972 box office hit – in town tonight, but everybody wants to go to Mexico

City with Dylan. [He] also just called a 6.30 rehearsal for Monday morning because he knows we won't be back 'til after eight. But I don't care, man. I got to get away." Wurlitzer's diary notes certainly reflect the need for people to escape from the confines and soullessness of Durango and to take a break from Peckinpah's increasing psychosis.

Those travelling to Mexico City were assembled in the airport lobby at 6:30 on Saturday evening. The flight was from Durango Airport direct to Mexico City; a couple of hours and almost 500 miles aboard a worryingly dented Aero Mexico 727. Wurlitzer was heard to mutter, "That plane, man. It don't look too good." James Coburn, brandy in hand, wasn't happy either, asking Rudy, "Is the Big D coming?" Wurlitzer checked his watch for the umpteenth time and then, just as boarding was due to begin, a car rolled up and 'Big D' got out. Completely unfazed by the condition of the aircraft, Dylan got on board and proceeded to go to sleep. On arrival, Bob checked into room 734 at the Sheraton. It was almost 10 in the evening before Dylan and the others arrived at Discos studios, a vast barn of a place in the suburbs of Mexico City.

All the discographers and commentators are in total agreement that Dylan's only recording session in Mexico was on Saturday, January 20, 1973. However, the aforementioned Michael Watts, who was there at the time, said this about the session: "The following day ... it was a Sunday, and in the afternoon practically everybody went over to the [recently opened] Fiesta Palace [hotel], where a suite had been booked, to see the Miami Dolphins beat up the Washington Redskins." The problem is, the Dolphins, Redskins Super Bowl VII took place on Sunday, January 14, 1973, a week before the supposed date of Dylan's Mexico City session! Could Watts' memory be faulty? Highly unlikely considering his piece about Dylan in Mexico was published less than three weeks after the event.

Furthermore, *Rolling Stone's* Chet Flippo, who was also present, concurs with Watts' account: "It was four in the morning, and [Dylan] ordered another bourbon and sat, impassive behind his shades, as he listened to the tapes. Just after Kristofferson, Coburn and Wurlitzer left to get some sleep before watching the Super Bowl..."

Problems with filming and Peckinpah's moods were compounded by illness! The influenza epidemic, a strain of 'Hong Kong flu,' which swept the United States in 1972, had hit Durango in early December. It overwhelmed the film crew with almost everyone contracting the virus, including Peckinpah. On December 8 he was confined to bed for three days with a temperature of 104°.

Actor LQ Jones, who had worked on four films with Peckinpah over the previous 10 years, couldn't believe what he saw when he arrived on the set. "My first impulse," Jones said, "was to say, 'My God Sam, I didn't realise you'd died.' He had the sickest, weakest look I'd ever seen in my life ... He wasn't coherent. He'd tune out in the middle of a conversation ... Probably it was a combination of the drinking and the flu."[25]

Sam was sick on and off throughout the remainder of the production. The virus was responsible for the deaths of many hundreds that winter in the state of Durango, among them Bud Hulburd, Peckinpah's special-effects coordinator on *The Wild Bunch*. By early February, two of the Dylan children were taken ill and the family was forced to relocate to Los Angeles where they were able to receive better medical attention. Dylan rented a house in Malibu, which would eventually result in him moving the family to live at Point Dume.

Burbank Studio Sessions

Dylan knew that the single session in Mexico City was well short of capturing what he needed for the soundtrack so sessions were booked for February 1973 at Burbank Studios, California. At this stage, Peckinpah brought in his regular arranger, Jerry Fielding, who he asked to compose "around" Dylan's songs. Fielding was a jazz musician, bandleader, arranger, and film composer who re-emerged in the Sixties after a decade on the blacklist. He had begun working with Peckinpah in 1966 and by the time he arrived in Burbank Studios to work with Dylan he had already scored 14 films and had been nominated for an Academy Award for Peckinpah's *The Wild Bunch*, the success of which ensured that whenever possible, Peckinpah would employ Fielding as his composer and arranger.

Although a political free-thinker, Fielding held extremely conservative views when it came to pop and rock and he treated Dylan's music with disdain. Fielding's memory was that the Burbank sessions were nothing short of "a total frustration" and "wasted effort." "I give Bobby Dylan credit for writing seven great pieces of music and a lot of nonsense which is strictly for teenyboppers," Fielding said. "I also give him credit for having a way with words that is often very effective but just as meaningless. He plays a simple blues pattern and a number of repetitious chords that I honestly must say offend me as a musician. On that basis, considering the complexities of scoring a picture, Bobby Dylan has no more business attempting it than Sam Peckinpah has of selling popcorn ... But he was their boy and I was supposed to make it happen."[26]

"Just because you play a guitar and sing doesn't qualify you for scoring a picture," Fielding said. "All [Dylan] could do was look at me, and all he could see was 'establishment.' So he wouldn't listen to me at all. And I resent that superficial shit. I paid my dues..."[27]

Fielding had not been present for the session in Mexico City but he had flown out to Durango during the third week of January to listen to the results of the session.

Fielding: "Dylan had this song ['Billy'] he'd written for which he had a limitless number of verses that he would sing in random order. Actually, Kris Kristofferson had written a song as well which I thought had more potential in terms of scoring the picture, but I was overruled. So I had to tape Dylan's song, because he had nothing written down, and have it transcribed. It was my idea that by having Dylan sing the relevant verses as it fit the story at roughly nine separate points throughout the picture, it might be coherent. Dylan never understood what I wanted. At the same time I asked that he write at least one other piece of music because you cannot possibly hope to deal with an entire picture on the basis of that one ballad."[28]

Wurlitzer: "One night when we were returning to Durango from Mexico City – I forget why we were there – [Dylan] said he wanted to write something for Slim Pickens' death scene, which was due to be shot the next day. He scrawled something on the aeroplane and showed it to me line by line and when we got off the plane, there it was, 'Knockin' On Heaven's Door.'"[29]

This was sometime near the end of January; Wurlitzer was bowled over by the song and shortly before leaving for California, and close to the time that Sam began shooting the film's climactic sequence on January 26, Dylan showed 'Heaven's Door' to Peckinpah.

Bob recorded the song almost as soon as the Burbank sessions began and Fielding was, to say the least, not impressed with the new song.

Fielding: "So finally he brought to the dubbing session another piece of music – 'Knock-Knock-Knockin' on Heaven's Door.' Everybody loved it. It was shit. That was the end for me."[30]

Fielding described the lyrics as "infantile." "It was sophomoric ... The kind of stuff you learn not to do the second year you score a piece of film." Fielding walked out of the session and with the blessing of producer Gordon Carroll, Dylan finished the soundtrack his way with poor ol' Sam caught somewhere in the crossfire.

Jim Keltner: "It was very early in the morning. I think the session was 10 am. ... This was for a particular scene in the movie when Slim Pickens is dying and that's the first time I ever cried while I played. It was the combination of the words, Bob's voice, the actual music itself, the changes, and seeing the screen ... In those days you were on a big soundstage, and you had this massive screen that you can see on the wall, [with] the scene ... running when you're playing. I cried through that whole take."[31]

Although the Burbank sessions were far more successful than the one in Mexico City, Dylan was still frustrated. He told Gordon Carroll, "This is the last time I work for anyone in a movie on the music. I'll stick to acting." Dylan's interest in making films had become heightened. "I want now to make movies," he said. "I've never been this close to movies before. I'll make a hell of a movie after this."

Apart from Heylin, most biographers view Dylan's escapades in Mexico as a sideshow and a minor episode in the Dylan story. In fact, the work Dylan did in creating the film soundtrack was a major factor in getting him writing again. Moreover, the two-and-a-half months spent in Durango, coupled with his time in Arizona, helped convince Dylan that he should not return to the trials and tribulations of life in New York City and that he and his family should head for warmer climes. After filming and recording was completed, the Dylans made one last dash for freedom. This time the move would take them two-and-a-half thousand miles west of New York to California.

Chapter Six

No Direction Home

In 1965, Bob Dylan wrote: "I'm used to four seasons/ California's got but one." Now, however, he was considering moving the family to Southern California. Would this next move be the answer to Dylan's continuing troubles or was there now really No Direction Home?

In 1971, Dylan had been looking to expand his portfolio of property investments and, at the suggestion of Victor Maymudes, he looked at an unpopulated area three miles west of the affluent beach city of Malibu. Dylan found a suitable property perched high above the stark cliffs at Point Dume. The house, which overlooked the Pacific Ocean, belonged to legendary Los Angeles sportswriter Jim Murray. Murray, clearly no music aficionado, knew Dylan only as "some guitar player." The purchase was completed in December 1971.

On April 24, 1973, Dylan signed a one-month rental lease and moved his family to a three bedroom property belonging to actor Martin Milner at 21336 Pacific Coast Highway in the La Costa Beach neighbourhood of Malibu. Once installed in the rented house he began work extending his investment property at Point Dume, which Sara thought needed an extra bedroom and a little remodelling, with a view to the house becoming the family's main residence. The projected cost of the work was $50,000. At this time Dylan decided to sell his Woodstock house, though he retained close to 100 acres of land on Ohayo Mountain.

BOB DYLAN TOO MUCH OF NOTHING

As soon as contractors arrived at Point Dume, however, Sara began "expanding" her ideas for the property. Architect Dave C Towbin said the house took on "several new directions." "It's kind of hard to put a label on it," Towbin said, "but I guess I'd call it stick-and-timber eclectic." A Los Angeles County Building Inspector went somewhat further calling the house, "a terrible mishmash" (a mix of Santa Fe, Spanish and Moorish styles). The previous owner, Jim Murray, said: "I've only seen it from the outside but I'd say it looks something like the Madonna Inn."*1

The salient feature and crowning glory of the house is a huge onion-shaped copper dome protruding from the centre section of the property. "The dome was originally going to be an eagle's nest. You know, just a little hideaway," says Towbin, "Then it was going to be a [whale watching] observatory, then something else."2

Dylan said of the house: "It's just a place to live for now. The copper dome is just so I can recognise it when I come home." The one bedroom extension project took on a life of its own in which only one wall of the original house was left standing, and that only remained to satisfy Californian building regulations. "[T] he thing began to grow and grow and grow ... Let's just say there were a lot of major changes, mainly because it had to feel right ... But asking Bob Dylan if he's happy with it, you never come up with a simple answer ... You have to understand him. It's like no other project any of us has ever worked on, but it's for an unusual client."3

* *The Madonna Inn is a motel in San Luis Obispo, California. Opened in 1958, the celebrated motor inn quickly became a prominent landmark on the Central Coast of California. The property is decorated with a pseudo-Swiss-Alps exterior and lavish common rooms accented by bright pink roses, Western murals, and lots of hammered copper. Each of the 110 guest rooms and suites is uniquely and individually designed and themed in what many would say are completely over-the-top and garish colours; even the outside tennis and basketball courts are bright pink.*

180

The finished house, which Bob called his "own fantasy," contains around 20 themed rooms including a cathedral room and a storytelling room. There is also a Great Room with a spectacular vaulted ceiling. This room was the bane of architect David Towbin's life because plans for the room, which Dylan had informed Towbin should be, "large enough to ride a horse through," were continually being changed. So much so, the building contractor, Frank Neisner, resigned on more than one occasion and had to be persuaded by Towbin to return to work. Another design feature that caused much consternation was the enormous fireplace which was said to have been ripped out and replaced almost weekly. There is a vast bedroom wing with each room having an en suite bathroom. The Dylans' master bedroom was on the second floor, away from the rest of the bedrooms.

While on a visit to Minnesota, Bob found one of his first cars. He bought the car and then phoned Towbin to inform him that he wanted it suspending from the ceiling of the Great Room. By now, used to such bizarre requests, Towbin nonchalantly asked, "With or without the engine?"

Work on the house took three years to complete. Fifty-six "hippie" artisans camped on site in tepees and gypsy caravans for two years at Bob's expense, producing handmade bricks in flaming kilns. Thousands of tiles were also made on site as were wood carvings and various other fixtures and fittings. Every door in the house was handmade and all were different. Along with Robert Gilbert, who was well-known for his work on the homes of rock stars and top athletes, designer Martin Newman was heavily involved with the project.[4]

Newman: "We were showing the Dylans these books of architectural features like arches," he recalls. "In architecture, there are seven classic arches, and Bob said: 'Just use them all.' That was kind of his attitude ... there's a million dollars' worth of hand-made tile in this house. It's an extraordinary place."*[5]

Bob didn't want the house to look new so almost everything, including the plaster, was distressed to give the property an aged feel. At the back of the house a vast lake-size pool was constructed. It contains huge artificial mushrooms and a bridge with supports shaped like a woman's legs. In the end, the cost of remodelling the home was said to be in the region of $2.25-million (approx. $8.5 million in 2019);[6] a mere $2.2-million over budget.

Almost before the distressed plaster was dry, the Dylans began experiencing distress from outside. The press soon became intrigued by the new onion-domed house and helicopters were dispatched to take aerial photos of the property, which then appeared in a local LA newspaper. Perhaps unsurprisingly, curiosity seekers and unwanted visitors soon began to arrive and as was the case with their time in Woodstock and Greenwich Village, the Dylans suffered from frequent acts of trespass. To help combat these intrusions, Bob had a guardhouse erected near the entrance to his land which was manned by 24-hour security guards. When problems with his new neighbours occurred it must have felt like Groundhog Day for Bob! In September 1976, the Dylans were sued by the Primmers over the use of an access road to the property. In the great scheme of things this was relatively insignificant; the case nevertheless dragged on for almost two years before being settled. Bob would eventually purchase eight neighbouring parcels of land which included several private roads. The Dylan "compound" ultimately covered 12 acres.

---

* *Sara Dylan had seen one of Martin Newman's coats fashioned from an Indian blanket in Beverly Hills. She contacted Newman and asked if he could come out to Malibu to measure Bob and her for "a couple of these great coats." Newman said he and "Uncle Bob" became friends and that the two men were together: "every day for four years after that." Part of that time was spent on the Rolling Thunder Revue tour, for which Newman designed everything from the feathered cowboy hats and Norfolk jackets to cases for Dylan's guitars and harmonicas.*

The Point Dume house, which remains Bob Dylan's main home today, is of significant importance to our story because many commentators believe that tensions began to appear in Bob's marriage to Sara as a result of the "remodelling" of the property. Logic dictates that the break-up of the marriage was far more complicated than the size and design of a fireplace but nonetheless, it was at this time that the strain of their harried and complicated life together began to come to the fore and cracks in their marriage appeared. Several close friends have said that they had never seen the couple argue before the move to California and work on the house began.

"That [house] was Sara's folly," Jonathan Taplin said: "Bob went along with it, but it just got out of control in terms of the cost of building it. I think from Bob's point of view it was like, 'When is this gonna end? When are all these people gonna get out of my house?.'"[7]

As the problems began to mount, Dylan started to think in earnest about going back out on tour. It had been seven long years since his 1966 world tour. Maybe, just maybe, it was time to get back to doing what he'd always done best.

My Head Tells Me it's Time
to Make a Change

With his Columbia contract now expired, Dylan began 1973 by signing a deal with David Geffen's Asylum Records label. Columbia Records' boss Clive Davis had been in the process of negotiating a new contract with Dylan but when Davis was fired in May things turned sour and Dylan signed a deal with Geffen's newly established West Coast label.

Although having a bunch of kids who call him "Pa" was for a while "what it's all about," sidelining his musical genius couldn't continue forever and by the end of 1973 the conflict between the two sides of his Gemini self had begun to pull Dylan in very different directions. It seemed the more he had tried to escape from fame, the tighter its grip became. The deal Dylan signed with Geffen would allow him to stage the tour that he had been considering and the shows, which would be with The Band, also raised the possibility of an accompanying live album. Before all of this, however, Dylan went into Village Recorder Studios in West Los Angeles to record a new album, *Planet Waves*. The album was cut during six sessions over an extremely short seven-day period.

Apart from a conga player by the name of "Ken" and Harry Dean Stanton, who it seems had survived the rage of knife throwing film director Sam Peckinpah, the musicians were Dylan's old and trusted pals from The Band. Old and trusted maybe, but amazingly, this would be the first time that Robertson, Danko, Manuel, Hudson and Helm had appeared on a full album of Dylan songs!

As was the case with much of Dylan's work from the past four years the album deals with domestic themes and taken at face value some tracks seem like uncomplicated love songs, particularly the opener, 'On a Night Like This.' 'Wedding Song,' 'Never Say Goodbye' and 'You Angel You,' which Dylan dismissed in 1985 as having "dummy lyrics," also fit the love song bill. 'Forever Young,' which on one of those big black CDs closes side one and also opens side two of the album, was as previously noted, written the previous year in Arizona for his then six-year-old son Jesse. The opening line of the song: "May God bless and keep you always" alludes to the Aaronic blessing: "The Lord bless you and keep you." The songs released on *Planet Waves* were registered to Bob's new publishing company, Ram's Horn Music, a reference to the Shofar, the ram's horn in the Scriptures that is blown to awaken slumbering souls at Jewish New Year.

The album began life with the working title 'Love Songs', which then became 'Wedding Song' and after that Ceremonies of the

Horsemen – a reference to a line in the 1965 Dylan song 'Love
Minus Zero/No Limit' – but finally *Planet Waves* won the day. This
late change delayed the release of the album by two weeks. As
pointed out by several music critics, many of the songs take on
darker overtones, the darkest of which is the track 'Dirge.' Listed on
the recording sheets as 'Dirge for Martha,' the song begins and ends
with: "I hate myself for lovin' you." As much as the lyrics sound as
though they could be directed to a woman, the song probably goes
deeper than that and fame, drugs or even his audience could be the
target. Whatever, Dylan seems only to have himself to blame for the
position he now finds himself in. He intends to do something about
it. But what?

'Tough Mama' is a tough one to crack. Parts of the song seems to
refer to Dylan's career, maybe his muse or muses? The final stanza
must surely be aimed at Columbia Records, the label he has just
parted company from. Dylan tells them straight: "I ain't a-haulin'
any of my lambs to the marketplace anymore" ... "I've gained some
recognition but I lost my appetite."

In 'Going, Going, Gone,' Bob is again moving on but this time
there is a feeling of sheer desperation. "I am closin' the book/ On
the pages and the text/ And I don't really care/ What happens
next," Dylan sings with a voice that sounds almost tortured. "I been
hangin' on threads/ I been playin' it straight/ Now, I've just got to cut
loose/ Before it gets late."

A Trip Down Suicide Road

Arthur Rosato, who carried out a plethora of duties for team Dylan
from December 1973 until November 1981 and who worked as
monitor engineer on the 1974 tour told me: "I think the Stones [1972]
tour had a big influence on [Dylan]. That was the biggest thing
going at the time. Bob's a major rock'n'roll fan; he loved the Stones
thing, and he takes in everything."[8]

As one might have expected after such an extended break from the road, the 1974 tour received a vast amount of coverage in the music press. The average ticket price was $8 and top-dollar tickets were $9.50, an extravagant sum for that time. The tour received a mind-boggling 5.5 million pieces of mail applying for up to four tickets each. Sold by mail-order only, promoter Bill Graham claimed there were requests for more than 12 million tickets for the 658,000 available seats. According to Clinton Heylin, it was estimated that $92 million worth of checks and money orders were sent in. With so many applications for so few tickets, monies had to be returned, but even so the tour generated more than $5 million gross.

On January 2, 1974 Dylan left his sad-eyed lady behind in California and went off on tour for the first time in eight years. "[Sara] despised the rock'n'roll lifestyle," Band road manager Jonathan Taplin said: "People who just wanted to talk about music were boring to her."[9]

Going from show to show in a private jet, Starship 1, Dylan and The Band played 40 concerts over 43 days in 21-cities. "This event is the biggest thing of its kind in the history of show business," David Geffen bragged to the press. Although as stated previously, deep cracks had started to appear with the move to California, going back out on tour was probably the true beginning of the end for Bob and Sara. With the advent of "Tour 74," Dylan began to smoke and drink heavily again and worse still his once roving eye again began to wander. One month into the tour he met 24-year-old Columbia Records' A&R executive Ellen Bernstein whom he continued seeing for much of that year. Actress Ruth Tyrangiel has maintained that Dylan began a 19-year affair with her in the same month. Tyrangiel, who appeared in *Renaldo & Clara*, in which she played the part of "The Girlfriend," would file a palimony suit in 1995 in which she alleged that between 1974 and 1991 she had acted as "nurse, confidante, home-maker, housekeeper, cook, social companion [and] advisor" to Dylan. Though her case was dismissed by Los Angeles Superior Court, there are those who believe that at least some of her claims were true. Although there is no suggestion that Dylan was involved, there are stories about the debauched depths that rock music tours had sunk to in the early/mid-Seventies. It is alleged that during the 1974 tour The Band instructed roadies to take Polaroid photos of girls wanting to get backstage. The girls not chosen by the band were left for the road crew.

With Tour 74, David Geffen and promoter Bill Graham presented Bob on a grand scale. This tour was eight years and several galaxies away from 1966. Gone were the town halls and cinemas with seating for a couple of thousand and in were sports arenas, more usually used for staging basketball and Ice hockey games, with typical capacities of 15,000. To quote Bob Dylan, "Things Have Changed." The tour opened in Chicago at the 18,500-seat Chicago Stadium and in New York, at the end of January, there would be two shows at the 20,000-seat Madison Square Garden. Although the song arrangements were altered, these performances felt a little like a collection of "greatest hits" concerts. There were a couple of songs per show from the new album but otherwise the set-lists were stuck inside of the Sixties.

In these changing times songs like 'The Lonesome Death of Hattie Carroll,' 'Ballad of Hollis Brown,' and 'Song to Woody' appeared a little passé, especially if Dylan was trying to shake off his protest mantle. As for 'Blowin' in the Wind,' which was added as a second encore halfway through the tour, it's a great song, a crowd pleaser and one that he probably should have played. Nevertheless, you might remember that when George Harrison requested the song at the Concert for Bangladesh Dylan objected and was said to have performed it there, "begrudgingly."

A slightly confused Dylan seemed to want to move on but didn't know how and the tour was understandably seen by the press and many of his audience as one of nostalgia. But nostalgia for what exactly? The last time Bob and The Band had gone out on tour together they were booed, heckled and pilloried at almost every show and yet on this tour they were greeted like old friends and returning heroes. But hang on a moment, on the '74 tour the same group of musicians were playing all of the seven numbers from Bob's 1966 acoustic set plus 'I Don't Believe You (She Acts Like We Never Have Met),' 'Just Like Tom Thumb's Blues,' 'Maggie's Farm,' 'It Ain't Me, Babe,' 'Ballad of a Thin Man,' 'Leopard-Skin Pill-Box Hat,' 'One Too Many Mornings' and 'Like a Rolling Stone' from the reviled '66 electric set. A quick calculation will reveal that of the 12 'electric' songs across the entire 1966 world tour only four were absent from Tour 74! "Everybody cheered and acted like, 'Oh, I loved it all along,'" guitarist Robbie Robertson sneered: "There was something kind of hypocritical in it." Instead of booing and walking out as they had done in 1966, the audiences, in some cases the same people, were now holding aloft thousands of matches and cigarette lighters in gestures of unity with Dylan. Photographer Barry Feinstein was there to capture the sea of tiny lights for the front cover of the ensuing double live album, *Before the Flood*.

When Arthur Rosato asked Dylan about the tour a few years later Bob said: "it was just okay." When others have asked, however, Dylan has said that he "hated every moment of [the] 1974 tour" and that he knew it would be, "the hardest thing [he'd] ever done." Although the tour was very much a retrospective affair, there was one poignant moment, during Dylan's solo acoustic sets, where contemporary events allied with the performance. Early in 1974, just as the tour got underway, the cover-up and efforts to impede the Watergate investigation began to unravel and the scandal was dominating the headlines. Against this background, when Bob performed 'It's Alright, Ma (I'm Only Bleeding),' the line: "Even the President of the United States sometimes must have to stand

naked" was greeted with cheers, hoots and raised arms. The
tour closed with two nights, February 13 and 14, at The Forum,
Inglewood. Sara was present at those shows and on the last night
(Valentine's Day), Bob played her favourite song, 'Mr Tambourine
Man.' It was only the second outing for the song on that tour.

In April 1974 Bob was back in New York. While there, he began
attending art classes at the eleventh-floor Carnegie Hall annexe
studio of Norman Raeben. Raeben was a 73-year-old painter with
a radical approach to teaching. Dylan had first heard about him in
early 1974 when several of Sara's friends from New York had visited
the Dylans. "They were talking about truth and love and beauty and
all these words I had heard for years, and they had 'em all defined,"
Dylan said. "I couldn't believe it ... I asked them, 'Where do you
come up with all those definitions?' and they told me about this
teacher."

When the two men first met, Raeben had no idea who Dylan was.
Concerned that the scruffy looking individual might have nowhere
to stay, the painter told Bob he could sleep in the studio in return for
cleaning and tidying.

Carolyn Schlam, a student who was there when Dylan first
arrived, said, "I remember the day that Bob Dylan came to our
classroom for the first time. I walked in as usual to grab my spot for
the day and saw Norman standing by the radiator and speaking to
a prospective new student. Squinting, and incredulous, I realised
the student was the famous folksinger Bob Dylan. But the students
soon realised that Norman had no idea who he was, and more
importantly, couldn't care less ... We subsequently chuckled when
Norman, even after being informed of Dylan's pedigree, continued
to speak to him as casually and emphatically as to the rest of us. He
called Bob Dylan 'an idiot' ... He sent him down to get coffee for us,
which was a regular assignment for the rest of us."

Raeben was, "more powerful than any magician," Dylan later

claimed. "Five days a week I used to go up there, and I'd just think about it the other two days of the week ... I used to be up there from eight o'clock to four. That's all I did for two months ... Needless to say, it changed me. I went home after that and my wife never did understand me ever since that day. That's when our marriage started breaking up. She never knew what I was talking about. What I was thinking about, and I couldn't possibly explain it."[10]

In mid-1974, Bob and Sara separated and Dylan spent much of that summer in Minnesota. He had recently bought an 80-acre arable farm on the banks of the Crow River and Bob's brother David came to live on the farm full-time, building a house next-door to Bob's. While at the farm Dylan began writing the songs that would become Blood on the Tracks, an album that reflects the problems he and Sara were experiencing at the time. Ellen Bernstein spent many long weekends at the farm and, according to Clinton Heylin, one of the songs from Blood on the Tracks, 'You're Gonna Make Me Lonesome When You Go,' is directly addressed to her. The final stanza: "I'll look for you in old Honolulu/ San Francisco, Ashtabula," manages to mention Bernstein's hometown of Ashtabula, Ohio, her then home of San Francisco and the fact that she was shortly planning a trip to Hawaii.[11]

By this time Dylan's short dalliance with Asylum Records had come to an end. Columbia quickly decided they wanted their man back and sent word that they, "will spare nothing to bring Dylan back into the fold." In the short time he had been with them Bob seemingly had several gripes with Asylum. He was annoyed by the number of unfulfilled ticket requests for the 1974 tour– though Geffen should not shoulder all of the blame from that. Also, although Planet Waves had reached Number 1 on the Billboard Chart, Geffen's label had only managed to sell 650,000 copies of the album. In actual fact, a lack of record sales had become a perennial problem for Dylan, one that he had hoped Geffen would be able to rectify. It was a huge conundrum to Dylan – and also to me – as to why his 1974 tour, with ticket prices as high $9.50, could attract mail-order applications in excess of 12 million but *Planet Waves* could only manage to sell around half a million copies on initial release!*

The central reason for Dylan's return to Columbia, however, was doubtless the vast amount of material residing in their vaults. Columbia had already released one "revenge" album Dylan (1973) and in all probability there would have been more to come. "He has a lot of stuff in the vault that's about to come out," Geffen told *Rolling Stone*. "But with this [new] deal [with Columbia], ownership of his masters reverts to him at the end of five years. Also, he gets a retroactive raise on his past records. What I did [by signing him to Asylum] was make it possible for him to get back his masters from Columbia. He should thank me. At the time he went with me, they weren't that interested in him."[12]

During the selection process for the live tracks to be included on *Before the Flood*, Dylan began to have doubts about letting Asylum have the record. In theory, the album was promised to David Geffen but out of the blue Bob began to get edgy telling Robbie Robertson: "I don't think I want to do this Asylum Records deal with Geffen. It doesn't feel right to me." Was he concerned that Columbia would continue rifling through their vaults for more previously unreleased material? Had they offered him a better deal for the album? Or was it just some mysterious vibe? According to Robertson, Dylan couldn't explain. He just repeated that, "it didn't feel right." The Band, Dylan, Bob's lawyer David Braun, and Geffen had a meeting

* *David Geffen: "The bottom line is that "Planet Waves" was number 1 for three weeks and it's probably one of his bestselling albums … Three [Asylum] albums were released January 1: Carly Simon ["Hot Cakes"] sold 1,080,000 and Joni Mitchell ["Court and Spark"] sold 1,400,000 … We shipped 771,000 "Planet Waves" albums and we've taken back less than 15%, which is standard for the industry, around 110,000, so it will end up around 600,000 probably. That's fantastic for Bob. His influence and importance have always been greater than his sales and he's naïve to think otherwise."*

and there was a vote which came down on the side of Columbia. When Braun tried to explain the reasons for their decision, which were about as vague as Bob's, Geffen walked out. In the end, however, the record came out on Asylum. The album broke into the Top 10 on both sides of the Atlantic which for a double album was a considerable achievement.

Lord Knows I've Paid Some Dues

Released January 20, 1975, Blood on the Tracks, Dylan's first album under his new Columbia contract, was initially received with mixed reviews but has since been rightly acclaimed as one of his finest records. With this album Dylan was again on the move and the results were an extraordinary return to form.

The songs were more or less fully realised in Dylan's head by the time the tapes started rolling. Bob certainly seems to know his songs well before he starts singing. For this album Bob has returned to his old stomping ground on New York's 54th Street. Although now A&R Studios, this space had previously been Columbia Studio A where Bob had cut his first half a dozen albums. Confident in what he had in the bank, and maybe because the songs were so personal to him, he decided to record for the first time without a producer.

To begin with, Bob ran through half-a-dozen songs solo before bringing in other musicians. He wasn't happy with the results, however, and apart from bassist Tony Brown, quickly dispensed with Eric Weissberg's band Deliverance. Overall, however, the sessions went well and Dylan left A&R on September 25 with one hell of an album in the can. This record was enormously important to Dylan and maybe because of the personal nature of the songs he seemed to need as much reassurance as possible regarding the material. Even before he had gone in to record the album he played the songs for a mass of friends including David Crosby,

Riding his 1964 Triumph Tiger 100-SS

Working at home in Woodstock, 1968

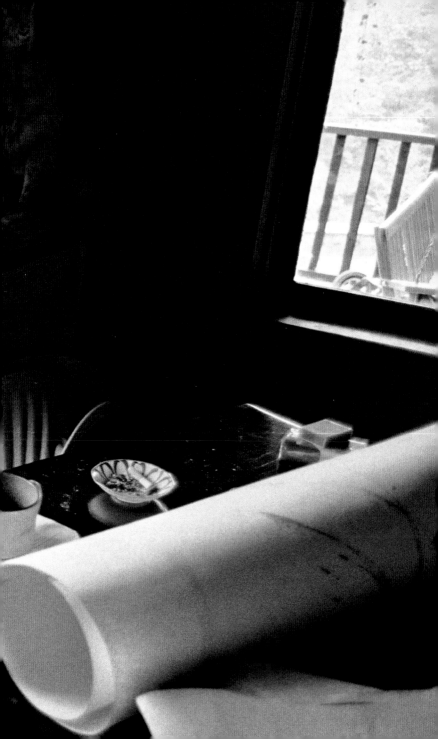

Above: Hippie Bob at the Mariposa Festival, Canada, July 15, 1972
Opposite: Bob with Sara and family, at home in Woodstock, 1968

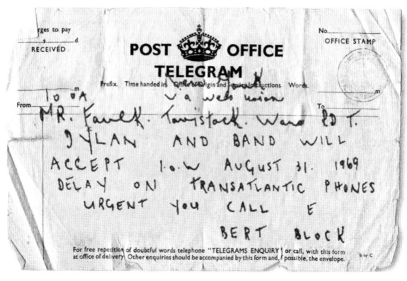

Telegram to promoter Ray Foulk confirming that Dylan
will play the 1969 Isle of Wight festival

Tennis with George Harrison shortly before his
August 31, 1969 Isle of Wight Performance

With The Band at the Woody Guthrie Memorial Concert,
Carnegie Hall, January 20, 1968

On tour 1975, reading Crystal Magick

Bob Dylan as Alias in the film *Pat Garrett and Billy the Kid*, 1972

At his son Jesse's Bar Mitvah in Jerusalem. September 20, 1983

Dylan & Grossman at Hamlet's Castle, Denmark, 1966

Rolling Thunder Tour, 1975

Above: Bob Dylan and Joan Baez, 1975
Opposite: Dream Away Lodge, while on tour, November 7, 1975

Dylan at Jack Kerouac's grave in Lowell, MA, 1975

Wearing the silver cross at the Omni Coliseum,
Atlanta, Georgia, December 12, 1978

Melody Maker

JULY 15, 1978   15p weekly   USA 75 cents

CLASH talk on page 8

Moodies interview — page 10

Talking Heads A great album: p 23

BOB DYLAN returns to Britain on Saturday for the climax to his European tour — his Picnic at Blackbushe for 100,000 adoring fans.

As well as promising a revised set from his six Earls Court shows, the show offers fans the likelihood of Dylan jamming with his buddy Eric Clapton, who plays with his band as support to Dylan after sets by Merger, Lake, Joan Armatrading and Graham Parker and the Rumour.

The prospects of Clapton and Dylan playing together on stage has been fuelled by the burgeoning friendship between the two — a friendship sealed when they got together in Dylan's hotel room after his Nuremberg festival appearance last week and spent all night playing and writing songs.

On top of the changed Dylan set, other surprises are promised for the show — including a firework display, courtesy of his record company, CBS.

To be in with Blackbushe, MM today presents a four-page supplement with all the fax 'n' info about the festival that many fans see as THE show of the year.

● On page 31 is a how-to-get-there guide complete with road maps and transport details.

● On page 32, Michael Gray reviews Dylan's show in Paris last Friday — a concert that gives a fair indication of what to expect at Blackbushe.

● Colin Irwin talks to Joan Armatrading, rock's first lady a couple of years back, who was personally invited onto the Blackbushe bill by Dylan.

● On page 34 Chris Welch interviews Harvey Goldsmith, the promoter who opened Earls Court for six nights to 94,000 people to see their hero, and who is the man behind the Blackbushe enterprise

IT'S DYLAN'S PICNIC

BLACKBUSHE
4-page focus
SEE PAGE 31

Melody Maker front page, July 15, 1978

Graham Nash, Stephen Stills, Tim Drummond, Peter Rowan, Mike
Bloomfield and the wonderful writer-cartoonist Shel Silverstein!
Now, with a finished New York City test pressing in his hands, he
required still further confirmation that all was well. Back in Malibu
he played the album to Robbie Robertson and probably anyone else
who would listen. This constant seeking of reassurance was very
unlike Dylan. He usually knew exactly what it was he wanted and
he also knew when he'd got it. There have been many occasions
over the years when his choice of songs or his choice of the right
take to be put in front of his public would be argued as wrong, but
they were his choices.

Bob went up to the Crow River farm in December intending to
spend Christmas there with his brother. Upon arrival, one of the
first things he did was to play David the test pressing. Bang! If he
tried long enough, he was bound to find a naysayer somewhere.
David seemingly told his big brother that the album might not sell.
A producer of radio and TV jingles and the manager of a couple of
local artists, it has been said that David felt the recording lacked
commercial appeal and therefore might not attract radio airplay.
Despite comments by other writers, David didn't persuade his
brother to rerecord the album, Bob was already convinced that what
he had was possibly not right for public consumption and if he
played the test pressing to enough people someone was bound to
confirm those reservations.

David suggested that Bob might go into his local Minneapolis
studio with musicians that David could muster and rerecord some
of the tracks. In the end, five of the 10 songs were re-done ('Tangled
Up in Blue,' 'You're a Big Girl Now,' 'Idiot Wind,' 'Lily, Rosemary and
the Jack of Hearts' and 'If You See Her, Say Hello'). In the case of
the lengthy 'Lily, Rosemary and the Jack of Hearts' the rerecording
brought about improvement, predominantly in the re-writing
and telling of the complex tale. Unhappily, this would be the only

improvement, the biggest casualty being 'Idiot Wind' on which the original New York vocal had been simply glorious. Regardless of the version though, the song is nothing short of a masterpiece.

Dylan's decision to recreate the album came so late in the process that the first pressing was housed in a sleeve that credited the original musicians and also featured liner notes written by Pete Hamill which quoted lyrics that were now not on the record. Ironically, the notes were pulled from the second pressing just as Hamill got a Grammy nomination for them! Now with a dilemma on their hands, Columbia had little choice but to reinstate the notes that quote from the original lyrics for 'If You See Her, Say Hello' ("If you're makin' love to her/ Kiss her for the kid/ Who always has respected her / For doin' what she did").

Engineer Phil Ramone commented: "Emotionally [Dylan] was in a state of revealing his life, and most writers don't want to tell you they're writing their autobiography, but it's there in the atmosphere..." In a New York Times profile of Jakob Dylan, former Wallflowers manager Andrew Slater recalled a conversation with the young Mr Dylan in which he said: "When I'm listening to 'Subterranean Homesick Blues,' I'm grooving along just like you. But when I'm listening to Blood on the Tracks, that's about my parents."[13]

Although much of it is, in interviews Dylan the elder has denied that the album is in any way autobiographical. In an April 1975 radio interview with Mary Travers, Dylan said: "A lot of people tell me they enjoy that album. It's hard for me to relate to that. I mean ... people enjoying that type of pain, you know?" Enquiring whether the album expressed his own pain, Dylan responded by saying that he didn't write "confessional songs."

In 1978 Dylan told Matt Damsker: "There might be some little part of me which is confessing something I've experienced and I know, but it is definitely not the total me confessing anything."[14]

In the 1985 interview with Cameron Crowe that accompanied the *Biograph* boxed set, Dylan expressed his annoyance with the common belief that the songs contained on *Blood on the Tracks* were about the breakup of his marriage: "I don't write confessional songs. Emotion's got nothing to do with it. It only seems so, like it seems that Lawrence Olivier is Hamlet... Well, actually I did write one once and it wasn't very good–it was a mistake to record it and I regret it... back there somewhere on maybe my third or fourth album ('Ballad in Plain D'). That one I look back and I say, 'I must have been a real schmuck to write that.'"

"I've read that that album had to do with my divorce," Dylan told interviewer Bill Flanagan in 1985. "Well, I didn't get divorced 'till four years after that. I thought I might have gone a little bit too far with 'Idiot Wind'... I didn't really think I was giving away too much; I thought that it seemed so personal that people would think it was about so-and-so who was close to me. It wasn't... I didn't feel that one was too personal, but I felt it seemed too personal. Which might be the same thing, I don't know." Nevertheless, after Flanagan pressed the subject asking: "[it] must at least be somewhat about that?" Dylan's replied: "Yeah. Somewhat about that. But I'm not going to make an album and lean on a marriage relationship.[15]

Regardless of Dylan's denials, there is no doubt that the majority of the songs on *Blood on the Tracks* are autobiographical. Nevertheless, although the breakdown of Dylan's marriage can easily be spotted in nearly every song, it is faulty thinking on the part of the many critics who simplistically refer to the record as Dylan's marriage breakup album. For starters, as previously stated, the person who will make Dylan lonesome when she goes is not Sara, but rather Columbia Records' executive Ellen Bernstein.

In 1974, Bernstein headed up Columbia's San Francisco A&R office and the August 3, 1974 trade magazine *Billboard* wrote a piece about her complete with photo. At the time Columbia was the only label with an A&R office in the Bay Area and the piece made a big thing out of the fact that Bernstein had two "Fems" as her assistants and went onto speculate that this was "probably the only all-woman A&R setup in the nation." Bernstein's Bay Area roster of artists, which included Boz Scaggs, Mike Bloomfield, Taj Mahal, Herbie Hancock, New Riders of the Purple Sage and Dr Hook, was only 15 artists strong and Dylan was not on that roster and in fact they did not meet through Columbia but rather through a party thrown for Dylan by Bill Graham. The party was on the evening of February 10 at Trident restaurant on the waterfront in Sausalito in Marin County. Owned by The Kingston Trio, Trident was a musical entertainment venue, natural foods restaurant and the in-place for the young and beautiful to hang out. During the evening, Dylan sidled up and sat next to Bernstein and they chatted. She lived in Sausalito and so Dylan walked her home. She invited him in and they stayed up all night playing backgammon, which according to Bernstein, Dylan was very good at. The next day Bob had afternoon and evening concerts in Oakland and at Dylan's insistence Bernstein attended the evening show. He left the next day to complete the remainder of Tour 74 but as soon as the tour finished he invited her to visit him at his home in Malibu after which they meet regularly in Malibu and also up at Crow River Farm. She was present during the recording of *Blood on the Tracks* but after this, according to Bernstein's own words, there was a "downswing" in their relationship. Bernstein: "The press had written about the musicians [on Blood on the Tracks] and I remember him calling me, and not coming directly out and saying, did you give the information out? But he was trying to find out."[16]

'Simple Twist of Fate' is another song that has nothing whatsoever to do with Sara. Just as 'Girl from the North Country' had come about because of his split from Sixties girlfriend Suze Rotolo, but was in fact about a previous girlfriend, possibly Bonnie Jean Beecher, so the break with Sara made Dylan reflect on a previous love, Suze Rotolo. The giveaway clue for this is the working subtitle of the song, which was '4th Street Affair' (Bob and Suze had lived together in an apartment on West 4th Street in Greenwich Village). If further confirmation were needed, in the performance of 'Simple Twist of Fate' on June 30, 1981 in London, Dylan sang: "He walked along through the city blocks/ I remember Suze and the way that she talked."

Although not explicitly referring to Blood on the Tracks, in 1985 Dylan opened up to Scott Cohen: "A lot of myself crosses over into my songs. I'll write something and say to myself, I can change this. I can make this not so personal. And at other times I'll say, I think I'll leave this on a personal level ... Other times I might say, 'Well, it's too personal, I think I'll corner it.'"[17]

'If You See Her, Say Hello,' a song clearly about Bob and Sara, became less personal when it was subjected to the Minneapolis mauling. The original lyric to the song: "If you're makin' love to her/ Kiss her for the kid" would seem to be a sly reference to Billy the Kid. Or should that be Bobby the Kid? As one might expect, some of the more personal songs were the ones that either got altered or cut from the album. With Sara gone, a lyric like, "I've only got me one good shirt left and it smells of stale perfume/ In fourteen months I've only smiled once and I didn't do it consciously" ('Up to Me') would seem to sum up Dylan's situation quite succinctly. Another song that failed to make the cut is 'Call Letter Blues.' Said to have been developed from the lost Dylan song, 'Bell Tower Blues,' which in turn had its tangled roots somewhere in the works of Skip James and Robert Johnson, 'Call Letter Blues' was so painfully confessional and direct that it was never going to make the finished album.

"Well, your friends come by for you/ I don't know what to say. I just can't face up to tell 'em/ Honey, you just went away ... Well, children cry for mother/ I tell them, 'Mother took a trip.' Well, I walk on pins and needles/ I hope my tongue don't slip."

This song was attempted three times on September 16 before being completely abandoned. In total contrast to Dylan's usual ways of working he appears to have recorded the song's replacement, 'Meet Me in the Morning,' by singing wholly new lyrics over the backing track of the second of the three abandoned takes.*

Rated by many as one of Bob Dylan's finest songs, 'Tangled up in Blue' is probably the best example of what Dylan referred to as his "painting period.' With the line: "Me I'm still on the road/ Heading for another joint," Dylan appears to be contrasting his life on the road playing concerts, and even his recent domestic nomadic existence, to the home life that Sara, and for a while, Bob himself, craved. 'Tangled up in Blue' is really tangled up in blues; in fact the original working title for the song was the rather unattractive sounding 'Dusty Sweatbox Blues' ("Lord knows I paid some dues/ Wish I could lose, these dusty sweatbox blues.") The narrative of the song is engaged with time. Dylan credited painter Norman Raeben for transforming his understanding of time. The song, which is told in both the first and third person narrative, is a tale of the past, present and a vision of the future all rolled into one.

In 1978, Dylan told Peter Oppel: "This guy [Raeben] ... He looked into you and told you what you were." "He taught me how to see ... in a way that allowed me to do consciously what I unconsciously felt ... when I started doing it, the first album I made was Blood on the Tracks. Everybody agrees that was pretty different, and what's different about it is there's a code in the lyrics, and also there's no sense of time."[18]

* There are several reasons why lyrics might change or a song may get abandoned during the writing process. All songwriters endeavour to create the best work possible and so lines and rhymes will change in the quest for perfection. Bob Dylan is not unique in this so anyone attempting to interpret his lyrics has to understand that some lines will exist purely to aid the composition. It is also understandable that final drafts will often be amended to exclude names and ensure that the song for public consumption is less autobiographical.

When reviewing Dylan's work from the mid-Seventies onwards *Blood on the Tracks* has become a benchmark album for music critics. Dylan's marriage had gone off the rails but his music was back on the tracks. Even so, he had no wish to take this album on the road. For now, he seemed to view the writing and recording of these songs as an autonomous episode. Born in the moment, they were a way of purging himself of his recent experiences. In *Chronicles*, Dylan wrote: "I would even record an entire album based on Chekhov short stories. Critics thought it was autobiographical – that was fine."[19] Make of that what you will!

On March 23, 1975, Dylan was the surprise guest at a benefit concert for SNACK (Students Need Athletic and Cultural Kicks). City budget cuts had meant an end to all extracurricular activities in San Francisco's schools so promoter Bill Graham staged a one-day concert at the city's vast Kezar Stadium with an incredible list of performers and guest celebrities. The concert was a way for Graham to give back to the San Francisco community. He told radio station K-101: "We make our living from the youth of San Francisco. This is one way we hope to thank them." The event raised enough money to keep extracurricular activities in schools going for a year.

There had been rumours of a very special guest but station K-101 would only identify the guest as "The Man from the Fairmont [Hotel]." Dylan, along with three members of The Band plus Neil Young, Tim Drummond and Ben Keith, played for half an hour. Dylan contributed vocals on 'Are You Ready for the Country,' a slightly rewritten 'I Want You,' 'Knockin' on Dragon's Door,' and 'Will the Circle Be Unbroken.' He also provided backing on piano and guitar for the five other songs. Sara accompanied Bob to the show and after the concert, along with Bill Graham and Marlon Brando, they dined at the home of Francis Ford Coppola. The following day, March 24, Bob and Sara attend a party given by Paul and Linda McCartney to celebrate the completion of the Wings album *Venus*

and Mars. The party was in Long Beach onboard the ocean liner
Queen Mary.

Still trying to work out their marital problems, the Dylans seemed
to be doing the rounds. A few weeks earlier, during the first week
of March, they had attended a Warner Brothers' party for Rod
Stewart and the Faces at the Greenhouse restaurant on Wilshire
Boulevard, Los Angeles. It was during this star-studded gathering
that Dylan famously cut the notorious Peter Grant down to size.
The 6-foot 5-inch ex-doorman and professional wrestler was used
to throwing his considerable weight around and from all accounts
at this party he was even more obnoxious than usual. According
to one partygoer, Grant grabbed Richard Fernandez's cowboy hat
off his head. Fernandez, the Faces Road Manager who would later
fill that same role in Dylan's organisation, "stood rooted to the spot,
amazed at this show of ignorance." Grant clearly had no intention
of returning the hat so when he turned his back someone snatched
it off his big head and surreptitiously slipped it back to Fernandez.
Grant then strutted over to where Dylan sat, brushing people aside
as he walked. Arriving at the table he said: "Hello, Bob. I'm Peter
Grant, I manage Led Zeppelin," to which Dylan replied, "I don't
come to you with my problems."

In early May Bob flew to the south of France to stay with his
friend, the painter David Oppenheim, (whose illustration had
recently graced the rear sleeve of *Blood on the Tracks*). Dylan stayed at
Oppenheim's home in Savoie in the French Alps for six weeks. Sara
was supposed to join him there to celebrate his 34th birthday but
although, according to Oppenheim, Bob rang her daily, she didn't
come. The painter's assessment of Dylan, who he said, "talked
about nothing but love," was one of complete despair and isolation.
With Sara as a no-show, Oppenheim took Dylan down to the south
coast to celebrate his birthday at a Gypsy festival which fell on the
same date, May 24.

The Gypsy Festival, or Gitan Pilgrimage, has been formally taking place in Les Saintes Maries-de-la-Mer on the same date since 1448. Situated in the Rhône River delta, close to the mouth of the Petit Rhône, the area is almost exotic with its tall marsh grasses, pink flamingos, black bulls and white horses all roaming freely. Van Gogh painted Gypsies in the Carmargue during his time living unhappily in Arles and the extraordinary Romani jazz guitarist Django Reinhardt was a regular visitor to the festival.

The Romani come to Les Saintes Maries-de-la-Mer to pay homage to Black Sara in the town's 9th-century church. Although not recognised by the Vatican, Black Sara is the patron saint of the Gypsies. The legend of Sara (or Sarah) tells that in 42 CE a boat without a sail or oars drifted across the Mediterranean from Jerusalem and landed on the Isle of Ratis, the fishing village that is now Les Saintes Maries-de-la-Mer. Its occupants, who had been cast out by their Roman persecutors, were said to be Joseph of Arimathea, Mary Jacob (sister of the Virgin Mary), Mary Salome (mother of the apostles James Major and John), Lazarus and his sisters Mary Magdalene and Martha. At this point the legend varies, some say a dark-skinned girl named Sara was also on the boat while others say she was already living in the village and when she saw the boat flounder her prayers helped it to reach land safely. Legends also vary wildly as to Sara's identity. One interpretation is that the girl was an indigenous princess of one of the Camargue tribes while another very different tale tells that she was merely a servant girl or an Egyptian slave. The most radical claim is that the girl was the daughter of Mary Magdalene and her husband Jesus. At any rate, for many hundreds of years Roma – largely drawn from French and Catalan-speaking communities – have come together here to affirm their faith and culture.

According to Dylan, he spent a week in Les Saintes Maries-de-la-Mer and while there he met the self-proclaimed King of the Gypsies.

Dylan: "I went to see the king of the Gypsies in Southern France. This guy had 12 wives and 100 children. He was in the antique business and had a junkyard, but he'd had a heart attack before I'd come to see him. All his wives and children had left. After he dies, they'll come back. They smell death and they leave."[20]

The six weeks in France away from Sara were a fertile time both for songwriting and also for ideas for new songs. 'One More Cup of Coffee' is a song that clearly comes from this period and the lyrics, "a wanderer by trade" and "Your sister sees the future/ Like your mama and yourself" plainly allude to a Gypsy way of life. The lyric: "He oversees his kingdom" would also seem to refer to Dylan's meeting with the King of the Gypsies. Dylan would later say that the song came to him in a dream one week after his visit to Les Saintes Maries-de-la-Mer. There is also little doubt that while there Dylan was exposed to the legend of Black Sara.

The very fact that Saint Sara's feast day happens to fall on Dylan's birthday and that the wife he was missing so much both have the same name must have resonated deeply with him. There is also a very strong connection between Black Sara and the Egyptian goddess Isis. Isis was a major goddess in ancient Egyptian religion whose worship spread throughout the Greco-Roman world. In the Osiris myth, she used her considerable magical powers to resurrect her slain husband, the divine king Osiris. In the Hellenistic period (323–30 BCE), when Egypt was ruled and settled by Greeks, Isis came to be worshipped by both Greeks and Egyptians and her cult then spread into the wider Mediterranean world. Her Greek devotees credited Isis with the invention of marriage and interestingly, on the Rolling Thunder Tour, Dylan would introduce 'Isis' with the words: "Here's a song about marriage." As Hellenistic culture was absorbed by Rome in the first century BCE, the cult of Isis became a part of Roman religion and numerous homes housed statues of a black Isis. Although the worship of the goddess was ended by the rise of Christianity her adoration influenced some Christian beliefs and practices, such as the veneration of Mary. Shrines to Isis were founded all around the Mediterranean and the church of Saintes-Maries-de-la-Mer itself was built on the site of one such temple. It is quite possible therefore that the Black Sara legend was built on the legend of Isis.

Author John Baldwin wrote: "Whether Dylan took the next step to uncover the association between Sarah and Isis is conjecture but that connection is ... something well known to the locals. Faced with the knowledge (if he was) that Sarah and Isis were one and the same, could that have been the impetus he needed to start work on 'Isis'?

The song – possibly a re-telling of the Isis/Osiris myth – is also one that, in coded terms, may tell of Bob's marriage to Sara and his hopes for reconciliation ... we do know that he came back from his visit with Oppenheim and very soon after met up with [Jacques] Levy with at least the framework for the song in place."*[21]

We know that Bob bumped into Jacques Levy in Greenwich Village during the first week of July, less than six weeks after the Gypsy festival and about three weeks after he had returned from France. We also know from interviews with Levy that Dylan had already started writing 'Isis' before the two men had met.

"When we first met, Bob had a few basic partly-worked tunes" Levy informed me: "I guess the only reason that 'Isis' was chosen as the [first] song to work together on was that we were at my loft apartment and Bob didn't have a guitar with him. I didn't have a guitar there either, but I had a piano, and 'Isis' was the one song that he had started to write on the piano ... It was so slow and rather stately and sad; it would have taken a whole side of an album!"[22]

I think from the above information we have to conclude that 'Isis'

* *The main premise of Bob's film Renaldo & Clara, one of death and rebirth, would be the same as the song 'Isis.' This theme would continue through 1978 with the Street-Legal album.*

must have originated from Dylan's visit to Les Saintes Maries-de-la-Mer and that there is a connection between Black Sara and the Egyptian goddess Isis. Exactly when Bob began work on the song 'Sara' however is much less clear. When I asked Levy about the song he answered with, "Bob had been working on 'Sara' for a long time. He'd got the chorus all worked out but the verses were [later] written out at East Hampton. Bob and Sara had stayed there many times. That's where the images of the dunes and the kids playing on the beach and all that stuff is from. He would hit me with some lyrics– use me as a sounding board, but it was a very personal song for him."[23]

(Dylan's rented house in East Hampton was on Nichols Lane, which is off Lily Pond Lane, and Bob even managed to work the house address into the lyrics for 'Sara'.)

Levy's comments give the impression that Bob had been writing 'Sara' for quite some time. However, in another conversation I had with Jacques, he was more specific: "Well, I didn't mean that Bob had been writing the song that we get on *Desire* for a long time. What I meant by that was that he'd been thinking about writing something along those lines for quite a while. Just fooling around; kicking the idea about. He told me it was an idea he'd had for years but you might be right that he only started writing the actual song around the time of 'Isis.' I don't know for sure."[24]

Writer Tim Riley noted that with Emmylou Harris' vocal contribution to the song, 'Oh, Sister' became "a discourse on the fragility of love." That would certainly seem to be the case but John Baldwin has also found possible connections between this song and ancient Egypt. The tarot website 'tarot-online' states that *Desire* "contains anguished songs around the Isis-Osiris dynamic – the famed 'Isis' and 'Oh Sister' (Isis and Osiris were soul brother-sister and husband-wife)." To a lesser extent, Baldwin also writes about possible Egyptian connections with the *Desire* outtake 'Golden

Loom.'

In any event, an interest in ancient Egypt appears to be in evidence in the Dylan household way before Bob's visit to Les Saintes Maries-de-la-Mer. One visitor to the newly finished Point Dume mansion informed me that the home contained many Egyptian objects and images. It has also been noted by Larry "Ratso" Sloman that Sara not only wore an Isis pendant/amulet of her own design, but she constructed an altar for the Empress card* While discussing *Renaldo & Clara*, one of Dylan's girlfriends, Faridi McFree, told me that there was an element of Egyptology in the film and that some of the people who were involved with *Renaldo & Clara* were also involved with Egyptology, "especially Sara Dylan."[25] The Empress card from the Tarot of the Rider-Waite deck is of course featured on the back cover of the *Desire* album.

in Egyptian Tarot Arcanum III, The Empress card is called Isis Unveiled.

Chapter Seven

Rolling With The Thunder

After his visit to France, Dylan decided not to return to California but instead to spend some time in New York City. He borrowed a vacant loft on Houston Street and settled into the sweltering heat that had arrived in the Big Apple that June. Maybe he was looking to spend a little time away from his wife. In any event, Sara turned up in New York for the July 31 *Desire* recording session. Dylan's co-writer on that album, Jacques Levy, told me in 1999 that Sara arrived seemingly unannounced: "She was in the control booth listening when Bob recorded 'Sara,'" Levy said, "As soon as Bob sang that first line: 'When the children were babies and played on the beach,' you could see her face change! Every verse was like a confessional. And when he got to that very last line, 'Don't ever leave me/ don't ever go,' well, I tell you, you could have heard a pin drop. Sara was completely astounded by the song. At this point it looked like they would get back together. It definitely seemed on the cards."[1]

On August 2, two days after the session, the couple left New York for Minnesota where they spent time together on the farm. Having toured in the United States the previous year, Dylan now planned a European tour for November 1975. However, during his time in New York City he had begun thinking about what would become The Rolling Thunder Revue. Europe was still on the cards, but it would now be pushed back, probably to spring '76. While Tour 74 had been hugely successful in terms of ticket sales, Bob had not enjoyed it and one source said, "He loathed it." Unhappily, after taking an age to embrace the decision to get back out on the road, Dylan had found no pleasure in it. In spite of all his efforts to move forward he was still floundering, bereft of any real sense of direction. With the advent of stadium tours, things had changed greatly since he was last on the road and to a certain extent Bob had been left behind.

What he now had in mind would be a complete antidote to Tour 74. Forget advance postal ticket applications for huge nosebleed arenas; this time he would play intimate venues with a vast troupe of musicians forming some sort of travelling caravan. He would take Greenwich Village on tour. Spontaneity would be the name of the game. To begin with, there wasn't any advance publicity for the shows and in some instances tickets only went on sale on the day of the performances. A band of counterfeit gypsies rolling from town to town was an idea that Dylan had harboured for quite some time. This was probably as close as any artist of Dylan's stature could come to recreating Levon Helm's much-loved Walcott's Rabbits Foot Minstrels* or even Ronnie Lane's The Passing Show which had toured Britain in the summer of 1974.**

*Walcott's Rabbits Foot Minstrels was a variety troupe of African American entertainers that toured the American South as a tent show from 1900 to the late 1950s. A number of these troupe existed but the Rabbit Foot Minstrels was one of the most popular. The shows presented a wide range of comedy routines, song-and-dance numbers, and a marching band. In the 1910s blues was added to the existing repertoire of ragtime, classical and popular vaudeville music. The "Foots" played a major role in promoting the blues across the South. The Band song 'The W.S. Walcott Medicine Show' relates the memories of drummer Levon Helm who went to minstrel and medicine shows during his youth in Arkansas. The song was released The Band's 1970 album Stage Fright.

** In 1974, Ronnie Lane took his Romany caravan across the English countryside rolling into towns with a rag-tag troupe of jugglers, fire-eaters, dancing girls and his newly discovered band, Slim Chance. Also on the tour was what Lane described as "the world's unfunniest clowns." Christened The Passing Show, this brilliant but tragically fated rock circus tour has entered the annals as one of the boldest but ill-judged tours ever. Lack of advance publicity, permits, safety issues and other unfortunate factors all resulted in Ronnie Lane pitching his Big Top and watching his money disappear.

One of Bob's Malibu neighbours was Roger McGuinn. "[Bob] used to come and hang out," McGuinn told Record Collector. "And he noticed my basketball court, and asked if I had a basketball." McGuinn hadn't, but the next day he went out and bought one. He rang Bob's house and Sara answered. "Tell Bob I've got a basketball," Roger said. Sara replied, "Oh, he'll be thrilled." When Dylan arrived to shoot hoops he immediately began telling McGuinn about his idea for a tour. "I'm thinking of doing something like a circus," Dylan told the Byrd.

The Rolling Thunder concerts were not held under canvas but Dylan did have a yellow decorated circus-type drape to help create an effect. At larger venues the drape was used as a front curtain and at smaller shows as a backdrop. A huge Persian rug was laid over the stage and Master of Ceremonies, Bobby Neuwirth, invited the audience to join the troupe in the "Rolling Thunder living room."

In the beginning it was hoped that his record company would finance the tour and Columbia employee Faris Bouhafa sent a four-page memo to the label outlining the idea. According to Larry Sloman, a few days later Bouhafa received the proposal back with the words "Bullshit! That'll never happen" pencilled in along the top-left of the opening page.

Robbie Robertson: "[Rolling Thunder was] looser, it wasn't done with as much seriousness [as Tour 74]. [The Revue] has been a thing that Bob's been talking about for years. I'm sure he would have liked to take it all the way and done it by train, he's always wanted to have that kind of gypsy caravan situation happening where it was loose and different people could get up and do different things ... I think his anticipation and nervousness on [Tour 74] didn't allow for any laid-back stuff ... I missed that, all those different moods. On Rolling Thunder I heard more of that and I like that."[2]

Dylan said that he would have liked to have got some sort of Jug band together but that never happened. To begin with, he toyed with the idea of calling the tour the Montezuma Revue but later he decided on the Rolling Thunder Revue. The name for the tour was derived from the Native American shaman Rolling Thunder. Born John Pope in 1916, of a white mother and according to Pope, a Native American, (Paint Clan) Cherokee father, Pope, who passed in 1997, was a controversial figure who lived most of his life in Nevada with the Western Shoshone. He was an activist for Indian rights, an excellent herbalist and powerful healer who helped thousands of people. There were many, however, mostly in the media, who mocked and disbelieved Thunder's powers. One of the main charges against him was that he was not a real Native American. This accusation was often backed up by the fact that he was not on the official register of Native Americans. According to Rolling Thunder, he failed to register himself as a protest to the fact that Native people should have to register at all. Nevertheless, questions about his legitimacy as a Native American teacher followed him for the rest of his life.

During the late Sixties, the Grateful Dead sought him out, much in the same way the Beatles had sought out the Maharishi Mahesh Yogi. In 1972, the Dead's Mickey Heart paid tribute to Thunder when the drummer released his first 'solo' album which he titled *Rolling Thunder* (Pope's voice can be heard on the short opening track, 'Rolling Thunder/Shoshone Invocation'). It was the Grateful Dead who introduced Dylan to Thunder and from that introduction Bob read the book *Rolling Thunder* in late 1974. Written by Doug Boyd and first published by Dell, the book was originally sub-titled A Personal Exploration into the Secret Healing Power of an American Indian Medicine Man.

When asked about the origin of the name Dylan said: "I was just sitting outside my house one day thinking about a name for the tour, when all of a sudden, I looked into the sky and I heard a boom! Then, boom, boom, boom, boom, rolling from west to east. So I figured that should be the name."[3]

In 2017, I asked Arthur Rosato about the origins of the name and although he could not confirm for sure, he believed that the tour name did come from the medicine man. Rosato told me he met and talked with Rolling Thunder in Niagara Falls in November 1975 during the first leg of the Revue tour.[4]

In the 2019 Martin Scorsese Rolling Thunder film, Ratso Sloman repeated Dylan's "boom, boom, boom" story of how the tour name came about. A few minutes later, however, Bob says that he took the name from an American Indian. Dylan goes on to say that he was told later that Rolling Thunder meant "walking with the truth," which he liked. He may have liked it even more had he known that Rolling Thunder has two meanings: "walking with the truth" and perhaps even more appropriate, "song of the gods."

Jacques Levy: "Well, after *Desire* Bob talked about going out on tour. I directed the first leg of Rolling Thunder. I insisted that we have rehearsals. Not so much rehearsing the music but deciding what the other musicians should play and what the running order would be and how we would get all of these people on and off the stage smoothly. The trick was to make it look and feel like everyone was just coming on stage and doing impromptu songs but that wasn't the case at all. I had scripted the whole thing. If an artist wanted to change a song from time to time they could, but on the whole they had a set routine. Bob had very little to do with putting the Revue together; he left all of that to me. He knew what he wanted to do in his own set but after that he wasn't concerned. He really just wanted to be part of the whole and this also enabled him to feel free because he was only responsible for his own performance and not the tour. He knew that I was taking care of everything else and that allowed him the freedom to do his own thing.

Bob told me in no uncertain terms that he wanted something completely different from the previous tour. He couldn't stand that tour. He called it the 'planes and limos tour.' He absolutely hated it. I told him it didn't have to be that way and suggested we do the exact opposite, a bus and trucks tour. Bob talked to Bobby Neuwirth about putting something together and it gained momentum from there. The core of the band was bass and drums so Neuwirth got Rob Stoner and Howie Wyeth on board. I'd worked with Roger McGuinn and I liked him a lot so I suggested Roger.

We had been going down to Paul Colby's [Greenwich Village] club, The Bitter End, trying out the songs we'd written for *Desire* and after that Bob continued turning up there and began using the place for impromptu rehearsals. Musicians heard what was going on at Colby's and they just started turning up. I think Bob wanted the tour to take on a life of its own and it did. The original concept was that it might even become self-perpetuating. As musicians got tired of the Revue, they might drop out and someone else would take their place. It was even suggested that another artist could eventually take Bob's place and keep the thing going."5

Arthur Rosato: "Bob just wanted to get away from the big production. It was easier to be part of a travelling troupe of fellow musicians ... [He] was infamous for asking people to join the tour. That was Bob, 'Come on down I'm doing this or I'm doing that.' ... Looking around the rehearsal room and seeing Bobby Neuwirth, Ramblin' Jack Elliot, Joan Baez, Joni Mitchell, Roger McGuinn, and the other odd assortment of musicians, including a very tall T-Bone Burnett and actress Ronee Blakley, it was hard to say who really stuck out. They all did. It was like something out of *Mad* Magazine."6

Even amongst the *Mad* Magazine crew there was a musician who stuck out and that was the Spider from Mars, Mick Ronson. After David Bowie broke up his band the spider with the platinum hair had joined forces with his Mott the Hopple pal Ian Hunter but when that went nowhere in particular Rono found his career hitting the skids. He began spending time hanging out in various Greenwich

Village haunts where he met the likes of Rob Stoner, Bobby
Neuwirth, T-Bone Burnett and David Mansfield.

Mick Ronson: "I was down at the Other End with Ian [Hunter]
and Bobby Neuwirth, who I'd met recently and he was there with
another guy. It was like, I recognise this bloke, shit, it's Dylan!
Anyway, I got drunk and the owner, Colby, threw me out, like three
times and I just kept coming back in. Anyway, I talked with Dylan
for a while and out of the blue he invited me to go out on the road
with this tour he was putting together. Of course, I said 'yes,' but
I didn't think for a minute that I'd hear any more about it. In fact,
I thought it was some kinda joke, but he asked me for a contact
number. Bobby [Neuwirth] said that Dylan had been showing up
at the club most nights at around midnight and jamming. Not long
after that he called and asked me to come down to rehearsals.
This was like a Friday and the rehearsals started, I think, Sunday. I
remember it so well because it saved me. I desperately needed to
work and things were shit at the time. I got to tell you though, and
don't pass this on [laughs] but I didn't really like Dylan's stuff that
much. That was before he offered me a job [laughs]. The rehearsals
were in the City [New York], Midtown, at a place called Studio
Instrumental Rentals. Some of the people there didn't even know
it was for a tour. It wasn't really a rehearsal; it was like a jam. There
were like six or seven guitarists there so I still didn't think I'd be on
the tour. I thought it was an audition. Roger McGuinn was there.
I'd never even heard half of the numbers they were playin'. Two
days we were there. That first day they must have got through, I
don't know, maybe 150 songs! Then, the next day, they ran through
maybe another 80-100. It was fuckin' madness.

On that first day I wasn't comfortable at all. It seemed like all
the rest knew each other and they knew the songs. I knew three
or four of the musicians and only half the fuckin' songs! I thought
I was terrible but Bobby [Neuwirth], and Rob [Stoner] and T-Bone

were great; they really helped me through it. And Dylan, Dylan helped too. Dylan never said what he wanted from you. That's why I thought it was an audition. It seemed to me that he wanted to see just what you had. What your contribution could be. But that wasn't it. It was more like he wanted you to find your part in things. He wanted you to do your thing and see if it would fit with him.

It was mostly Bobby [Neuwirth], and Stoner who ran the rehearsals. Dylan mostly left it to them but he knew what was goin' on. He was right on the ball. I've said before, Dylan doesn't have to say anything. With Bob, you just know. He's someone very special and that tour was just this massive thing for me; a lad from Hull."[7]

The Circus Is In Town

"Shaman don't care about eating now, he's got his paint on he's ready for jive ... shaman's going to finish what he started, shaman grows old & never changes ... shaman speaks occasionally ... swings his guitar like a baby, is a baby, is sometimes a woman ... shaman bites down hard on the wind, you'd better well listen to shaman."

(Shaman Hisses You Slide Back into the Night is journal-type poem written by Anne Waldman during the 1975 tour)

"There's no fear allowed on Rolling Thunder"

(Bob Neuwirth)

The circus left town on October 27. Seventy people, including a film crew of 15 and Bob's beagle, Peggy, took to the road. Although artistically the tour is seen by many as Bob Dylan's finest hour, the size of the troupe would ensure that it would not be a financial success. Transportation for the tour included two buses, one of which, a converted Greyhound called 'Phydeaux,' was hired from Frank Zappa.

Dylan took a bright red Cadillac and his Winnebago motor-home, dubbed 'The Executive.' "He was driving himself," McGuinn told *Record Collector*. "[He was] wearing dark prescription glasses. And as it started to get dark he was having difficulty [seeing]."

Arthur Rosato: "To begin with we had no idea what we were going to do, there were no itineraries, we all just got on the bus and where we woke up was where we were."[8] The Revue opened in the historic town of Plymouth, Massachusetts on October 30, 1975. Low-key was certainly the name of the game here. Few artists ever bothered to play the small town which was described by Sam Shepard as, "The kind of place you aspire to get out of the second you discover you've had the misfortune to have been raised there."

Arthur Rosato: "As the tour went on the shows were getting longer, and Bob noticed how long it would be before he would get back on stage. He said: 'I have time to go to a movie.' To keep him from doing that we got him a TV for his dressing room. If you watch the 'Isis' clip from the *Renaldo & Clara* film, you'll see Bob is wearing a watch. That's my watch. I loaned it to him every night so that he could keep track of the show time."[9]

There were so many highlights on this tour it would be unfair of me to single one out but how can I not mention my magazine's namesake, 'Isis'? White-face with his wide-brim hat adorned with fresh flowers Bob performed 'Isis,' sans guitar, his eyes as wide as saucers, his fists clenched, wrists crossed in the sign of a cross. All eyes were fixed on Dylan. He had taken back complete control of his art. Talking about Bob's performances on Rolling Thunder, Joan Baez has said that she has never seen anybody with such charisma, either before or after.

Dylan told tour photographer Ken Regan that the whiteface was so the people at the back of the halls could see his eyes. The whiteface was also designed to differentiate between Bob Dylan on stage and Renaldo offstage, which is the reason that the makeup only arrived at the 4th show in Lowell, MA– the first night of filming for *Renaldo & Clara* (November 4). Dylan had kicked-off the tour on October 31 (All Hallows' Eve) wearing a plastic Bob Dylan mask!

Those on the '75 tour talk of a party atmosphere and there was certainly a lot of heavy drinking and plenty of cocaine use. Bass player Rob Stoner said of the tour, "You were suspicious of anybody who didn't do drugs back then."

If Bob wanted to keep his marriage alive he seemed to be going about it in a very unconventional way. The Revue tour formed the backdrop to the shooting of Dylan's proposed film *Renaldo & Clara* and, because Bob had cast Sara in the role of Clara, she was present for most of the '75 tour. Had she not agreed to take this lead role her disdain for the road would almost certainly have kept her at home in California. To add to the perplexity of an already bewildering movie, as well as having Sara playing Clara, Bob also cast her as a whore!

Also, he invited his ex-lover, Joan Baez, to join him on tour and, as previously stated, actress Ruth Tyrangiel was also on board. In one scene, Baez, who plays The Woman in White, asks Dylan: "What would've happened if we ever got married, Bob?" To which Dylan replies, "I married the woman I love." As an acknowledgement to Sara and as a probable mark of respect, he named his production company, Lombard Street Films, Inc.– Sara was born in North Lombard Street in Wilmington, Delaware.

Mel Howard – associate producer of *Renaldo & Clara* – told Howard Sounes that Bob's old girlfriend's, "were coming out of the Woodwork" and that, "Some of them travelled with Bob; it was quite an open thing." There was certainly plenty of gossip amongst the troupe about who Bob might be sleeping with. From the outside – and probably from the inside also – the situation certainly seemed far more complicated than it needed to be. It was almost as if Bob was caught up in some sort of love-hate relationship with Sara and he appeared to be working things out as they toured and filmed! It was a good cop / bad cop routine with Bob playing both cops– his Gemini personality was working overtime.

Bob told his audience in Montréal, Quebec that 'Isis' was a song "about marriage." When the lady in the song asks the narrator if he's going to stay, he answers with a resounding "YEAH!" The reality of the situation, however, was that going back out on the road at this time was bound to put a significant strain on his already tense relationship with Sara. You could maybe make sense of this if Bob had gone on the road to get away from the situation– a little breathing space, a time out, but to take Sara with him so that she could witness firsthand the excesses of the road seems quite eccentric to this mere mortal! Maybe he was hoping to force her hand. Sara certainly tired of the tour quite quickly and although she was used to such events, on the morning of November 21 she was reminded of the insanity of it all when Larry Sloman came to her Cambridge, Massachusetts hotel room to inform her that a strange guy was hanging around the hotel lobby asking questions. The rest of the travelling caravan had already left for Boston so Sloman appointed himself as Sara's bodyguard and informed her that they needed to get out of the hotel as quickly as possible. Sara finished packing and asked if Sloman was sure the guy was dangerous, "I mean," she said, "we get a Christ every six months coming up to our house. Even the kids are used to it. We even had a John the Baptist last year."[10]

In the spring of '75, shortly before Dylan had left for France, Richard Solomon, a fund organiser for the campaign to get middleweight boxer Rubin "Hurricane" Carter a retrial, had written a letter to Dylan's New York office explaining Carter's plight and asking for Dylan's support. Several weeks later, Solomon received a phone call from Dylan asking, "What do you want from me?" Solomon explained the situation and asked Dylan if he would be willing to meet with Rubin. Bob said that he would "give it some thought" but in any event he was about to fly out to France. Heartened by the fact that Dylan hadn't given him a straight 'no,' Solomon mailed Bob a copy of Carter's autobiography. Published in 1975 by Warner Books, The Sixteenth Round, which had been written by Carter while he was in prison, arrived with Dylan just before he left for France and he took the book with him. Dylan read the book while on vacation and his interest was immediately sparked.

The product of a hard and difficult childhood, growing up in Forties to Fifties black America, Rubin Carter, having won 15 of his last 17 bouts, had become a top contender for the middleweight boxing crown. His career in the ring, however, had come to a sudden halt when on May 26, 1967 he and another black man, John Artis, were found guilty of the murder of three people in a Paterson, New Jersey bar. While in prison, Carter had chronicled the events that led to his sentence of three consecutive life sentences and 10 years in solitary confinement in the hope that the story would alert people to his plight. It did, and one of those people was Bob Dylan. Dylan visited Carter in Trenton State Prison – a maximum-security facility in New Jersey – and immediately felt an affinity with the boxer. Dylan later said of that meeting: "The first time I saw him, I left knowing one thing ... I realised that the man's philosophy and my philosophy were running down the same road, and you don't meet too many people like that."

As well as writing and releasing the song 'Hurricane,' Dylan also participated in two benefits in aid of Carter's defence fund. The first concert, December 8, closed the 1975 leg of the Rolling Thunder Revue. It was a very successful evening which paved the way for more of the same. The second benefit, which took place on January 25, was first slated for New Orleans and only relocated to Houston Astrodome 10 days before the event took place. Unlike the Madison Square Garden show, The Night of the Hurricane II was organised entirely by Carter's defence committee, 'Freedom for All, Forever,' and

Dylan did not confirm that he would appear until he was sure who else would be on the bill. Nonetheless, quite a number of the press reports managed to somehow tie the event down to Dylan, especially when things started to go awry. With the change of venue, time was too short to properly promote the event and even posters that read "The Night of the Hurricane II" lead some locals to believe the concert was a benefit for the victims of a tropical disaster!

Rehearsals for the Astrodome concert were held at S.I.R. soundstage in Hollywood and Dylan spontaneously instigated a shopping expedition to Nudie Cohn's Rodeo store. Dylan bankrolled stage clothing for the entire entourage and picked up the tab for unlimited room service at the luxury Sunset Marquis Hotel in West Hollywood. After the rehearsals and buying spree, which was said to have cost Dylan $50,000, he flew everyone to Houston.

"Bob bought this gorgeous Jesus coat with Jesus' head and rainbows and palm trees," remembers Kinky Friedman: "God knows what it's worth today. He got it from Nudies, wore it for a show or two and then gave it to me. I wore it for a little while, kept it for some years, and eventually the jacket was sold at auction. I told Bob years later that I had hit some hard times and sold the coat. He said, 'Bad move, bad, bad move.' It was a bad move."[11]

The Night of the Hurricane II began at two in the afternoon with the 1619 Bad Ass Band, a local New Jersey disco group that Carter had requested because they had previously played prison concerts. By the end of the staggeringly long seven-hour concert the 1619 Band weren't the only ones with bad asses! The star-studded but seemingly endless line up included Stevie Wonder, Isaac Hayes, Dr John, Richie Havens, Carlos Santana, Shawn Phillips, Steven Stills, Kinky Friedman, Levon Helm, Rick Danko and Ringo Starr. The Rolling Thunder Revue took the stage around dusk and performed for the usual three hours.

"All the good intentions and noble gestures in the world can't make up for a tediously long and sloppy performance," wrote Dale Adamson in the Houston Chronicle. With knives sharpened the press quickly began dissecting the event and as early as the morning after the concert rumours were rife that the rental of the stadium, coupled with extravagant hotel and transportation costs, had resulted in the event losing money. According to *Rolling Stone* magazine, by the Tuesday after the concert the promoter was unable to say how much money Carter's defence committee would receive but he was confident that the concert would show a profit after the Astrodome's rental, initially pegged at an astronomical $100,000, "was renegotiated." Nevertheless, sources at Bill Graham's FM Productions, which was called in just before the event to handle the technical side, criticised the deal which allowed the concessionaires to keep their entire proceeds. Dave Furano, FM's vice-president of operations said the promoters were "rookies on every level." Exactly how much this second concert made or lost isn't clear but the two concerts combined only raised $100,000 net and most of that came from the Madison Square Garden concert.

Although Dylan was not responsible for the Astrodome event he might have been wise to have taken it as a warning of what was to come. However, still high on the triumphs of the '75 tour, in March, Dylan travelled to Britain in the hope that the Revue might play shows there. In early April he reassembled the Revue to begin 10 days of rehearsals at the grand historic Belleview Biltmore hotel in Clearwater, Florida. The atmosphere however was very different from the previous leg. Rather like the now ageing hotel in which they rehearsed, the Rolling Thunder Revue was about to go into steep decline.

Filming for *Renaldo & Clara* had finished so the film crew had gone and the entourage was significantly smaller. With no filming taking place, there was no longer any need for Sara to accompany Bob on tour and this gave him even more scope, if indeed any was needed, to chase women. According to those present, on this tour Bob's various affairs were even more brazen.

One of those alleged lovers was Stephanie Buffington who, a decade before, age 19, had been the subject of the Arthur Lee song 'Stephanie Knows Who,' in which she was the focus of a romantic triangle involving three members of the American band Love. Buffington joined the Revue tour during the Clearwater rehearsals to, amongst other things, teach Bob to tightrope walk! Some might say that Dylan had been walking a tightrope well before Buffington joined the troupe! Joan Baez described her as the "girl with henna hair and Salvation Army clothes." She remained with the caravan for most of the '76 tour.

Buffington: "[Dylan was] curious about my own spiritual practice and experience. I think that was the focus between us ... Big things were happening in his life: the dissolution of his marriage ... Friends dying [Phil Ochs, April 9, 1976]. That changes you on a deep level. It makes you think of your own mortality ... Everything is all screwed up in a personal way, it's part of the quest ... I think he was doing a lot of soul-searching at that time."[12]

Buffington was under the impression that Bob and Sara had split four months before they had met so she was surprised when, in early May, Sara arrived on the tour. Although Buffington had forgotten about the meeting, Sara had visited her at her home a couple of years earlier to buy some "Tibetan artefacts."

Joan Baez: "Sara showed up late in the tour, wafting in from a plane looking like a madwoman ... her hair wild and dark rings around her eyes. In two days, she had regained what I called her 'powers.' Bob was ignoring her, and had picked up a local curly-headed Mopsy who perched on the piano during his rehearsals in a ballroom ... Sara appeared airily at the front door dressed in deerskin, wearing her emerald necklace ... [We] talked distantly about nothing in particular, all the while eyeing the closed door to the ballroom. I had the impression that she had her magic powers set upon that room, and that whatever plans Bob had would soon be foiled. The door to the room opened and Mopsy tumbled out. 'Who's that?' said Sara, looking at the girl sideways with her big, lazy, suspicious eyes. 'Some groupie. No one likes her,' [Baez answered]." "It was true. We liked the tightrope walker, who vanished quietly when Sara was around, but Mopsy was a lawless intruder and I realised how much I supported Sara.

[Then] ...Through a curiously wide-open dressing room door ... I saw Sara ... Her husband was on one knee in front of her, bare-headed and apparently distraught. It was like a silent movie, Bob in whiteface and Charlie Chaplin eyeliner, Sara all ice and coal and bits of rouge. That night I sang 'Sad-Eyed Lady of the Lowlands' and dedicated it to Sara."[13]

It's very clear that Dylan had been doing a great deal of soul-searching since he vacated his Woodstock home in 1970 and the songs on this tour say it all. A new acoustic rendition of 'If You See Her Say Hello' with especially poignant lyrics summed up Dylan's mood: "She left in a hurry/ I don't know what she was on" ... "I know that she'll be back someday/ Of that there is no doubt/ And when that moment comes, dear Lord/ Give me the strength to keep her out." A savage 'Idiot Wind,' which had begun life with the title 'Selfish Child,' was also introduced into the set and Dylan spat venom at the song's recipient like never before ("bloooood on your saddle," indeed). The previous six years of Dylan's life can be succinctly summed up with: "I haven't known about peace and quiet now for so long/ I don't even remember what it's like."

On May 23, 1976, at the Fort Collins concert, which was being filmed for a TV special, the Dylan family gathered in readiness to celebrate Bob's 35th birthday the following day. Perhaps in the hope of salvaging something from their marriage, Sara was there. However, this meant that Sara, the children, and Bob's mother all stood side stage while Bob belted out this emotion-filled rendition of 'Idiot Wind'!

Just how serious Bob was is open to debate, but he told several people that it was his intention to keep Rolling Thunder rolling indefinitely. As mentioned previously, he had talked about this with Jacques Levy before the tour started. Dylan had commented on the musical *The Fantasticks*. "It's been running for 10 years off-Broadway, man," Dylan said, "how come they won't let us do that?" In actual fact, by 1975, *The Fantasticks* had been running for 15 years. The musical featured Jerry Orbach whom Dylan had recently been introduced to by Jacques Levy. Orbach was a friend of mobster Joey Gallo, which is how Bob first learned about Joey's life and death.

While having a meal, Dylan insisted to Joan Baez that he wanted to keep the tour going and begged her to help him. He said they should be blood brother and sister and took out his pocket knife. Baez asked a waiter for a clean steak knife and dunked it into whisky. She then made a small scratch on both their wrists, "just deep enough to draw blood, and we stuck our wrists together." In truth, by the end of the 1976 leg, the Revue had run its course. For all sorts of reasons the enjoyment that Bob had found in touring again in '75 had begun to dissipate. Nonetheless, in an extremely potent version of 'Knockin' on Heaven's Door,' as performed on the Revue tour, Bob sings: "Mama, wipe the blood off of my face/ I can't see through it anymore/ I need someone to talk to in a new hiding place/ Feel like I'm looking at heaven's door".

"The Rolling Thunder Revue, so joyful and electrifying in its first performances, had just plain run out of steam," wrote music critic Janet Maslin for *Rolling Stone*. Regardless, as the lyrics to 'Knockin' on Heaven's Door' state, Bob needed "someone to talk to in a new hiding place" and for now that hiding place was on the road.

Arthur Rosato: "I don't think I said two words to [Bob] on the whole second tour, in '76 ... That tour was very strange! That tour was more like an obligation rather than something he wanted to do at that time. It became like a fad thing. You know, now everybody wants one. He wasn't too keen on assembly line anything. I don't think he even wanted to call that [second] tour Rolling Thunder ... He did the first one for his own reasons. The second one was like the Hollywood version of a sequel. People were looking for the big payoff ... That's just my speculation."[14]

Joel Bernstein: "'76 seemed to me to be done in the shadow of the previous tour. I mean it wasn't new for a start, and Bob's rapport with the players was gone. I mean at rehearsals he wasn't talking to anybody."[15]

Like most of the rest of the troupe, Scarlet Rivera felt the change. "Something had definitely changed in 1976," Rivera told *Record Collector*. "Bob was personally going through a lot. He eventually realised he was going to go through a divorce, and that might have coloured it." Rob Stoner agreed. "The train only goes as fast as the locomotive, and the locomotive was definitely dragging. The sound had changed. It became less folk and more of a rock show." It seems with the second leg of Rolling Thunder Dylan and the troupe were trying to recreate something that simply couldn't be duplicated. The revue had been founded on spontaneity but by the second tour that spontaneity had gone.

Not only was enthusiasm for the tour waning amongst the musicians but tickets sales were also sporadic. The fall tour of '75, which played the north-eastern seaboard including Canada, had been really well accepted but the spring '76 shows in the American south and southwest were much less so, most notably in early May when the tour rolled into Texas. The May 6 show scheduled for Lake Charles, Louisiana, 30 miles from the Texas state line, was cancelled due to poor ticket sales while the next show, May 8 at Houston's 11,000-seat Hofheinz Pavilion, failed to sell-out despite the late addition of Willie Nelson to the bill. A second night intended for that same venue was scrapped altogether. These disappointments were followed by the May 11 concert in San Antonio having to be moved from the Hemisfair Arena to the smaller Municipal Auditorium, again due to poor tickets sales. May 12 should have seen afternoon and evening shows in Austin, TX but the afternoon concert had to be called off. May 15 in Dallas was yet another casualty of poor tickets sales and that date became a free concert at the Gatesville State School for Boys, a juvenile corrections facility in Gatesville, Texas. It appears that interest in the Revue was so poor in Texas that the audience had to be locked in! The final show, May 25, Salt Palace in Salt Lake City, played to a half-empty 17,000-seat arena. The tour had become emotionally exhausting for Dylan who pushed both his performance art and his private life to the absolute limit and then some. Except for the November '76 "Last Waltz" farewell concert with The Band, Salt Lake City would be Dylan's last performance for 21 months. Any thoughts of playing concerts in Europe were now quickly banished from his mind.

Chapter Eight

All That False Instruction

With the Revue now behind him, Dylan returned to California to begin work editing *Renaldo & Clara*. This was a long and difficult task but time spent with Howard Alk in the editing suite was time away from his problems with Sara. The Dylans moved fully into their new Malibu house in January 1977 but by the end of February Sara had moved out! On the morning of February 13, Sara told her lawyer, Marvin Mitchelson, that she came down to breakfast to find Bob, the children and a woman by the name of Malka Marom sitting around the breakfast table. The reason for Marom's presence in the Dylan home at that hour in the morning is far from clear but a violent argument is said to have erupted between Bob and Sara during which Bob allegedly struck Sara on the face and told her to leave.

A Canadian acquaintance of Leonard Cohen and Joni Mitchell, Malka Marom had been introduced to Dylan by Mitchell in December 1975 when the Revue made a two-night stop at Toronto's Maple Leaf Gardens. According to Marom, she wasn't interested in meeting Dylan and only did so at Mitchell's unrelenting insistence. Mitchell introduced Marom to Dylan with the words, "Bobby, I want to introduce you to the only person I know who doesn't want to meet you."[1] She would probably live to regret the introduction because when Sara filed for divorce on March 1, 1977, Marom unwittingly became a key person in the divorce statement. Nevertheless, Marom wasn't the new woman in Dylan's life [she] 'just happened to be there, that's all.' Clinton Heylin makes an

insightful observation about the situation in his Dylan biography
Behind the Shades: "It was classic Dylan behaviour: rather than
simply ask his wife to leave (or leave himself), he preferred to allow
an intolerable situation to develop, forcing the other party to show
their hand first."

The Fortune-Telling Ladies

The next woman in Bob's life was one Faridi McFree. Shortly after
the Dylans had split, McFree was introduced to Sara Dylan by a
mutual friend, Rosanna Taplin – wife of road manager Jonathan
– with a view to her helping Sara with the children, and to do "Art
Healing" with them. Sara and Faridi were quite alike, they shared
a common interest in psychic energy and all things "New Age"
and McFree, who at the time was meditating under a six-foot
copper pyramid – sometimes for as long as 16 hours a day – was
immediately hired. Faridi spent part of each week in the carriage
house on Sara's rented property at the Malibu Colony. Sara had
moved to the Colony, located a half mile west of the Malibu Pier,
after she and Bob had split. Believing that she was being treated
more like a housemaid than an art teacher, McFree's relationship
with Sara soon deteriorated and she decided to leave her
employment. Before she left, however, McFree agreed to look after
the house while Sara took the children on vacation to Hawaii.[2]

At this point McFree barely knew Bob Dylan; they had met in
1974 when they both attended the wedding of McFree's next-door
neighbours, Rosanna and Jonathan Taplin. Nevertheless, on June
30, 1977, directly after his divorce from Sara was finalised, McFree
rang Dylan on what she described as the "forbidden number." A
neighbour had read about the divorce in the local newspaper and
had brought the paper round to McFree's house. "Last night, Bob
had gone to court in Santa Monica and got the divorce. It was a
short news release in the middle pages of the Santa Monica News,"

Faridi said. "I doubted whether anyone noticed the article, it was so hidden ... [but it was true], Bob had beaten Sara to the punch! He got the divorce!"[3]

As one might expect, Bob seemed upset but was appreciative that Faridi had bothered to ring him; he told her that none of his friends had called. He invited her over and Faridi said she reluctantly agreed. She had been having strange dreams and feelings of "danger and foreboding" all of the previous week. She nevertheless jumped into the old Ford station wagon that Sara had given her as part of their financial arrangements and drove to the "monster castle." "The castle," Faridi said: "could be perceived as unusual because of the lack of originality of the surrounding houses." Faridi liked the monster castle. "It was big – very big and well designed" and the architecture evoked her imagination as she flashed on fairy tales she had read as a child where prince charming had rescued the princess who was being held prisoner. The guards at the entrance had been given orders to let Faridi pass through the front gates. The guards seemed scary that night but she didn't know why. After all, she had driven through those gates many times with the children when they visited their father.

"For the next three hours, Bob never stopped talking," Faridi said. "It was non-stop ... disappointments, sorrows, and torment he had endured throughout the years ... He sure did need to release a lot of the excess baggage he'd been carrying around for a very long, long time."[4]

Faridi spent the night with Dylan and fell hopelessly in love with him. She would remain in love with him for the rest of her life. "The very first time I met Bob there was a spark, a connection and I'd never forgotten it so when I read that piece [in the paper] I just knew I had to try and help him ... Bob needed someone around him. Someone he could share his thoughts and emotions with." Dylan told McFree that the main problem with his marriage was that, "Sara couldn't handle his fame," and that she, "hated being in the spotlight."[5]

Sara had not only been a wife and mother, but according to those close to him, she was also Bob's astrologer and psychic guide. Al Aronowitz has said that Bob depended greatly on Sara's advice, advice that often came through the cards. It is perhaps not surprising therefore that soon after Bob and Sara split he began consulting with prominent L.A. psychic Tamara Rand. Bob had already been taking advice from Rand for some months before Faridi entered his life. On one occasion, when Rand visited Bob at his Point Dume home, he introduced her to McFree, who also had psychic abilities. Faridi felt that Rand's gift was not that accurate (Rand predicted that Bob would win custody of the children). At the time, Bob said that Tamara's predictions were "very positive" and it's possible that he continued consulting with her simply because she was telling him what he wanted to hear. That was certainly Faridi's belief at the time and 30 years later her view remained unchanged.

"Bob had been very dependent on Sara for a lot of things," McFree told me. "He was very interested in psychic astrology and had been guided by Sara in this. Bob is the archetypical Gemini. Gemini is ruled by the planet Mercury, which in mythology is the winged messenger of the gods. Of course, that is where the name *Planet Waves* had come from. The main thing with Gemini's though is the duality of the twin self. There is also a keen nervous awareness. He was certainly spontaneous, which is another Gemini trait. But on the other hand, he was also very careful and would take advice from Sara.

Gemini's have vast amounts of mental energy that must be expressed and Bob did this through his music, so when he wasn't doing music, there was a conflict. Sara wanted a 'normal' life and one half of Bob wanted that too but the other half of his Gemini self would keep pulling him back to that intellectual creativity. The trick was to try and do both but that was an extremely hard balancing act.

To have the love of a Gemini can be a hugely joyful experience but only if they don't become restless. Bob had held his creativity back for quite some time in Woodstock, he got into painting and stuff, but that was just a pastime, it wasn't a substitute for his music and never could be so inevitably he became restless. Also, because Bob was so famous, there was massive added pressure. Even if he could manage to split his 'self' between his music and his family, the time he had with his family was often intruded upon by his fans and the media. Sara couldn't cope with this. He would withdraw from the world and was also very guarded, even from those he knew well.

Later, I created the character of 'Zimmie the Zipper' for Bob because he was in his own bubble, "zipped up" from the outside world. He was a lost soul and needed guidance, but in my opinion, Tamara was not the right person to turn to for help."[6]

Although she is not mentioned in any of the Dylan biographies, the name Tamara Rand did crop up in a November 1977 interview with Ron Rosenbaum. Rand's association with Bob Dylan was also reported in the British "red top," the *Daily Mirror*. This is what Ron Rosenbaum had to say about Rand in the introduction to his original *Playboy* magazine interview; a preamble cut from the reprints of this piece.

Rosenbaum: "Late one afternoon, Dylan began telling me about Tamara Rand, an L.A. psychic reader he'd been seeing, because 'when the world falls on your head,' he said, 'you need someone who can tell you how to crawl out, which way to take' ... Dylan seemed concerned that I understand that Tamara was no con artist, that she had genuine psychic abilities."

Dylan: "There's this lady in L.A. I respect a lot who reads palms. Her name's Tamara Rand. She's for real; she's not a gypsy fortune-teller. But she's accurate! She'll take a look at your hand and tell you things you feel but don't really understand about where you're heading, what the future looks like. She's a surprisingly hopeful person."

According to the *Mirror* newspaper: "Many top stars go to the beautiful Tamara for around £75 an hour." In the same piece, Rand is quoted as saying: "I have a kind of doctor-patient relationship with Dylan," and that, "Bob sees me as a solid, stable person with solid values of right and wrong ... I hear things when I touch his hand. He has the hand of an inventor, but his vehicle is words. He is a graphic artist with words. He has the hands of a healer, so his words – his message – are healing in spirit."

Rand said that Dylan would marry again, "but not yet." She also said that Bob, "will be with us for a very long time." The *Mirror* stated that Dylan kept in constant contact with Rand by phone, "If he's out of town or abroad," and that, "he consulted her before he signed his contract to appear at Earls Court [1978]." Dylan is quoted as saying, "You need someone who can tell you which way to take."

It's not entirely clear when Dylan started consulting with Rand but a comment she made to the *Mirror* in the June 1978 interview indicated that she had met him, "just over a year ago." This dating would, therefore, coincide with his split from Sara, something that was confirmed to me by Faridi McFree. Robert Shelton, who knew Bob and Sara in the mid-Sixties, wrote that Sara, "had a Romany spirit, seeming to be wise beyond her years, knowledgeable about magic, folklore and traditional wisdom."

Aronowitz: "In the years following his motorcycle accident ... More and more, he depended on [Sara's] advice as if she were his astrologer, his oracle, his seer, psychic guide. He would rely on her to tell him the best hour and the best day to travel."[7] In 1978, Dylan told Jonathan Cott: "I meet witchy women. Somehow I attract them. I wish they'd leave me alone."

Dylan's fascination with fortune-telling goes as far back as the early Sixties: "Well, I've spent my time with the fortune-telling kind," Dylan wrote in 1963. While performing in the clubs around Greenwich Village he would also sing the traditional song 'West

Texas' that contained the lines: "Get me a fortune-telling woman/ One that's gonna read my mind." A couple of years later Dylan found his "fortune-telling woman" in the shape of Sara Lownds and there is little doubt that she reinforced a belief that Bob already loosely held about the cards and palmistry. Dylan would later use playing card imagery, in the form of an incomplete deck of cards, to illustrate that Sara, like everyone, had some imperfections: "With your sheets like metal and your belt like lace/ And your deck of cards missing the jack and the ace."[8]

When Dylan performed 'Ramblin' Gamblin' Willie' for Cynthia Gooding in early spring 1962, he said: "I can't read cards. I really believe in palm reading, but for a bunch of personal things ... personal experiences. I don't believe too much in the cards. I like to think I don't believe too much in the cards, anyhow."[9]

Rand portrayed an air of respectability through the Rand Institute which operated from high-class offices on Cienega Boulevard in Los Angeles. Her reputation nevertheless took a severe bashing when she was persuaded to make a fake prediction on US television. On January 6, 1981, on *The Dick Maurice Show*, Tamara Rand predicted that a fair-haired young man with the initials "JH" would shoot President Reagan sometime in late March. Her incredible powers to see into the future were apparently confirmed when John Hinckley attempted to assassinate President Reagan in Washington, D.C. on March 30, 1981. NBC, ABC and CNN all replayed the footage that showed her making the prediction and Rand soon began appearing on TV shows across the United States. However, when sceptical AP reporter Paul Simon began to analyse the footage he was of the opinion that the segment showing the prediction might have been spliced into the tape. Simon confronted Dick Maurice with his suspicions and Maurice confessed that the prediction had indeed been a hoax. He admitted that the so-called "prediction" had been filmed on the day after Hinckley had shot Reagan. Rand insisted that she had predicted the assassination attempt but admitted that she taped a "dramatisation" of her prediction on March 31 at Dick Maurice's request. Rand then filed a $10 million slander suit against Maurice claiming that he had defamed her by his accusation that the prediction was a hoax. It didn't take a psychic to predict that her suit went nowhere.

During the second half of the Seventies, tarot card imagery came very much to the fore in Dylan's work and several examples are to be found on *Blood on the Tracks*. ("I knew it had to be that way/ It was written in the cards.") As previously mentioned, on the subsequent album, *Desire*, released in January 1976, The Empress tarot card is in evidence on the rear sleeve. The Empress is associated with Isis, and said to be the object of Desire.

During the Rolling Thunder tour, Dylan was photographed by Ken Regan posing with *Crystal Magick*, a book by Carlyle A. Pushong. Published in 1968, *Crystal Magick* was a follow up to Pushong's *The Tarot of the Magi*, a book that Sara would have certainly known about or more probably would have owned. Bob even took his own astrologer with him on the Rolling Thunder Tour. The most explicit use of tarot card imagery is to be found on two songs, 'Changing of the Guards' and 'No Time to Think,' from the 1978 *Street-Legal* album.

"Fortune calls/ I stepped forth from the shadows, to the marketplace," Dylan sings in the second stanza of 'Changing of the Guards.' The first explicit mention of the tarot comes with The Tower. The Tower is a card that reflects change and a sense of betrayal. It is likely that some people/situations that you have counted on in the past may no longer be there in quite the same way. Nevertheless, you must keep a positive attitude because new understandings and insights may come to you in the blink of an eye.

The next piece of tarot imagery in 'Changing of the Guards' is The Moon. This card shows a crayfish crawling from the abyss of water to the land, but the road ahead to the mountains is long.

This symbolises the early stages of consciousness unfolding. The following description of the meaning of The Moon card can be found in most tarot readings and it certainly describes Dylan's long hard road through the second half of the Seventies. "Oftentimes, the Moon appears in a reading when you are not sure of your destination … You may have lost your way and are now left to walk in the dark, guided only by your inner light and intuition. You need to go on without a clear picture of where you are, where you are going or where you have been."

The next tarot figure is The Sun. The naked children are usually portrayed with "long golden locks." Their innocence is renewed through discovery, bringing hope for the future. By the time we arrive at the seventh stanza Dylan is nearing the end of his journey (1978). The Sun is an image of optimism and fulfilment; the dawn that follows the dark moon. In the final stanza, Dylan sings: "Peace will come/ With tranquillity and splendour on the wheels of fire." Bert Cartwright suggests that this lyric echoes Daniel 7:9. However, the wheel could also represent the tarot card Wheel of Fortune ("the wheel's still in spin.") This card represents: karma, life cycles, destiny, and a turning point in one's life. In the closing lines to the song, "Cruel death surrenders with its pale ghost retreating/ Between the King and the Queen of Swords." The Death card is probably the most feared and misunderstood of all the cards in the tarot. In actual fact, the card can be one of the most productive and positive in the deck. According to Eden Gray, a key writer on the esoteric meanings of tarot cards, it is unlikely that this card represents a physical death. Instead, the card is the ultimate purifier. The bringer of abrupt change; all things are reborn fresh, new and pure. Typically, it implies the end of a relationship. Gray interprets this card as a change of thinking from an old way into a new way. *Street-Legal* represents a significant turning point and a clearing of the ways for Bob Dylan. His long search is nearing a conclusion.

And so to 'No Time to Think.' This song opens with: "In death, you face life with a child and a wife/ You sleep-walk through your dreams into walls." We have already discussed the Death card so I'll move on to the third stanza and The Empress. This card symbolises female dominance. Although The Empress attracts him (desire), he has to recoil from that attraction because of the oppression it now brings. "The empress attracts you but oppression distracts you/ And it makes you feel violent and strange." The two may not be connected, but in her statement to her lawyer, Sara said that Bob had been "violent" towards her and that he allegedly hit her, injuring her jaw, on the morning she found him with Malka Marom.

Five stanzas on, we run into The Magician. Depending on the card's placement in relation to other cards, the message is to tap into one's full potential rather than holding back, especially when there is a need for transformation and when there are choices and directions to take; a ceaseless search for meanings.

Dylan's deep interest in the tarot graphically illustrates how hard he was searching at this time for guidance in his life. Whether *Street-Legal* was influenced in any way by Dylan's dealings with Tamara Rand will probably never be known but it should be noted that Rand's "expertise" was in Palmistry and not the tarot, and in any event, Bob was attracted to the cards through Sara long before he met Rand.

McFree: "You must not overlook the fact that most women were obsequious and said anything to Bob to be on the good side of him. He always said to me, 'Faridi, when God made you, he threw away the mould' ... because I would tell him the truth, as I perceived it, and Bob wasn't used to such 'reality checks.'"[10]

"Bob's birth chart," McFree said: "made it very difficult for him to settle into family life. From 1967 to 1973, most of which he spent happily in Woodstock, Saturn, the planet of responsibility, was crossing his chart. That was good for his marriage, but it blocked many other things. It prevented him from performing."[11]

In January 1974, before embarking on "Tour 74," Dylan made mention in Newsweek that he had been off the road for quite some time because "Saturn has been an obstacle in my planetary system. It's been there for the last few ages," Dylan said: "and just removed itself from my system. I feel free and unburdened." When asked about this on January 12 by Ben Fong-Torres, Dylan replied: "I can't read anybody's chart, but the thing about Saturn is ... it's a big, heavy obstacle that comes into your chain of events, that fucks you up in a big way. Came into my chart a few years ago and just flew off again a couple of months ago." When asked who it was that told him about Saturn, Dylan replied: "Someone very dear to me, told me."

Detour over, we return to the summer of 1977:

After spending time with Bob at the Point Dume mansion, McFree accompanied him on a summer (July and August) retreat to his Crow River farm. Bob always enjoyed his visits to the farm and even with his recent personal turmoil the summer of 1977 was no exception. The Dylan children were with them and Bob's mother was also there and even though at times he was feeling down, the family had some idyllic moments together. The one huge low point came when Bob heard about the death of Elvis Presley on August 16. McFree was on hand to witness Bob's anguish. He locked himself away in his music studio and didn't speak for a couple of days. He told Faridi that if it wasn't for Elvis, he would never have started in music. In August 1987 Dylan reiterated: "When I first heard Elvis' voice I just knew that I wasn't going to work for anybody and nobody was gonna be my boss. Hearing him for the first time was like busting out of jail."[12] "It was so sad," Dylan told Robert Shelton in July 1978: "I had a breakdown! I broke down ... one of the very few times I went over my whole life. I went over my whole childhood. I didn't talk to anyone for a week after Elvis died. If it wasn't for Elvis and Hank Williams, I couldn't be doing what I do today."

By the time Bob and Faridi left the farm and returned to Point Dume he had written most (probably six) of the songs for *Street-Legal*. He had also decided that he wanted permanent custody of the children. There is little doubt that his decision to apply for custody had been partly fuelled by Sara's trip to Hawaii. He was alarmed that she might be intending to make a home for her and the children there. Following advice from his lawyers, at the court hearings Bob wore a suit, which he borrowed from the wardrobe department of a film studio. Sara's lawyer, Marvin Mitchelson, cited McFree as being the children's surrogate mother and accused her of being unfit to care for them. He obtained a court order demanding that the children be returned to Sara. However, due to the tight security at the Point Dume property, the process servers were unable to gain access and were therefore unable to serve the notice. In any event, Sara was eventually awarded custody after which she moved from her temporary home in the Malibu Colony to Beverly Hills. Bob was allowed to spend time with the children but he had to agree that McFree would have no contact with them. He signed a document agreeing to that and although she continued in his employment for a time, Faridi McFree disappeared from his personal life.

McFree: "In a healthy world, people will live their lives authentically and individually – not imitating others! One of the major obstacles I was to face once we left the farm was Bob's fame and money. It was disgusting to observe people who were obsequious – it made us both sick – especially the women. I began to realise that Sara had experienced a very difficult situation living with an icon. There was no trust – no loyalty. People forgot about integrity. They forgot who they were when they were in Bob's presence. Idolatry is spiritual unconsciousness and there were many spiritually lazy people surrounding Bob Dylan.

Without warning, Bob became suspicious of me. There were so many people buzzing in his ear – so much jealousy – and Marvin

Mitchelson was creating most of this chaos! It became difficult to relate to Bob. He was losing his balance. Too much was hitting my angel poet from all sides ... Mitchelson put him in an impossible situation. He made Bob choose between his children and me!"[13]

Marvin M. Mitchelson, the "chameleon with a law book," had made his name representing Lee Marvin's girlfriend in her groundbreaking palimony lawsuit (It was Mitchelson who coined the term 'palimony'). Under California State law, Sara was entitled to half the Dylan "community property" acquired during their marriage (November 22, 1965 – June 29, 1977). That included houses and land in five US states, cash, and most valuable of all, half of Bob Dylan's music rights; rights that spanned the albums from *Blonde on Blonde* to *Desire*. Mitchelson: "Those musical rights were enormous. That was the real value."[14]

Mitchelson's biggest task was to compile a list of the songs Dylan had written and recorded between 1965 and 1977. "It went on for pages and pages," Mitchelson said. "I became sort of a fan [because] I realised how good Bob was." Music rights boosted Dylan's notional wealth to approximately $60 million but because Bob wanted to keep the Point Dume mansion, real estate was traded against cash and Sara's share rose to $36 million. If Bob ever sold his music catalogue, Sara would be entitled to a further payout and all the time he retained ownership, she would share in the royalties. "They keep coming in, year after year," Mitchelson said: "We're talking about millions."[15]

During his time in Woodstock, Dylan had become a staunch family man and there is little doubt that separation from Sara and the children meant far more to him than money. A visibly shaken Dylan told Robert Shelton: "No one in my family gets divorced," and that he "figured it would last forever."[16]

Before the divorce settlement was finalised, and unable to take any more pressure, Faridi McFree left for New York City. McFree: "While I was in NYC, the heat of the custody trial in Los Angeles became very intense. There were many telephone calls between [Bob and me]. He described his torment between heaven and hell – the anguish over his deep love for me and the legal document that Mitchelson wanted him to sign ... never to see me again ... Bob had insisted I stay at his townhouse on MacDougal Street in Greenwich Village, which was an extraordinary experience itself. The energies of the environment ... I had no idea that Dylan had a reincarnational connection with the tortured poet, Rimbaud..."[17]

With the divorce finalised and work on *Renaldo & Clara* completed, Dylan's thoughts again turned to escaping onto the road. In December 1977 he told Jonathan Cott: "I have to get back to playing music because unless I do, I don't really feel alive. I have to play in front of the people in order just to keep going."[18]

Sometime around September 1977 Dylan had taken out a five-year lease on 2219 Main Street, Santa Monica. The rather dilapidated three-story building, which Bob jokingly christened Rundown Studio, was converted into a rehearsal space, offices for his touring company, a pool room and an 'apartment' for Dylan. Bob had an extensive tour in mind and wanted the rehearsal studio up and running by Christmas. Arthur Rosato and Joel Bernstein were brought in to help transform the space into something workable and on Boxing Day 1977 Dylan, Steven Soles and Rob Stoner, ran through 13 songs, half-a-dozen of which would be worked up for Dylan's next album, *Street-Legal*.

A New Day at Dawn

Bob Dylan's public face had been well hidden during 1977 but in stark contrast in 1978 we would see a high profile Dylan. On January 25, *Renaldo & Clara* was released to poor reviews and, after opening in New York City and Los Angeles, the film's initial limited theatrical run was terminated after just a few short weeks. A hectic

1978 would also see a huge world tour, for which rehearsals began in early January, and a brand new studio album.

In 1978 Dylan said that it took a week to make *Street-Legal* and that they mixed it the following week and it was released the week after that. Bob went on to say that if they hadn't done it that fast the album wouldn't have been made at all because they were ready to go back on the road. In actual fact, *Street-Legal* was recorded over five sessions between April 25 and May 1, during a break in Dylan's 1978 world tour. The break in touring was, however, two full months so Dylan's assertion that they only had a couple of weeks to make the album is a little heavy on poetic licence. *Street-Legal* was released June 15, which by any standards is a speedy turnaround but again Dylan was exaggerating when he said it was put out the week after mixing. In any event, with time tight Bob decided to record the album via a 24-track mobile truck parked outside of Rundown. Cables would be run through a studio window and down to the truck. Dylan would later recall that he didn't want to record this way but that he couldn't find the right producer. The thought was that they might achieve a live sound. Ultimately, however, the sound quality of *Street-Legal* would come in for stiff criticism.

Unlike many artists, including Dylan contemporary Neil Young, Bob strives for the feel of the music rather than necessarily the sound quality. Dylan's soundman, who is credited with being "Second in Command" during the *Street-Legal* sessions, told me: "Bob knows that most people will be listening to his music on their car radios, boom boxes and [cheap] turntables. Most people don't have $10,000 home systems. Bob wanted to make sure it sounded good the most common way. If all the sound in the world came through a transistor radio, [Bob] would be happy" Rosato said. "So what he had us do was disconnect some of the speakers in the floor monitors and replace them with four-inch speakers! So you have this little radio sound coming out and that was his monitor.

In your own home, it would sound fine, but when you're on stage with all these amps you just hear hisssss ... He'd have us tearing these thousand dollar speakers apart and have us put these little $2 Radio Shack speakers in there! He would do that too at recording, especially in Santa Monica, at Rundown. That wasn't the official name for the place. That was another Bob thing, calling it Rundown Studio. He just threw that out one day and next it became the official thing ... It was another Bobism. We would record something and put it on cassette, and he would go sit out in his car and listen to it and then say, 'Okay, yeah, that's a take.' Or he would listen to it in the pool room [at Rundown], there was a tiny little boombox and he'd listen on that. That's the way we did it. We'd never listen to it on playback through the studio speakers." According to Rosato, the title *Street-Legal* has no deep or special meaning. "Bob asked me what street legal meant," Rosato said. "He had heard the word somewhere but he didn't know exactly what it meant. So I explained to him that it was about cars and that sort of thing and he was happy with that. He just liked the expression."[19]

One of his most revealing albums, *Street-Legal* brought down the curtain on Dylan's majestic Seventies while also "Closin' the book/ On the pages and the text" of yet another challenging chapter in his life. Probably because of the poor sound quality and production, plus coming hot on the heels of a pair of exquisite albums – *Blood on the Tracks* and *Desire* – *Street-Legal* well and truly fell between the cracks. With its big band, including sax, trumpet and female backing singers, the album, a serious musical departure for Dylan, could be described as his Marmite album. Personally, I hate Marmite, but I love *Street-Legal*. In November 1977, Dylan told Ron Rosenbaum: "I have new songs now that are unlike anything I've ever written ... I mean, unlike anything I've ever done. You couldn't even say that *Blood on the Tracks* or *Desire* led up to this stuff ... It's that far gone, it's that far out there."[20]

Street-Legal was the first in a long line of records that would fail to realise their potential in the studio either due to unfortunate song selections or poor or unsuitable production. One of the most startling things about *Street-Legal* is the marked difference in reception between audiences and critics in the US and those in the UK. The album, which stalled at number 11 on the *US Billboard chart* – his first studio album not to make the US Top 10 since 1964 – became Dylan's best selling album across the pond in the land of the right-hand drive, reaching number 2 on the chart and achieving platinum status.

Writing for *Rolling Stone*, Greil Marcus, who appears to be incapable of constructing a balanced review of Dylan's work, criticised the singing on *Street-Legal* as, "simply impossible to pay attention to for more than a couple of minutes at a time." According to Marcus, the performances are "wretched" and "most of the stuff" is "dead air, or close to it." "There have been bad Dylan albums before..." Marcus continued: "but *Self Portrait* had 'Copper Kettle,' 'New Morning,' 'Sign on the Window' and 'Went to See the Gypsy,' *Planet Waves* 'Wedding Song' and *Desire* 'Sara.' The collapse of Dylan's timing ensures that there are no such odd gems on *Street-Legal*." If we are to believe Marcus, then *Self Portrait, New Morning, Planet Waves, Desire* and *Street-Legal* contain just five gems between them! Even by the standards of the holy Greil, that is plain ridiculous!

Nonetheless, in his quest for yet more worthless foam from the mouth, the *Rolling Stone* critic delivered perhaps the biggest insult of all. According to Marcus, although 'Señor (Tales of Yankee Power)' is, "the most musically striking number" on the album, he felt it was, "really just a pastiche of the best moments of the Eagles' 'Hotel California.'" When Jonathan Cott interviewed Dylan in November 1978, Bob was quick to mention Marcus' *Rolling Stone* review. "They had the nerve to run the reviews they did on *Street-Legal*," Dylan told Cott: "why should I give them an interview anyway?."

It is vital to view *Street-Legal* in the context of the blues tradition, something that Marcus seemed oblivious to. 'Is Your Love in Vain?' is accused of not being politically correct because it asks questions of the woman in the song like, "Can you cook and sew/ Make flowers grow?." In one of his many nonsensical assertions, Marcus claimed that Dylan was "speak[ing] to the woman like a sultan checking out a promising servant girl for VD." Although entirely over the top with his smart-ass language, Marcus was not alone in his way off the mark allegations of sexism. Scratch beneath the surface of the song and you will reveal a universal blues that is inspired by Robert Johnson and his sad, romantic 1937 recording, 'Love in Vain.'

By the time of *Street-Legal,* Robert Johnson had long been one of Dylan's key inspirations. Dylan's first published book of lyrics is dedicated to the legendary bluesman and his influence is apparent in songs across Dylan's canon. Nonetheless, nowhere is this influence more in evidence than on *Street-Legal*. The album is drenched with the dark foreboding and soulfulness of Johnson's work and at least four of the songs borrow his lyrics; one, mentioned above, even borrows a title.

"All my love's in vain" ('Love in Vain') – "Will you let me be myself/ Or is your love in vain?" ('Is Your Love In Vain').

"Blues is an achin' old heart disease/ It's like consumption, baby, killing me by degrees" ('Preaching the Blues') – "Horseplay and disease is killing me by degrees' ('Where are You Tonight?').

"You can squeeze my lemon 'til the juice runs down my leg" ('Traveling Riverside Blues') – "I bit into the root of forbidden fruit, with the juice running down my leg" ('Where are You Tonight?').

"It's the last fair deal gone down" ('Last Fair Deal Gone Down') – "Merchants and thieves, hungry for power/ My last deal gone down" ('Changing of the Guards').

Even Dylan's first single from *Street-Legal,* 'Baby, Stop Crying,' clearly borrows from Johnson's 'Stop Breakin' Down Blues.'

In 1995, Dylan told John Dolan of the *Ft Lauderdale Sun-Sentinel*: "Robert Johnson only made one record. His body of work was just one record. Yet there's no praise or esteem high enough for the body of work he represents. He's influenced hundreds of artists. There are people who put out 40 or 50 records and don't do what he did."

In *Chronicles*, Dylan wrote: "When Johnson started singing, he seemed like a guy who could have sprung from the head of Zeus in full armour. I immediately differentiated between him and anyone else I had ever heard. The songs weren't customary blues songs. They were perfect pieces ... They were so utterly fluid ... The songs were layered with a startling economy of lines ... I fixated on every song and wondered how Johnson did it ... Johnson's words made my nerves quiver like piano wires. They were so elemental in meaning and feeling ... There's no guarantee that any of his lines... happened, were said, or even imagined ... Also, all the songs had some weird personal resonance." Dylan's exaltation for Johnson continues for a full eight pages.

Never before or since has anyone succeeded in conveying the hardships of this world like Robert Johnson. Born in Mississippi – a dirt-poor, African-American – Johnson, who grew up around Robinsonville (at the top of the Delta), was uniquely able to take personal experiences and give them a universal relevance. For many people, the intensity of his music changed the way the world looked. Eric Clapton has said: "I have never found anything more deeply soulful than Robert Johnson." He also said that Johnson is the most important blues singer that ever lived.

His cursed adult life began in April 1930 when his 15-year-old wife, Virginia Travis, died during childbirth. Virginia's surviving relatives told blues researcher Robert McCormick that her death was divine punishment for Robert's decision to sing secular songs, known as "selling your soul to the Devil." Any notion that he had been punished for performing secular music was confirmed to Johnson when just 18 months later history repeated itself when his second wife, Caletta Craft, also died during childbirth. Johnson himself accepted this fate and chose to abandon a settled life to become a full-time nomadic musician.

Like many bluesmen of his day, Johnson became an itinerant "walking" performer, playing whenever and wherever he could. He plied his craft on street corners, in jook joints, and at Saturday night dances. As Dylan suggests, if it were not true, it would be implausible to believe that Johnson's status as perhaps the greatest bluesman ever is based on just 29 songs written and recorded in Dallas and San Antonio from 1936 to 1937.

Bluesman Son House, a contemporary of Johnson, tells of how young Robert would hang around in the hope of learning from him. According to House, Johnson was a decent enough harp player, but his ability as a guitarist left much to be desired. That all changed when Johnson disappeared for what was said by some to be a "few weeks" and returned having somehow miraculously acquired an unbelievable guitar technique and mastery of the blues.

Part of the enduring mythology surrounding Johnson is the Faustian tale of how he gained his extraordinary musical talent. Legend has it that Johnson took his guitar to the crossroads of Highways 49 and 61 in Clarksdale, Mississippi, where he was met by a large black man (the devil) who took the guitar and tuned it. The devil then returned the guitar to Johnson who now had complete mastery of the instrument. The price the devil required for bestowing Johnson with this formidable talent was nothing less than his soul. Those who doubt the legitimacy of the devil tale will have to settle for the more mundane story that his tutor was mortal. Originally a farmer from Alabama, Isaiah 'Ike' Zimmerman was a few years older than Johnson. He had a rare gift for the guitar and an even greater gift for teaching. It seems when Johnson disappeared it wasn't for a few weeks but for a year; a year spent living with Ike Zimmerman and his family.

Bargain with the devil or not, the death of both his wives seemed to have convinced Johnson that he was indeed cursed and a number of his songs support the notion of a hell-bound man troubled by emotional demons ('Hellhound on My Trail,' 'Preaching Blues (Up Jumped the Devil)' and 'If I Had Possession over Judgment Day'). In 'Me and the Devil Blues' Robert sings: "Early this morning, ooh/ When you knocked upon my door/ And I said 'hello Satan I believe it's time to go.' It is interesting that the original lyrics to Dylan's 'New Pony' contained the lyric, "It was early in the mornin' / I seen your shadow in the door/ Now, I don't have to ask nobody/ I know what you came here for." In the song 'Crossroads Blues,' Johnson isn't waiting at the junction for the devil but instead to ask the Lord for his salvation ("I went to the crossroad, fell down on my knees/ Asked the Lord above 'have mercy, now save poor Bob, if you please.'")

Sadly, Robert Johnson died at the cursed age of 27 in a jook joint on the Star of the West Plantation, just north-west of Greenwood, Mississippi from undetermined causes. The date was August 16, 1938. There are several differing accounts of Johnson's death, the most popular involving a woman, a jealous husband and a couple of bottles of poisoned whiskey. Bluesman Sonny Boy Williamson said he was there when the poisoning took place and that he warned Johnson, knocking the first bottle out of his hand, cautioning him to never drink from a bottle that he had not personally seen opened. Soon after, Johnson was offered a second bottle and accepted it. He is reported to have begun feeling ill soon after and had to be helped back to his room in the early hours of the morning. Over the next three days his condition gradually worsened and eyewitness reported that he died in a convulsive state of severe pain. Writer Robert McCormick claims to have found the man who murdered

Johnson and to have obtained a confession from him but he declined to reveal the man's identity.

In a 2004 *60 Minutes* interview for CBS Television Dylan talks about "destiny" and how "a long time ago" he made a "bargain" with the "chief commander on this earth and in a world we can't see." In a reversal of Johnson's supposed bargain with the devil story, Dylan seems to be saying that he made a similar bargain but that his was with God.

Street-Legal opens with the Johnson influenced seven-minute epic, 'Changing of the Guards.' This was likely the first song that Bob penned for his 17th studio album and the first line of the song: "Sixteen years/ Sixteen banners united over the field," sets the scene not only for that song but for rest of the album. With this lyric Dylan is alluding to how far he has travelled since his professional musical journey began 16 years before and that during this time he has made 16 albums. Fortune called Bob Dylan and he stepped from the shadows of ambiguity into the marketplace where he had to deal with merchants and thieves, hungry for power. Here "merchants" represent music business people, record execs and managers, the "suits," all hungry for power, while "thieves" are those who cover his songs. He will allude to these cover artists again in the fifth stanza with: "Renegade priests and treacherous young witches/ Were handing out the flowers that I'd given to you." In the penultimate stanza Dylan addresses those same record execs and managers with: "Gentlemen, he said/ I don't need your organization, I've shined your shoes/ I've moved your mountains and marked your cards/ But Eden is burning, either getting ready for elimination/ Or else your hearts must have the courage for the changing of the guards."

Street-Legal, like some of his previous work and most of his work to come, is typically shrouded in deliberate ambiguity and is a sea change from the direct narrative approach which dominated the

Desire album. This dark-sounding record is a painstaking description of the singer's long and arduous journey from the beginning of his career through his marriage and divorce and up to the thorny problems that he now has to battle with.*

According to Dylan, this song underwent a major rewrite before being recorded and in the 2004 publication of *Lyrics 1962-2001* we are privy to a couple of those changes. The penultimate stanza seemingly started out very differently. The verse is changed from a first to a third person narrative.

"Baby be still she said, can y spare me a moment's passion/ Can I shine yr shoes, print yr money or mark yr cards." So, where the released version has Dylan addressing "gentlemen," this earlier draft has a woman talking to a man (Sara talking to Bob?). The original song was turned on its head and the finished version is far more dramatic, apocalyptic even. But who is it that is facing these End Times? Mankind, Bob Dylan or the record company execs? The song appears to have undergone such a radical transition that Dylan himself is no longer sure what it all means. In an interview with Paul Zollo, Dylan was asked: "Your songs often bring us back to other times, and are filled with mythic, magical images. A song like 'Changing of the Guards' seems to take place centuries ago ... How do you connect with a song like that?" After quite a long pause, Dylan replied: "A song like that, there's no way of knowing, after the fact, unless somebody's there to take it down in chronological order, what the motivation was behind it..."21

In telling his story, both in this song and on much of the album, Dylan employs the 'Christ allegory' or 'Christ figure,' a literary technique that authors use to draw allusions between their characters, in this case Dylan, and the biblical Jesus. The Christ association – "Betrayed by a kiss," "Pieces of change," "Starlight

* *The tarot laden images in this song are covered earlier in this chapter.*

in the East" – is in evidence throughout *Street-Legal*. The 'Christ figure' technique had of course been very obvious in 'Shelter from the Storm' where he sang, "Took my crown of thorns" and "In a little hilltop village, they gambled for my clothes." 'Changing of the Guards' closes with Eden burning and a warning to get ready for "elimination," "Or else your hearts must have the courage for the changing of the guards." This end of the world scenario appears again in 'Señor' ("Can you tell me where we're headin'?/ Lincoln County Road or Armageddon?"). This eschatological approach – the science of last things (end times) a part of theology concerned with death, judgment, and the final destiny – will become prevalent in Dylan's work following *Street-Legal*.

In 'New Pony,' a song suggested to have been inspired by Dylan's infatuation with backing singer Helena Springs, he sings: "Come over here pony/ I wanna climb up one time on you." This imagery, which leaves little to the imagination, has been seen, perhaps understandably, as contemptuous. But this is a blues; a straight blues – nothing more, nothing less. Here, Dylan is employing a tradition that harks back to 1928 and the father of the Delta blues, Charley Patton. The song 'Pony Blues' was one of Patton's earliest compositions and his first released recording. In blues-speak, a pony is something fine, often a woman, and there have been many "pony" variants across the years. The song that Dylan mostly borrows from is the Son House version and he makes this borrowing manifestly clear by titling his song 'New Pony.' "New" being the operative word here. In his version, House, an early mentor of Robert Johnson, sings: "I say, the pony I'm ridin'/ He can fox-trot, he can lope and pace," while Dylan sings: "Well, I got a new pony/, She knows how to fox-trot, lope and pace."

Charley Patton's 'Pony Blues' contains the lyric: "I'm gonna find a rider, baby, in the world somewhere." This lyric, plain and simple, relates to Patton's search for a woman; his rider. In early 1978, Dylan formed a new music publishing company. The name of that company, Special Rider Music, was very much influenced by the blues.

Dark and menacing, 'No Time to Think' is one of the many complex highlights of the album. By any standard this is a major work and along with 'Changing of the Guards' and 'Where Are You Tonight?' the song, which at almost eight-and-a-half minutes is the longest on the record, forms the central core of this album of rebirth. In the opening line, Dylan sings of death ("In death, you face life..."). The song suggests a conflict between spirituality and materialism; one that will take a little time to resolve.

In the sixth stanza Dylan sings of "duality," and "Mercury rules you and destiny fools you..." This is the duality of Gemini, Dylan's birth sign, which as we have already established is ruled by the planet Mercury. With *Blonde on Blonde*, he even described his electric music as "that wild, Mercury sound." Dylan's concern with the push-pull of his Gemini self will feature again in 'Where Are You Tonight?' ("I fought with my twin, that enemy within/ 'Til both of us fell by the way").

My examination of Dylan's songs in this book is primarily designed to enhance an understanding of the lyrics and to aid with an appreciation of Dylan's mindset during this period. Nevertheless, I can't leave this song without mentioning the clever way he rhymes "one real" with "Camille" and "all virtue" with "the dirt you."

Many of the images on *Street-Legal* appear to be connected to his recent divorce and it is possible that 'Baby, Stop Crying' is addressed to Sara. In 1978, Dylan said of the song: "The man in that song has his hand out and is not afraid of getting it bit." Again, this song has some of its roots in Robert Johnson. Dylan is asking the woman in his song to "stop crying" while Johnson asks that she stops "breakin' down." Both songs certainly feature pistols ("She jumped up and throwed a pistol down on me," Johnson sings in 'Stop Breakin' Down Blues.'

Structured around a long string of questions, 'Señor (Tales Of Yankee Power)' is a powerful and evocative song that appears to bring Dylan a little closer to the end of his search. From the beginning of the song the narrator's hope of finding the woman in question ("do you know where she's hidin'?") is tempered with an increasing knowledge or fear that that particular quest is now all but lost. The question, "How long [are we gonna be ridin'?]" is reminiscent of the repeated, "How much longer?" chorus in 'New Pony.' It seems that Dylan has become inpatient– He still wants Sara back but if that goal is not attainable, then he wants to get on with his journey. He simply, "Can't stand the suspense anymore." How long must he keep his eyes glued to the door waiting for his wife and children to return? And even if she does return, will there be any comfort there?

He is desperate to know where he is going on this journey, "Lincoln County Road or Armageddon?" In an early version of the song (Rundown Studios rehearsal December 26, 1977), he sings "Portobello Road or Armageddon?." The fully realised version works much better and the use of Lincoln County Road brings to mind *Billy the Kid* and Dylan's experiences filming with Sam Peckinpah. Billy the Kid was very much associated with Lincoln County and was involved in the so-called Lincoln County War.

Although I don't know quite why, the line: "He took dead-centre aim but he missed just the same/ She was waiting, putting flowers on the shelf," brings to my mind an image of the social bandit Jesse James standing on a chair cleaning a dusty picture and being shot in the back of the head by the bounty seeking coward, Robert Ford. Dylan had sung: "Ain't gonna hang no picture/ Ain't gonna hang no picture frame/ Well I might look like Robert Ford/ But I feel just like Jesse James" in the 1965 song 'Outlaw Blues.'

The gypsy with the broken flag and flashing ring probably harks back to Dylan's visit to the gypsy festival two years earlier. The dream, or nightmare, that Dylan had become embroiled in had now become "the real thing." The significance of the "broken flag" lyric is something of a mystery to me. *Broken Flag* is a Mexican drama film and also a track on the Patti Smith Group album Wave, but these were released in June and May 1979 respectively. Whatever the meaning, and there may be none, it is possible that Dylan wasn't completely happy with the lyric because in a beautifully impassioned rendition from Portland, Oregon (December 3, 1980), which he dedicated to a young lady in the audience named Victoria, whom he met in Durango in 1972, it is the gypsy's "hand" that is broken and not the flag.

At the onset of the song the narrator doesn't know which way to turn but as the story develops he grasps the nettle and asks his companion, to whom he has been posing the questions: "Well, give me a minute, let me get it together/ I just gotta pick myself up off the floor/ I'm ready when you are, señor." It appears that after his long search for salvation he is now ready to walk the final mile. But who is this señor that he is currently travelling with? Is he simply a Mexican on a train, or is he the "chief commander?" In the final stanza, the narrator gives his reasoning for now accepting that he must make the journey. "This place don't make sense to me no more," he says before impatiently enquiring: "Can you tell me what we're waiting for, señor?" The preceding lyric: "Let's ... overturn these tables," is a clear illusion to Christ overturning the tables of the money changers in the temple (Matthew 21:12). Robert Shelton argues that this lyric could be a comment on "Yankee power" and a "rueful political statement" on "American foreign policy."

This song, possibly more than any other on the album, is a pretty good barometer of where Dylan was emotionally at this time. His search, like the train he's on, is beginning to pick up speed. The song's narrator wants to progress with his journey to salvation but the last thing he remembered before he stripped and kneeled was a trainload of fools bogged down in a magnetic field. This lyric brings to mind the Ship of Fools allegory about a ship, its dysfunctional crew and a captain who is a little deaf, has poor eyesight and whose knowledge of navigation leaves something to be desired. The Grateful Dead utilised the idea of a ship in a state of mutiny in the song 'Ship of Fools' released on their 1974 album *From the Mars Hotel*.

Interestingly, by the back-end of the 1978 tour, Dylan was introducing the song with one of his eccentric raps. This introduction, about an elderly Mexican, is very reminiscent of his 1966 introduction to 'Just like Tom Thumb's Blues.' In his Tom Thumb introduction, the Mexican, who is a regular traveller between North Mexico and Del Rio Texas, is, "about 125 years old but ... still going." In his 'Señor' rap, the Mexican is, "about 150 years old" and is travelling between Mexico and San Diego. The rap changes from show to show but always involves Dylan riding on a train. Initially, he only reveals that the experience happened on a train bound for Mexico, but later he puts flesh on the bones of the tale.

To begin with, the train is going from Monterrey to San Diego but in a later version the journey begins in Chihuahua. The story involves the ancient Mexican boarding the train and sitting across the aisle from Dylan. He is wearing only a blanket. "I felt this strange vibration," Dylan tells his audience, "so I turned to look at him ... Both his eyes were burning. There was smoke coming out of his nostrils. I immediately turned away, but I kept thinking that this is a man that I want to talk to. So I waited a little while longer and the train pulled out of the station. Then I turned to talk to him [but] he had disappeared." Before Dylan arrived at this fiery tale he had introduced the song with, "This song is inspired by a man named Harry Dean Stanton." Dylan and Dean Stanton had of course worked together in Durango but after becoming good friends, they had also undertaken a three-day road trip together from Guadalajara to Kansas City. It is significant that these raps began just a few days after an audience member threw a cross on stage during a show in San Diego (November 17, 1978). More about this down the line, but from the timing of these raps it seems Dylan believed that his train encounter was important and that señor brought a message of salvation. Of course, Dylan's lady in the song had, "a cross still hangin' down from around her neck."

A relatively straightforward song of regret, 'True Love Tends to Forget' deals with the common problem of taking a loved one for granted; the apathy trap ("I'm getting weary looking in my baby's eyes"). 'We Better Talk This Over' could be True Love Tends to Forget Part Two as this song tells much the same story of parting but the break up is a little further along ("This situation can only get rougher/ Why should we needlessly suffer?"). An original draft of this song has Dylan spilling his guts in plain sight ("We can work it out/ There is no doubt/ Without having to shout/ Notify yr advisor/ That yr not greedy & I'm not a misor"). This lyric and much more was lost before the song was recorded. Nevertheless, although the final version is much less intimate, you don't need to scratch the surface too deeply to discover the message. At the time that Dylan wrote this song, reconciliation was possible but extremely unlikely.

A long time in the making, 'Where Are You Tonight? (Journey Through Dark Heat)' is the third song in this closing trio of break up songs. By this stage, however, the couple have well and truly parted ("There's a woman I long to touch and I miss her so much"). The song borrows two separate lyrics from Robert Johnson ('Preaching the Blues' and Traveling Riverside Blues').

A physical and spiritual journey through dark heat, 'Where Are You Tonight? is an incredibly powerful song with a plethora of wonderfully vivid imagery. Dylan once said of 'A Hard Rain's a-Gonna Fall,' "Every line in it is actually the start of a whole song," and the same can be said of 'Where Are You Tonight?.' The opening image of a train ploughing through the pouring rain is wonderfully juxtapositioned with the tears on the letter he is writing. Dylan's thoughts then retreat to New York City and Elizabeth Street. Midway between The Bitter End and Gerdes Folk City, Elizabeth Street runs north-south parallel to the Bowery. The north end is at Bleecker, just a few short yards from Weberman's apartment, which is why he believes the song is about him. The opening verse continues, "And a lonesome bell tone in that valley of stone/ Where she bathed in a stream of pure heat." Anyone who has experienced the sweltering mid-summer heat in amongst the Manhattan tower blocks, "that valley of stone," won't need this lyric explaining.

As he had done with *Blood on the Tracks*, with the lyric "Blood on your saddle," with *Street-Legal* and 'Where Are You Tonight,' we get the lyric, "Her father would emphasize you got to be more than streetwise." In the final version her father was a full-blooded Cherokee but in an earlier version he was a prince.

Dylan plants plenty of clues as to the meaning of this song but as the piece progresses it becomes an extended mystical journey, a journey through dark heat which Dylan undertakes with "Marcel and St John." In all probability, the two people here are the French Christian existentialist philosopher Gabriel Marcel and St John the Evangelist, said by some to be the author of the fourth gospel. Dylan had previously mentioned St John the Evangelist in the unreleased 1975 song 'Abandoned Love.'

"There's a babe in the arms of a woman in a rage/ And a longtime golden-haired stripper onstage" certainly congers up an image of Sara. Although not a golden-haired stripper, in the early Sixties she was a Playboy bunny and a model and had appeared in Harper's Bazaar as the "lovely luscious Sara Lownds." A woman in a rage with a babe in her arms certainly rings true, as does, "Oh, if I could just find you tonight." This song was written shortly after the break up at the time Sara was in Hawaii with the children and Bob was unconvinced that she would return. Faridi McFree, who was with

Bob at Crow River farm when he was working on the songs that would become *Street-Legal*, certainly believed that the lyrics referred to that situation.

The entire album can be summed up with: "There's a new day at dawn and I've finally arrived/ If I'm there in the morning, baby, you'll know I've survived/ I can't believe it, I can't believe I'm alive/ But without you it just doesn't seem right/ Oh, where are you tonight?."

With this song, a part of Dylan's physical journey is complete, and although his spiritual journey was still hanging in the balance, he is nearing his salvation; even so, without Sara "it just doesn't seem right."

Chapter Nine

Almost Didn't Have a Friend In The World

Dylan had signed Jerry Weintraub as his business manager in late April 1977. He had been without proper management since his unofficial parting of the ways with Albert Grossman some seven years earlier. Dylan, who had long since decided that he would never again be part-owned by anyone, used Weintraub as his personal manager and concert promoter. Weintraub's sphere of activity therefore did not cover Dylan's music publishing companies; those affairs were handled by Dylan's own office, which he had set up during the summer of 1968. Naomi Saltzman (formerly of Trio Concerts, a Grossman-owned company) ran the office, which operated out of Manhattan. In early May 1977, Weintraub made an official statement to the effect that Bob Dylan had signed with his company for "personal legal representation." Dylan later said of his involvement with Weintraub, "At the time I got Jerry to manage me, I almost didn't have a friend in the world."

By the mid-Seventies, Weintraub, who had founded Management III in 1965 with two partners and just three clients, was well established both as a manager and also as a leading concert promoter. His landmark successes had been the staging of Elvis Presley's first arena tour, since which time his reputation had grown and led to the formation of Concerts West, a company that handled shows for such artists as Frank Sinatra, Judy Garland, Led Zeppelin, The Moody Blues, The Carpenters, Jimi Hendrix, the Beach Boys, one hit wonders Zager & Evans, and Neil Diamond, whom Weintraub also managed.

According to Robert Shelton, Weintraub, who once boasted that he worked the phones the way Jimmy Page worked the guitar, was known for non-interference with his clients and, whilst he was very much involved in the staging of Dylan's 1978 world tour, and even accompanied the troupe on the Japanese leg, he was becoming far more interested in producing movies and as his involvement with films grew, much of the day-to-day work at the management company was handled by ex-rock-station radio DJ Dick Curtis.[1]

Weintraub felt that Dylan needed to go in, "a different direction." He said that Bob had been to see Neil Diamond in concert (possibly in August 1976) and that some of Dylan's '78 stage show was based around what he had seen at that concert. Weintraub went on, "I think Bob felt that he was in danger of being stuck inside the Sixties."[2]

After the American press had tired of the "Alimony Tour" tag, they would dub Dylan's US '78 shows as the "Vegas Tour." Even *Rolling Stone* magazine, usually avid champions of Dylan's work, ran the headline "Dylan Going Vegas," and noted his debt to Neil Diamond. At the time, much of the responsibility for the change in Dylan's approach to touring was heaped at Weintraub's door, but are we to believe that Dylan's new management was the sole instigator of this change in style and direction? Writer Paul Williams said, "This idea – Bob Dylan marketing himself like a Las Vegas crooner, packaged music and showmanship for the mentally middle-aged – is so repellent to the average Dylan fan that the public backlash that resulted is not surprising."[3]

Many Bob fans may find it extremely difficult to accept the premise that Dylan's 1978 concert tour borrowed anything from Neil Diamond's live show. However, the first thing that doubters need to appreciate is just how big Neil Diamond was in the US at that time. During the 18 months from June 1976 to the end of '77 he had three hit albums: *Beautiful Noise*, which went gold on the week of its release and quickly gained platinum status; *Love at the Greek*, which went gold after just two weeks and qualified as platinum within six months, and *I'm Glad You're Here with Me Tonight*, which went gold on release and platinum within a month. Also in January 1978, Dylan's record label, Columbia, awarded Diamond a Crystal Globe for world sales in excess of five million albums.

Bob Spitz wrote: "They [Columbia] treated him [Diamond] like royalty, they even put up billboards [of Diamond] on Sunset Boulevard that Bob had to look at every time he drove out to see friends in the Hills ... He decided he should investigate." Dylan fans were also incensed over a supposed incident that happened between Diamond and Dylan backstage at The Band's lavish November 1976 Last Waltz concert. The story originated from the Dylan fan journal *The Telegraph* and was reprinted in Q magazine, issue 75, in December 1992.

Ron Wood: "At The Last Waltz, Neil Diamond, who's one of my pet hates – in fact, none of us could understand what he was doing there anyway – came off stage and Bob is just about to go on. And as he came off, Diamond said: 'you're really gonna have to go some to follow me, man, I was so great.' And Bob says, 'What do you want me to do, go on stage and fall asleep?'"

At the London film premiere of *The Last Waltz* when Neil Diamond came on screen people actually booed the film because of his supposed disrespect for Dylan. The story features across the Internet and in various books and magazines but according to Neil Diamond what really happened is somewhat different from the Ron Wood story. Diamond has spoken on two separate occasions about this but his comments have almost gone wholly unnoticed. He was first asked about The Last Waltz incident by *Rolling Stone* in 1988.

Diamond: "I had fun. [Got to] hang out backstage with people like Bob Dylan ... I did feel like the odd man out ... but I got to see Dylan perform for the first time there. Before Bob went out, I was kidding with him backstage. I said, 'You'd better watch because this is my audience and I'm gonna kick them in the ass!' Knowing, of course, that these people probably didn't have the vaguest idea who I was. He kind of looked at me. But he went out there and he really kicked ass."

Asked again in 2010 by *Rolling Stone* Diamond replied: "Well, something like that happened. Actually, it was before we both went on. He was tuning his guitar and I came over to him and I said: 'You know Bob, those are really my people out there.' He kind of looked at me quizzically. I said it as a joke, but I think it spurred him a little bit and he gave a hell of a performance."

In the 1988 *Rolling Stone* article, Diamond also refers to a recording of 'Sweet Caroline' that Dylan personally sent to him. This is mentioned again in 1992 when Neil Diamond appeared on American syndicated late-night talk show *The Arsenio Hall Show*. Neil Diamond: "Bob Dylan sent me a version of him singing 'Sweet Caroline' with his band ... which is like nothing you've ever heard before."*

On July 1, 1976, Diamond made his Las Vegas debut at the Aladdin Hotel. He was paid a hefty $650,000 ($2.80 million in 2019) for his five-night residency which opened the Aladdin's new $10 million Theater for the Performing Arts. At the time, this fee made many artists, probably even Dylan, sit up and take note.

By the time Dylan's 1978 tour went on the road, the comparison with Neil Diamond's shows had become quite startling. Dylan's big band set-up very much echoed the configuration of musicians that Diamond had used on his transitional album *Beautiful Noise*, which featured tenor sax and trumpet, keyboard, a separate percussionist and three female backing vocalists. Released in July 1976, the songs that made up *Beautiful Noise* fit together as a semi-autobiographical concept album of Diamond's rise to fame, and its personal cost, as well as a memoir of New York's Tin Pan Alley. The track 'Signs'

---

* *Bob Dylan recorded 'Sweet Caroline,' a song that Diamond later revealed was about JFK's daughter, Caroline Bouvier Kennedy, during rehearsals at Rundown Studios, 1980.*

is evidence of Diamond's interest in all things cosmic, while the album's central theme is best captured in a song titled 'Street Life.' A further possible connection is that *Beautiful Noise* and Diamond's 1977 live double album, *Love at the Greek,* were produced by Robbie Robertson who had recently taken up residence not too far from Dylan's home and who was a regular visitor there and no doubt discussed his new found friend with Dylan.

Dylan's use of Stanal Sound, the company that had supplied the sound system which Diamond was then using, also meant that Stan Miller and Patrick Stansfield, who had worked extensively with Diamond, would be involved with the Dylan tour. One of the best in his field, Stan Miller was the founder of Stanal and Patrick Stansfield was head of production. Another connection to Diamond would be that the same clothes designer was now dressing both men! Dylan and all of his tour musicians wore costumes that were designed for the '78 tour by Bill "Spoony" Whitten. Neil Diamond had been the first performer to discover Whitten back in 1974 after he had opened a custom shirt business called Workroom 27. Located on the second floor of a building on Santa Monica Boulevard in West Hollywood, the tiny shop was almost invisible, and until Diamond found it, Whitten had virtually no customers. Diamond immediately became an advocate of Whitten's designs, and he spread the word. While Dylan liked Whitten's clothes, some members of the band were less than happy with the stage-wear. Lead guitarist Billy Cross said: "The band looked like a large aggregation of pimps," while backup singer Debi Dye-Gibson said she and the other women: "looked like hookers."

Clearly, some of the above comparisons between Dylan and Diamond came about simply because both artists were, at the time, from the same management stable. Also, although many of the connections were much more than simple twists of fate, some of those working with Dylan at the time are less convinced.

Arthur Rosato: "A lot of people say [he was copying Diamond]. Maybe they want to give a label to something they can easily identify. At the time Bob was actually listening to a lot of Phil Spector. The sound of a Phil Spector production is something that is uniquely his. What I was hearing in the studio and [during the tour] rehearsals was maybe Bob's interpretation of the Phil Spector sound done live."[4]

It is often too easy to make connections that in reality aren't actually there. One such case is the bogus connection between the Dylan tour and Stanal Sound, which Arthur Rosato informed me was entirely his decision and had nothing whatsoever to do with Dylan. Arthur Rosato: "...I chose Neil [Diamond's] PA company [for Dylan] but I could have easily chosen Clare Brother's or any number of companies that I've worked with. I knew Neil's production manager and he said: 'If you want to check out his system come up to Seattle.' So I flew up with Neil and his band ... and I checked out the sound system. It was really nice. It was everything we needed for the venues that we were going to be playing. So I worked out how much it was going to cost. It comes down to bidding and quality and availability. It's called the process, but that was totally my decision. Bob had nothing to do with those sorts of things."[5]

Rob Stoner: "[Dylan] had in mind to do something like Elvis Presley, I think. The size of the band and the uniforms. [But] he wasn't very sure about it, which is why he opened way out of town. I mean, we didn't go any place close to Europe or England or America [for] forever, man ... and I don't blame him. I think he knew, subconsciously, he was making a big mistake."[6]

Interestingly, during extensive rehearsals for the 1978 tour, Dylan tried out 'Tomorrow is a Long Time,' playing it no fewer than 11 times on January 28 and also attempting it once each at the next two sets of rehearsals. Dylan said that he "treasured" Elvis' recording of the song and considering it hadn't been given a live outing at a Dylan show since 1963, one must assume that Elvis was likely occupying Bob's mind at this time.

So who was Dylan emulating, Elvis Presley, Neil Diamond, Phil Spector and was it as Rob Stoner believed, all "a big mistake"? Regardless, he seemed to be going against his own intuition because in a 1978 interview Dylan told Ron Rosenbaum: "If you try to be anyone but yourself, you will fail; if you are not true to your own heart, you will fail."[7]

Death Is Not the End

In 1980, Dylan's friend and neighbour Howard Alk told author Paul Williams that the one thing he had failed to explore in his book about Dylan's Christian conversion – *Dylan: What Happened?* – was a major probable factor in that conversion: an awareness of and fear of death.

The Seventies had been a harrowing time in rock/blues circles. During the first two years of the decade the world had lost Jimi Hendrix, Janis Joplin, Jim Morrison, Gene Vincent, Duane Allman, Mississippi Fred McDowell and Dylan's good friend Reverend Gary Davis, to name but a few. Soon to follow would be the Grateful Dead's Ron 'Pigpen' McKernan, Gram Parsons, Jim Croce, Bobby Darin, Arthur 'Big Boy' Crudup, Lightnin' Slim, Cass Elliot, Tim Buckley, Howlin' Wolf, another of Dylan's friends, Phil Ochs, and of course Elvis Presley. The list seems to go on forever and Dylan couldn't fail to be shocked by these deaths. In a 1980 interview Dylan told Paul Vitello: "I used to walk out on the street [after a concert] and look up in the sky and know there was something else ... A lot of people have died along the way–the Janises and the Jimis. People get cynical, or comfortable in their own minds, and that makes you die, too, but God has chosen to revive me."[8]

Street-Legal is choc full of death, be it physical, mental or spiritual. "If I'm there in the morning, baby, you'll know I've survived/ I can't believe it, I can't believe I'm alive," Dylan signs in 'Where Are You

Tonight?.' "In death, you face life," "cruel death," "death can disarm you" and "Armageddon" also turn up across the various songs on the album. Elvis' death, which had occurred shortly before Dylan began writing the songs for *Street-Legal*, was probably the catalyst. We know from Faridi McFree that Bob was very badly shaken by Presley's passing and that he had told Robert Shelton, "I had a breakdown!"

At this time Dylan was still charting a way forward but he was also taking stock of his past. Maybe sometimes you do have to look back. Although still extremely popular, it has to be recognised that by 1978, in the wake of a much-changed music scene, Dylan was becoming part of the old guard. His response was to look back to his musical heroes; chiefly Elvis Presley.

The Amnesia is Finished

Other than his appearance at the Isle of Wight festival, 1978 was the first time Dylan had played concerts outside of North America for 12 years. His arrival in London therefore prompted French journalist Philippe Adler to ask Dylan if his return to the stage meant that his, "journey through the wilderness had ended," Dylan replied, "Yes, I believe so. I'm back on the tracks." Adler continued, "We won't need to wait another 12 years to see you again?" To which Dylan replied, "No, no. The amnesia is finished."[9]

European audiences had been starved of Bob Dylan for so long there was never any doubting that his reception would be anything other than rapturous. In stark contrast to our American cousins, who had been graced with a Dylan tour in 1974 and regional shows in '75 and '76, British and European fans, plus the press, lapped up the 1978 shows while seats remained unsold for some of the fall/ winter US concerts.

The press of course needed to find a reason as to why Dylan should be undertaking a lengthy tour after such a long break and his recent high profile divorce provided them with the perfect answer and the tour was promptly dubbed "The Alimony Tour." "I've got a few debts to pay off," Dylan told the *Los Angeles Times* candidly: "I had a couple of bad years. I put a lot of money into the movie, built a big house ... and there's the divorce. It costs a lot to get divorced in California."*[10]

When asked by Philippe Adler if he was touring for the money, Dylan said: "No. Of course I need the money and I know how to spend it, but basically it's because I wanted to do the only thing I've ever known how to do, sing and play. I'm a musician that's all."[11]

Accordingly, after a 21-month break from touring, a great deal of preparation and rehearsal, not to mention a recent bout of flu, Bob Dylan flew into Tokyo on February 16 in a leased BAC-111 that had two suites, a bedroom for Dylan with a feature fireplace and a fully stocked bar. The musicians and their back-up, totalling 44 persons in all, travelled in style, stayed in the best hotels side-by-side with Dylan, and prior to arriving back in the United States for the final leg of the tour, no expense was spared. The personnel included an 18-man road crew that would be augmented by local help in the various locations along the way.

The initial proposal was for a tour of Japan, a country not played on the 1966 world tour. Once Japan was agreed, however, extending touring to Australia and New Zealand made perfect logistical sense. The promoter for these shows was AGC Paradine, a promotions company that had initially been put together in Australia in 1974 by Australian Pat Condon and two Englishmen, Robert Paterson and the well-known television host and media personality, David

---

* *Bob Dylan invested $1.25-million ($4.6-million as of 2019), of his own money into the movie,* Renaldo and Carla. *The Dylan house at Point Dume cost $2.25-million ($8.5-million as of 2019) to "remodel." Dylan's divorce settlement was $36-million ($138-million as of 2019). All figures quoted here, including inflation, are approximate.*

Frost (Paradine was Frost's middle name). The company had been responsible for bringing Neil Diamond to Australia and New Zealand in early '76 and Diamond had thanked the promoters in the trades for putting together a great and enjoyable tour.

While there is absolutely no doubt Dylan needed to recoup some of his recent losses, if the sole motive for the tour had been money, it could have been structured in a far more cost-effective manner! The 1978 world tour played in front of almost two million people and grossed in excess of $20-million (about half the amount that Dylan had recently spent or lost on his house, divorce and *Renaldo & Clara*), but the cost of putting this show on the road with such a large band travelling in style was enormous. The huge 114-date world tour would take Bob from Japan to Australia, New Zealand then on to seven concerts in Los Angeles, six in London, plus dates in northern Europe, including five shows in Paris, a big open-air event in Nuremberg, and of course the mammoth English Blackbushe festival. "I'm ready to have a regular band," Dylan told Cameron Crowe, "I want to be able to tour and record again with a group of musicians I know I'll work well with."[12]

When Robert Shelton commented in June that the band was "impressive," Dylan replied gloomily, "It's about the only thing I've got together now ... I started recruiting this band in January," Dylan said. "It was difficult, hard. A lot of blood has gone into this band. They understand my songs. It doesn't matter if they understand me, or not."[13]

The band that departed Los Angeles for Japan consisted of:

Bob Dylan – rhythm guitar, harmonica, vocals
Billy Cross – lead guitar
Ian Wallace – drums
Alan Pasqua – keyboards

Rob Stoner – bass, vocals
Steven Soles – acoustic rhythm guitar, vocals
David Mansfield – violin, mandolin, guitar, dobro
Steve Douglas – saxophone, flute, recorder
Bobbye Hall – Congas and assorted percussion

Helena Springs – vocals
Jo Ann Harris – vocals
Debi Dye – vocals

This band, eight players and three female backing singers, was, and still is, the biggest that Bob Dylan has ever put together. But not only was the band bigger, it also sounded very different from what had gone before. Selecting the musicians, however, was a long and arduous task. David Mansfield: "It wasn't at all like picking up where the Rolling Thunder tour left off. I remember I brought my steel guitar [to] rehearsals and every time I'd go to unpack it, Bob would go, 'We don't need that.' All of a sudden the instrument that I'd played all over the place in the previous band, he didn't wanna see it, let alone hear it."[14]

For the most part, the December-January '77-78 rehearsals were little more than shambolic jam sessions. Rob Stoner said that Dylan always seemed to be in a "really bad mood." "No one could do anything right," Stoner told Tom O'Dell: "[Dylan] was having to deal with the custody battle and then there was the movie. He didn't even turn up for most of the early rehearsals."[15]

Once Bob became fully engaged with the rehearsals, the tide turned, but by that time the Japanese leg was almost upon him! Drugs, it seems, played a key role in the availability of musicians. One of the players Dylan deemed as crucial to the tour was drummer Howie Wyeth. Wyeth, who had played on *Desire* and been an integral part of the Rolling Thunder Revue, attended rehearsals but when word came down from Jerry Weintraub that there would be no drugs allowed on the tour, Wyeth reluctantly told Dylan that he was unable to make it.

Anecdotal evidence points towards Dylan auditioning close to a dozen drummers and he was about to settle on Denny Seiwell when disaster struck again. Known mainly as a session drummer, Seiwell had featured in the first of several incarnations of Paul McCartney's Wings, playing live with them from 1971-73 and appearing on the *Ram, Wildlife* and *Red Rose Speedway* albums. Unfortunately, shortly before the Dylan world tour line-up became set in stone it became evident that Siewell would not be allowed into Japan because of the infamous Wings drugs bust which had occurred in Sweden six years before. So, another man done gone!

Another drummer that Dylan called on was his 1966 world tour drummer, the affable Mickey Jones. There is no doubt that Mickey's playing style was perfectly suited to Dylan's 1965/66 Judas tour. He cheerfully boasted to me on more than one occasion that he played "hard and loud" and that he had a right foot like a "105 Howitzer," but what possessed Bob to think that he would be suitable for the '78 big band with all its subtleties is way beyond my ken. The words Mickey Jones and flute don't even belong in the same sentence, let alone the same band!

It has been rumoured that drummer Jim Gordon auditioned. If so, I can't imagine why he didn't get the gig. Beginning his time with the Everly Brothers, Gordon had gone on to be one of the most requested session drummers on the West Coast and his experience in big bands should also have stood him in good stead. In 1972, he was part of Frank Zappa's 20-piece Grand Wazoo tour and the subsequent 10-piece Petit Wazoo band. And in any case, the very fact that he played on Neil Diamond's *Beautiful Noise* album should have got him the gig with Bob!

The legendary Jim Keltner came down but after some thought

he decided against the tour. In the end, the place on the drum stool went to Ian Wallace, the man Rob Stoner once disparagingly said, "Had a beat like a New York cop." Stoner also said that Wallace couldn't "swing from a rope" and alleged that the ex-King Crimson drummer only got the gig because he was in the right place at the right time. Time was now tight and Wallace was just about the only man left standing. Others were less fortunate. Bob apparently had some people rehearse for weeks and then let them go without giving any reason. "Bob didn't even break the news," one of the tour personnel told me: "He would have one of his assistants tell them, 'Sorry, you're not going to be on the tour,' or 'We don't need you anymore,' and that was that!"

One guy who was at the rehearsals for quite some time but who didn't make the gig was Native American guitarist Jesse Ed Davis. Davis, who had a pretty good pedigree and a great tone, had played on Dylan's 'Watching the River Flow' single and had also been part of George Harrison's Concert for Bangla Desh extravaganza. The reason Davis didn't make the tour is lost in the mists of time but it is well documented that by the late Seventies he was having chronic problems in dealing with an alcohol and drug addiction. Billy Cross, who had recently played with Rob Stoner in the trio Topaz, and had just recorded an eponymous album for Columbia, got the gig.

When it came to the keys, before choosing the unknown quantity that was Alan Pasqua – who had previously played in the jazz fusion quartet The Tony Williams Lifetime – Dylan again ignored his own mantra of don't look back and talked with Sixties associates Al Kooper and Barry Goldberg. Neither man was available for such an extensive tour.

Several of the musicians that made the final cut had outstanding pedigrees but they didn't come cheap. Steve Douglas had been a key member of the celebrated 'Wrecking Crew,' a top-class group of hired guns who worked with producer Phil Spector at Goldstar Studios in L.A. Douglas had played on countless sessions, which saw him working with the likes of John Lennon, the Beach Boys and Elvis Presley. He had also been a member of Presley's road band in the early Seventies. Dylan couldn't decide as to whom he wanted on sax and in the end, Douglas was just about the only option left open to him. Stoner told Clinton Heylin: "We had to get Steve Douglas in, who cost a fuckin' fortune." Dylan paid Motown veteran percussionist Bobbye Hall $2,500 a week (the equivalent of nearly $10,000 in 2019) to compensate her for session work she would have to forego while on tour with him.

The tour arrived in the Land of the Rising Sun on February 17, 1978. The first three Japanese concerts were staged in the now famous Nippon Budokan. A 14,000-seat arena located in Chiyoda, Tokyo, the venue was originally built for the judo competition at the 1964 Summer Olympics, hence its name, which translates into English as Martial Arts Hall. The tour would then move 300 miles to Osaka for three shows before then returning to the Tokyo Budokan for a further five nights.

Dylan's record label decided to record the Budokan concerts and a selection of songs from two of the shows (February 28 and March 1), were put out as a Japanese only release. The double LP was issued on August 21, 1978. Later that year, the album was released in Australia and New Zealand and was extensively imported into many other world territories. At least one counterfeit edition could be found in Europe. Columbia decided therefore that the album should be released worldwide. The official release date was April 23, 1979. The album peaked at number 4 on the UK chart, which for a double LP was a great commercial success. In hindsight, however, releasing the album outside of Japan was a poor decision since it captured the tour in its infancy before the big band had fully gelled and before the

Street-Legal songs had been integrated into the sets. The release contains just one *Street-Legal* song, 'Is Your Love in Vain?,' and overall the album is a very poor representation of the tour as a whole.

It was not at all unusual for concerts at the Budokan to be immortalised in plastic. Six years before Dylan, CBS/Sony had released *Chicago Live in Japan* and one month after the Dylan recording Epic would capture the band Cheap Trick in concert. As with the Dylan album, *Cheap Trick at Budokan* was designed only to be released in Japan but when an estimated 30,000 import copies were sold in the United States the double album was released worldwide.

Dylan's Japanese dates were followed by an 11-hour flight and a one-night stand in Auckland, New Zealand. While heading out for a 5 am jog, Dylan spotted an attractive young woman in the foyer of Auckland's Intercontinental Hotel, where Dylan's entourage occupied the entire 14th floor. The striking longhaired lady, 24-year-old Ra Aranga, was said in one report to be a Maori princess from the ruling family of the Ngai Tuhoe tribe. Ra later said that Dylan, who was "disguised" to avoid fans, approached her asking if she would like to go for a run with him. She agreed and the two of them, minus any security, went for a jog around the waterfront. Dylan had to leave the following day for shows in Australia (Brisbane, Adelaide, Melbourne, Perth and Sydney; 11 dates in all), but after phoning her at all hours of the day and night, he returned to New Zealand on April 3 to spend what Ra later referred to as "Three beautiful days together" in a mountain hideaway. Dylan is said to have invited Ra to visit him in California.*

* The initial newspaper report made no mention that Ra Aranga was a princess. This 'information' appeared almost six months later in the Australasian Post (August 31, 1978) and may well be erroneous.

Ms Aranga wasn't the only new friend that Dylan met while in Auckland. He is said to have befriended two young 'hippie-type' fans, one male and one female, and invited them to join him on tour to Australia! Bob seemed to enjoy their company and they spent quite some time just hanging out together.

After the shows in Japan and Australasia, Dylan returned to the United States for seven consecutive nights at the 2,500-seat Universal Amphitheater in Los Angeles. Cameron Crowe reviewing for *Rolling Stone* wrote: "Dylan's first American concerts since his much-acclaimed Rolling Thunder appearances in 1976 were glibly professional ... Dylan left most die-hard fans and reviewers puzzled on opening night." Crowe did, however, go on to say that: "By the end of his Amphitheatre run, Dylan had won over many doubters."[16]

Over the years, much has been made of the fact that during rehearsals for the '78 tour Dylan received a telegram from Japanese promoters, Seijiro Udo and Tats Nagashima, stipulating which songs he was expected to play on the Far Eastern leg of the tour! According to Howard Sounes, Dylan even sent guitar tech Joel Bernstein to a bookstore to buy a copy of *Writings & Drawings* so that he could look back over his old songs. The information regarding this telegram was given to Clinton Heylin by Rob Stoner: "A telegram arrived from the Japanese promoter, and in it he had a manifest of the songs he expected Bob to do on this tour. In other words he was a jukebox, he was playing requests."

Based on this information, Howard Sounes and many others have adopted the attitude that the 1978 world tour was, to quote Sounes: "Essentially a greatest-hits show." Well, I don't buy into that view. Apart from Stoner, I don't know of anyone who saw this telegram. If we assume that it did exist, what exactly did it say? How many songs were requested? There certainly isn't sufficient evidence to accuse Dylan of pandering to the promoter and touring as some sort of Dylan jukebox!

As Paul Williams said: "[Dylan] set out to play the songs that people wanted to hear ... He had to consciously strip the songs of their nostalgic value in order to be able to freely perform them." Of course, this is precisely what Dylan has been doing now for the past 40 plus years. Yes, in part the 1978 sets did include a goodly amount of what could be called greatest hits, but I believe that was always Dylan's intention for this tour; and why not?

Harvey Goldsmith

When asked by *Melody Maker*'s Chris Welch in 1978 if he was a Dylan fan, promoter Harvey Goldsmith answered: "Yeah. Very much so. When I was at college, for me it was Dylan and Leonard Cohen and Buffalo Springfield. And Dylan was the god ... I didn't see him at the Isle of Wight – I didn't go. But I saw him at the Royal Albert Hall."

Although Harvey Goldsmith would help in promoting Bob Dylan's 1981 and 1984 tours of Britain, he is perhaps best known for arranging more auspicious one-off extravaganzas like the star-studded 1996 Prince's Trust concert or for helping to turn Bob Geldof's dream into the fundraising miracle that was Live Aid. Regardless of these significant accomplishments, Goldsmith will always be best known by British Dylan fans as the man who brought Bob back to the British mainland in 1978 after a 12-year absence and for that, we will always be grateful.

Harvey Goldsmith was a 20-year-old student in 1966 when he began promoting Club 66, a successful weekly live music venue for students in Brighton. The son of an East End tailor, Goldsmith soon dropped out of his college course in pharmacy to travel to San Francisco where he found the most popular pharmaceutical was LSD. The first big event that Goldsmith was involved in promoting was the April 1967 14 Hour Technicolor Dream. By 1978,

Goldsmith had seen it all. He was looking on at the 1971 Crystal Palace Garden Party when Pink Floyd filled the lake with dry ice, killing all of the fish. He was present when Keith Moon threw his first television from a hotel window (to see which would reach the floor first, the TV or a feather) and didn't raise so much as an eyebrow when Alice Cooper stipulated that he required a separate hotel room for his python. When the guest arrived at a Glasgow hotel, booked under the name of "Mr Snake" (what else?), the receptionist immediately fainted.

An uncomplicated and uncompromising risk taker, Goldsmith's biggest gamble was bringing Bob Dylan and Eric Clapton together in 1978. Harvey Goldsmith: "You have to risk all to achieve anything … [one of my biggest risks] was when I brought Bob Dylan and Eric Clapton over to play an aerodrome called Blackbushe and paid the highest fee ever to an artist at that time; one million pounds. I didn't have a million pounds, so that really was betting on the 3.30. Thank god, we ended up selling 175,000 tickets and with the proceeds I bought a Fifties Mulliner Park Ward Bentley Flying Spur. One of only six."[17]

Although the June 18 issue of *The Observer* newspaper reported that: "[Dylan] and his band required pinball machines in their dressing rooms," Goldsmith said that Dylan was, "easy to work with" and that there were, "no unusual or special requests," for the '78 concerts. "They're not looking for anything outrageous," Goldsmith told *The Daily Mail*, "Not like the Stones, they wanted 100-year-old bottles of tequila."[18] In fact, Goldsmith put pinball machines, table tennis tables and a few other assorted amusements in the various Earls Court dressing rooms at the cost of £1,000. He told the Mail reporter that he had to "put in" dressing rooms in Earls Court at a cost of £6,000 and that over the week a total of £10,000 was spent on food and wine for Dylan and his guests.

Coming in from Los Angeles

Dylan arrived at London's Heathrow Airport from Los Angeles on Tuesday June 13, two days before his first London concert which would also coincide with the release of his new album, *Street-Legal*. Expectations for the London shows were running sky high; both in the media and with Dylan fans starved for so long of seeing their hero play live. Tickets, which were limited to four per person, went on sale on Sunday May 7 at 15 locations around the country. Queues started forming at least 48 hours before the box offices opened and at some sales outlets fans slept on pavements for three nights. All six dates in London's 15,700-seat Earls Court arena sold out. The *Daily Telegraph* reported it as being, "The fastest selling series of large scale concerts in history." Touts, asking up to £150 for a £7.50 ticket, had a field day.

After routinely clearing customs, Dylan was greeted by a posse of over-excited record company executives and an assemblage of hired muscle who attempted to hold back a scrum of anxious photographers and a hoard of reporters. A slightly bemused-looking Dylan remarked, "Hey man, it's like a circus here." He had obviously forgotten that after the Isle of Wight festival he had said, "No more, they make too much of singers over there." Now he was back on British soil, one reporter asked why it had been so long since he had visited Britain, to which Dylan joked that the English weather had kept him away. Then, having been in the country for all of 10 minutes, another Jackass reporter asked if a further British tour was planned! I sometimes wonder how these people get their jobs. "I don't know, I might do," said Dylan, "So far all I've done is thoroughly enjoy myself. I just sort of stand around and watch while everyone else gets upset."[19]

With that, and before being hit with another dim-witted question, Dylan slid outside and onto a waiting coach to the Royal

Garden Hotel on Kensington High Street where he and the band occupied the entire 18th floor. The band that accompanied Dylan to Europe was still eight plus three, but changes had occurred since the tour had left for Japan three months earlier. At the close of the first leg (April 1), an unhappy Rob Stoner (who had been the bandleader), left the tour. However, he appeared to rewrite history a little when he told Clinton Heylin that it was he who had decided to quit.

In Tom Odell's 2006 filmed interview with Stoner the bandleader said: "There were no written arrangements ... they were all head arrangements. So this involved people remembering their parts and executing them identically from performance to performance. The backing singers – two of them were very skilled at this and one of them was not. The one who wasn't just happened to be somebody that Bob was very fond of and I had to stay on her case a lot because she was messing up the sound from night to night! And of course, this created problems between Bob and myself. And so I was between a rock and a hard place with this." Stoner then went on to admit to Odell that he also became very unpopular with the other musicians: "They came to resent me," Stoner said, "Because they couldn't get an answer from Bob. They would have to get an answer from Bob through me ... And eventually it was decided that it would be better if I left."

The role of bass player was taken on by Jerry Scheff. Scheff, like horn player Steve Douglas, had made his reputation playing in Presley's road band in the early Seventies and continued to work with Presley until the singer's death. As well as his live work, Scheff was a hot session player, contributing to a host of albums including working with, you guessed it, Neil Diamond. Previous biographers have written that Scheff took over Stoner's role as bandleader but according to Scheff's autobiography, *Way Down*, this is was not the case. Scheff had only leant half of the live set when Dylan announced that he had some new songs and they were going to record an album, *Street-Legal*. The album sessions drastically reduced the time available for Scheff to rehearse for the next leg of the tour so he was given a tape of the songs to enable him to prepare for the seven shows in Los Angeles (June 1-7). Fortunately, everything went well and Scheff was now ready for the European tour which began in London eight days later.

The other change to Dylan's tour personnel was a little more complicated. The tour had started in Japan with Helena Springs, Debi Dye-Gibson and Jo Ann Harris on backing vocals. Debi Dye and Jo Ann had worked together for several years in stage shows including *Hair*, but it seems that like Stoner, neither girl rated Helena Springs. Dye has been quoted as saying that Springs was chosen more for her looks than for any musical ability, and commented that: "As a singer, she was a hell of a dancer." Stoner talked with Springs about the situation but it soon became apparent – as previously hinted at – that Dylan was having an affair with the singer, which might explain her inclusion in the band. At any rate, as the first leg of the tour progressed, tensions grew, and Dye, like Stoner, left the tour after Australia, partly because she was pregnant, but mainly because she could not get along with Springs. Carolyn Yvonne Dennis, daughter of singer Madelyn Quebec, was brought in to replace Dye, but it also seems that she may have replaced Springs as Dylan's lover!

At his June 19 Earls Court concert, Dylan introduced the backing singers as: "On the background vocals tonight, yeah, on the left, my fiancée Carolyn Dennis. And on the right, my ex-wife's best friend, Jo Ann Harris. And in the middle, my current girlfriend, Helena Springs."

On September 27, during a show at Nassau County Coliseum, Dylan was still announcing Carolyn Dennis as being his fiancée but on this night he followed the statement with, "Wishful thinking!" Maybe it was, but as we now know, Dylan and Dennis married in the June of 1986.*

Now in London, Dylan was enjoying being on the road again. He was "hanging" with the band and, for the most part, appeared to be pushing his many troubles to the far reaches of his mind. David Mansfield: "He generally fraternised with the help quite a bit. He was part of the band – he'd hang out, he'd drink, he'd talk his head off, he'd play, total reverse of '76. He was having a ball. He had all kinds of stuff booked. He just wanted to get on an aeroplane or bus, and keep playing forever."[20]

Not only was Dylan 'fraternising with the help,' but he was also talking to the press and to his audience. This was a very different Bob Dylan from the one that had toured the world in 1965-66. He appeared more mature, but that was hardly surprising considering everything he had been through during the ensuing years. It had been a long hard road since his motorcycle spill but now, especially with his divorce finally behind him, things were beginning to take a slight turn for the better. His mind was very much back on his

---

* *Dylan dated Dennis off and on after the 1978 tour. Their liaison cooled and Dennis eventually married. The marriage failed and after her divorce she re-established her relationship with Dylan and on January 31, 1986, Dennis, then 31, bore him a daughter at the Humana Hospital, in Canoga Park, California. The child was named Desiree Gabrielle Dennis-Dylan. The name of the father listed on the birth certificate was Robert Dylan. Six months later, on June 4, The couple married. Three days after the marriage Dennis was on stage with her new husband in San Diego as a member of Dylan's backing group, The Queens of Rhythm. Dylan's friend, guitarist Ted Perlman, said of the wedding: "We were all sworn to secrecy never to mention it." The couple went to extraordinary lengths to keep their marriage out of the public-eye and as one might expect, the secrecy, coupled with Dylan's time spent on the road, meant that the marriage was a little unconventional. Dennis did not live at Dylan's house at Point Dume, instead, the couple set up home in a bungalow in the Los Angeles suburb of Tarzana. On August 7, 1990, after four years of marriage, Dennis filed for divorce; the marriage was dissolved in October 1992. To keep the divorce secret, court records listed Dylan under the name, R Zimmerman and the judge made an order to seal the file.*

music and previous half-hearted efforts to organise a concert tour outside of North America had finally come to fruition. Peace and relaxation had been scarce commodities for far longer than Dylan would care to remember: "I haven't known peace and quiet for so long/ I can't remember what it's like," Dylan sang in 'Idiot Wind.' In any case, from the various reports, he made the most of his free time in London. By day, he spent much of his time shopping and managed to relax most mornings by swimming. According to Robert Shelton, "[Dylan] churned up several laps at a north London public pool, where few of the other swimmers recognised him."[21]

The pool in question was a council-owned swimming pool at Swiss Cottage, less than 10 minutes by chauffeur-driven Mercedes from the Royal Garden Hotel. Although a few fans and some press hung around the Kensington hotel entrance, the crowd mania of the Sixties wasn't really in evidence. Bob spent his first afternoon in the capital shopping, buying mainly clothes and records for his children. He then went on to see the 1977 movie *The American Friend*, a mystery-thriller starring Bruno Ganz who played a terminally ill picture framer, Jonathan Zimmermann. Presumably, Dylan was attracted to the film, not because of the lead character's name, but because it featured two of his American friends, Dennis Hopper and David Blue. That evening and the next, Dylan made the rounds of London music clubs with CBS Records' Press Manager, Brooklyn-born Ellie Smith. On Tuesday evening they went to the 100 Club on Oxford Street where a twice-weekly Roots Reggae Night was held. They also visited Dingwalls at Camden Lock, where they enjoyed a set by the blues band George Thorogood and the Destroyers.

Dylan was extremely interested in what was happening in the recently turbocharged British music scene and as well as guiding him around London, Smith also furnished Bob with a copy of The Clash's eponymous debut album which had been released on CBS the previous summer. Dylan liked the album very much and later his son Jakob would become greatly influenced by the band. On the afternoon of Wednesday June 14, there was a soundcheck at Earls Court, after which, Bob endured a small CBS party in his honour at Covent Gardens' newest trendy nightspot, The Club Next Door. Eric Clapton declined his invitation saying that he intended to watch World Cup football on the television. At the earliest opportunity Dylan and Ellie Smith slipped away and what happened after that depends whose recollections you care to believe.

In a piece written for *Melody Maker*, Robert Shelton wrote that from the CBS party Dylan and Smith made an aborted trip to the Cloud Club in Brixton, which was closed. The two then made their way to the Four Aces in Dalston Lane, which according to Shelton was, "open, but not swinging," and from there they moved on to the Music Machine. Jerry Scheff, however, tells a very different and far more interesting tale. In Scheff's version, Dylan called Scheff in his hotel room and asked the bass player if he liked reggae, to which Scheff replied in the affirmative. Dylan then asked Scheff to meet him in the hotel garage where he had a Mercedes at his disposal. When he arrived, he found Dylan waiting with backing singer Helena Springs and percussionist Bobbye Hall.

Scheff: "Bob drove us across town and found a parking space about a block away from the club." Scheff does not refer to the club by name but we must assume it was the Four Aces in the old Dalston Theatre building which, by the Seventies, had become a centre for West Indians in cultural exile. There was, however, a problem. When the party arrived at the ticket booth, the dreadlocks wearing cashier informed Dylan that it was members only and that membership was £100 per person! According to Scheff, Bob willingly stumps up for four memberships; handing over £400. One hundred pounds in 1978 was an awful lot of money, about £550.00 in 2019. If correct, that would mean – taking inflation into account – Dylan was changed in the region of £2,200 for four memberships to what was in effect a backstreet reggae club! Either Scheff has the figure hopelessly wrong, he is employing a truckload of poetic license, or Mr Dread saw Dylan coming! Anyway, according to Scheff they gained entrance only to discover that there was no live music that night, just a DJ and a lone couple on the dance floor! Dylan apparently saw the funny side of the experience and he and his party were soon back in the car and on their way over to the Music Machine on Camden High Street to catch Robert Gordon, whose excellent band then featured a Dylan favourite, guitarist Link Wray, and Bob's recently departed bandleader, Rob Stoner.

Steven Soles and David Mansfield had independently decided to go to the gig and after the show everyone was lead backstage to meet with Stoner. According to Ireland's Mr Music, BP Fallon: "Sid Vicious' Nancy [Spungen] wobbled up, tits hanging out and eyes closing down ... A sloppy floppy messy deadweight bodybag of mascaraed custard," she hurled herself at Dylan who winced. Nancy said something about Sex and Dylan again recoiled until it is explained that Sex was a clothes shop run by Vivienne Westwood and her partner Malcolm MacLaren. In this story, there is no mention of a knife. According to Stoner, however, Vicious lived up to his assumed name by brandishing a knife in Dylan's direction. "Sid Vicious was the only person I ever saw threaten Dylan," Stoner said, "Sid ... started waving a knife around the room hassling Bob. He was saying: 'Hey, you're Bob Dildo then, aren't you? Eh! Fuck you, Bob Dildo.' Bob asked me, 'Rob who is this guy?.' He wasn't freaked or anything, Bob boxes; he's a tough little guy and can take care of himself. We just grabbed Sid and hustled him out of the room." According to Scheff's autobiography, however, it was Steven Soles who ended the evening with a knife being waved around his face by an intoxicated Mr Vicious. Who knows, Sid could well have pointed the knife at more than one of the group!

At this time, Dylan's eclectic taste in music had grown to

encompass reggae, especially Bob Marley, a fact reflected in some of the new arrangements of his own material. Although Ray Coleman believes that Dylan heard the reggae band Merger, whom he invited to appear with him on the Blackbushe festival bill, at Dingwalls, Bob actually caught them live on the first of his two visits to the 100 Club. Dylan had already played a reggae-infused rendition of 'Knockin' on Heavens's Door' at the LA shows and a 'reggaeised' version of 'Don't Think Twice, It's All Right' would be in evidence from February to July.

On another night Bob attended a well-heeled late-night Chelsea party where he was greeted by Andy Warhol, Bryan Ferry and a few other scene-makers. Ellie Smith's job was to deal with the barrage of requests from the media. There were more than 50 requests for interviews and several hundred applications for backstage passes. In an interview conducted for *ISIS* magazine, Robert Shelton told Chris de Souza:

"Dylan was very open to meeting people during his stay. He saw a lot of people backstage on that tour. George Harrison, Paul McCartney and Ringo were there [at Earls Court], as were the Rolling Stones, Bianca Jagger and her daughter. Jack Nicholson and Shelley Duvall were in London filming [for Stanley Kubrick's The Shining]; Jack's a big fan. Dylan saw quite a few old friends including Bob's old Woodstock pal Happy Traum and his family … [Also backstage were photographer David Bailey and Monty Python's Eric Idle]."[22] As the residency continued Jack Nicholson, Billy Connolly and TV presenter Michael Parkinson were spotted as was the Secretary of State for Education and Paymaster General, Shirley Williams (she held both posts!).

Ray Coleman wrote in *Melody Maker* (June 20, 1978): "The singer did no formal interviews, hardly surprising in view of the fact that when he emerged early in the week from the Royal Garden Hotel, Kensington, a national foot-in-the-mouth type yelled: 'You're doing it for the money, aren't you, Bob?' That incredible piece of insensitivity reduced everyone's interview chances from nil to nil-plus ... And anyway, oddly enough, most artists do perform for money. Dylan, unlike some, actually earned his." Coleman went on to say that the opening night was the best concert he had ever seen: "If I had to choose one concert to mark my life," Coleman wrote, "just one that mattered much, much more than any of the countless performances attended in the past 25 years – it would have to be Bob Dylan's opening show at Earls Court."

After the final Earls Court concert (June 20), Harvey Goldsmith organised a thank you dinner. All his staff and the crew were invited, as was Dylan. Bob told Robert Shelton that he would be at the party and that Shelton should meet him there so that they could talk. Dylan told him to bring along his notebook as he wanted to give an informal interview. Shusha Guppy accompanied Dylan to the restaurant. Born in Iran, Guppy, a singer of Persian and Western folk songs, performed several Dylan songs at her concerts, which, like Bob in 1978, usually ended with 'Forever Young.' Dylan, who was a fan, especially of her 1975 album *Before the Deluge*, had telephoned Guppy the day before and asked her to attend his final Earls Court concert. Shusha, who at the time was living in Chelsea, tells the story of their meeting in song on her 1980 album, *Here I Love You*. Also with Dylan that night were Carolyn Dennis, Helena Springs, and Jo Ann Harris.

Robert Shelton: "San Lorenzo is a very smart restaurant in Knightsbridge, just down the road from where Dylan was staying. I arrived just a few minutes before Bob and managed to get a good table [in the corner] that I knew would suit him. Bob came in the door and headed straight for me, he was very talkative. There's always that something when he's around, a tension, a feel of excitement and anticipation that he generates wherever he is."[23]

Shelton wrote in *Melody Maker:* "Although I've known and studied him for 17 years, it is always exciting to be around him. The air still crackles a bit when he walks into a room ... Dylan was filled with nervous energy, but his dark glasses gave him some refuge ... Dylan speaks with the same sort of rhythm that he brings to his singing. Sometimes his lines are gentle. Sometimes they bite.

Bob nibbled at his food and kept working on a bottle of Courvoisier that was near him." He told Shelton: "I'm just the postman. I deliver the songs. That's all I have in this world are those songs. That's what all the legend, all the myth is about – my songs ... All you really have to please is yourself, in any area of life ... You can't depend on an audience to tell you that you're good. You have to know yourself. If you know it, they'll know it! I earn everything I make! ... Reggie Jackson of the New York Yankees gets three million dollars a year, for striking out! For every dollar I make, there's a pool of sweat on the floor ... I put in an eight-hour day in two hours onstage."

Shelton asked Dylan if he could put his finger on the "enemy within." "Dylan laughed at the question and pointed his index finger toward his heart ... 'It's all in those two verses of that last song ... the enemy within is suspicion ... It is true that a man is his own worst enemy, just as he is his own best friend. If you deal with the enemy within, then no enemy without can stand a chance.'"

Shelton continued: "Although bristling with drive, Dylan left me with the general impression that he is far from happy these days. Naturally, the great reviews and ovations he's gotten pleased him. But it's difficult to recall protracted periods when Dylan has been happy. Perhaps it's all what is called, "the divine discontent of the artist ... For all the rapport he has with millions around the world, I still sense a foreboding loneliness about him ... 'A lonely man with money is still lonely...' (Dylan wrote in 1964). Two years later, he said: 'It's always lonely where I am.'"

According to Shelton, nearly every eye in the restaurant was on

Dylan. "I wondered," Shelton said, "if he could ever find those secret little cafés, like he used to in Greenwich Village, where he could scribble down lyrics and ideas for songs … I offered him his old line: 'Be invisible.' 'Yes,' he went on, 'I'm invisible now, I don't have that kind of fame. In reality, I'm not that famous.'

To show my appreciation for his survival as a great artist who is always busy being reborn, I wanted to give him some token … I handed him a Judgement card from my [tarot] deck. It shows a winged angel blowing a trumpet, raising the dead from their graves, and they are reborn again as little children. The Judgement card is like 'Forever Young,' telling us that music can revitalise and renew us. Dylan thanked me warmly for the token gift. 'But you shouldn't break up your pack of cards,' he said. Dylan accepted the card. What else can you give a man who has given us all so much?"[24]

It was now time for Dylan to visit mainland Europe before returning for the Blackbushe Picnic. With several free days before and after his June 23 concert at Feijenoord Stadium, Rotterdam, Bob took in the sights of the city of bikes, Amsterdam, visiting the Van Gogh Museum, the Rembrandt House Museum and Anne Frank House, where the wartime diarist wrote while in hiding from the Nazis. The concert, Dylan's first in Holland, was exceptionally well received by a crowd of some 55,000.

Bob and the band travelled in a private train carriage from Amsterdam to Essen, Germany, where Dylan stayed for four nights at the Hotel Broadway, a 25-minute ride from Dortmund where he played two shows, June 26 & 27 (his first ever concerts in Germany). On June 28, Bob journeyed by train from Essen to Berlin for a concert to be held the next evening at Deutschlandhalle. Then, on June 30, he travelled, again by train, from Berlin to Nuremberg. Although his memory would appear to be faulty, in the long out of print German language book *Accountant of Dreams*, concert promoter Fritz Rau says that he "flew" with Dylan from Berlin to Nuremberg.

In fact, excluding the short excursion to Sweden, for the most part Dylan and company travelled around mainland Europe in a private train. They occupied five carriages including a dining car. During the Nazi years in Germany the train, including the red DSG dining car, had been at the disposal of Hitler's deputy, Hermann Goering.

Dylan was unhappy with some of the pre-concert press coverage and of the audience reaction to the show in the German capital. A small segment of the Berlin audience, seemingly Anti-Semitic, racist, or both, began booing Dylan and or his black backing singers. Before this concert, Fritz Rau said: "[Dylan] raved about Berlin. He stated that Berlin fascinated him and that he would like to live there for six months." After the concert, however, Rau said, "[Dylan] had abandoned this intention. The city had hurt him too deeply. When we flew to Nuremberg, he was very silent and very reflective." Dylan had intended to visit the site of a concentration camp while in Germany, but that excursion had to be cancelled due to lack of time.

Over the years, there has been much talk about problems with neo-Nazis when Dylan played Nuremberg (July 1). The concert there was held at Reichsparteitagsgelände, the so-called Zeppelinfeld; a rallying ground for the Nazi Party between 1933 and 1938. While it's true that before the concert threats were made by the neo-Nazi group Wehrsportgruppe Hoffmann, which resulted in a heightened state of security, those who attended the event say there was no trouble at the concert itself.

In stark contrast to this, one prominent biographer has written that in response to Dylan's performance of 'Masters of War,' which Dylan introduced by saying: "It gives me a great pleasure to sing it in this place," "a couple of dozen neo-Nazis ... threw things at [Dylan] for his effrontery." In his book *Day by Day*, Clinton Heylin went further, saying: "[A] small group of neo-Nazis [threw] things at the stage throughout the show," an assertion vigorously denied by the attendees that I have interviewed on the subject. The consensus is that the only time anything was thrown was when those further back threw objects, mainly drinks cans, at the people standing near the stage. This is a common occurrence at festivals when people close to the stage stand and block the view of those further back. The same thing happened at Blackbushe when Clapton took the stage and people at the front stood. Shouts of "Sit down," occasionally accompanied by missiles, continued through parts of Dylan's Blackbushe performance.

In conjunction with Dylan's tour supervisor Patrick Stansfield, German tour promoter Fritz Rau decided that the stage for Dylan's Nuremberg concert should be set up on the opposite side from the Führersteig, the dais where Hitler stood to give his rallying speeches. This would mean that the crowd would turn their backs to the Führersteig to watch Dylan play.

In *Accountant of Dreams*, Rau tells of visiting Jerry Weintraub in Los Angeles. During the dinner party, at which Dylan was present, Bob was more interested in talking with Rau about the promoter's celebrated European "American Folk Blues Festivals" than he was about his own upcoming concerts in Germany.

Dylan told Rau that in 1963, "he had hitchhiked through Europe and attended the Festival in Copenhagen." Rau, however, said: "I was more concerned with the Dylan million-dollar-tour and moved on to that as soon as possible. I told him that we had planned concerts for Westfalenhalle in Dortmund, Deutschlandhalle in Berlin and for Zeppelinfeld, Nuremberg ... Dylan shakes his head: 'I think Nuremberg is the wrong place' ... [Dylan] ponders, and I realise that it is a tough decision for him," Rau says. "Suddenly, [Dylan] smiles and nods. He instinctively understood why we wanted him to appear at that exact location."[25]

Fritz Rau: "On the second evening, [Dylan] phones me at my hotel room and asks 'Fritz, what happened in Nuremberg? I didn't understand.' I told him, 'You should ask what happened in Nuremberg and in Berlin. They belong together.' And I once more explained to him why we had set up his stage opposite to the Hitler rostrum and that 80,000 Germans had turned their backs on Hitler and had turned to Bob Dylan and his music. He hesitated for a moment as if he was reflecting on that. 'Yes,' he said before terminating the call, 'it could have been like that... maybe.'"[26]

They're Planting Stories
in the Press

Both the British and European press were in raptures over Bob's 1978 concerts. *The Sun* called Dylan "The Living Legend," while the *Daily Mail* ran with the headline: "The Greatest Concert I Have Ever Seen," which coming from Ray Connolly, who was not always known for such generosity of spirit, was quite an accolade. The excitement even extended to English National TV news which for the first time gave a two-minute segment to a rock concert on the evening of Dylan's Earls Court début! In total, 10 minutes of news clips exist for June 15, though they consist mostly of audience interviews and footage of long queues. As for the music press, *Melody Maker* led the way with an eight-page pull-out celebrating the Earls Court shows; a four-page centre-spread previewing Blackbushe in their July 15 issue, and another four-page pull-out reviewing the festival in their July 22 issue.

"Angry Dylan in Empty Seats Row" read the headline in the June 17 *Daily Express*: "Bob Dylan had to be persuaded to go on stage to open the first of his six concerts, it was revealed yesterday. The backstage drama came only a minute before he was due to go on at 8 pm at the 15,000 capacity Earls Court. He looked out in astonishment to find the lofty building half-empty and immediately went back to his dressing room. 'There's a bit of a to-do,' admitted one of Dylan's party yesterday. 'He refused to go out until everyone was in their seats. He didn't want people scrambling over each other after he started the show.'

Dylan remained in his dressing room for 25-minutes as officials pleaded with him to go out. 'He was very reluctant. He could not understand all the empty seats when it was supposed to be a sell-out,' said the spokesman. The management blamed a 'box-office mix-up' and a 'turnstile blockage.'"

John Collis writing in the June 23 issue of *Time Out* said: "On June 15, 1978, Bob Dylan took an Event and turned it into everything an audience could require ... Impossible to be sure in the vast hangar of Earls Court, but there was a curious lack of tension as we waited the standard 20 minutes before the advertised kick-off time.

As the lights go down, stimulating a hollow, pavlovian roar, one's greatest fear re-surfaces. Ever since that announcement 'Bob Dylan to play Earls Court,' I've been remembering the Rolling Stones fiasco. A horrid blur of noise, assaulting the ears from six directions, each signal a second behind its sibling, and somehow in the middle a little green Jagger prancing about. Of course tonight will be an Event, but I am trying not to bank too much on the music.

The group essay a finger-stretching, unremarkable instrumental, but at least it allays that 'greatest fear;' with the exception of the ghost acoustic, every instrument is clear, in its place and at ear respecting volume. An even bigger roar greets a dapper little chap in black and white, strolling on from the back and raising his arms in a boxer's salute ... The voice is in great flexible shape, and he's using it with care ... Why do I have to be working tonight; I shouldn't have to be scribbling, but sitting back with a big grin like everyone else."

Dave Kelly writing in *The Observer*, June 18, says: "According to all the precedents, the first of Bob Dylan's six London concerts shouldn't have been anything like as good as it was. Of course it was bound to be a great event. His enormous reputation and the rarity of his visits guaranteed massive media coverage, panic for tickets and grade-A hysteria all round. But great events are not usually great musical experiences. They are celebrations first and concerts secondly. Tuesday night at Earls Court, however, turned out to be a magnificent exception."

According to Russell Davies writing in *The Sunday Times* (June 18), "What this thoroughly convincing concert proved– and went on proving ... Was that an artist who can rely on his audience to bring some knowledge of his work to a concert need not coast or merely reproduce: he can afford to subject his material to drastic musical revision." Russell closed by saying, he doubts, "Whether London has ever heard a better evening of creative re-vamping since Duke Ellington stopped coming round with his savagely re-cycled oldies."

"They gave Bob Dylan an ovation simply for existing last night," Ray Connolly said in his *Daily Mail,* June 16 article: "At first the sound of the ecstatic thousands at Earls Court was an affirmation of loyalty, a thank-you for surviving. But by the end of a two-hour show the enthusiasm had generated into wild appreciation beyond anyone's expectations." Connolly went on to say that the show was "quite the most exciting, vibrant concert" he had ever seen. "It was," he said, "a celebration of the compelling music that has been the background to an entire generation. It would be easy to speak of Bob Dylan in terms of nostalgia. Easy, but facile and wrong ... Last night he did what he always did best: he became an entertainer again ... He turned his old songs into new ones ... He is a consummate artist."

In a very lengthy article in the *New Statesman* (June 23), Mark Kidel wrote: "It is [Dylan's] reluctance to play the hero's part, which has so endeared him to a generation that chose to worship the anti-hero, no longer trusting the cardboard cut-out qualities so characteristic of the Hollywood machine and its rockbiz successor ... For those who have grown up with him, Dylan has provided a myth, a model and a mirror-image. He is an enigma, someone with almost superhuman powers; he is also expected to live up to the promise of the alternative perfection, eschewing the corruption of commercialism, and more fateful than any other to the cause..." Kidel went on to say: "Only Dylan could have generated an AJ Weberman."

Chapter Ten

I Saw It Advertised
One Day

The day before the Blackbushe festival Bob Dylan told the *Daily Mirror*: "I've had a wonderful time. I've been away from here too long and I'd like to come back. England feels like a second home to me."[1]

The 94,200 tickets for the Earls Court residency had sold within hours of going on sale and Harvey Goldsmith was extremely keen for more of the same. For the staging of the Blackbushe event Harvey joined forces with Jamie and Laurence Bloom of Strutworth Ltd, who at the time were the owners of the soon to be ill-fated Rainbow Theatre. Goldsmith had supposedly paid Bob £350,000 for the six London shows and is reputed to have talked about Dylan earning in the region of £300,000 for "The Picnic." In any event, he persuaded Dylan to return to England after he had finished his mini tour of northern Europe. Consequently, just three-and-half weeks after completing his highly successful Earls Court residency, Bob Dylan was back in Britain for a grand finale. This final performance of the European leg would eclipse everything that had gone before (and anything still to come) on the 1978 world tour.

Two weeks before the event, promoter Harvey Goldsmith had this to say about festivals in general: "They're horrendous. They're absolute nightmares, from an organisational point of view ... Because of screw-ups in the past the authorities are making it more and more difficult. We're forced to put in permanent facilities for a temporary situation, and that's very difficult. It's past festivals like the Isle of Wight and the free festivals which didn't go down too well with anybody and weren't that much about music anyway, in my opinion, which haven't helped.

Woodstock and the Isle of Wight cropped up around the same time and there were no questions asked about having sufficient toilets. People just didn't think about it, I guess. They were disasters and, of course, the outcome was the Night Assemblies Bill and the Isle of Wight Bill ... It was all happening at that time [1969-71] but there was damage done, no security, and slowly but surely the authorities began to clamp down ... I had to make three trips to the States to secure Bob Dylan," Goldsmith said: "I first knew the Dylan thing was on at the end of January. It wasn't confirmed until nearly April, but we knew it was on the cards. Once he was committed to doing Japan and then the Australian thing came up, then I knew he was going to come to Europe ... When the artist feels ready to do something, they'll do it. If you push too hard, then it doesn't work out."[2]

Initially, Dylan had only wanted to play three or four outdoor stadiums in Europe– England, France, Germany and maybe something in Scandinavia. Nevertheless, it seems that others were fighting for the rights to stage Dylan concerts. Antonio Iriarte told *ISIS* magazine that CBS-Spain, "appeared to be willing to support any promoter who could lure Dylan across the Pyrenees." Relying on this support, Spanish promoter Gay Mercader decided to make a bid. He is rumoured to have offered $150,000 for a show in Spain. The concert would be at Barcelona FC stadium and the proposed date was July 8. However, when Mercader arrived in London to talk with Goldsmith he was informed that Dylan's management expected $250,000 and that the French promoter was willing to take up the option on July 8 for a second Paris date. Frantic phone calls to CBS-Spain and his bankers came to nothing and Mercader came away empty-handed.

With the planned outdoor concerts now confirmed, Goldsmith persuaded Dylan to play some indoor shows at Earls Court. "I felt he should be seen indoors in a controlled situation," Goldsmith said: "Fortunately they went for it and it worked. It was always in the back of my mind to do an open-air show [in England], and there was so much demand, and it was at the end of the tour, so we thought, let's make it into something really nice."[3] The main reason for choosing Blackbushe Aerodrome as the venue for the festival was its proximity to London, especially the rail link.

As was the case with the Isle of Wight, and for that matter most of the Sixties and Seventies music festivals, there was much local opposition to Blackbushe. Councillor Keith Hunch said: "When we first heard about the concert, our initial instinct was to stop it at all costs. This proved impossible but I would say the mood of the local residents is one of apprehension."

Goldsmith: "There's always a fear of drug-crazed hippies running all over their croquet lawn, and you have to allay their fears." The event was officially announced on May 25, 1978 but a local weekly newspaper, *Surrey & Hants Star*, had been tipped off by airport owner Douglas Arnold, the previous morning. Mr Arnold told the *Star*: "I am just an aeroplane man ... and I have to pay the bills somehow."

The airfield is on Yateley Common and one of the Commoners, Mike Chappell, said that they were considering an injunction to stop the concert. A meeting was held on Wednesday, May 31 between the promoters, the police and the public transport authorities concerning the arrangements to be put in place for a crowd estimated at 60,000! Even though matters were not yet settled, it was announced that tickets were due to go on sale at Harlequin record shops on June 5. At this point, however, there was still concern about the possibility of legal action from the Yateley Commoners. A representative of the co-promoters, Strutworth's Laurence Bloom, told the local paper (a little tongue in cheek): "The nineteen Commoners will all be offered special passes so they can come to the concert and graze their cattle – as long as they don't contravene Civil Aviation Authority regulations about livestock on runways." The local newspaper later reported: "Following a secret deal between Yateley Commoners, Goldsmith and airport owner Douglas Arnold, the Commoners have dropped their objections to the show." A press conference was convened but the nature of the deal was not revealed. The belief was that the withdrawal of the threat of injunction was, "reputedly on payment of a large sum of money which will be donated to a local charity." This now only left the local authority to agree.

Worryingly for the locals, the numbers expected to attend were rising – it was now at 100,000 – and the local paper reported that Hart Council wanted, "The promoter's signature on a document agreeing to stringent litter, noise and toilet controls and provisions." A three-man "action committee," with the power to serve a writ, "which would halt the festival at the 11th hour," was hastily set up. On July 4, the Council's public relations officer, Malcolm Arlott, stated "We are still trying to get the agreement signed," but, "I am very hopeful there will be an agreement." As the matter had not been settled, a briefing was set up for 2 pm on Monday, July 10 (just five days before the festival) to advise parish councillors, Hart's three Chambers of Trade and the press of the situation. "This is to give the press good time to publicise the news that the concert is definitely 'on' – or not," reported the local newspaper, adding that, "It will almost certainly go ahead." A couple of days later, the reporter confirmed that, "Promoter Harvey Goldsmith has now signed an agreement with Hart Council – the first such agreement ever in Britain – about the various standards to apply for the huge crowd, thus ensuring that the concert is on."

The size of the crowd had, however, grown once again. The official estimate of numbers was now at 120,000. Nonetheless, others suggested up to 150,000 tickets would be sold in advance with another 20,000 being sold on the day. At the July 10 press conference, a spokesman for Harvey Goldsmith said that estimates of 150,000 to 200,000 were "over the top." Chief Superintendent Reed told the press conference that, "Every single officer in Hampshire is working a 12-hour day from Friday to Sunday and all leave has been cancelled." He added that at least 300 police officers would be inside the concert arena – the eventual figure was probably half that.

The concert held at Blackbushe on Saturday July 15, 1978 was the first, and interestingly the last music event ever to be staged there. Promoter Harvey Goldsmith intended to continue the 'English Country Garden' theme he had created so successfully for his Crystal Place concerts. "We called it the Picnic," Goldsmith said, "because we hoped people would come along in the right spirit and have a good day."

Unfortunately, the barren airfield didn't come close to the picturesque setting of Crystal Palace. The aerodrome was featureless and uncomfortable, especially if you ended up sitting on one of the three runways that crisscrossed the arena. Although the event was rightly deemed to be a great success, for the most part, the Great British festival spirit seemed to be a little lacking; not for the Dylan faithful who occupied the first 50-60 or even 100 yards, but for the "civilians" further back who had difficulty in seeing in the days before video screens. Unlike the natural bowl at Knebworth Park, Blackbushe was dead flat; perfect for an airfield, but not so good for Bob watching.

Regardless of the imperfections, Blackbushe Aerodrome was a more attractive venue than the Nürnberg, Zeppelinfeld had been. With its giant stark concrete walls, inhospitable rolls of barbed wire and stern looking leather clad security guards, the venue was most uninviting; at least from the outside. It could be said that after witnessing the exterior of the Zeppelinfeld there wasn't any need for Dylan to visit a concentration camp!

So Many People There I
Never Saw in M'life

Situated two miles west of Camberley on the north side of the A30, Blackbushe Aerodrome, now known as Blackbushe Airport, lies some 40 miles south-west of London and a dozen miles south-east of the town of Reading. Contrary to every other text you will have read, including the tickets and official festival posters, Blackbushe is actually in the county of Hampshire (not Surrey).

Despite the many announcements regarding anticipated crowd figures given by the promoter, we are not privy to Harvey Goldsmith's private thoughts on the subject. On the one hand, he would have wanted to talk up the event as the largest and most important music spectacle ever, one that no one should miss, while on the other hand, he didn't want to scare the local populace and Hart Council shitless! The truth is that no one, including Harvey Goldsmith, knows precisely how many people saw Dylan perform that day because hordes of people arrived with forged tickets. Many of those who had unwittingly bought counterfeit tickets were escorted to a giant holding pen just outside of the arena where police and the promoters' representatives asked questions about where the tickets were obtained. In the end though, the organisers let those holding forged tickets in for free. Well done Harvey!

The stark truth is that the police and the promoter were expecting forged tickets. Scotland Yard had received a tip-off from a print company who had been approached by two men wanting a printing plate made for one side of a ticket for the festival. They told the company they would produce the plate for the other half of the ticket later! The print company agreed to make the plate but then informed the police who lay in wait for the men who were due to collect it the day before the festival. The two men didn't show up and police believe they may have become suspicious and had the plates made elsewhere. Nine people were charged with selling forged tickets at the festival site, but the actual counterfeiters were never found.

Although the *Sunday Times* erroneously reported that "Some 80,000 pop fans" were in attendance, the truth was far from that. In total, Goldsmith sold 175,000 tickets but taking into account those arriving without tickets and others who had bought some of the many counterfeits, the crowd was swelled to between 200,000-215,000. The most common figure quoted (and the one given by the police) was 200,000. The crowd was later classified in some quarters as being the "largest ever assembled to see one artist," which was a little disparaging toward Eric Clapton (and others). British music paper *Melody Maker* employed a substantial slice of poetic licence when they said the crowd was the largest peacetime gathering in British history. In truth, the 1970 Isle of Wight festival, which drew an estimated crowd of 250,000-350,000, was larger than Blackbushe. The revenue from ticket sales for The Picnic was said to have been £1,270,000, a record for a one-day paying festival.

With above average rainfall and below average temperatures, the British summer of 1978 had been a huge disappointment. It was all the more pleasurable therefore that July 15 was a warm and sunny day; a factor that might have helped to swell ticket sales on the day. Other oft-quoted statistics stated that the 23-acre site was fenced with 12,000 feet of corrugated fencing, which was decorated by artists and local school children with picnic murals and was manned by an assemblage of private security guards. Also in attendance inside the arena were 170 police, about 100 members of the St John Ambulance, five full-time doctors and a number of nurses. Five hundred portable toilet blocks provided the sanitation – though more were required. Goldsmith had anticipated this but he encountered problems in locating more.

The promoter hired several street theatre groups consisting of various entertainers including clowns on stilts, Chris the Pyss and his Nomads, who mingled with the crowd, and a Punch and Judy show which operated from a bus. Similar scaled-down entertainment had previously been provided around the outer concourse at the Earls Court shows. The Action Space Theatre company carried out three performances of their epic saga: "War of the Sexes." Bouncy inflatables and skateboarding facilities were also to be had. The entertainment area also contained a crèche with free jelly and cake. In keeping with the size of the event, the cake was a monster, measuring eight feet in length. Before you could enjoy any of this, however, you had to get to the festival site!

The most important part of any concert is of course the sound and on that front, no cost was spared. The rig for Dylan's world tour had been supplied by Stanal Sound of Kearney, Nebraska who had provided Neil Diamond with his sound system for the previous eight years. For the Dylan shows, Stanal's chief soundman, Tim Charles, handled the house mixing while Chris Coffin mixed the stage monitors. A new type of power-amp called an "incremental power system" drove the monitor speakers and these amps were so new the accompanying literature carried the words: "temporary operating instructions." Although the Stanal Sound system had performed wondrously throughout the tour more power was needed for the three big outdoor dates (Rotterdam, Nuremberg, Blackbushe) and for these concerts it was easier to supplement the rig with other, more local sound systems. So, while Stanal remained in charge as the 'general sound contractor,' Britannia Row, TFA Electrosound, and Tasco, three English companies, were also drafted in.*

* *Owned by Pink Floyd, the Britannia Row sound system was first used by the band for their 1975 Knebworth gig, after which they established the name (the company was based at 35 Britannia Row, Islington), and began hiring the rig to other bands. TFA Electrosound was owned by none other than Rikki Farr of Isle of Wight festival fame. Probably less well known than the others, Tasco had nevertheless built a 100 amplifier, 76,000 watt PA system for The Who's May 31, 1976 Charlton Athletic Football Ground concert. The PA got The Who an entry in* The Guinness Book of World Records *as the world's "Loudest Pop Group."*

The Road to Blackbushe

Harvey Goldsmith: "We're arranging special trains backwards and forwards so that people can get on a train at Waterloo, after parking their car in town, and then in 42 minutes they're down at the site... So there is no need to sit in traffic jams all day long. It's there so use it... The station is right near the site, and trains will run every 15 minutes."

It transpired that British Rail ran 66 additional trains from London's Waterloo Station. Even so, an estimated 60,000 vehicles turned up at the site and many more were simply abandoned or broke down on route. Despite advertising that people would not be allowed to camp overnight, some festival goers arrived on the site several days before the event and organisers did make basic provisions for people to camp.

Prior to the event the M3 motorway was completely blocked and in an attempt to get past the gridlock, many people drove down the hard shoulder until that too became jammed. The jams soon began to take their toll on the queuing vehicles. Many of the cars had been built in the late Sixties and when stationary for any length of time were prone to overheating; very soon an assortment of vehicles sat like so many tombstones strewn along the route. When the hard shoulder came to a standstill some people attempted to drive along the grass verges while others simply left their vehicles behind and walked the remaining six or seven miles to the festival site.

Journalist Chris Brazier recounted his experience in the July 22 edition of *Melody Maker*: "The travel arrangements sounded so simple and speedy in the Gospel according to Goldsmith ... Trains every 15 minutes to a 'station right near the site.' The reality was different though ... After a quarter of an hour at gate five the loudspeakers asked, 'Could all passengers for The Picnic at Blackbushe queue up at gate 11?' Which meant the back of the queue became the front – The first one now will later be last. Ten minutes later: 'Train cancelled– Could everybody return to platform five' ... [At the other end of the journey] the queue for buses looked to stretch for the half-a-mile that a policeman told me was all I had to walk to get to the aerodrome. Wondering why everyone was bothering to wait for a bus, I set out on what turned out to be a three-mile journey."

According to the August 1978 edition of *Rail News*: "Southern Regional Staff rose to the occasion to get American folk-singer Bob Dylan from London to his personal appearance unscathed ... With traffic jams to consider the answer was a specially chartered train, plans for which were kept secret. The South-West divisional manager masterminded the operation though he already had to contend with 40,000 fans making their way to Fleet by rail."

Dylan, who left his hotel wearing a leather waistcoat over a spotted shirt, which was open almost to his waist, was taken by coach to the taxi road parallel to the terminal on platform 11 at London's Waterloo Station. As he arrived a special four-coach train pulled in alongside, the carriage door opened and Dylan stepped the few yards from his coach to the train. Although booked to Fleet, the "Hush-Hush Special," as it was christened by British Rail, was stopped at Farnborough station where Dylan made a dash to a waiting motor coach with a motorcycle outrider escort. After Dylan arrived at the festival site the coordinator met with Harvey Goldsmith to finalise details for the return journey.*

* Over the years, many people have referred to The Concert at Blackbushe as the 'Hippies Graveyard,' the main reason being that many of the major routes leading to the festival site had signs along them which simply read 'Hippies Graveyard'. Over the years there have been various comments about these signs. Some assume that in the midst of new wave and punk the signs signalled the end of an era for artists like Dylan and Clapton, whilst others maintain the signs were erected as a direct protest over high ticket prices. Both are wrong. In 2015, I came across a 1978 single entitled 'Hippy's Graveyard.' The release date for the single was July 14, the day before Blackbushe. The song was written and released by "Johnny G" (John Gotting). Johnny, who is still on the circuit today, confirmed to me that the signs were put up by the promotional people at his record company, the UK indie label Beggars Banquet. Johnny told me that the signs were to promote his single and that they had nothing whatsoever to do with the festival itself. He was at pains to explain that they were in no way meant to disrespect Bob Dylan. Johnny was, and still is, a huge fan.

The VIP Experience

Concert-goer Johnny Haynes told me: "I arrived at Blackbushe without a ticket. I'd been to many festivals over the years and on all but one occasion had managed to get in without paying! The security at Blackbushe was very heavy and the fences very high! After searching for what seemed like an age, I spotted some buses parked up against the perimeter fence at the stage end of the arena. Then, as I walked toward the buses, I saw someone jump over the fence from the top of one of them! Not to be outdone and with no one looking, I climbed up on top of a bus. It was a long way to drop, but there seemed no other way to get in. Well, there was, but I didn't intend paying.

Once inside, I picked myself up and, as nonchalantly as possible, began walking toward the stage. I quickly realised, however, that I'd landed not in the main arena but in a VIP enclosure! This should have been very good news but unfortunately the VIP section only had a side view of the stage; and only the front section of the stage at that! Problem was, there was yet another fence between this section and the main crowd. There was a gate by which you could get out of the VIP section into the outside parking area – where I'd just come from! – but there was no way that I could see of getting from the VIP section into the public arena. I couldn't believe that a VIP section would have such a poor view of the stage; but, if the truth be known, most of the so-called VIPs were merely there to be seen or to procure free food, alcohol and gifts. So, my 'dropping in' to this area wasn't as fortuitous as it had first seemed. Not only was the stage only partially visible from this section, without the required passes there was no way you could gain access to any of the tents and with no pass at all I was constantly in fear of been thrown out. During the afternoon, and for reasons best known only to them, a group of hippies decided to tear down a section of the corrugated iron fence that separated the populace from the VIPs. As the militant hippie brigade came running into the VIP area I seized the opportunity and moved as swiftly as I could in the opposite direction! Free at last, I quickly found myself a great spot quite near the front and when I turned back to look from whence I came I fell back in laughter as the hippie horde that breached the fence was now falling over itself to get back out of the VIP area; two of them even helping security guards to re-erect the fallen section of fence!"[4]

Phil Sutcliffe reporting for the British music paper Sounds said: "Backstage it was one of the most sumptuous liggers' playgrounds yet constructed outdoors. A series of record company tents provided almost limitless food and drink for those with the aplomb to collect the various badges, stickers and cards that were needed to gain admission. The Saturday Night Fever Tax Loss Award was won by RSO [records], who managed to hang chandeliers inside their marquee."[5]

Chris Brazier writing for *Melody Maker* was in complete agreement with Sutcliffe regarding the Hospitality Enclosure which he described as "spectacularly disgusting" and catering for the "grotesquely pampered elite." He continued, "A more sickeningly artificial crew would be difficult to imagine, even by music business standards."

Phil Sutcliffe: "Unfortunately, anyone attending the concert with an official function to perform who wasn't directly employed by Harvey Goldsmith faced a lean time. Photographers were hassled to the point of extinction whether they had official passes or not. In fact a photographer's pass didn't actually permit you to photograph the stage at all! Despite the fact that dozens of these passes were handed out by press officer Alan Burry, no one was allowed access to any vantage points that might enable them to take a worthwhile photograph (with the exception of Harvey's own man of course)."[6]

Photographer Chalkie Davies recalls: "I was in America with the Rolling Stones when I got a call from promoter Harvey Goldsmith, he wanted me to fly home and be the official photographer for the Bob Dylan concert at Blackbushe Airport. I jumped at the chance of shooting Dylan and booked a seat on the first plane home and I went straight from Heathrow to the gig. But when I got there I was given the news that Bob had his own photographer and I was out of a job. His tour manager told me to put my cameras away and be sure not to take any photos of Bob, even when he was performing.

I was mightily depressed by this news and wandered around backstage in a daze. I bumped into Graham Parker and told him my tale of woe. Then, a voice behind us says 'Hey man, I just want to say, man, that I really like your albums, man.' We turn around and see Bob Dylan standing there, GP, suffering from shock looks Bob in the eye and says: 'Thanks, do you know my photographer, Chalkie?' I offer Bob my hand and receive the worst wet fish handshake ever. I ask Bob if it's okay to take a photo of them and he happily obliges, shaking like a leaf I take three frames. Bob and Graham then have a short but meaningful conversation before Bob bids us both farewell and wanders off into the sunset."[7]

During that conversation Dylan told Parker, "I really love that song of yours." There was then a painfully long pause while Parker waited to hear what the song was. "That song ... um ... erm .... errmmmm ... ahh ... ooh, man," was all Parker got from Dylan. Parker says he then started to sweat. "My lip went up above my teeth and I became so nervous it dried out and stuck there. Ah, 'Don't Ask Me Questions!'" Dylan eventually exclaimed to Parker's great relief.[8]

Martin Carthy: "Apparently he [Dylan] wanted me to be on [at Blackbushe], so he told Harvey Goldsmith, and Harvey tried to get hold of me. Not very hard... but I got the invitation to come down... It took me four hours to get backstage. There were at least three levels of security, and then his caravan. And he had no idea. So I went in and he said, 'Oh, how are you?' and then he said, 'How's Anthea?' [Joseph] And I said, 'She's fine. She's out in hospitality.' And he said,

'Why doesn't she come and see me?' I looked at him and said, 'Do you have any idea what the security is like here?' He turned to one of the blokes and said, 'Can you go and find Anthea Joseph? She's in hospitality.' They came back in five minutes and there she was, festooned in all the passes. You know, there's a level of innocence about him that's really endearing. He didn't have a clue."

Other "festooned" people spotted backstage and in the VIP area were Bianca Jagger and Ringo Starr. Ringo complained that he couldn't see the stage from the VIP enclosure so before Clapton's set began he and Bianca were supplied with folding chairs and taken to the open area between that stage and the front barrier. Like moths to a flame, the great and the good came to pay homage: Mick Jones and Joe Strummer (of The Clash) were both seen in the VIP area; as was Jimmy Page, Rory Gallagher, Wilko Johnson, Roger Chapman, Denny Laine, Barbara Dickson, Terry Wilson-Slessor (Back Street Crawler); the wonderful bard of Salford and Dylan lookalike, John Cooper Clarke, Annie Nightingale, 'Whispering' Bob Harris, one half of Gallagher & Lyle (the one with the long hair), and the entire cast of Dire Straits. Also present were Billy Connolly, Brian Lane (manager of Yes); writer and major counterculture figure, Barry Miles; graphic designer, publisher and underground denizen, Pearce Marchbank and actresses Susan George and Jenny Agutter.

The festival's biggest failure by far was the car parking facilities. Goldsmith had turned responsibilities for parking over to the "professionals," but the resulting chaos was not National Car Parks' finest hour! The bizarre thing was, when people arrived at the car park and paid their 50 pence all the bays were neatly numbered and taped into sections and those with presence of mind noted down the location in which their car was parked. Shortly after the festival had finished, but long before most of the attendees had returned to their vehicles, all of the section markers were removed and the situation rapidly degenerated into total chaos. It took hours for people to find their cars among 60,000 vehicles and even then they were probably hemmed in by other cars. Some people reported taking six hours to locate their vehicles and exit while others simply decided to sleep in their cars, leaving the following morning.

Regardless of any other problems – and they were few and far between – the crowd was very well behaved. One police officer said, "I'd rather deal with this lot than the average soccer crowd." The *Daily Mirror* newspaper reported: "The biggest open-air rock event for nine years, went off with hardly a sour note." Praise continued to be lavished on the crowd in the *Daily Express*: "The feeling of good-will was quite remarkable," a police spokesman said, "We could never have anticipated how calm the atmosphere would be." In total there were just 69 arrests on drug and theft charges. The St John Ambulance Brigade dealt out a few pills for headaches and mild cases of sunstroke, strapped up one broken arm and had few problems with drug overdoses; otherwise, things were relatively quiet.

During the afternoon's proceedings, a helicopter, which droned loudly overhead, began dropping small packages from on high. The packages weren't manna from heaven, but rather presents from Goldsmith! (actually, I believe CBS Records footed the bill). These mini-parachutes, which were about seven inches in length and officially called "paratwirlers," rained gently down on an expectant crowd; though quite what they were expecting is another matter. When the paratwirlers finally completed their spinning descent all was revealed. The card parachutes, which were in the shape of a pair of dark Dylan glasses, housed a souvenir badge advertising "Bob Dylan Street-Legal"– A lovely memento of the day Bob Dylan came to Blackbushe.

People had begun arriving at the festival site on Thursday afternoon. The arena was opened to the public at 9 am on Saturday and by 11 am more than 50,000 were already settled inside. With

Merger added to the bill, the 2 pm start was brought forward to 12.30. Their late addition meant the band was not featured on the festival posters. The London based reggae outfit kicked off the proceedings with a 45-minute set and although the crowd was still not fully formed there was a crush at the front and one injured attendee had to be strapped to a stretcher and lifted over the crash barrier. The concert was just two minutes old! Thankfully, this was pretty much an isolated incident.

The band's Jamaican/Ghanaian line up allowed them to play a wide range of often energetic reggae/jazz sounds. Their much-hyped début album, *Exiles in a Babylon*, created something of a stir when it appeared in 1977 and the band just about lived up to their reputation.

Next up was Lake; a six-man line-up comprising two keyboard players, two guitarists, a bassist and drummer. I have to admit that after Blackbushe the only thing I could remember about Lake was that I couldn't remember anything about them! *Melody Maker* said the band was, "Europe's answer to Boston," but then we all have our crosses to bear! An Anglo-German keyboard driven outfit, Lake had received rave reviews in Germany. Signed to CBS, the label had already taken the opportunity of getting them on to the Dylan bills in Nuremberg and Rotterdam before pushing them forward for Blackbushe.

Next came Graham Parker, a local lad from Deepcut near Camberley. A former petrol pump attendant, Parker placed an ad in *Melody Maker* that read: "Singer-songwriter needs tasteful musicians for Stones-Dylan style band." The line-up that came together and remained together at Blackbushe featured legendary Brinsley Schwarz on lead guitar, Brinsley's keyboard player Bob Andrews, ex-Ducks Deluxe guitarist Martin Belmont, plus Andrew Bodnar on bass and Steve Goulding on drums.

By the time of Blackbushe, Parker and the Rumour had built a solid reputation for delivering extremely powerful live performances of which Blackbushe would be no exception. Two days before The Picnic, Parker had appeared at the three-day Manchester carnival, arranged jointly by the Anti-Nazi League and Rock Against Racism, an organisation that Dylan had talked with CBS Press Manager Ellie Smith about while in Germany. I can't imagine what Parker, a staunch anti-racist, thought about Clapton's inclusion in the Blackbushe line-up. Although Dylan was not unaware of the situation, Clapton had been receiving bad press in Britain due to a hideous rant he made on August 5, 1976 during a concert in Birmingham, England. On that night, Clapton made a drunken declaration of support for former Conservative Minister Enoch Powell (known for his anti-immigration 'Rivers of Blood' speech). Clapton began his rant with: "Do we have any foreigners in the audience tonight? If so, please put up your hands. Wogs I mean, I'm looking at you ... So where are you? Well wherever you all are, I think you should all just leave. Not just leave the hall, leave our country ... I think Enoch's right, I think we should send them all back. Stop Britain from becoming a black colony. Get the foreigners out ... Keep Britain white. I used to be into dope, now I'm into racism." The Birmingham Odeon quote is lengthy, it gets much worse and for the most part the language used is too vile and repulsive to repeat here. This incident was the main inspiration for the formation of Rock Against Racism. "It [was] just an idea until ... Eric Clapton made a drunken declaration" said one of the organisers. These comments were all the more galling when you consider that much of Clapton's music was borrowed from the blues and that his most recent hit was with a cover of a Bob Marley song (Clapton had specifically included Jamaicans on his list of those who should leave). Rock Against Racism wrote a letter to *NME* expressing their opposition to Clapton's comments: "Come on Eric," they wrote, "Own up. Half your music is black. Who shot the Sheriff, Eric? It sure as hell wasn't you!" In the years since his horrendous outburst, Clapton has repeatedly been required to reckon with those words, frequently chalking them up to being out of his brain on drugs and alcohol. "I sabotaged everything I got involved with," Clapton said in one interview, "I was so ashamed of who I was, a kind of semi-racist, which didn't make sense. Half of my friends were black, I dated a black woman, and I championed black music."

It might be difficult to comprehend now, especially for those not born at the time, just how high racist feelings were running in Britain and parts of mainland Europe in the Seventies. Andrew Muir, author and editor of the now-defunct Dylan magazines Homer, the slut and Judas!, encountered these bigoted attitudes during his long coach ride from Scotland to Blackbushe. As his coach passed through a predominantly black area of the English Midlands, racist slurs were hurled at people on the pavement outside. Only a short time before, those responsible had been singing along to 'The Lonesome Death of Hattie Carroll.' Andrew tried to comfort himself that it was probably a one-off, but a friend later told him that the same thing had happened on his coach journey.

Back at the festival, Parker and the Rumour opened their set with a ferocious version of 'Stick it to Me,' the title track from their most recent studio album. He could easily have been fazed by being on the same stage as one of his biggest influences, Bob Dylan, but on this afternoon the diminutive Parker was, as usual, punching way above his weight. As was always the case, his songs, direct and uncomplicated, were delivered with total conviction.

Joan Armatrading was initially scheduled to appear next, but it was decided it would be better if she played between Clapton and Dylan, acting as a sort of buffer between the two main artists. In any event, the gap between Graham Parker's set and Eric Clapton taking the stage was overly long. Clapton, who had arrived by helicopter, appeared wearing a black leather jacket, an open neck shirt and faded blue jeans, a far cry from the Armani suits that would later become his trademark. The crowd had mostly remained seated until Clapton came on, but Eric's arrival, which was greeted by at least one "Clapton is God" banner, got people onto their feet. Those standing were quickly pelted with cans and security asked everyone to sit down. Although his set was reasonably well received, at times Eric was so laidback he was in danger of falling over. His nonchalant approach may have worked well in a more intimate setting but in front of a massive outdoor festival crowd he was frequently in danger of losing the audience's attention. To me, it was a seemingly indifferent performance, but Harry Doherty writing in *Melody Maker* was much less complimentary, in Harry's opinion, Wonderful Tonight, Clapton wasn't.

"If The Trade Descriptions Act applied to rock concerts," Doherty wrote, "Eric Clapton would be hauled in front of the appropriate committee and asked to explain his lacklustre performance." What Dylan thought of Eric's show isn't known. He did, however, watch the proceedings from side stage. As an interesting aside, the initial report in the local Star newspaper suggested that David Soul and/or Eric Clapton would be support to Dylan. Maybe David Soul would have been a better choice!

Clapton was followed at just after 7 pm by Joan Armatrading, or Joan armaplating as she was popularly known back then. Even though Dylan liked Armatrading's music and she was therefore one of the artists he recommended for the event, Joan admitted that she had only recently got into Dylan through *Blood on the Tracks*. Armatrading told *Melody Maker*: "Yeah... That was very late ... But that was the first Dylan album I got ... I never went out of my way to listen to a lot of people ... It was only when I started to teach myself to play that [music] became prominent." Joan, who is always nervous before gigs, said she was particularly anxious about playing on the same bill as Dylan.

Born the third of six children in St Kitts, West Indies, Joan

Armatrading came to live in Birmingham, England at the age of seven. Hugely underrated musically, she would go on to have a long career. Nevertheless, when Joan signed to A&M America in 1974, Derek Green, the then head of the company's British arm, was less than enthusiastic, believing her to be un-commercial with no image to project. What's more, she was black, female and a poor investment! Green cautioned her first producer Pete Gage: "Don't spend too much money." Armatrading, who by 1978 had four albums to her name, delivered an unbelievably good 60-minute set which couldn't have been easy, sandwiched as she was between Clapton and Dylan.

Considering the size of Dylan's tour band, the changeover between Armatrading and Dylan was pretty slick. A special (at the time) rolling stage built for Dylan's '78 tour was used at Blackbushe. The stage, with the musicians' equipment already set up, was rolled on top of the main stage and rolled off again after the performance.

Chapter Eleven

The Picnic Performance

By the time he got to Blackbushe, Bob Dylan was well and truly basking in the grandeur of performing with his big band. He was now very much at ease, was happy with the proficiency of the musicians and was revelling in the almost unlimited capacity they gave him to reinvent not only his Sixties material, but also later songs.

   The start of the tour had been tentative, especially the concerts in Japan and the resulting *At Budokan** album, but, by the time the tour reached Europe, Bob and the band were far more confident and many of the arrangements had taken on more of a rock feel. There was a radical re-imagining of his familiar songs, an approach that would become a well-loved and expected hallmark of his concerts in the future. At this time, however, many critics and fans were utterly dismayed at the treatment of these "sacred" anthems. Be that as it may, those who dismissed the entire 1978 tour out-of-hand as being showbiz, Vegas, lightweight, and lacking in sincerity, are somehow missing the passion that exudes from Dylan during his performances of songs like 'Tangled Up In Blue' (especially during the European leg), or the rewrites of many other songs like 'Going, Going, Gone.'

* At Budokan *received some of the worst reviews of Dylan's career. Critically savaged, it was derided as "slick" and "sterile." Music critic and author Jimmy Guterman included* At Budokan *in his 1991 book:* The Worst Rock 'n' Roll Records of All Time... *Bob Dylan said of the album: "They twisted my arm to do a live album for Japan ... We [the band] had just started findin' our way into things on that tour when they recorded it. I never meant for it to be any type of representation of my stuff, or my band or my live show."*

Plaudits should be bestowed on Janet Maslin writing for *Rolling Stone* in July 1979 for understanding that to stand still is to stagnate and to die. "However much they may offend purists," Maslin wrote, "These latest live versions of his old songs have the effect of liberating Bob Dylan from the originals. And the originals – however lasting, however beautiful – constitute a terrible burden."

"What I like about this band," said Dylan: "Is that I can get everything I want from them – the blues, soul, country, Cajun, American music – everything. This is not a rock band. Soul has always been in me, and I've listened to Red Prysock, the greatest horn player I've ever heard. Then years ago I used to go to the Apollo and listen to the Bobby Blue Band (sic). Lonnie Johnson and Muddy, these people are the guys I've come up with, so the soul element is natural."[1] Interestingly, Dylan gave much of the credit for the new arrangements to Steven Soles.

The Stage Was Set, the Lights Went Out…

The time has arrived to set the scene: guitarist Billy Cross, resplendent with a Gibson Les Paul Goldtop, is a way to the left as we view the stage, with Bobbye Hall on congas behind him and further still to the left. Alan Pasqua, who plays a Baby Grand piano, a Clavinet, a Fender Rhodes and a CS-80 Yamaha Synth, is on the extreme left of the stage with his main keyboard facing across towards Dylan and with his other keyboards to both sides.

In a line to Dylan's right as we view the stage are Jerry Scheff (bass), Steve Soles (rhythm guitar), David Mansfield (mandolin, violin) and Steve Douglas (tenor sax, flute, recorder). Standing on a small raised platform to the extreme right and close to the edge of the stage are Helena Springs, Jo Ann Harris and Carolyn Dennis. The girl backing singers are now much further to the right than they were when the tour started. Dylan told Ray Coleman in June that he was beginning to think that the back-up singers were maybe, "A bit Las Vegas." "I turned round in Japan and saw a pair of breasts on stage ... I thought then that something's gotta be done about this." If Dylan did think that, then he was monumentally slow in ringing the changes because backing singers, whether a trio or a quartet, would be part and parcel of Dylan's live shows for several years to come and would be a feature of his recorded output for almost the next decade. Bringing up the rear, Ian Wallace's drum kit is pointing very slightly diagonally across the stage towards Pasqua's keyboards.

As was the case throughout 1978, for much of The Picnic, Dylan plays a stunning black custom Fender Stratocaster. He also uses a blonde maple-neck Fender Telecaster on some songs. The white National Glenwood 98 (aka The Map), on which Bob played slide during 'Shelter from the Storm' on the second leg of the Rolling Thunder tour was at the back of the stage but wasn't used (in fact, although The Map – Dylan christened the guitar "Rimbaud" – appeared on stage throughout much of the 1978 tour it was never played). At the start of the Japanese leg of the tour Bob either bought or was given three Yamaha acoustic guitars– an L-6, an L-51 and a very distinctive black and white L-52. Dylan talks about his new guitar(s) in a March 1978 interview with Craig McGregor: "I'll tell you one reason [why I haven't been playing much acoustic stuff], but you wouldn't probably believe me, is because I haven't found a magic guitar. I think I might have found one now." At Blackbushe, the new Yamaha L-6 was used for the one-off acoustic performance of 'Gates of Eden.'

The 34-song (depending on how you count them) Blackbushe set is longer than any other on the tour. In fact, at three hours and five minutes, the performance is Bob Dylan's longest continual concert ever. The content of Dylan's show is something of a surprise (leastways to those who had not seen the setlist from Nuremberg; remember these were pre-Internet days when news of this sort travelled slowly, if at all). Although it is only a short time since Dylan finished his Earls Court residency, Blackbushe sees the introduction of eight songs not performed in London ('Just Like Tom Thumb's Blues,' 'It's All Over Now, Baby Blue,' 'Girl From the North Country,' 'Is Your Love in Vain?,' 'Where Are You Tonight? (Journey Through Dark Heat),' 'Gates of Eden,' 'True Love Tends to Forget' and 'Changing of the Guards') and a further two, 'Simple Twist of Fate' and 'To Ramona,' that have only received one outing each. Until Paris (July 4) Dylan's sets had usually opened with a sort of instrumental overture of 'A Hard Rain's A-Gonna Fall'– sans Dylan. From the second Paris show on, however, the opening instrumental, still minus Dylan, changed to 'My Back Pages'; an appropriate choice to announce these career retrospective – or should that be greatest hits? – shows.

Twilight has now arrived; it's a magical time of the day, even though the disappearance of the warm July sun means the night is rapidly growing cold. At the front there is a clear and definite air of excited anticipation running through the crowd and everyone is now standing. What is to come will be the climax both to The Picnic and to Dylan's all-conquering European tour.

As the band takes the stage for 'My Back Pages,' the crowd instantly erupts; those more than halfway back are probably unaware that Bob has not yet arrived on stage! Shouts of "sit down" ring out from all quarters and, when those at the front fail to respond, the requests grow louder and more forceful. Missiles, mostly drinks cans, begin to rain down on the transgressors while the band takes it in turn to introduce themselves via their instruments: mandolin is followed by lazy phrases of brass, then keys and finally lead guitar. It's only during the last few bars of the song that the man himself emerges into the deep red light that will remain with us for pretty much the whole concert. This time the crowd's roar rolls from the front to the back of the site like a not yet thought of Mexican Wave. After less than a month away, Bob is back in London.

Dylan takes the stage wearing black trousers, a heavy looking black leather jacket and a white collarless shirt under a fancy black waistcoat. The ensemble is topped off with a splendid black top hat. Although he previously wore similar headgear in Auckland in March, this magnificent specimen is borrowed from a doorman at London's Royal Garden Hotel (Bob asked the doorman if he could borrow the top hat as he left the hotel and returned it safely when he arrived back there after the show). Other fashion accessories include dark glasses (for part of the show), a chunky bead necklace and no less than five rings which were not in evidence at the beginning of the tour.

Black Strat in hand, he takes up his position centre-stage, his mic-stand a couple of paces forward of the rest of the musicians. There's a short pause and the band moves into the second number, the first to feature Dylan. As has been the case for most of the tour, Dylan sings a Tampa Red song; tonight it's the Chicago blues 'Love Her with a Feeling.'*

When the fast-paced blues comes to an end Bob dives straight into his brand new album, *Street-Legal*. He's been playing the song since June 1; two weeks before the release of the album and the vast crowd seems familiar with it. Leastways it's greeted with another massive roar of appreciation. The song in question, 'Baby Stop Crying,' would also be released on July 31 as a single. Although there is a little more edge to Bob's vocals, as with the majority of the *Street-Legal* songs, tonight's arrangement of 'Baby Stop Crying'

* When originally released in 1938 on Bluebird, the title on the record was 'Love With a Feeling.' It was only when Tampa Red recorded an updated Chicago-style blues version for RCA in 1950 that "her" was added to the title. Dylan played this song at all his London shows so those of us who attended the Earls Court concerts probably wouldn't be aware that while in Europe this slot had been occupied by another Tampa Red song, 'She's Love Crazy.'

is pretty much identical to the released version. Almost without fail the live performances of this song are emotionally charged and tonight is no exception.

We now move back in time to the *Highway 61 Revisited* album for a pleasant if slightly lightweight version of 'Just Like Tom Thumb's Blues.' Where once there was harmonica, tonight there's sax and organ. It's clear that Bob is very happy for the musicians to come to the fore and tonight guitarist Billy Cross obliges with three separate short solos.

'Shelter from the Storm' is next up. With its radically new choppy arrangement the jerky, jagged, stiff guitar riffs almost impart a reggae feel to the number. The song is nicely understated with a great guitar solo and some lovely sax from Steve Douglas. As 'Shelter...' closes, Bob puts down his guitar, takes a few steps forward and grabs hold of the mic stand with one hand. He looks slightly uncomfortable, or maybe he just looks like Bob Dylan always does on stage. He seems unsure quite what to do with his hands now that he's not holding his guitar but he soon discovers that the borrowed silk top hat makes a good prop and tips it slightly in recognition of his audience; something he will do several times before the long night is over. Relinquishing the guitar signals an abrupt change of pace as we are transported back to 1965 for a great rendition of 'It's All Over Now, Baby Blue' during which he produces a harmonica which until that moment has been concealed in the palm of his left hand. Unsurprisingly, this first rasping harp solo of the night is greeted with whoops of recognition and huge applause.

The exceptional 'Tangled up in Blue' is sidelined tonight in favour of a mournful 'Girl from the North Country' on which Dylan is accompanied only by Pasqua on piano and some evocative sax lines from Douglas. Almost a torch ballad, Bob pays great attention to his singing on this one.

Next up is a dramatic, maybe overly dramatic, 'performance'

of 'Ballad of a Thin Man' on which Dylan keeps the customers satisfied with a few theatrics. As Cross cranks it up, Bob continues ridiculing Mr Jones for failing to understand just what's happening. Without his guitar and with mic in hand, Bob paces the stage taking tiny exaggerated Thunderbird puppet like steps; at times spinning around on the spot. During the time it takes Bob to retrieve and strap on his Stratocaster we are treated to some fine crashing keyboard from Pasqua. Although the visuals may be hammed up a little on this one, the way in which the song is sung is nothing short of breathtaking.

Off comes the top hat and on go the shades. 'Maggie's Farm' takes the form of a very energetic shuffle that sees Bob bounding around the stage bending at the knees and rocking like a demon. This one is followed by a dramatic 'Simple Twist of Fate.' There are some nice vocals here but in the end this version lacks a little of the intimacy of the original.

Those in the crowd who have been calling for 'Like a Rolling Stone' now get their wish granted and soon the multitudes are singing and clapping along with the greatest pop/rock single ever written. Bob straps on his Telecaster for this one and we are transported back a dozen years to the Judas tour! This song wasn't played in 1975-76 and, although it's been performed regularly on this tour, tonight's version, complete with some great lead guitar from Cross, ranks as one of the best we've heard. Some of the crowd like the backing vocals on this one, while others find them superfluous or even a burden.

A song that many in the crowd associate more with The Band than Bob Dylan, 'I Shall be Released' is very well sung and everyone seems to agree that the girls are a valuable addition on this one. Bob's jerky movements and theatrical hand gestures keep us transfixed. Wonderful stuff!

For most of the European tour a nice tight 'Going, Going, Gone' has occupied the number 13 slot but tonight 'Going' has gone and the rarely performed 'Is Your Love in Vain?' gets an outing. Introduced as "a new song," 'Is Your Love in Vain?' is slightly lacking when compared to the album version. Dylan's voice is pitched high above the music and at time he tends to shout out the ends of some of the lines.

'One of Us Must Know,' which was a regular in this spot at the Earls Court shows and for much of the first half of the European tour is now replaced with yet another *Street-Legal* number, 'Where Are You Tonight? (Journey Through Dark Heat).' The top hat returns for this one. Unlike 'Is Your Love in Vain?,' 'Where Are You Tonight?' follows the album version almost exactly; albeit at a slightly slower tempo. This is a great performance, especially when you consider this is the first ever outing of the song. The lyrics seem to sum up precisely where Dylan is at this time.

We've reached the halfway point in the show and Dylan takes a break. "Thank you. Yes, there's some other people in the group too," Bob informs us. "I wanna introduce you to a girl I know you're gonna like. All three girls over here sing. Also, these guys sing too ... He sings. Just for now we're just gonna have three girls and maybe one of the guys sing. I'm getting tired. So, we're gonna have Carolyn Dennis come first. I want you to meet Carolyn Dennis." Dylan then removes the top hat and drops back alongside Billy Cross where he plays some perfunctory rhythm guitar while Dennis sings the Sam Cooke Sixties classic 'A Change is Gonna Come.'

Next, Helena Springs sings 'Mr Tambourine Man,' a song that Dylan himself performed during his Earls Court residency. Much later in the tour he will play the song again in the form of a stunning, slow-paced, radical rearrangement, but sadly tonight it's left to Helena. Bob moves forward again to introduce the song: "This is Helena Springs," Dylan says. "This is her song. She might sing awhile. She's gonna sing 10 songs for you now." After this introduction Bob again withdraws from front stage. Thankfully, Springs only performs one song and not the threatened 10! Next up we have Jo Ann Harris. Again Bob makes the introduction: "All right, thank you. Jo Ann wants to sing a Paul McCartney song that she likes a lot. Jo Ann Harris." The song in question is 'The Long and Winding Road.' The final song in this interlude comes from Steven Soles. "Oh, there's another person here," Dylan says. "You gotta hear this guy sing. He writes his original songs too. He's gonna come and sing one for you. You must hear him, you really must. He really is a genius; Steven Soles. Maybe you've heard of him, maybe you haven't but I'm sure you'll remember him after you hear him tonight; Steven Soles."

At this point, Dylan leaves the stage (I'm told he made a telephone call! If so, time would have been very tight). Soles' performance, which he dedicates to the French people in the crowd, is a mandolin-driven 'Laissez-Faire,' a David Ackles song that Soles previously performed on the Rolling Thunder tour.

It's now getting quite dark and the stage lighting, which has been deep red for almost the entire set, starts to take effect, creating a mood that will enhance the stage show during the remainder of the evening. With Dylan now bathed in a blue spotlight and with the L-6 Yamaha acoustic guitar across his shoulder, we are treated to a truly stunning 'Gates of Eden.' Well played and beautifully sung, this rendition of 'Gates,' complete with a harmonica break that has Dylan swaying and leaning to his right, might even surpass the original! The only slight distraction is a firework that was let off midway through the song. Anywhere else in the set might have been acceptable!

We are now back to a full band line-up and also back to *Street-Legal* for a brilliant version of 'True Love Tends to Forget.' Well sung, this rendition again follows the album version closely. 'One More Cup of Coffee (Valley Below)' is one of the countless highlights in tonight's show. This, almost gospel sounding arrangement, is terrific. Don't even think about comparing this outing to the *Desire* version. They don't bear comparison. There's some great sax here and Bobbye Hall also earns her corn on this one.

As one might expect, 'Blowin' in the Wind' receives a great reception. The flute, which is endlessly annoying on the *At Budokan* album, works quite well here as it skips in and out of the proceedings. By the time this one is over, many thousands of tiny lights are held aloft in appreciation as sections of the crowd sway to this Sixties anthem. The lighting now reverts to deep red and a slow, deliberate 'I Want You' is played. Still seated, Pasqua rocks back and forth violently as though in a trance.

'Señor (Tales of Yankee Power)' receives a mumbled intro from Dylan: "Thank you. This is a recently written song. Written and inspired, this song is inspired by a man named Harry Dean Stanton. Some of you may know him, some of you maybe not. He's in the house tonight! Stand up and take a bow! Put the light on him! Yes, put the light on him! Yes put the light on this man! Anyway, this is called 'Tales of Yankee Power.'" This performance, on which the girl back-up singers are quite effective, is as dark and menacing as you'll hear. Steve Douglas' recorder is rather nice on this one.

The first few bars of the hard rock 'Masters of War' sound like the band are going to play 'Louie Louie'! Bob sings this one like he means it, almost spitting venom over Billy Cross' biting lead guitar. Steve Douglas' honking sax works well and he gets to perform a great little solo.

'Just Like a Woman' is also sung with extreme passion tonight. At the end of the song, Bob lets the guitar fall to his waist and the sax break gives way to his harmonica. Dylan rocks back and forth, harp cupped in both hands blowing for all he's worth. Are the crowd won over by this new arrangement or is it just nostalgia that brings such enthusiastic applause at the close of the song? Hopefully it's the arrangement because Dylan really pulls this one apart and then stitches it back together to create a brand new tapestry of words and music. The back-up vocals again work very well on this one.

'To Ramona' contains some really soulful violin. Dylan told Ray Coleman: "I think [David Mansfield] is the best guy around on that instrument, but they're all special to me." In any event, this is a stunning version. At the song's close, Steven Soles begins playing the intro to 'All Along the Watchtower.' The song is not due yet. Perhaps Soles is ready for his supper. What we do get next is a dose of "Southern Mountain Reggae" in the guise of, 'Don't Think Twice, It's Alright.' "Thank you," Dylan says: "we wanna play a reggae, our reggae version for you. Sort of reggae, not really reggae. What we call Southern Mountain Reggae. This is a particular sound you get in the States in the Southern Mountains." (Sure thing, Bob!). Whatever the sound is, it's unique to Dylan; his own genre! With its emphatic cross-rhythms, the song sounds like it's floating along on a whistle (in actual fact it's Steve Douglas' flute). With Hall's congas in the foreground the song revolves around percussion and bass. During the instrumental break, Bob moves around the stage in a sort of cross-stepping motion that I can only assume are Southern Mountain Reggae dance steps!

Next up, thank you Mr Soles, are the unmistakeable opening chords to 'All Along the Watchtower.' This is a stunning flute and fiddle-driven hard rock rendition of the song on which Mansfield seems to be channelling Jimi Hendrix while Bobbye Hall's congas pound out the beat. The high-speed fiddle solo at the close of the song is truly amazing and Bob stands and stares for a while, almost transfixed by Mansfield's speed and dexterity. During the Nineties, the Dylan faithful would tire of this overly familiar song but at this point in Dylan's career the number was still fresh, bold and vibrant.

Although some might argue that the carnival, honky-tonk arrangement of 'All I Really Want to Do' is slightly throwaway, I can't agree. Tonight's outing is certainly a vast improvement on the half-baked version released on the *At Budokan* album. The arrangement of this one continued to develop throughout the tour and by June/July it had become fully realised. As previously stated, the hugely altered arrangements of some of the songs performed on this tour paved the way for what was to come on future tours.

"All right," Dylan says, "I've just been notified we've been running out of time. Anyway, let me run through who the band here is real quick." After the introductions we get a fast-paced, heavy rock version of 'It's Alright Ma (I'm Only Bleeding).' This one has been improving throughout the tour and tonight we are treated to a standout performance on which the female backing vocals work well. "I got nothin', Ma, to live up to." Indeed. The stage lighting is still deep red but the super trouper now has Bob engulfed in white light.

A perfect closer, the final song of the set is 'Forever Young.' Dylan: "All right, we gotta go; the stage manager just said it. They're gonna send us home. Anyway Eric Clapton's back. And he's gonna stay with us and play. So we've ended the shows so far with this song and we're gonna do it again. I hope we can meet again real soon. I want to come back." Eric Clapton then walks out on stage grinning from ear to ear. Clapton: "God I was drunk. So drunk. He called me on to play and I started walking from the back of the stage and thought I was going to walk straight off the front. You know when you are really drunk and once the forward motion has started there isn't any stopping it. A real lurch. Funny night. I was sober when I played my own set, but in the interim I think I drank a bottle of vodka."

Clapton, who doesn't appear drunk, plays off Billy Cross and also trades a few riffs with Dylan. In truth though, his contribution is pretty minimal. The song features some nice sax and a fine Billy Cross guitar solo after which the instrumentation falls into discord for a few seconds. Partway through, thousands of tiny lights are again set against the now black night sky. "Thank you very much," Dylan mumbles. More guitar, another "thank you," something that resembles a salute, and he's gone.

As Dylan leaves the stage the crowd begin to stand and a rhythmic chant of "more, more, more" cuts through the now chilly night air. Then, after a short wait the band, including Eric Clapton, are back on stage for the encore. The encore provides us with yet another surprise; two songs instead of one. At all of the Earls Court shows the encore was restricted to 'The Times They Are A-Changin,'" but, while in Europe, Bob had upped the ante by performing two encores. Although the extra song – the first encore – 'Changing of the Guards,' is virtually identical to the album version, Bob seems to race through it a little here; not the best performance of the night. Like Soles before him, perhaps Bob is now ready for supper!

Finally, Bob delivers 'The Times They Are A-Changin',' which tonight is an anthem re-born. At the end he raises both arms in salute and leaves the stage. "That's the end of the show; the best we've ever had," he says. Predictably, the crowd shouts for more but at three hours plus Bob has already delivered far more than anyone could have hoped for! A truly compelling and hypnotic performance. Harvey Goldsmith later said: "Dylan was on fire during that tour and at Blackbushe we couldn't get him off the stage."

On the subject of fire, the only thing missing from the show was the fireworks display. On either side of the stage and directly above the vast PA system were a pair of firework rigs. Although the rigs were covered with white fabric, when the wind blew against the sheets the words "Bob Dylan" (stage left as we view it) and "Blackbushe 78" (on the other side), could just about be seen. A fireworks display was also planned for behind the stage but unfortunately the wind was deemed to be too strong and the health and safety crew decided against the pyrotechnics.

Blackbushe, July 15, 1978:

My Back Pages (Instrumental with no participation from Dylan)

Love Her with a Feeling (Tampa Red)

Baby Stop Crying

Just like Tom Thumb's Blues

Shelter from the Storm

It's All Over Now, Baby Blue

Girl from the North Country

Ballad of a Thin Man

Maggie's Farm

Simple Twist of Fate

Like a Rolling Stone

I Shall Be Released

Is Your Love In Vain?

Where Are You Tonight? (Journey Through Dark Heat)

A Change is Gonna Come (Sam Cooke)(sung by Carolyn Dennis)

Mr Tambourine Man (sung by Helena Springs)

The Long and Winding Road (Paul McCartney) (sung by Jo Ann Harris)

Laissez-faire (David Ackles) (sung by Steven Soles)

Gates of Eden (solo acoustic)

True Love Tends to Forget

One More Cup of Coffee (Valley Below)

Blowin' in the Wind

I Want You

Senor (Tales of Yankee Power)

Masters of War

Just Like a Woman

To Ramona

Don't Think Twice, It's All Right

All Along the Watchtower

All I Really Want To Do

It's Alright Ma (I'm Only Bleeding)

Forever Young (with Eric Clapton on guitar)

Encores

Changing of the Guards (with Eric Clapton on guitar)

The Times They Are A-Changin' (with Eric Clapton on guitar)

Later on as the Crowd Thinned Out

After the show Dylan raced to Camberley train station to pick up the special train that was to take him to Waterloo. No definite departure time had been fixed so the train simply stood by for the appropriate moment. Dylan told the station supervisor David Humphrey how pleased he was with the secret rail arrangements, before giving him a cassette copy of *Street-Legal*. The guard was also given a similar gift. A message from Dylan's management thanked British Rail for: "outstanding cooperation from all staff met."

Regrettably, the rest of us didn't get away from the festival site quite so effortlessly! I've previously mentioned the six-hour delays in getting out of the car park but those heading to London by train experienced their fair share of problems. As people stumbled away from the site on foot they were quickly greeted by a police loudhailer informing them that there were no buses due to, "the volume of pedestrians." This was bad news, especially as the £3.00 travel ticket should have included this bus ride back to the station! In actual fact, just one bus ran from the site after which all others were cancelled because of the danger to pedestrians walking on the roads. With the buses cancelled, the weary festival goers now had to endure a three-mile hike to the train platform. Unfortunately, the cancelled bus service was not the end of the misery. A derailment on the track caused severe delays to the train service back to Waterloo and crowding at the station became extremely uncomfortable. Nevertheless, the day had been such a great experience that few complained.

Thomson Prentice writing for the *Daily Mail* (July 17, 1978) said of Blackbushe: "For just a few hours, the spirit of the Sixties lived again among 200,000 pilgrims. A vast denim army gathered for probably the last reunion of their generation at The Picnic." In hindsight, Prentice's prediction was right, with Blackbushe, the last great one-off music festival, the times had well and truly changed. By 1979, almost every remnant of the counterculture had gone and on May 3 of that year, in their infinite wisdom, the people of the United Kingdom put the daughter of a Grantham grocer in charge of the country. When Bob Dylan returned to Britain in 1981, Michael Jackson would be at Number 1 and Margaret Thatcher at Number 10. The times had well and truly changed. There would be no room for liberal thinkers on Maggie's Farm.

Chapter Twelve

You Changed
My Life

The 1978 world tour contained many 'firsts': Dylan's largest ever band, his only ever use of brass, the first use of female backing singers, his first ever concerts in Japan, New Zealand, Holland and Germany, and the first electric performances of a rake of songs including 'Love Minus Zero/No Limit,' 'Girl From the North Country,' 'Don't Think Twice, It's All Right,' 'To Ramona,' 'All I Really Want to Do,' 'Tomorrow is a Long Time,' 'It's Alright, Ma...,' 'The Times They Are A-Changin'' and 'Masters of War.'

By the time the final leg of the tour got underway in Augusta, Maine on September 15 Dylan had been on the road for seven months and much of the band's energy had begun to dissipate and in general the musicians were not particularly relishing the prospect of a further 65 lengthy concerts. Ian Wallace: "I think we were playing like six nights a week ... and those were three-hour shows and, even though we had our own plane and everything, that's pretty demanding ... Things started getting out of hand at one point. There was all kinds of rumours flying around, who was doing this to [whom]."

As one might expect, the majority of the gossip and intrigue focused on Dylan and his relationship with the band's backing singers: "I never got involved with anything like that," Jo Ann Harris told Howard Sounes, "but eventually [it] seemed to be that the girls who were singing always had something going on with [Bob]." Dylan would of course marry backing singer Carolyn Dennis in 1986.

This was the first nationwide tour of the States since 1974 and while tickets for those shows could not be had for love or money, the lack of demand four years later was quite hard to fathom. Demand for the earlier legs of the 1978 tour had been high and as we know in England Dylan sold-out six nights at Earls Court and then returned to play in front of some 200,000 at Blackbushe.

Although the band continued to travel from town to town by private plane, other expenses were now very much curtailed and as was the case in 1976, the overall mood of the tour had become somewhat subdued. The American audiences were not alone in their indifference towards the '78 shows. As had been the case earlier in the year with *Street-Legal*, the US press was also less than enthusiastic. Dylan told Robert Hilburn: "The writers complain the show's disco or Las Vegas. I don't know how they came up with those theories. We never heard them when we played Australia or Japan or Europe. It's like someone made it up in one town and the writer in the next town read it. I don't know what the reviewers mean half the time. I don't even care."[1]

According to the *Chicago Sun-Times*, the American shows were, "a funny cross between Name That Tune and That's Entertainment." *Time* magazine used the word "tiresome" and as previously mentioned, even Dylan champion Paul Williams described the shows as, "Packaged music ... for the mentally middle-aged."

As the tour progressed through to its December 16 finish, the woes increased when band members began going down with illness. Said to be influenza, it was being passed along like an unwanted birthday gift. Everyone seemed able to continue playing so maybe it was wasn't influenza. Whether flu or a just some nasty bug, Ian Wallace remembers feeling so ill that at one point he had to drum with a bucket next to him on stage.

Dylan's moods varied greatly at this time and tour personnel are divided as to his position on the Subjective Happiness Scale.

According to David Mansfield, Bob was: "Part of the band. He'd hang out, he'd drink, he'd talk his head off ... He was having a ball ... He just wanted to get on an aeroplane or bus, and keep playing forever."[2] There is no doubt that Dylan did consider extending the 1978 tour into the next year and he had called Jerry Weintraub on several occasions requesting that he should book more shows. The simple fact was, however, wanting to stay on the road did not necessarily mean that he was content in his private life. According to the often unreliable biographer Bob Spitz, who quotes a nameless entourage member: "Bob was at the lowest point in his life ... He was drinking heavily, just slugging down one brandy after the next [and] his moods were more inconsistent than usual."[3] As Dylan had told Robert Shelton when they met in London six months before: "[This band] is about the only thing I've got together now." Even so, when he returned to the studio in April 1979 and to the road in the November of that same year, he did so with an entirely new band. Before all of that, however, there is the small matter of the Jesus epiphany.

According to legend, on a cold November night in 1978, Bob Dylan experienced a vision of Jesus Christ. The Jesus epiphany is said by some to have occurred in a hotel room in Tucson, Arizona, near the end of the 1978 world tour. A little earlier in the tour, during a concert at the Sports Arena in San Diego (November 17), someone had thrown a small silver cross on stage which Dylan had quite uncharacteristically picked up and kept. When he returned to play San Diego, almost a year to the day later, Bob described this event to his audience:

"Last time I was here in San Diego, I think it was about a year ago ... wasn't it a year ago? I don't know but I was coming from someplace and I was feeling real sick when I got through here. And on the day of the show, I don't think it was in here, in this [venue] – I think it was in another place ... anyway ... just about towards the end of the show somebody out in the crowd – they knew I wasn't feeling too well, I think they could sense that – and they threw a silver cross on the stage. Now, usually I don't pick things up that are thrown on the front of the stage. Once in a while I do, but sometimes, most times, I don't. But, uh, I looked down at this cross and I said, 'I got to pick that up.' I picked up that cross and I put it in my pocket. It was a silver cross, I think maybe about so high – and I put it, brought it backstage and I brought it with me to the next town which was off in Arizona, Phoenix. Anyway, ah, when I got back there I was feeling even worse than I had felt when I was in San Diego, and I said, 'Well, I really need something tonight,' and, I didn't know what it was, I was using all kinds of things, and I said, 'I need something tonight that I never really had before.' And I looked in my pocket and I had this cross that someone threw before when I was in San Diego. So if that person is here tonight I want to thank you for that cross."[3]

A week after the '78 San Diego concert Dylan was photographed wearing the cross on stage in Fort Worth, Texas (November 24). Then, two nights later, at The Summit in Houston, Bob suddenly sang altered lyrics to 'Tangled Up in Blue.' The lady in the topless joint no longer had a book of poems. Instead, she is quoting from a Bible ("She opened up the Bible/ And started quoting it to me/ The Gospel according to Matthew/ Verse 3, Chapter 33"). In actual fact, Chapter 33 does not exist, but in any event Dylan gradually changed this line from night to night before settling upon Jeremiah. A quote from Jeremiah will later appear in the sleeve notes to the *Saved* album. It's interesting that Dylan seems to have begun his readings with Matthew. As the first book of the New Testament, the Gospel According to Matthew is of course a logical place to start. Nevertheless, the author, be it Matthew or an anonymous writer from AD 80, was almost certainly a male Jew who stood precariously on the margins between traditional and non-traditional Jewish values. The Gospel was written to convince fellow Jews that Jesus was the Messiah and it serves as a bridge between the Old Testament and the New Testament.

The above – picking up the cross, later wearing it and penning lines about Matthew and Jeremiah – is all fact but where the oft-told tale becomes vague is Dylan's supposed visitation by Christ. Clinton Heylin: "Stuck in a Tucson hotel room, after a lifetime of visions that caused divisions, Dylan experienced a vision of Christ, Lord of Lords, King of Kings." Heylin continues: "His state of mind may well have made him susceptible to such an experience. Lacking a sense of purpose in his personal life since the collapse of his marriage, he came to believe that, when Jesus revealed Himself, He quite literally rescued him from an early grave." This text is taken from the Dylan biography *Behind the Shades*, but where do these 'facts' originate? No source is given and as far as I'm aware Bob Dylan has never said that this epiphany took place in Tucson, or for that matter in Arizona. Nevertheless, the tale has been repeated countless times but never with any proper attribution. Also, there appears to be a slight shifting because in his latest book, *Trouble in Mind*, Heylin writes: "[Dylan] heard a voice in a hotel room in Arizona, of all places. It was November 18th, 1978." On November 18 Bob was in Tempe, Arizona not Tucson as quoted in *Behind the Shades*.

The first mention in interview regarding Dylan experiencing Jesus did not arrive until some 18 months after San Diego / Tucson. In May 1980, three days before his 39th birthday, Dylan told Karen Hughes: "I guess He's always been calling me. Of course, how would I ever know that, that it was Jesus calling me? I always thought it was some voice that would be more identifiable. But Christ is calling everybody; we just turn him off. We just don't want to hear ... But God's got his own purpose and time for everything. He knew when I would respond to His call ... Jesus put His hand on me. It was a physical thing. I felt it. I felt it all over me. I felt my whole body tremble. The glory of the Lord knocked me down and picked me up."[4]

In this interview, Dylan doesn't say where or when this experience happened. The next meaningful interview was given to Robert Hilburn on November 19, 1980. In this conversation, Dylan said: "I truly had a born-again experience, if you want to call it that ... It happened in 1978." However, at the July 1981 Travemunde press conference he said: "A few years [ago] I guess, in about the winter of '79 ... Jesus did appear to me as King of Kings and Lord of Lords." In truth then, the date and place of the Jesus epiphany appears to be supposition and if you dig a little deeper, there is some evidence that Bob had been drawn to this calling even before the San Diego cross episode.

Talking to Jonathan Cott of *Rolling Stone* in late 1977 Dylan said: "You know, I tell you. Lately I've been catching myself. I've been in some scenes, and I say, 'Holy shit, I'm not here alone.' I've never had that experience before the past few months. I've felt this strange, eerie feeling that I wasn't all alone, and I'd better know it."[5] Also, Bob's old friend from Minneapolis, Dave Whitaker, has said Bob gave his 11-year-old son, Ubidube Whitaker, his first electric guitar; a brand-new Fender Stratocaster. This occurred directly after Dave and Ubi met Dylan following a concert in Oakland, California on November 13, 1978. The guitar arrived bearing a quotation by the Apostle Paul. This gift was given four days before the San Diego cross episode and six days before Tucson.

It is also debatable just how susceptible Dylan might have been to the Jesus experience. When Robert Hilburn asked Dylan if Jesus came to him at a crisis point in his life, Bob answered, "No." He then continued, "The Funny thing is a lot of people think that Jesus comes into a persons' life only when they are either down and out or are miserable or just old and withering away. That's not the way it was for me. I was doing fine ... I was relatively content..." I would suggest that when Dylan spoke to his November 1979 San Diego audience about "feeling real sick," he wasn't referring to an emotional dilemma – although he may have had those as well – but that he was literally "feeling real sick." We have previously established that some sort of bug was tearing through the camp at that time and it would seem to me that even the great Mr Dylan was not immune to such an infection.

A Different Set of Rules

While it is an interesting conundrum, the exact moment that Jesus Christ entered Bob Dylan's life is far less important than the fact that He did enter. Some will say that they are not interested in Dylan's faith and that they are in it solely for his music. This, however, ignores the mportant fact that Dylan's faith changed that music from 1979 through to the present day. In all likelihood, Dylan's belief in Jesus came about in stages and not in one blinding flash and it is probably fair to say that Bob Dylan had always had a restless lifelong search for spirituality and that he seems to have always had a belief in one God, or in the oneness of God. Johnny Cash once said: "I knew Bob Dylan was searching for the truth and had been for years. And anyone who really wants the truth ends up at Jesus."

There are numerous early examples of Dylan's bluesman preoccupation with death and meeting his maker. A good illustration is the 1962 composition, 'I'd Hate to Be You on That Dreadful Day' ("Well, your clock is gonna stop/ At Saint Peter's gate/ Ya gonna ask him what time it is/ He's gonna say, 'It's too late' ... You're gonna yell and scream/ 'Don't anybody care?'/ You're gonna hear out a voice say/ 'Shoulda listened when you heard the word down there."). In another composition from around the same time, 'Quit Your Low Down Ways,' the narrator tells a woman that reading the Bible and praying to the Lord won't save her if she doesn't quit her low down ways here on earth. Journalist Maureen Cleave had picked up on the fact that Dylan was, according to her, "interested in religion," as early as 1963: "I realised he had been reading the Bible," Cleave told Matthew Tempest, "because of the line, 'The first one now will later be last,' which is directly from one of the Gospels. It's part of Christ's teaching.

We have already established that the Bible had become prominent in Dylan's life and work by 1967 (the Bible on the lectern and the *John Wesley Harding* album), and we have evidence at various points throughout the Seventies that Dylan was searching for spiritual fulfilment and was asking questions of those who had already found Christ. In 1970, he talked with his old friend the American radio disc jockey Scott Ross about Christian conversion. "I started to tell [Dylan] the story about what happened with the Lord in my life," Ross told *ISIS* magazine, "and he was asking me a lot of questions. It was a good conversation."

Dylan was referencing Matthew in 1974, but at that time the Apostle hadn't gotten through: ("Now we heard the Sermon on the Mount and I knew it was too complex/ It didn't amount to anything more than what the broken glass reflects."). While on tour in January 1974, Dylan rode his 10-speed bicycle to a Jesus People rally in Miami's Peacock Park. He wanted to talk with one of the speakers, Arthur Blessitt. During their short 10-minute conversation, which unsurprisingly was all about Jesus, Dylan asked Blessitt if Jesus really was the way. Two days later, during a private chat with the then governor of Georgia, Jimmy Carter, the conversation turned to Christ. In 2015, Carter told *The Atlantic*: "Bob and I spent a long time in the garden that night just talking about matters concerning theology and religion." Exactly how much of these various conversations rubbed off on Bob is pure conjecture but in November 1975 *People Weekly* printed an interview with Dylan: "I didn't consciously pursue the Bob Dylan myth," Dylan told Jim Jerome, "It was given to me– by God."

He continued, "I don't care what people expect of me. I'm doin' God's work. That's all I know."

Allen Ginsberg, who spent time with Bob on the Rolling Thunder tour, said that at this time Dylan would sometimes say that he didn't believe in God and then on other occasions he said that he did believe. Ginsberg: "That's why I wrote 'Lay Down yr Mountain Lay Down God.' Dylan said that where he was, 'on top of the Mountain,' he had a choice whether to stay or to come down. He said, God told him, 'All right, you've been on the Mountain, I'm busy, go down, you're on your own. Check in later.' And then Dylan said, 'Anybody that's busy making elephants and putting camels through needles' eyes is too busy to answer my questions, so I came down the Mountain.' Asked about 'Father of Night,' Ginsberg said, "I think that is, in a sense, a penultimate stage. It's not his final stage of awareness."[6]

According to Ginsberg, Dylan was always searching, but around the mid-Seventies his search appeared to be much deeper than before. "It took a long time," Ginsberg told me, Dylan finding God was a gradual thing. It didn't happen overnight." David Mansfield agreed: "His conversation wasn't one of those things that happens when an alcoholic goes to AA ... The simplest explanation is that he had a very profound experience which answered certain lifelong issues for him."[7]

In an interview with Neil Hickey, published in the September 11, 1976 issue of TV Guide, Hickey asked: "How does Bob Dylan imagine God?" Bob laughed abruptly and then said: "How come nobody ever asks Kris Kristofferson questions like that?" After a pause, he then answered with: "I can see God in a daisy. I can see God at night in the wind and rain. I see creation just about everywhere. The highest form of song is prayer. King David's, Solomon's, the wailing of a coyote, the rumble of the earth. It must be wonderful to be God. There's so much going on out there that you can't get to it all. It would take longer than forever." It is clear from this that Dylan believed in a monotheistic and omniscient God, the one God that made everything and therefore knows everything, a belief shared by many faiths including Judaism, Christianity, Islam and Sikhism.

In the Name of Religion

In Bob Dylan's case, and also in the lives of many others, faith is separate from religion. In a 1983 interview Dylan told Martin Keller: "My so-called Jewish roots are in Egypt. They went down there with Joseph, and they came back out with Moses, you know, the guy that killed the Egyptian, married an Ethiopian girl, and brought the law down from the mountain." Then, after a protracted history of the Jewish people, he concluded: "I ain't looking for [my roots] in synagogues, with six-pointed Egyptian stars shining down from every window, I can tell you that much." He continued by saying: "Religion is a dirty word. It doesn't mean anything. Coca-Cola is a religion. Oil and steel are a religion. In the name of religion, people have been raped, killed and defiled. Today's religion is tomorrow's bondage."[8]

That same year, while performing in Buffalo, New York, Bob told his audience: "I've been walking around today ... I noticed there's many tall steeples and big churches with stained glass windows. Let me tell you one thing; God's not necessarily found in there. You can't get converted in no steeples and stained glass windows."

During the summer of 1991 in Europe, Dylan began talking about 'Gotta Serve Somebody' as his "anti-religion song." The first mention of this came in Milan in June. At this show, Bob simply said: "This is one of my anti-religion songs," but by Munich the introduction had become: "Here's one of my anti-religion songs. There are many in my repertoire." When the tour recommenced in the States in July the rap was still there and by Pittsburgh (July 16), it had become: "Anybody here heard that song 'Losing My

Religion'? You can't lose what you never had, though!" Although
Bob now had a deep faith it is clear that he did not align himself
with any prescribed religion. Eighteen months prior to the summer
'91 concerts Dylan had told *USA Today*: "People who work for big
companies, that's their 'religion.' That's not a word that has any
holiness to it."

In 1997, Dylan told David Gates of *Newsweek*: "Here's the thing
with me and the religious thing. This is the flat-out truth: I find the
religiosity and philosophy in the music. I don't find it anywhere
else. Songs like 'Let Me Rest on a Peaceful Mountain' or 'I Saw
the Light'–that's my religion. I don't adhere to rabbis, preachers,
evangelists, all of that." That same year (1997), in an interview
published in *The New York Times*, Dylan told journalist Jon Pareles
that he: "now subscribes to no organized religion."

Even at the time he was attending Bible Classes, Dylan was
dismissing organised religion. In December 1979 he told Bruce
Heiman: "Religion is another form of bondage which man invents to
get himself to God ... Christ didn't preach religion. He preached the
Truth, the Way and the Life ... He talked about life, not necessarily
religion."[9]

In 2007, in reply to Jann Wenner's question: "What's your faith
these days?" Bob answered: "Faith doesn't have a name. It doesn't
have a category. It's oblique. It's unspeakable. We degrade faith by
talking about religion."

Contract with the Lord

Dylan became involved with the Vineyard Christian Fellowship
Church in early 1979 through his then-girlfriend. Thought to be the
inspiration for the songs 'Precious Angel' and 'Covenant Woman,'
Mary Alice Artes, referred to as "Queen Bee" on the *Street-Legal*
cover, was living with Dylan in Brentwood, a neighbourhood on Los
Angeles' Westside, until she recommitted herself to her long lost

Christian faith.*

Musician Keith Green and his wife Melody first met Dylan through an elder at the Vineyard. Melody said that Artes had gone to a Vineyard service, "Where she gave her heart to Jesus." Green said that after Artes received, "Some basic Christian counselling that she shouldn't be living with her boyfriend, she decided to move out. The elder at the Vineyard had no idea that the boyfriend was Bob Dylan."[10] Artes requested that the Vineyard talk to her boyfriend and explain why she was unable to continue living with him. The Vineyard's Kenn Gulliksen has said that he knew that the man in question was Bob Dylan while others have said that initially they had no idea. In any event, Artes spoke with Dylan and he agreed to talk with the Vineyard. Two pastors, Larry Myers and Paul Emond, were dispatched to Dylan's home.

Founded by Pastor Kenn Gulliksen in 1974, the 'Vineyard,' a Biblical metaphor for God's people, began as a small Bible Study group in Southern California but by the time Dylan arrived, almost five years later, it was a fast-growing evangelical church, one that emphasised redemption over judgement. Larry Myers: "[W]e met a man who was very interested in learning what the Bible says about Jesus Christ. To the best of my ability, I started at the beginning in Genesis and walked through the Old Testament and the New Testament and ended in Revelation."[11]

"I was willing to listen about Jesus," Dylan said, "I was kind of sceptical, but I was also open. I certainly wasn't cynical. I asked a lot of questions, questions like, 'What's the son of God, what's all that mean?' and 'What does it mean – dying for my sins?'."[12]

In 1999, Kenn Gulliksen said: "I tried to clearly express what is the historical, orthodox understanding of who Jesus is. It was a

---

* In early 1980, Dylan is said to have bought Artes a $25,000 engagement ring. He is believed to have written the song 'The Groom's Still Waiting at the Altar' after she returned to the east coast to continue her career as an actress.

quite intelligent conversation with a man who was seriously intent on understanding the Bible. There was no attempt to convince, manipulate or pressure this man into anything. But in my view God spoke through His Word, the Bible, to a man who had been seeking for many years." Myers added: "Sometime in the next few days, privately and on his own, Bob accepted Christ and believed that Jesus Christ is indeed the Messiah. After yet more time and further serious deliberation, Bob was baptized."[13] Another Pastor, Bill Dwyer, who took Bible classes in Reseda, California, said that Bob was very diligent and made considerable sacrifices to attend the daily classes with 19 other students including turning down an overseas tour.

Kenn Gulliksen: "I did my best to stay out of Bob's immediate circle so it wouldn't look that I was personally trying to capitalize on the relationship. I thought that was the godly, wise thing to do. Again in retrospective, I wish I had given more of myself because Bob subsequently, because of who he was and the pressures in his life, got caught back into the world ... It was absolute craziness," Gulliksen said, "because we all of a sudden had 30 or 40 media showing up at our services, writing absolutely ludicrous stories. If Bob wasn't there, they'd make up stories about why he wasn't there. They would talk about us having sections cordoned off just for him. It was at that time, I discovered that you can't believe everything that you read ... So we did our best to try to create another venue for Bob. I assigned one of my pastors, Larry Myers, to spend as much time with him as possible and Bob did go through our school of discipleship. He spent four months, every day in a classroom and it was out of that came the albums of *Saved* and *Slow Train Coming*."[14]

In total, Dylan studied with six pastor-teachers. Al Kasha: "Dylan would keep us up until three or four o'clock in the morning asking us all kinds of questions going from the Old Testament to the New Testament ... He would want to try to see consistencies, you know, like Isaiah– he loved that book ... In fact, if you look at his songs, he took a lot from Isaiah."[15]

The Vineyard's fervent evangelical preaching focused very much on end times and a belief that they were close at hand; that the Lord might return to earth at any time. A belief that the battle of Armageddon could be imminent interested Dylan greatly, a fact that is evident both from his stage raps and from much of the music he made at that time. This belief was advanced by the Christian Zionist Hal Lindsey, author of the 1970 book, *The Late Great Planet Earth*. This idea, coupled with Lindsey's belief in the Jewish Messiah, was of great interest to Dylan and he was able to discuss these philosophies with Lindsey who in the late Seventies was spending time on the fringes of the Vineyard church.

The Alpha Band

After abandoning drugs, many Sixties musicians turned to what the cover of *Time* magazine dubbed "The Jesus Movement" (June 21, 1971). Musicians like Roger McGuinn (Byrds), Dan Peek (America), Ritchie Furay (Poco), Al Perkins (Manassas), BJ Thomas, Barry McGuire and Leon Patillo (Santana) and Keith Green all turned to Christ during the Seventies. Those closer to Dylan were also giving themselves to the Lord.

After coming off tour with Bob Dylan in 1976, T-Bone Burnett, Steven Soles and David Mansfield formed The Alpha Band and almost immediately signed a ludicrously lofty six-million-dollar record deal with Arista Records' founder Clive Davis. With the industry awash with money and A&R people clueless as to what was going to be the next big thing, The Alpha Band, over the course of three years, made three sometimes dazzling but always commercially unacceptable records.

The band's second album, *Spark in the Dark*, was "humbly offered in the light of the triune God" while their third and final effort, *The*

Statue Makers of Hollywood, an even more overtly Christian record, spotlighted man's fall from grace. Side one opens with 'Tick Tock,' a boastful eight-minute account of the biblical Genesis. The overly ambitious record also contains a cover of Hank Williams' 'Thank God,' a song that eight years later Dylan would introduce into his live sets.

Although Burnett had been raised in The Episcopal Church, he was still searching and by the early Seventies he described himself as a Christian mystic. Nevertheless, when reading books like *The Aquarian Gospel of Jesus Christ* – a text dating from 1908 that in the Seventies had been adopted by New Age spiritualists – had failed to move him, he turned back to a less complicated Christian view.

After *The Statue Makers of Hollywood*, Arista chose not to renew the band's contract and Alpha's back catalogue was hastily deleted. The trio disbanded in 1978 with two of the members, Soles and Mansfield, rejoining Dylan. Nevertheless, *Spark in the Dark* had been a turning point for T-Bone. It was "a revelation," Burnett said, "Before that album, things looked pretty dark, but I turned around to where I could see the spark–The light."

Mansfield: "[I]n many ways [Statue Makers] was pretty fierce ... But T-Bone (and Steven Soles in a lesser sense) had this mission having been recently converted ... On many of the songs, he did this Old Testament jeremiad kind of take on the whole thing. It was his chance to take the moral high ground ... So it was very intense."[16]

The unanswered question is, what part if any did Burnett, and to a lesser extent Soles, play in Dylan coming to Christ? T-Bone Burnett has often been credited as being instrumental in Dylan's Christian conversion and while Burnett believes that, "The whole story of Bob Dylan is one man's search for God," he has denied playing any part in swaying Dylan toward Christianity.

According to Bob Spitz, however, in 1976, "In the waning hours of the Rolling Thunder Revue," T-Bone Burnett, "babbled rapturously

about the Word of God, righteousness, and the blessing of salvation."
Spitz wrote that Rob Stoner had confirmed that Burnett was a major
factor Bob's spiritual conversation. Nonetheless, on more than one
occasion Burnett has denied that he was the catalyst for bringing
Dylan to Christ and Spitz gives no sources, either for his T-Bone
Burnett story, or Rob Stoner's supposed confirmation of it.

In a September 1999 interview with author Scott Marshall,
Burnett was more than happy to debunk Spitz account again: "[It
is] total fiction," Burnett told Marshall. "There's not a word of truth
in it ... It's yellow journalism ... cheap melodrama really." Burnett
continued by saying that he didn't think that any of the band
was going to church at that time [1976] and that Spitz's writing
and interpretation of what happened was not even, "imaginative
fiction." Regardless, something incredibly powerful and seemingly
infectious seems to have happened during Rolling Thunder because
T-Bone Burnett went on to tell Marshall that, "Spontaneously, about
10 to 15 people from the tour started going to church, and either
going back to church or becoming Christian or something. I don't
know what that was or why that happened."

Burnett's objection to Spitz description of him as, "an early
disciple of born-again fundamentalism" is perhaps understandable
because as a lifelong Episcopalian, Burnett was neither born-again
nor a fundamentalist. Even so, according to Lloyd Sachs in his 2016
biography, T Bone Burnett: *A Life in Pursuit*, Burnett and his wife did
attend Bible classes at the Vineyard Christian Fellowship in West
Los Angeles, probably from around 1976-77, at least two years before
Dylan began studying there. Shortly after Burnett began attending
the Fellowship, Soles, Mansfield and other friends followed. Soles
started writing songs, which were performed at the Vineyard and
Mansfield told Sachs, "Sometimes people were dragging their friends
there just to hear the music. T-Bone talked about this stuff all the
time." When he formed The Alpha Band in July 1976, Mansfield

had not yet committed to Christianity but he says that he almost immediately came under intense pressure: "T-Bone and Steven were laying it on pretty thick. They challenged me pretty hard." Nevertheless, in conversations with Sachs, Burnett clearly resented the fact that people have said that he put pressure on others to become Christian. In an interview, T-Bone Burnett said: "I'm not going to get into an argument with anyone about the relative merits of Judaism and Christianity, and what it means for a Jewish kid to be a Christian – I'm just not interested in that argument."

After becoming an enthusiastic member of The Vineyard Fellowship, Steven Soles is said to have spent time during the 1978 tour talking about Christianity with Dylan. In retrospect, however, Soles, like Burnett, doesn't feel that his conversations had much of an effect on Dylan. Soles does, however, remember Dylan telling him, on more than one occasion, "You can't place your faith in man."[17]

Drugs aside, musicians turning to the church had come about in part due to disenchantment with the changing music business in the Seventies. Not only had the money involved become obscene, but there was a great deal of sycophantic behaviour and a window to this was available through Bob Dylan. Burnett: "I watched what was going on from the shadows. I watched the fact that Bob Dylan could make somebody famous just by sitting across the table from him. And I saw onstage, the right spot to be was singing on the same mike as Bob. That repulsed me so much that I got as far away from his mike as possible– not as a virtuous thing, but just as reverse snobbery."[18]

Our Forefathers Were Slaves

During a 1978 *Playboy* interview with Dylan, Ron Rosenbaum asked if Bob grew up thinking about the fact that he was Jewish. Dylan: "No, I didn't. I've never felt Jewish. I don't really consider myself Jewish or non-Jewish. I don't have much of a Jewish background. I'm not a patriot to any creed. I believe in all of them and none of them."

Although at the time, Bob's comment regarding not being
a patriot to any creed was probably true, he appears to be
downplaying his Jewish upbringing.

In 1968, Bob's father told Robert Shelton that his son could speak
400 Hebrew words: "Literally, he could speak Hebrew like they
do in Israel today," Abe Zimmerman said. At this time, Bob was
seemingly very interested in Hebrew observances and rituals and
was keen to learn; so much so, his teacher, Rabbi Reuben Maier,
showed his student off in public one Friday evening. "The Rabbi
would say the sentence in English," Abe told Shelton, "and Bobby
would say it in Hebrew."

One of the real highlights of Bobby's summers for the five years
from 1953-57 was attending Herzl camp. According to its Mission
Statement, the Wisconsin camp is somewhere that, "young people
become self-reliant ... create lasting Jewish friendships and develop
a commitment and love for Judaism and Israel."

The fact is, Bob's family were at the centre of the Jewish
community in their adopted hometown of Hibbing and Bobby was
well aware of the family's heritage. In 1906, under Czar Nicholas
II, Dylan's family had fled the last, biggest and most terrifying
of the five anti-Jewish pogroms undertaken against Jews in the
city of Odessa. He had Yiddish speaking grandparents – whom
the family shared a home with for a while – and a very Orthodox
great-grandfather. Benjamin Harold Edelstein, or BH as he liked
to be called, died in 1961, around the time Bob left the Midwest to
search for fame and fortune in New York City. A bearded, yarmulke-
wearing man, BH partook in daily prayer and Torah study. He also
spent a great deal of time reading volumes of the Talmud. Although
like the majority of Hibbing, the family were not Orthodox, the
grounding that Bobby received from the Bible would later become
an important source of imagery for many of his songs, especially up

to and including John Wesley Harding.

Dylan told Paul Zollo: "When I was young, my life was built around family. We got together all the time. There weren't many Jews around." Beatty's aunt, Ethel Crystal, concurred with this: "It was quite difficult for us because there weren't too many young Jewish people. So we used to go to Duluth to visit our relatives."[19]

The fact is, growing up Jewish in Hibbing – like many working-class towns in the US – set Bobby apart. Most of the businesses in Hibbing were owned by Jews: Feldman's department store, where Bob's mother worked part-time, Herberger's department store, Sher and Mackoff insurance, Sapero dress store, Stein's law office, Shapiro's pharmacies, David Shapiro's market and Jolowsky's auto wrecking were all Jewish owned businesses on Howard Street. Bob's family owned their fair share: Ben Stone had a clothing store, Bobby's father and his two brothers owned Micka Electric, and the family had a stranglehold on the picture and entertainment business in Hibbing. The town had four movie theatres, the double-matinee Gopher and the State, both on Howard St, and the Homer and the Lybba, both on 1st Avenue. The Lybba was named after Lybba Edelstein, BH's wife, and all of the theatres were owned, at least in part, by the Edelstein Amusement Company.

Over the years, American Jews have faced much prejudice, especially during periods of economic hardship. Many working-class towns were hotbeds of anti-Semitism and some Catholic priests are known to have blamed Jews for the Great Depression. In a 1938 American opinion poll, approximately 60 per cent of the respondents held low opinions of Jews, labelling them: "greedy," "pushy" and "dishonest" and by 1945, 58 per cent of respondents thought that Jews had, "too much power in the United States." All of this meant that many Jews, including a young Bobby Zimmerman, felt they were outsiders. While the family rarely spoke of their migrant past, notions of separation did not fade quickly. I pity the poor immigrant, indeed.

In 1976, Dylan told Neil Hickey: "I'm interested in what and who a Jew is. I'm interested in the fact that Jews are Semites, like Babylonians, Hittites, Arabs, Syrians, Ethiopians. But a Jew is different because a lot of people hate Jews. There's something going on here that's hard to explain."[20]

Bob's family were comfortably off but that didn't apply to everyone in Hibbing and from various accounts he was not altogether comfortable with the brisk way his family dealt with customers who owed their business money. On occasions he accompanied Abe's brothers when they were forced to repossess electrical items and domestic appliances from people who had fallen behind with their payment plans. On the 1978 tour, Dylan would perform a song entitled 'Repossession Blues.' Originally recorded by Dylan favourite Billy Lee Riley, it has been suggested that Bob may have had an affinity with this song because of his recent divorce. While there might be an element of truth in that, I doubt Bob had concerns that he was going to receive a visit from the repo man anytime soon. If Dylan had any connection at all with 'Repossession Blues' it is more likely to have come from his experiences at Micka Electric ("Well they took my television/ Now they're coming for my radio/ They don't like the way I'm doing / They say I pay my bills too slow.").

So, importantly, Bob Dylan was raised as a Jew but what is Jewishness anyway? Is it a religion? A tribe? An ethnicity? Or is it merely a group of people who share a common and often tragic history? According to Bob Dylan in 1981: "Some people say they're Jews and they never go to a synagogue ... Judaism is really the laws of Moses. If you follow the laws of Moses you're automatically a Jew."

Over the years, many secular Jewish intellectuals, most especially from the left, have ventured beyond the boundaries of their Jewish background and have adopted universal and humanist outlooks rooted in Jewish thought. Many of these people have taken the label "non-Jewish Jew" as a badge of their identity. The phrase was coined in a 1958 lecture by the Marxist historian and scholar Isaac Deutscher to describe Jewish intellectuals like Baruch Spinoza, Sigmund Freud, Leon Trotsky, Karl Marx and Heinrich Heine who "dwelt on the borderlines of various civilisations, religions, and national cultures." Despite being an atheist, Deutscher emphasised the importance of his Jewish heritage. He believed that a person could be a Jew without subscribing to the Jewish religion or any religion for that matter. Surely that is the point; you can be an atheist while still cherishing your Jewish heritage in the same way that you can believe in Jesus Christ without abandoning your Jewish upbringing and values.

In the early Seventies, as more young Jews became believers in Jesus as their Messiah, a non-profit group, "Jews for Jesus," was founded. Begun in 1973, this controversial Messianic Jewish organisation seeks to share its belief that Jesus is the promised Messiah of the Jewish people. Although Bob Dylan has no connection to this organisation, it does illustrate that he was far from alone in being a Jew who found Christ. Al Kasha, a young Jewish record producer at CBS when Dylan joined the label in 1961, became a follower of Jesus. A sufferer from chronic agoraphobia, Kasha believes he was healed after praying and giving his life over to Christ. He became an ordained Southern Baptist pastor and later started taking weekly Bible studies at his home in Beverly Hills. In 1979, Dylan attended those studies for six months. Kasha gave Bob a key to his home and he would spend time there alone writing the songs that became *Slow Train Coming* in front of Al's fireplace. Kasha: "Bob was, at that time, going through a spiritual search and if you look at his track record as a writer, he was always seeking after Jesus and he finally realised that Jesus was his Saviour."[21] Kasha said that Dylan prayed the 'Sinner's Prayer' with him and accepted Jesus into his life. Inevitably, Kasha had to fend off questions about

Dylan from the media: "We didn't give interviews," Kasha told Scott
Marshall. "They would ask me if Dylan was still Jewish, and I said,
'Like myself, you don't leave that, but he's a Jewish Believer.'"[22]

Terry Botwick, a teacher at the Vineyard who took another of the
classes that Dylan attended, was another Jew who had become a
believer in Jesus in 1975. Botwick took classes in a hall used by the
Vineyard church at Point Dume, close to Dylan's home. Yet another
Jewish believer in Jesus was Keith Green. Dylan and Green became
friends in the spring of 1980 and Bob contributed harmonica to the
track 'Pledge My Head to Heaven,' which was released on Green's
1980 album, *So You Wanna Go Back to Egypt*. Raised in Christian
Science, Green was another open-minded seeker and after drugs,
eastern mysticism and free love, "[God's] love broke through," and
he became a Jewish believer in Jesus the Messiah. A week later,
Green's wife Melody, whom he had married in 1973, followed Keith
in becoming a Jewish believer in Jesus. Like Dylan, the couple
became involved with the Vineyard Christian Fellowship.

Melody Green: "Somewhere along the way, [Dylan] got turned
onto Keith's music ... which is why he wanted to meet Keith. By
the time we actually met, Bob had already been studying the Bible
and learning about Jesus. We had invited him over for dinner, and
I cooked him hamburgers at our house ... Bob Dylan was one of the
most famous people in the world, and here we were just having
a casual meal together on the second-hand fold-out table in our
living room!

[W]e spent time with Bob at his apartment and office near Santa
Monica ... [H]e was the same as anyone who wanted to know more
about God–full of eager questions and fresh excitement about his
spiritual discoveries. He told us that he loved to pick up hitchhikers
and tell them about Jesus. They never recognised him because
he drove a beat-up old car and wore a knit ski hat over his famous
curls. He also told us that he didn't like to get out of bed before

reading ten chapters of the Bible.

...Bob fell in love with Second Chapter's music and asked them to open for him on his upcoming [Saved] tour. They prayed, but didn't feel a release to do it. We were a bit surprised. Had Bob asked us, we would have gone with him in a heartbeat just to hang out with this man who had written the musical soundtrack for our lives."[23]

Melody Green's was quite clear that she had no difficulty in squaring the fact she could be a Jew and still be a believer in Jesus. Green: "The book of Acts showed clearly that you don't need to be Jewish to follow the Jewish Messiah. It also seemed clear in the New Testament that following Jesus was the most natural Jewish thing a Jew could do ... One prophecy in particular impacted me deeply. I couldn't believe it was actually in the Old Testament ... The Jewish prophet Isaiah talked about the kind of punishment and death the Messiah would suffer. That when he died he would be pierced for our sins. Pierced! That blew my mind. If that didn't describe Roman crucifixion, I don't know what did! There was no prescribed Jewish death penalty that included piercing ('He was pierced through for our transgressions') ... I read it over and over again all week, and it pretty much sealed the deal for me on the Jewish side of things."[24]

Even when Dylan was performing his newly minted Christian songs there was proof positive that he had not forgotten Moses or that he was abandoning his Jewish heritage. At two of his 1979 concerts – Santa Monica, November 21 and Albuquerque, December 5 – Dylan introduced a song to be sung by backing singer Mona Lisa Young with an important and lengthy rap about the Passover (Pesach), the story of the Exodus from Egypt as described in the Hebrew Bible.

Dylan's affinity with his heritage was again made public in June 1980 with the released of the album *Saved*, the inner sleeve of which carried a quotation from Jeremiah Chapter 31:31: "Behold, the days come, saith the Lord, that I will make a new covenant with the house of Israel, and with the house of Judah." This quotation is regarded as one of the greatest messages in the Old Testament. Dylan is telling us here that these words of comfort are not only for Israel, but for everyone.

In 2003, Dylan's friend and co-conspirator in the film *Masked and Anonymous*, Larry Charles, gave his opinion on the subject of Jew and Christian: "I think when he was 'born again,' [Bob] was just expanding his feeling about religion and God. In his mind – this is my interpretation – I don't think that he saw a disconnect between his Judaism and his Christianity. I think he sees it all as streams running from the same source. His definition of religion, his definition of God, is a very broad one and encompasses a lot of traditions, and I don't think they are in conflict with each other."

Bob's friend and fellow musician Leonard Cohen was initially shocked by Dylan's "conversion." After some thought, however, he decided that Bob must still be Jewish but that he had been deeply touched by the figure of Jesus. Interviewing Dylan in 1981 for *New Musical Express*, Neil Spencer asked Bob if he felt that his previous interest in Judaism was compatible with his present beliefs? Dylan replied: "There's really no difference between any of it in my mind." In fact, rather than conflicting with his Jewish upbringing, the way of Christ was more at odds with a hedonistic rock and roll lifestyle; an ingrained way of life that Bob would find very much more difficult to abandon! Bob's mother told Fred A Bernstein, writing for The Jewish Mothers' Hall of Fame: "What religion a person is shouldn't make any difference to anybody else. I'm not bigoted in any way. Rabbis would call me up. I'd say, 'If you're upset, you try to change him.'" And that is exactly what they did!

If Bob was coming to terms with being both a Jew and a believer in Christ, others were not! Several people remember Rabbis arriving backstage at Dylan concerts while others recall them visiting Dylan in his office at Rundown. Dave Kelly, who worked as Dylan's personal assistant from October 1979 to November 1980, recalls the first of these visits beginning during the recording of *Saved*. Persuading Bob Dylan back into the fold must have been of some significance to the Jewish world because one of the men dispatched to talk with him was the top banana amongst Orthodox Jews, Rebbe Menachem Mendel Schneerson. Known by his followers simply as 'the Rebbe,' Schneerson, the seventh leader in the Chabad-Lubavitch dynasty, is considered to have been one of the most influential Jewish leaders of the 20th century. His religious knowledge was encyclopaedic and his scholarship and published teachings fill more than 300 volumes of work. Dylan was hugely taken with 'the Rebbe' and when Schneerson died in June 1994, he made a significant donation to Chabad in his honour.

Another Rabbi who worked extensively with Dylan was Manis Friedman, author of *Doesn't Anyone Blush Anymore?*, a book published in 1990 that Dylan personally endorsed. Friedman had been introduced to Dylan by Louie Kemp, an old friend from his youth in Minnesota. Louie and Dylan had remained close friends since their childhood and in 1975 Kemp helped organise and run the Rolling Thunder tour

In December 1980, Kemp flew up to Duluth for a visit with his mother. The flight involved a short layover at Minneapolis airport and Louie arranged to meet up with an old friend – who was also a long-time friend of Bob's – Larry Kegan. Kegan was aware that Kemp had many spiritual questions and he brought along a rabbi, Manis Friedman, to meet and talk with Kemp.

Rabbi Friedman impressed Louie and while in Minnesota Kemp arranged to sit in on his classes at a Chabad House in Saint Paul. He attended class for three weeks and came away a very different person.

At the time, Dylan was renting a house in Brentwood, LA. Bob used the house regularly when he needed to be in the city as it meant he wouldn't have to drive the hour each way from his main home in Point Dume. After Mary Alice Artes had moved out of the Brentwood house and returned to the East Coast, Kemp, who at the time had a condo on Wilshire Boulevard, spent a great deal of time with Bob in Brentwood and the dynamics there were, to say the least, interesting. Kemp was now an Orthodox Jew, while Bob was very much occupied with his studies of the New Testament. Kemp said that Dylan "understood Jesus as part of the Holy Trinity: Father, Son, and Holy Ghost," whereas Kemp saw Jesus as a "rabbi, teacher, and another Jewish boy who'd made good."

"Nearly every day, Bobby and I would engage in intense discussions of theology," Kemp wrote in his book *Dylan & Me: 50 Years of Adventures*. "I soon realized I didn't have a deep enough knowledge of my faith to counter Bobby's arguments; I was outmatched. After one such discussion, I went to my room and called Rabbi Friedman. I told him I had a close Jewish friend who was absorbed in the New Testament, and that I didn't feel equipped to debate him. I asked if he would be willing to come to L.A. and meet with my friend ... It had become my mission to help Bobby find the spiritual fulfilment his soul was yearning for in Judaism..."

Kemp now made it his mission to "bring Bobby home" to the faith of his forefathers. Dylan was happy to talk with Rabbi Friedman and the rabbi flew out to LA. According to Kemp, the two men hit it off and the time they spent together was the "beginning of Bobby's Jewish education."

"Once he dipped his toe in," Kemp said, "Bobby developed an abiding passion for Judaism – while maintaining his profound appreciation for Jesus as a historical and spiritual figure."

Dylan's publicist Paul Wasserman remembers the appearance of the first Rabbis as being somewhat earlier than this. According to Wasserman, during the Warfield run of concerts (November 1979)

Dylan was visited backstage by a lot of his new Christian friends, but in the battle for Bob's soul, mysterious Jews were also said to be appearing on the scene which, according to Wasserman, "made it confusing." "[T]here were all these very religious Jews in the background too, who had come in and were hanging out. And I speak a little Hebrew and I had an Orthodox upbringing, so I knew what was happening ... they would come and visit and Dylan would also study the Torah with them [at his office in Santa Monica and at their homes]."[25]

Later, in 1981, Dylan would also study the Torah and Talmud with Rabbi Moshe Feller in Saint Paul. There is some anecdotal evidence that Rabbis may have encouraged top brass at CBS to try and dissuade Dylan from releasing the *Saved* album. The record label wouldn't have needed much persuading. Finding execs at CBS who wanted to see *Saved* put in front of the record buying public was like trying to find a Turkey that would vote for Christmas. Even the album's cover picture proved contentious. As per Dylan's request, artist Tony Wright created cover art that depicted a large hand, that of Jesus Christ, reaching downward to touch a sea of smaller hands; those of His believers. Dylan told Wright that it was perfect and that he had previously had a vision of this hand while he was recording the *Slow Train Coming* album. In stark contrast to Dylan's opinion, CBS hated the cover with a passion and rumours began to circulate that they would not actively promote the album. They changed the cover in 1985, scrapping the sea hands picture for a painting of Dylan on stage. The picture used on the new US front sleeve had initially appeared on the inner bag of the original release. Now promoted to the front cover, this picture had also been drawn by Tony Wright and was taken from a photograph of Dylan on stage in Montreal, Canada in April 1980.

Where is he now?

In my role as editor of *ISIS* magazine, one of the questions I'm asked regularly is: "Where is Bob Dylan's faith now. Is he a Christian or a Jew?" Very few people ever consider that he could be both!

For many people over the past half-century, Messianic Judaism, the acceptance of Jesus Christ as the Messiah prophesied in the Old Testament, merely completes their Jewishness, rather than negating it. Nonetheless, some, I'm sure, will be surprised to learn that a 2013 study by the American think tank 'Pew Forum' showed that 34 per cent of American Jews thought that a belief in Jesus as the Messiah was "compatible with being Jewish." Like many other Jews, through Messianic Judaism, Dylan is able to live as a Jew and continue to celebrate his rich heritage while also recognising Jesus Christ as his saviour. And although very few people recognise this, almost everything he has said and done concerning his faith since finding Christ in 1978 accords with this dual association.

In the early Eighties Dylan, along with Alen Ginsberg, had attended a Sheva Brachot for an old friend at Rabbi Shlomo Freifeld's Sh'or Yoshuv Yeshiva in New York. Bob was so taken with Rabbi Freifeld and with Yeshiva (a Jewish institution that focuses on the study of traditional religious texts), that he talked about buying a place in Far Rockaway, Queens, near the Yeshiva. Dylan was quoted as saying, when visiting Rabbi Friefeld on a freezing cold New York night: "It may be dark and snowy outside, but inside that house, it's so light."

At around the same time, Dylan was also a regular visitor to Eastern Parkway in Crown Heights. He studied Jewish scripture at the main Lubavitcher synagogue, listened to the teachings of Rebbe and prayed in Hebrew. "We never know when he is coming – he can come and go any time," said Rabbi Yehuda Krinsky, a spokesman for the Lubavitch movement.

A copy of a cartoon drawn by Aislin (aka Terry Mosher) from April 20, 1980 has appeared on the Internet. Dylan wrote a message on the cartoon and sent it to Mosher. The note read: "To Aislin, 'the Law was given by Moses but grace & truth thru Jesus Christ' (John) Love Bob Dylan." This is early proof that Bob was already embracing being a Jew and a believer in Jesus Christ.

Some of the arguments used to illustrate Dylan's supposed backsliding on his belief in Jesus are both absurd and feeble. One such argument, which appeared in the March 15, 1982 issue of *New York* magazine and was widely syndicated, concerns the bar mitzvah of Dylan's third child, Samuel Abram. The New York piece, entitled: "Dylan Ditching Gospel?," read: "Singer Bob Dylan, who strayed from his Jewish roots in the mid-Seventies to espouse evangelical Christianity, seems to have been born yet again– back into Judaism." The reasoning behind this assertion was that: "Dylan was asked to present the National Music Publishers Association Gospel Song of the Year award during a visit to New York," but that he was unable to do so because he would be in California attending his son's bar mitzvah. For the unnamed writer, this is evidence enough that Dylan's Christian period "is over." In fact, according to an undisclosed 'source,' Dylan was never converted! "Despite a rumour that he was baptized in Pat Boone's swimming pool," the piece continued, "Dylan has never formally converted [to Christianity"].[26]

All of this presupposes that Dylan had left Judaism in the first place. Also, as author Scott Marshall rightly points out, one must wonder quite why Bob would choose to present an award to someone he didn't know in favour of attending his own son's bar mitzvah! Still, we should never let common sense get in the way of a newspaper story.

Many true believers were confident that Dylan would release a fourth evangelical album and many in the Christian community

were shocked by the arrival, in 1983, of *Infidels*, which they saw
as a return to secular music after a trilogy of evangelical records.
Surely nobody expected that Dylan would continue to make only
"Christian" albums for the remainder of his career? Nevertheless,
with *Infidels* it is clear that Dylan had become even more connected
with his Jewish roots, especially by his expression of solidarity with
Israel through the song 'Neighborhood Bully.' After the release of
Infidels articles began appearing in the press stating that Bob Dylan
had already moved away from his recently acquired Christian faith
and returned to Judaism.

In 1983, word spread around Crown Heights that Dylan was to
marry an Hasidic girl. The forthcoming wedding was said to be
the chief topic of conversation at 770 Eastern Parkway, the world
Lubavitch headquarters. That September, Dylan's mother Beatrice
decided to take a break in Israel with her 17-year-old grandson,
Jesse. His younger brothers had already been bar mitzvahed so
Beatty thought it would be a good idea to have Jesse's overdue bar
mitzvah while they were holidaying in Jerusalem. She suggested
this to Bob and he agreed. Bob flew over to Israel with Sara and they
attended the September 19 ceremony. As mentioned previously,
while at the Western Wall, Bob, Jesse and Moshe Schlass, the
officiating Rabbi, were photographed by Zavi Cohen and the picture
was widely syndicated in the United States and elsewhere. Beatty
begged the photographer not to take the picture but her plea fell
on deaf ears. Despite the unwelcome intrusion, Beatty told Fred
Berstein that the bar mitzvah was the high point of her life.

It was some time before Dylan went back to Crown Heights, but
when he did there was no further mention of marriage. At about the
same time, letters signed "R.Z., Hibbing, Minn.," began appearing
in issues of the short-lived *Mendy and the Golem*, "The World's Only
Kosher Comic Book," that featured the offbeat misadventures of
Mendy, an Orthodox Jewish boy, and his pet Golem.

In 1984, Bob distanced himself from the 'born again' label when he informed Kurt Loder of *Rolling Stone* magazine: "I've never said I'm born again. That's just a media term. I don't think I've been an agnostic. I've always thought there's a superior power, that this is not the real world and that there's a world to come." During a May 1984 press conference in Hamburg, Germany, Dylan was asked point blank if he was a Christian or a Jew. To which Bob replied: "Well, that's hard to say." This response was taken as Dylan being his usual evasive self while in actual fact, he was quite accurate with his answer. When asked to elaborate, Dylan told the reporter: "It's a long story ... It'd take too long to tell you." Again, he was telling the truth. A full and proper answer would have taken the remainder of the press conference. In 1987, however, Bob gave us a huge clue that he was still paying close attention to his Jewish heritage while also following Christ. At the opening show on his 1987 European tour (Hayarkon Park, Tel-Aviv, September 5) Bob performed 'In the Garden,' a song about Jesus, and 'Go Down, Moses,' a traditional number with sentiments firmly rooted in the Old Testament.

As the Eighties continued Dylan became increasingly close to the Chabad-Lubavitch movement. Then, during the 1989 Chabad Telethon, Bob appeared on the live fund-raising TV programme *L'Chaim – To Life!* wearing a yarmulke and accompanying his son-in-law, Peter Himmelman, on harmonica. Dylan took part on the Chabad again in 1991, telling viewers in no uncertain terms: "Give plenty of money to Chabad. It's my favourite organization in the world. Really, they do nothing but good things with the money. The more you give, the more it will help everybody." According to a piece in Jewish Journal, at the time Chabad rabbis were helping, "Dylan return to Judaism." The mid-Nineties saw Bob worshipping with Brooklyn Lubavitchers and in 2005 it was reported that he attended Yom Kippur (the holiest day of the year in Judaism) in the hamlet of Woodbury in Nassau County. Two years later, during Yom Kippur in 2007, he was seen in Atlanta, Georgia at Congregation Beth Tefillah where he was called to the Torah for the sixth aliyah.

There is plenty of evidence that Bob Dylan is still very much involved with his Jewish roots but as for leaving Jesus behind, there is an equal amount, or even more proof, that he is still very much a true believer.

In 2017, I asked Clinton Heylin for *ISIS* magazine where he thought Dylan's faith now lay: "I've never had much truck with people who thought that in 1983, Dylan pulled a switch and became Jewish again," Heylin told me. He cites Dylan playing 'In the Garden,' which he did extensively from 1979 to 1995 and occasionally thereafter, as being proof positive that Bob has remained a believer in Christ. Heylin told me that he had argued with Allen Ginsberg over dinner about this because Ginsberg believed that Dylan had returned to Judaism by the mid-Eighties and that he was no longer a Christian.

Clinton Heylin: "I was saying, 'I don't understand Allen how you can think Dylan is an apostate when he's singing 'In the Garden' tonight. Unless Dylan is the most appalling hypocrite, I do not see how an apostate can sing that song. And that's not the same as a non-believer. Elvis Costello can sing 'Full Force Gale,' that's fine, he doesn't have to believe the message. Being an agnostic or an atheist and singing a song of religious conviction is one thing, but for an apostate to sing it is a totally different thing ... There is ample evidence that Dylan still believes'."[27]

There is no doubt that 'In the Garden' has meant a great deal to Dylan over the years and as late as February 1991 he was telling his audience in Glasgow, Scotland: "All right, this is one of my lesser known songs, but it's still one of my favourites." Although the song was played a number of times on this tour, Glasgow was the only time it got an introduction. Five years before, however, Bob was introducing the song at every opportunity. During the Down Under leg of the 1986 True Confessions Tour, the song was prefaced with a rap about other peoples' heroes. Dylan: "This is a song about my hero. Everybody got heroes, right? For lots of people Mohammed Ali's a hero, right? Yeah. And Albert Einstein, he sure was a hero. I guess you could say even Clark Gable was a hero. Michael Jackson, he's a hero, right? Bruce Springsteen. I care nothing about them people though. None of those people are my heroes, they don't mean nothing to me. I'm sorry but that's the truth. I wanna sing a song about my hero." (Entertainment Centre, Sydney, Australia, February 11, 1986).

The rap changed from night to night and included Sylvester Stallone, Rudolph Valentino, Richard Price, Ronald Reagan (often to boos) and even Mr Woody Woodpecker were mentioned. Dylan's one hero was, of course, Jesus Christ.

The first year of the Nineties saw the release of Bob Dylan's 27th studio album, *Under the Red Sky*. The cover art made a powerful statement even if most of the music did not. The front of the album featured a black and white photograph of Dylan kneeling on Israel's soil while the record included the song 'God Knows,' which contained the potent line about End Times: "God knows there's gonna be no more water/ But fire next time." Another line, found in the third stanza: "It was supposed to last a season/ But it's been so strong for so long," could well be a comment of Bob's enduring faith.

Dylan returned to faith songs in a big way during 1999. 'Gotta Serve Somebody' kicked off the tour that year and the rather beautiful hymn, 'Pass Me Not, O Gentle Saviour,' arrived in the set on February 23. Composed by blind poet and gospel writer Frances J Crosby (words) and William H Doane, who later provided the music, Dylan came to the song via The Stanley Brothers.

By June 11, the traditional 'Hallelujah, I'm Ready to Go' had begun opening the shows. "I let my Saviour in and he saved my soul from sin/ Hallelujah I'm ready to go" sang Dylan. An old traditional bluegrass number, this one is again associated with The Stanley Brothers. A month later, 'Hallelujah...' was replaced by another traditional number, 'Somebody Touched Me.' The two songs then began to take turns in opening the evening's proceedings. An up-tempo traditional gospel bluegrass number, 'Somebody Touched Me' was released by the Stanley Brothers on their 1961 album, *Old Time Camp Meeting*.

On September 4, the second evening of the next leg of touring, Dylan introduced 'I Am the Man, Thomas' to the setlist; again as the opening number. During this period as one faith song disappeared it was replaced by another. Written by Ralph Stanley and Larry Sparks and performed and recorded by both The Stanley Brothers and the Clinch Mountain Boys, Bob would go on to play 'I Am The Man, Thomas' some 59 times over the ensuing years ("Oh, I am the Man, Thomas, I am the Man/ Look at these nail scars here in my hands."). Interestingly, this was the first number in almost 20 years in which Dylan speaks in the first person as Jesus.

On November 9 there was a one-off performance of 'A Satisfied Mind.' Written by Joe 'Red' Hayes and Jack Rhodes, the song, which appeared in the number four slot in the set, had previously opened the *Saved* album. Also featured in the show was a track from the *Infidels* album, 'Man of Peace.'

On November 20, 1999 at the University Of Delaware in Newark, Dylan performed 'This World Can't Stand Long.' Written by Jim Anglin, who then sold the copyright to Roy Acuff, the song is about the impending destruction of the world and its passing into the Messianic age, something Dylan had spoken about in 1985 with Scott Cohen of *Spin* magazine. In his rambling and not entirely accurate explanation, Dylan described how we have to pass through this world to get to the Messianic world. "This world is scheduled to go for 7,000 years," Dylan told Cohen. "Six thousand years of this, where man has his way, and 1,000 years when God has His way … The last thousand years is called the Messianic age. The Messiah will rule … People don't know what God wants of them. They'll want to know what to do and how to act … They don't teach that stuff like they do math, medicine, and carpentry, but now there will be a tremendous calling for it. There will be a run on godliness, just like now there's a run on refrigerators, headphones and fishing gear. It's going to be a matter of survival. People are going to be running to find out about God, and who are they going to run to? They're gonna run to the Jews, 'cause the Jews wrote the book, and you know what? The Jews ain't gonna know. They're too busy in the fur business and in the pawnshops… They're too busy doing all that stuff to know… I know people are going to say to themselves, 'What the fuck is this guy talking about?' But it's all there in black and white, the written and unwritten word. I don't have to defend this. The scriptures back me up."[28]

'This World Can't Stand Long' would remain in the sets when touring recommenced in March 2000 and would make frequent appearances after that until September 2002. 'Ring Them Bells,' 'Rock of Ages' and 'Every Grain of Sand' would also make appearances during this final leg of 1999.

April 2002 saw 'Solid Rock' come into the setlist for the first time since November 1981. The song was played at numerous shows until October that year. I don't intend to write about them in detail here, but the faith songs just kept coming. August 15 saw the live debut, and the first of seven outings, for the Bill Monroe song, 'A Voice from on High.' On the next leg of the 2002 tour 'In the Summertime' made its first appearance since 1981 and was played eight times. In February 2003, 'Saving Grace' came into the set and remained a regular until 2005. It would appear again in 2012.

In 2008, Bob performed 'I Believe in You' in Mashantucket,

Connecticut. The concert was on the evening of August 15 and Dylan's old producer Jerry Wexler had died earlier the same day. The song was almost certainly a tribute to him. Although until that point it had not been performed live for a year, it was a favourite with Dylan who played the *Slow Train Coming* song 259 times between recording it with Wexler in 1979 and April 2009. On October 4, 2009 in Seattle, Washington, Dylan performed a totally re-written 'Gonna Change my Way of Thinking.' This re-write had appeared on the 2003 album *Gotta Serve Somebody: The Gospel Songs of Bob Dylan*. The album was a tribute to Dylan but he appeared on 'Gonna Change my Way of Thinking' in a duet with Mavis Staples. The song would continue appearing in Dylan's sets in 2010 and 2011.

Just when we thought that Dylan couldn't spring any more surprises, on October 13, 2009 he released the Christmas album, *Christmas in the Heart*. Bill Flanagan made reference to Bob's "heroic performance" on the track 'O Little Town of Bethlehem,' saying that Dylan, "delivered the song like a true believer." To which Dylan replied quizzically, "Well, I am a true believer."

In Toronto on July 15, 2013, Wilco's Jeff Tweedy and My Morning Jacket frontman Jim James joined Dylan for a rendition of the gospel standard 'Twelve Gates to the City,' a song Bob would have known through Rev. Gary Davis and probably others. Why this song was chosen on this night is anyone's guess but it was Tisha B'Av, an annual fast day in Judaism. The 12 gates in Revelation 21 belong to the New Jerusalem, which comes down from heaven to the new earth shining with the glory of God. The gates were inscribed with the names of the 12 tribes of Israel. On the previous evening, in the same slot in the setlist, song 14, the audience had been treated to the Richard Thompson song '1952 Vincent Black Lightning.' There would seem to be no religious connection here, unless, of course, your religion is motorcycles. On July 19 in Bridgeport, Connecticut, Tweedy and James again joined Dylan on stage, this time for a rendition of the Blind Willie Johnson gospel number, 'Let Your Light Shine on Me.'

For our next foray into faith songs we have to wait 15 months until Dylan reaches the last night of a three-show residency at the Dolby Theatre in Hollywood. The encore that night, and for the next 40 plus shows, is 'Stay with Me,' not the Rod Stewart and the Faces song, but the Main Theme from the 1963 American drama *The Cardinal*. An inspirational prayer and a lesser known Sinatra song, 'Stay with Me' will remain in Dylan's sets until April 2017. This song was the precursor to Bob Dylan's lengthy incursion into Frank Sinatra and the Great American Songbook.

Strong indications of Dylan's faith also continue to be apparent in recent interviews and also in his lengthy MusiCares speech. In a 2012 interview with *Rolling Stone*, referring to his then-new album *Tempest*, Dylan told Mikal Gilmore: "I wanted to make something more religious. I just didn't have enough [religious songs]." Later in the interview, a seemingly irritated Dylan responded vehemently to a question about his use of other peoples' works within his own. "These are the same people," Dylan said: "that tried to pin the name Judas on me. Judas, the most hated name in human history! If you think you've been called a bad name, try to work your way out from under that. Yeah, and for what? For playing an electric guitar? As if that is in some kind of way equitable to betraying our Lord and delivering him up to be crucified. All those evil motherfuckers can rot in hell." Despite the distinctly non-Christian forgiveness on show here, the word "our" is crucial.[29]

As the recipient of the MusiCares Person of the Year 2015 award, Bob Dylan delivered a 30-minute acceptance speech in which he again talked about recording gospel/Christian songs. Dylan: "The Blackwood Bros have been talking to me about making a record together ... Of course it would be a gospel album. I don't think it would be anything out of the ordinary for me. Not a bit. One of the songs I'm thinking about singing is 'Stand by Me' ... Not 'Stand by Me' the pop song. No. The real 'Stand by Me.' The real one goes like this:

When the storm of life is raging / Stand by me / When the storm of life is raging / Stand by me / When the world is tossing me / Like a ship upon the sea / Thou who rulest wind and water / Stand by me

In the midst of tribulation / Stand by me / In the midst of tribulation / Stand by me / When the hosts of hell assail / And my strength begins to fail / Thou who never lost a battle / Stand by me

In the midst of faults and failures / Stand by me / In the midst of faults and failures / Stand by me / When I do the best I can / And my friends don't understand/ Thou who knowest all about me / Stand by me.

That's the song. I like it better than the pop song. If I record one by that name, that's going to be the one..."[30]

Al Kasha, the man who spent six months giving weekly Bible study instruction to Dylan in 1979 has no doubt that Bob is still very much a believer in Jesus. In 2012, during an interview with Dan Wooding, Wooding asked Kasha outright: "So is Bob Dylan a believer?" Kasha replied firmly, "The answer is yes." Kasha then noted that Dylan's then-new album *Tempest* (2012) abounds with Christian lyrics. Kasha: "I am absolutely thrilled that Bob has shown through this new record that he has never lost God's calling in life. He's never given up. I get upset when people think that he has ... because you don't write all these songs ... It takes time to write them and they're all about Christ."

Leaving the interviews and the abundance of musical clues behind, *ISIS* reader Steve Jones commented to me in 2018: "[Evidence of] Bob still being a believer in Jesus continues to be found particularly in his artworks, especially in the recent *Beaten Path* body of work with its multi-various telegraph posts on the skyline as crucifixion crosses, etc." Jones continued: "Even the title *The Beaten Path* [2016/17] conveys spirituality on one's life journey with its many paths one man must walk ... It is very explicit in the "Jesus Saves" sign in blood red writing by the roadside and tall telegraph post in the Rural Route painting."

It is true to say that clues to Dylan's faith can be found all across his artwork and for this we can go all the way back to his first book of drawings, *Drawn Blank*, (1994) in which one pencil sketch contains a large, if faded, cross bearing the words 'Jesus' and 'Saved'.

This is where our journey with Bob Dylan ends. For Dylan, however, the story continues apace. His search for faith and a deeper meaning to his life may have concluded in 1979 but he continued to 'fine-tune' that search for many years after that. And who knows, he may still be fine-tuning it today.

Bob Dylan's achievements recognised by others are too numerous to mention here but they include being nominated for 39 Grammy Awards (11 of which he won), induction to the Songwriters Hall of Fame, a Kennedy Center Honors, GMA Dove Award, Pulitzer Prize, Presidential Medal of Freedom and a Golden Globe. He is only the second person in history to have received an Academy Award and a Nobel Prize and the only musician/songwriter ever to be awarded a Nobel Prize in Literature.

In 2015, when making his unexpectedly lengthy 30-minute acceptance speech at MusiCares, Dylan complained about critics writing that he had made a career out of "confounding expectations." This expression has been used many times over the years and even though Dylan mocked the 'label', I find it appropriate. Even more appropriate is "disturber of the peace," a term Dylan's friend and journalist Robert Shelton used as far back as 1986. Robert Shelton: "I think the born again phase for him solved a lot of problems for himself, did things for him rather than us. He has a talent to disturb.

Bob Dylan is a disturber of the peace, if not ours, then his."

Actor Jack Nicholson used the same phrase – did he plagiarise it from Shelton! – in one of the most insightful short assessments ever of Bob Dylan's long career. It was at the 1991 Grammy Awards and Nicholson was presenting Dylan with a 'Lifetime Achievement Award.' "He's been called everything from the voice of a generation to the conscience of the world. He rejects both titles and any others that try to categorize him or analyze him," Nicholson said with that unmistakable trademark grin: "He's been, and still is, a disturber of the peace, his own, as well as ours."

For too long Bob Dylan was doing too much of nothing; finding Jesus was the turning point. Currently, Dylan shows no signs of slowing down. Long may he persist in painting his masterpiece because while he continues to confound expectations and disturb the peace the world is a better and far more interesting place in which to live.

Sources

Chapter 1
1 Ben Fong-Torres, reprinted in *Knocking on Dylan's Door*, Straight Arrow, 1974
2 Howard Sounes, *Down the Highway: The Life of Bob Dylan*, Doubleday, 2001
3 Author interview with John Brandt, 2014
4 Robert Shelton, *No Direction Home: The Life and Music of Bob Dylan*, New English Library, 1986
5 Sam Shepard, True Dylan, *Esquire*, 1987
6 Joan Baez, And a Voice to Sing With, Summit, 1987
7 Howard Sounes, *Down the Highway: The Life of Bob Dylan*, Doubleday, 2001
8 Al Aronowitz, The Woodstock papers of Al Aronowitz, reprinted in *ISIS* issue 95
9 Ellen Willis, issue 6 of *Cheetah* magazine, March 1967
10 Clinton Heylin, *Behind the Shades: The 20th Anniversary Edition*, Faber & Faber, 2011
11 Robbie Robertson, *Testimony*, William Heinemann, London, 2016
12 Sean Egan (Editor), *The Mammoth Book of Bob Dylan*, Constable & Robinson, 2011
13 Robbie Robertson, *Testimony*, William Heinemann, London, 2016
14 Jann Wenner, *Rolling Stone*, issue 47, November 29, 1969
15 Robbie Robertson, *Testimony*, William Heinemann, London, 2016
16 Sam Shepard, True Dylan, *Esquire*, 1987
17 Bob Dylan, *Chronicles Volume One*, Simon & Schuster, 2004
18 Michael Iachetta, *New York Daily News*, May 1967
19 Toby Thompson, *Positively Main Street*, New English Library, 1972
20 Johnathan Cott, Fast On The Eye, *Rolling Stone*, March 4, 1971
21 *Sing Out! Vol. 18, #4*, October-November 1968
22 Ian Woodward interview for *ISIS* magazine, published in issue 79, June 1998
23 Michael Iachetta, *New York Daily News*, May 1967
24 Craig Harris, *The Band: Pioneers of Americana Music*, Rowman & Littlefield, 2014
25 Author interview with Al Aronowitz, 2000
26 Author interview with John Brandt, 2014
27 Bob Dylan, *Chronicles Volume One*, Simon & Schuster, 2004
28 Howard Sounes, *Down the Highway: The Life of Bob Dylan*, Doubleday, 2001
29 Lynne Allen, *Trouser Press*, Published December 1978
30 Robert Shelton, *No Direction Home: The Life and Music of Bob Dylan*, New English Library, 1986
31 Nat Hentoff, *The New Yorker*, October 24, 1964,
32 Robert Shelton, *No Direction Home: The Life and Music of Bob Dylan*, New English Library, 1986
33 Taped promotional interview with Bob Dylan (2014)

34 Clinton Heylin, *Behind the Shades: The 20th Anniversary Edition*, Faber & Faber, 2011

35 David Malachowski, *Albany Times Union*, December 2008, reprinted is *ISIS* issue 143

36 Jann Wenner, *Rolling Stone*, issue 47, November 29, 1969

37 Fredric Dannen, Hit Men: *Power Brokers and Fast Money Inside the Music Business*, McGraw-Hill, 1991

38 Taped promotional interview with Bob Dylan (2014)

39 Author interview with Al Aronowitz, 2000

40 Jann Wenner, *Rolling Stone*, issue 47, November 29, 1969

41 Howard Sounes, *Down the Highway: The Life of Bob Dylan*, Doubleday, 2001

42 Kurt Loder, *Rolling Stone*, issue 424, June 21, 1984

43 Jerry Hopkins, *Rolling Stone*, issue 42, September 20, 1969

Chapter 2

1 Michael Iachetta *New York Daily News*, May 1967

2 Matt Damsker, *Circus Weekly*, Broadcast October 1978. Transcribed in *Talking Bob Dylan* 1978

3 Clinton Heylin, *Behind the Shades: The 20th Anniversary Edition*, Faber & Faber, 2011

4 Dan Daley, *Mix* magazine, January 1, 2003

5 Clinton Heylin, *Behind the Shades: The 20th Anniversary Edition*, Faber & Faber, 2011

6 ibid

7 Anthony Scaduto, *Bob Dylan: An Intimate Biography*, Abacus Books, 1971

8 ibid

9 Jonathan Cott, *Bob Dylan: The Essential Interviews*, Wenner, 2007

10 Anthony Scaduto, *Bob Dylan: An Intimate Biography*, Abacus Books, 1971

11 *Sing Out! Vol. 18, #4*, October-November 1968

12 Bert Cartwright, *The Bible in the Lyrics of Bob Dylan*, Wanted Man study series, 1985

13 Robert Shelton, *No Direction Home: The Life and Music of Bob Dylan*, New English Library, 1986

14 ibid

15 Howard Sounes, *Down the Highway: The Life of Bob Dylan*, Doubleday, 2001

16 Rory O'Conner, *Musician* magazine, June 1987

17 Bob Dylan, *Chronicles Volume One*, Simon & Schuster, 2004

18 Rory O'Conner, *Musician* magazine, June 1987

19 Author interview with Al Aronowitz, 2000

20 Rory O'Conner, *Musician* magazine, June 1987

21 *Rolling Stone*, November 16, 1978

22 Author interview with Bob Johnston, 2012

23 Matt Damsker, *Circus Weekly*, Broadcast October 1978. Transcribed in *Talking Bob Dylan* 1978

24 Barney Hoskyns, *Across the Great Divide: The Band and America,* Hyperion,

1993

25 John Katsilometes, *Las Vegas Review-Journal*, May 31, 2017

26 Bob Dylan, *Chronicles Volume One*, Simon & Schuster, 2004

27 Christopher Ricks, *Dylan's Vision of Sin*, Viking, 2003

28 Andy Gill, *Classic Bob Dylan*, Carlton, 1998

29 Hubert Saal *Newsweek*, February 26, 1968

30 Al Aronowitz, The Woodstock papers of Al Aronowitz, reprinted in ISIS issue 95

31 Author interview with Al Aronowitz, 2000

32 Cameron Crowe, *Biograph* booklet notes, November 1985

33 AJ Weberman, *Bob Dylan vs. A.J. Weberman: The Historic Confrontation*, Folkways Records, 1977

34 Jon Landau, *Crawdaddy*, May 1968

35 Mick Farren *Record Collector News, USA* (date not known).

Chapter 3

1 Sue Clark, *Rolling Stone*, issue 6, February 24

2 *Sing Out! Vol. 18, #4,* October-November 1968

3 Barney Hoskyns, *Small Town Talk*, Faber & Faber, 2016

4 Timothy White, *George Harrison: Reconsidered*, Larchwood & Weir, 2013

5 Graeme Thomson, *George Harrison: Behind the Locked Door*, Omnibus Press, 2013

6 ibid

7 ibid

8 Rush Evans, *Goldmine*, February 8, 2011

9 Jann Wenner, *Rolling Stone*, issue 47, November 29, 1969

10 Jonathan Cott, *Bob Dylan: The Essential Interviews,* Wenner, 2007

11 Jann Wenner, *Rolling Stone*, issue 29, March 15, 1969

12 Jonathan Cott, *Bob Dylan: The Essential Interviews,*, Wenner, 2007

Chapter 4

1 Author interview with Mike Lang, 2013

2 Al Aronowitz, www.blacklistedjournalist.com re-printed in *ISIS* issue 95, 2001

3 ibid

4 Kurt Loder, *Rolling Stone*, 1984

5 Bob Dylan, *Chronicles Volume One*, Simon & Schuster, 2004

6 Al Aronowitz, www.blacklistedjournalist.com re-printed in ISIS issue 95, 2001

7 ibid

8 ibid

9 Brian Hinton, *Message to Love*, Castle Communications, 1995

10 On The Wight, radio interview with Ray Foulk, September 2, 2010, transcribed by author

11 Chris Hockenhull, *Fourth Time Around issue 3*

12 ibid
13 After the Crash, Film, Chrome Dreams, 2005
14 Chris Hockenhull, *Fourth Time Around issue 3*
15 ibid
16 Outtake, *After the Crash*, Film, Chrome Dreams, 2005
17 *After the Crash*, Film, Chrome Dreams, *2005*
18 Al Aronowitz, www.blacklistedjournalist.com, re-printed in ISIS issue 96 May, 2001
19 Chris Hockenhull, *Fourth Time Around issue 3*
20 ibid
21 King/Plumbley/Turner, Isle of Wight Rock, Isle of Wight Rock Archives, 1996
22 Al Aronowitz, www.blacklistedjournalist.com, re-printed in *ISIS* issue 96 May, 2001
23 Chris Hockenhull, Fourth Time Around issue 3
24 Al Aronowitz, www.blacklistedjournalist.com, re-printed in *ISIS* issue 96 May, 2001
25 ibid
26 Al Aronowitz, www.blacklistedjournalist.com, re-printed in *ISIS* issue 96 May, 2001
27 Chris Hockenhull, *Fourth Time Around issue 3*
28 Al Aronowitz, www.blacklistedjournalist.com, re-printed in *ISIS* issue 96 May, 2001
29 ibid
30 ibid
31 Chris O'Dell, Miss O'Dell, Touchstone, 2009
32 Dean Egan, *The Mammoth Book of Bob Dylan*, Constable & Robinson, 2011
33 ibid
34 Al Aronowitz, www.blacklistedjournalist.com, re-printed in ISIS issue 96 May, 2001
35 King/Plumbley/Turner, Isle of Wight Rock, Isle of Wight Rock Archives, 1996
36 Al Aronowitz, www.blacklistedjournalist.com, re-printed in *ISIS* issue 96 May, 2001
37 Michael Gray, *Rolling Stone*, September 20, 1969
38 Al Aronowitz, www.blacklistedjournalist.com, re-printed in *ISIS* issue 96 May, 2001
39 *After the Crash*, Film, Chrome Dreams, 2005
43 ibid
41 Author interview with Jonathan Taplin, 2013
42 Ray Foulk, *Stealing Dylan from Woodstock*, Medina Publishing Ltd, 2015
43 The Beatles Bible www.beatlesbible.com (retrieved 2014)
44 ibid
45 Alan Stroud, *Yesterday's Papers – Volume Six*, Now and Then Books, 2011
46 www.ukrockfestivals.com/iow69-aftermath.html

Chapter 5

1 Kurt Loder, *Rolling Stone*, issue 424, June 21, 1984

2 Bill Fanagan, http://www.bobdylan.com/news/qa-with-bill-flanagan/

3 Robert Christgau, www.robertchristgau.com

4 Douglas Brinkley, *Rolling Stone*, issue 1078 May 2009

5 Michelle Enghien , interview, Pairs, France, 1970

6 Bob Dylan, *Chronicles Volume One*, Simon & Schuster, 2004

7 Keith Badman, *The Beatles Diary Volume 2*, Omnibus Press, 2009

8 AJ Weberman, *Bob Dylan vs. A.J. Weberman: The Historic Confrontation* Folkways Records, 1977

9 *IT* (International Times), issue 132, June 19, 1972

10 Peter Doggett, *There's a Riot Going On*, Canongate Books (2008)

11 Robert Hilburn, *Melody Maker*, February 28, 1976

12 Clinton Heylin, *Behind the Shades: The 20th Anniversary Edition*, Faber & Faber, 2011

13 *Scottsdale Progress* Saturday Magazine, May 3, 1986

14 ibid

15 Scot Cohen, *Spin* magazine, December 1985

16 Rob Hart, *Cult*, September 2009

17 Rodger Jacobs, *PopMatters*, July 30, 2009

18 Chet Flippo, *Rolling Stone*, issue 130, March, 1973

19 Ben Fong-Torres, reprinted in *Knocking on Dylan's Door*, Straight Arrow, 1974

20 Chet Flippo, *Rolling Stone*, issue 130, March, 1973

21 Chet Flippo, *Rolling Stone*, issue 130, March, 1973

22 E Jean Carroll, *Rocky Mountain Magazine*, 1982

23 Donald Chase, *Los Angeles Times*, November 2, 1986

24 Liner notes, *Biograph*, Columbia Records

25 David Weddle, *If They Move... Kill 'Em!: The Life and Times of Sam Peckinpah*, Grove Press, 1994

26 Garner Simmons, *Peckinpah: A Portrait in Montage*, Limelight, 1982

27 ibid

28 ibid

29 Clinton Heylin, *Behind the Shades: The 20th Anniversary Edition*, Faber & Faber, 2011

30 ibid

31 ibid

Chapter 6

1 *Santa Cruz Sentinel*, September 8, 1976

2 ibid

3 ibid

4 *Variety*, April 23, 2013

5 ibid

6 Howard Sounes, *Down the Highway: The Life of Bob Dylan*, Doubleday, 2001

7 ibid

8 Author interview with Arthur Rosato, 2017

9 Howard Sounes, *Down the Highway: The Life of Bob Dylan*, Doubleday, 2001

10 Clinton Heylin, *Behind the Shades: The 20th Anniversary Edition*, Faber & Faber, 2011

11 ibid

12 Judith Sims, *Rolling Stone*, issue 169, September 12, 1974

13 Anthony Decurtis, *New York Times*, May 10, 2005

14 Matt Damsker interview with Bob Dylan (1978) transcribed by Gavin Diddle 1984

15 Bill Fanagan, http://www.bobdylan.com/news/qa-with-bill-flanagan/

16 Clinton Heylin, *Behind the Shades: The 20th Anniversary Edition*, Faber & Faber, 2011

17 Scot Cohen, *Spin* magazine, December 1985

18 Clinton Heylin, *Behind the Shades: The 20th Anniversary Edition*, Faber & Faber, 2011

19 Bob Dylan, *Chronicles Volume One*, Simon & Schuster, 2004

20 Jonathan Cott, *Bob Dylan: The Essential Interviews*, Wenner, 2007

21 John Baldwin, *Bob Dylan & the Fifth Day of May*, Desolation Row, 2017

22 Author interview with Jacques Levy, 1999

23 ibid

24 idid

25 Author interviews with Faridi McFree between 2005 and 2009

Chapter 7

1 Author interview with Jacques Levy, 1999

2 Larry Sloman, *On the Road With Bob Dylan*, Bantam Books, 1978

3 ibid

4 Author interview with Arthur Rosato, 2017

5 Author interview with Jacques Levy, 1999

6 Author interview with Arthur Rosato, 2017

7 Author interview with Mick Ronson, 1992

8 Author interview with Arthur Rosato, 2017

9 ibid

10 Larry Sloman, *On the Road With Bob Dylan*, Bantam Books, 1978

11 Mary Lou Sullivan, *Everything's Bigger in Texas...*, Backbeat Books, 2017

12 Clinton Heylin, *Behind the Shades: The 20th Anniversary Edition*, Faber & Faber, 2011

13 Joan Baez, *And a Voice to Sing With*, Summit, 1987

14 Author interview with Arthur Rosato, 2017

15 Clinton Heylin, *Judas* magazine, issue 1

Chapter 8

1 Malka Marom, Joni Mitchell in Her Own Words: Conversations with Malka Marom, ECW Press, 2014

2 Author interviews with Faridi McFree between 2005 and 2009

3 ibid

4 ibid

5 ibid

6 ibid

7 *Daily Mirror*, June 11, 1978

8 'Sad-eyed Lady of the Lowlands,' Copyright 1966 Dwarf Music; renewed 1994

9 Cynthia Gooding, Radio show for WBIA, possible broadcast date March 11, 1962

10 Author interviews with Faridi McFree between 2005 and 2009

11 ibid

12 US magazine interview, August 1987

13 Author interviews with Faridi McFree between 2005 and 2009

14 Howard Sounes, *Down the Highway: The Life of Bob Dylan*, Doubleday, 2001

15 ibid

16 Robert Shelton, *No Direction Home: The Life and Music of Bob Dylan*, New English Library, 1986

17 Author interviews with Faridi McFree between 2005 and 2009

18 Jonathon Cott, *Rolling Stone*, issue 257, January 26, 1978

19 Author interview with Arthur Rosato, 2017

20 Ron Rosenbaum, *Playboy* interview, November 1977, published March 1978

21 Paul Zollo, SongTalk, 1991

Chapter 9

1 Derek Barker (editor), *Anthology Vol. 2: 20 Years of ISIS*, Chrome Dreams, 2005

2 Author interview with Jerry Weintraub

3 Paul Williams, Performing Artist – The Middle Years, Underwood-Miller, 1992

4 Author interview with Arthur Rosato, 2017

5 ibid

6 Clinton Heylin, *Behind the Shades: The 20th Anniversary Edition*, Faber & Faber, 2011

7 Rosenbaum, Ron, interview for *Playboy* magazine, conducted November 1977

8 Paul Vitello, *Kansas City Times*, January 1980

9 Philippe Adler, *L'Express*, July 3, 1978. Translated by Sue Allen and reprinted in *Fourth Time Around*, issue 2

10 Robert Hilburn, *LA Times* Interview, May 22, 1978

11 Philippe Adler, *L'Express*, July 3, 1978. Translated by Sue Allen and reprinted in *Fourth Time Around*, issue 2

12 Cameron Crowe, *Rolling Stone*, Issue 269, July 13, 1978

13 Robert Shelton, *No Direction Home: The Life and Music of Bob Dylan*, New English Library, 1986

14 Clinton Heylin, *Behind the Shades: The 20th Anniversary Edition*, Faber & Faber, 2011

15 *Bob Dylan: Both Ends of the Rainbow,* Video, Pride, 2009
16 Cameron Crowe, *Rolling Stone,* Issue 269, July 13, 1978
17 *Mail on Sunday,* January 30, 2010
18 ibid
19 *Guardian,* June 13, 1978
20 Derek Barker (editor), *Anthology Vol. 2: 20 Years of ISIS,* Chrome Dreams, 2005
21 Robert Shelton, *Melody Maker,* July 29, 1978
22 Chris Souza, Interview with Robert Shelton for *ISIS* magazine, published July 1999
23 ibid
24 Robert Shelton, *Melody Maker,* July 29, 1978
25 Fritz Rau, *Fritz Rau: Buchhalter der Träume,* Quadriga, 1985. English translation Manfred Helfert
26 ibid

Chapter 10

1 *Daily Mirror,* July 15, 1978
2 Chris Welch, *Melody Maker,* July 15, 1978
3 ibid
4 Author interview with Johnny Haynes, 2015
5 Phil Sutcliffe, *Sounds,* July 22, 1978.
6 ibid
7 www.snapgalleries.com
8 Howard Sounes, *Down the Highway: The Life of Bob Dylan,* Doubleday, 2001

Chapter 11

1 Ray Coleman, *Melody Maker,* July 1, 1978

Chapter 12

1 Robert Hilburn, *LA Times,* May 22, 1978
2 Clinton Heylin, *Behind the Shades: The 20th Anniversary Edition,* Faber & Faber, 2011
3 Transcribed from concert recording at San Diego Golden Hall November 27, 1979.
4 Karen Hughes, *The Dominion,* New Zealand, August 2, 1980
5 Jonathan Cott, *Bob Dylan: The Essential Interviews,* Wenner, 2007
6 Peter Barry Chowka, The Allen Ginsberg Project, ginsberg75.rssing.com
7 Author interview with Allen Ginsberg, 1995
8 Martin Keller, Minneapolis City Pages, July 1983
9 The Bruce Heiman Interview, Tucson, December 7, 1979
10 Melody Green with David Hazard, *No Compromise: The Life Story of Keith Green,* Thomas Nelson
11 A letter from Larry Myers, *On the Tracks,* issue 4, Fall 1994
12 Robert Hilburn, *Los Angeles Times,* November 24, 1980

13 A letter from Larry Myers, On the Tracks, issue 4, Fall 1994

14 www.christianforums.com/threads/dylan.1253743/

15 David W Stowe, *No Sympathy for the Devil: Christian Pop Music and the Transformation of American Evangelicalism*, The University of North Carolina Press, 2013

16 Various, *Spiritual Journeys: How Faith Has Influenced Twelve Music Icons*, Relevant Books, 2003

17 *NME* 1979

18 Various, *Spiritual Journeys: How Faith Has Influenced Twelve Music Icons*, Relevant Books, 2003

19 Howard Sounes, *Down the Highway: The Life of Bob Dylan*, Doubleday, 2001

20 Neil Hickey, *TV Guide Magazine*, September 11, 1976

21 Dan Wooding, *ASSIST News Service*, October 2012

22 ibid

23 Melody Green with David Hazard, *No Compromise: The Life Story of Keith Green*, Thomas Nelson

24 ibid

25 Scott Marshall, *Bob Dylan: A Spiritual Life*, BP Books, 2017

26 Dylan Ditching Gospel? *New York Magazine*, March 15, 1982

27 Author interview with Clinton Heylin, 2017

28 Scott Cohen, *Spin*, Volume One, Number Eight, December 1985

29 Mikal Gilmore, *Rolling Stone*, issue 1166, September, 2012

30 *Rolling Stone*, February 9, 2015 from MusiCares Person of the Year 2015 acceptance speech

Acknowledgements

Permissions

All Along the Watchtower
Copyright © 1968 by Dwarf Music; renewed 1996 by Dwarf Music

As I Went Out One Morning
Copyright © 1968 by Dwarf Music; renewed 1996 by Dwarf Music

Call Letter Blues
Copyright © 1974 by Ram's Horn Music; renewed 2002 by Ram's Horn Music

Changing of the Guards
Copyright © 1978 by Special Rider Music

Dear Landlord
Copyright © 1968 by Dwarf Music; renewed 1996 by Dwarf Music

Dirge
Copyright © 1973 by Ram's Horn Music; renewed 2001 by Ram's Horn Music

God Knows
Copyright © 1990 by Special Rider Music

Going, Going, Gone
Copyright © 1973 by Ram's Horn Music; renewed 2001 by Ram's Horn Music

Idiot Wind
Copyright © 1974 by Ram's Horn Music; renewed 2002 by Ram's Horn Music

I'd Hate to Be You on That Dreadful Day
Copyright Copyright © 1964, 1968 Warner Bros. Music, Renewed 1992 Special
Rider Music

I Dreamed I Saw St. Augustine
Copyright © 1968 by Dwarf Music; renewed 1996 by Dwarf Music

If You See Her, Say Hello
Copyright © 1974 by Ram's Horn Music; renewed 2002 by Ram's Horn Music

I Pity the Poor Immigrant
Copyright © 1968 by Dwarf Music; renewed 1996 by Dwarf Music

Is Your Love in Vain
Copyright © 1978 by Special Rider Music

It's Alright, Ma (I'm Only Bleeding)
Copyright © 1965 by Warner Bros. Inc.; renewed 1993 by Special Rider Music

Million Dollar Bash
Copyright © 1968 by Dwarf Music; renewed 1996 by Dwarf Music

Minstrel Boy
Copyright © 1970 by Big Sky Music; renewed 1998 by Big Sky Music

New Pony
Copyright © 1978 by Special Rider Musicv

No Time to Think
Copyright © 1978 by Special Rider Music

One More Cup of Coffee
Copyright © 1975, 1976 by Ram's Horn Music; renewed 2003, 2004 by Ram's Horn Music

Outlaw Blues
Copyright © 1965 by Warner Bros. Inc.; renewed 1993 by Special Rider Music

Quinn the Eskimo (The Mighty Quinn)
Copyright © 1968 by Dwarf Music; renewed 1996 by Dwarf Music

Sad-Eyed Lady of the Lowlands
Copyright © 1966 by Dwarf Music; renewed 1994 by Dwarf Music

Sara
Copyright © 1975, 1976 by Ram's Horn Music; renewed 2003, 2004 by Ram's Horn Music

Señor (Tales of Yankee Power)
Copyright © 1978 by Special Rider Music

Shelter from the Storm
Copyright © 1974 by Ram's Horn Music; renewed 2002 by Ram's Horn Music

Sign on the Cross
Copyright © 1971 by Dwarf Music; renewed 1999 by Dwarf Music

Acknowledgements

Thanks to the following people who kindly gave up their time to provide me with Interviews: Al Aronowitz, John Brandt, Chris de Souza, David Geffen, Allen Ginsberg, Johnny Gotting, Clinton Heylin, Johnny Haynes, Levon Helm, Bob Johnston, Jacques Levy, Mick Farren, Mike Lang, Faridi McFree, Mick Ronson, Arthur Rosato, Jonathan Taplin, Jerry Weintraub.

The Isle of Wight music festivals form a significant part of this book and I would like to thank Isle of Wight festival promoter Ray Foulk for his help and understanding, *Message to Love* author Brian Hinton for his help and research, Chris Hockenhull for the groundbreaking work he carried out in 1986, Vic King, Tom O'Dell at Prism Films for giving me access to outtakes from his many filmed interviews, Alan Stroud.

The Blackbushe festival and the 1978 world tour also occupy a significant amount of pages in this book and I would like to thank Zac Dadic, Ian Woodward and Les Kokay for their invaluable contributions.

I would also like to thank Tracy Barker for keeping me (almost) sane, Paul Comley for his services, Andrew Muir for being Andrew Muir and the late John Baldwin who did so much to help and enrich the Dylan world and who tragically passed away shortly before the original hardback version of this book was finished.

I would also especially like to thank Dave Heath for starting the ball rolling on this project and to my publisher Mark Neeter, designer Harry Gregory and everyone at Red Planet.

Grateful thanks to Jeff Rosen and David Beal at the Bob Dylan office. And of course Bob Dylan.

Index

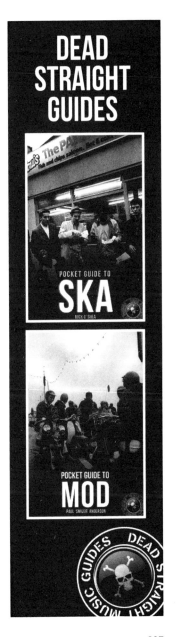

DEAD STRAIGHT GUIDES

POCKET GUIDE TO
SKA
RICK O'SHEA

POCKET GUIDE TO
MOD
PAUL 'SMILER' ANDERSON